Murdering Holiness

Law and Society Series
W. Wesley Pue, General Editor

Gender in the Legal Profession: Fitting or Breaking the Mould
JOAN BROCKMAN

*Regulating Lives: Historical Essays on the State, Society,
the Individual, and the Law*
Edited by
JOHN MCLAREN, ROBERT MENZIES, AND DOROTHY E. CHUNN

Taxing Choices: The Intersection of Class, Gender, Parenthood, and the Law
REBECCA JOHNSON

*Collective Insecurity:
The Liberian Crisis, Unilateralism, and Global Order*
IKECHI MGBEOJI

Unnatural Law: Rethinking Canadian Environmental Law and Policy
DAVID R. BOYD

People and Place: Historical Influences on Legal Culture
JONATHAN SWAINGER AND CONSTANCE BACKHOUSE

Murdering Holiness

The Trials of

FRANZ CREFFIELD

and

GEORGE MITCHELL

Jim Phillips and Rosemary Gartner

UBC Press • Vancouver • Toronto

09 08 07 06 05 04 03   5 4 3 2 1

Printed in Canada on acid-free paper

National Library of Canada Cataloguing in Publication Data

Phillips, Jim, 1954-
    Murdering holiness : the trials of Franz Creffield and George Mitchell /
Jim Phillips and Rosemary Gartner.

    (Law and society 1496-4953)
    Includes bibliographical references and index.
    ISBN 0-7748-0906-X

    1. Creffield, Edmund, 1867?-1906. 2. Church of the Bride of Christ. 3. Mitchell,
George, 1883?-1906 – Trials, litigation, etc. 4. Trials (Murder) – Washington (State) –
Seattle. 5. Northwest, Pacific – Social conditions. I. Gartner, Rosemary, 1952-
II. Title. III. Series: Law and society series (Vancouver, B.C.)
BP605.C546P44 2003   345.797′02523   C2003-910904-6

Canadä
UBC Press gratefully acknowledges the financial support for our publishing program of the Government of Canada through the Book Publishing Industry Development Program (BPIDP), and of the Canada Council for the Arts, and the British Columbia Arts Council.

This book has been published with the help of a grant from the Canadian Federation for the Humanities and Social Sciences, through the Aid to Scholarly Publications Programme, using funds provided by the Social Sciences and Humanities Research Council of Canada.

UBC Press
The University of British Columbia
2029 West Mall
Vancouver, BC v6t 1z2
604-822-5959 / Fax: 604-822-6083
E-mail: info@ubcpress.ca
www.ubcpress.ca

Contents

Acknowledgments

The research for this book took us to many archives and libraries, and we are grateful for the assistance of numerous staff at those institutions. We must first acknowledge John Nakamaru of the King County Medical Examiners' Office, where in 1996 we first encountered the murders of Franz Creffield and George Mitchell as part of an entirely different project. Subsequently we have benefitted greatly from the expertise and helpfulness of many people: Phil Stairs, Washington State Archives, Puget Sound Regional Branch, Bellevue, Washington; Deborah Kennedy, King County Archives, Seattle; the staff at the University of Washington Libraries, Special Collections Department; Dave Wendell of the Oregon State Archives, Salem; Connie Hagood, Salvation Army National Archives, Alexandria, Virginia; Kevin Moser, God's Bible School Archives, Cincinnati; Karen Tiverton, Inter-Library Loans Librarian, and Ted Tjaden, Reference Librarian, Bora Laskin Law Library, University of Toronto; and Carolyn Marr, Seattle Museum of History and Industry. A particular debt of thanks is due to Judy Juntunen and Marlene McDonald of the Benton County Historical Museum, Philomath, Oregon, for their enthusiastic and generous help.

Mike Balter, executive director of the Boys and Girls Aid Society, Portland, was very helpful in facilitating access to the Society's records, and we are greatly indebted to Professor David Peterson Del Mar of Portland for his advice and for examining those records on our behalf. Robert Blodgett of Corvallis, who has a long-standing interest in the Creffield story, provided us with some useful references and stimulating e-mail exchanges.

We have benefitted greatly from the help of some excellent research assistants. Joseph Berkovits of Toronto was especially helpful and conscientious, and Kelly de Luca of New York, Leslie Brinkley-Lawson of Portland, Torrie Hester of Eugene, and Lee Gentemann of Salem were of great assistance in various ways.

Financial assistance for the research was provided by the SSHRC and the University of Toronto Faculty of Law. The University of Toronto Centre of Criminology provided a collegial and stimulating academic environment for this and for all our work. Judy Phillips did a fine job of copy-editing, and Darcy Cullen of UBC Press helped bring the book to publication. Randy Schmidt, our editor with UBC Press, was a joy to work with and unfailingly helpful and perceptive.

We presented papers on aspects of this book in a variety of places, and our work always benefitted from doing so. We wish to thank participants in: the Toronto Legal History Group; the University of Toronto Centre of Criminology Seminar Series; the University of British Columbia, Green College Law and Society Series; the Symposium to Honour Professor Louis Knafla, held at the University of British Columbia; the Centre for the Study of the Pacific Northwest at the University of Washington; the Department of Sociology, University of Washington; the Faculty of Law, University of Victoria; and the 2002 Pacific Northwest History Conference.

Our time in Seattle was made especially pleasant and productive by the hospitality, friendship, and academic advice of Kathryn Baker, Bob Crutchfield, John Findlay, Edgar Kiser, Chuck and Pauline LeWarne, Marilyn and Dean Lytle, Kim McKaig, Susan Pitchford, Michael Reese, and Mary Wright.

For reading drafts of all or parts of this book and/or helpful discussions we thank: John Findlay of Seattle; Petra Fisher of Toronto; Jeanette Gartner of Ukiah, California; Christine Hayes of Calne, England; Anna Hoad and Allison Kirk-Montgomery of Toronto; Chuck LeWarne of Edmonds, Washington; Lynne Marks of Victoria; Michael Pfeiffer of Olympia, Washington; Michael Reese of Seattle; David Wright of Hamilton, Ontario; and, especially, Allyson May of Toronto. We also thank the anonymous reviewers who read the manuscript for the Press for their encouragement and useful suggestions. Michael Reese and Sara Howell of Seattle, Torrie Hester of Eugene, Susan Barker of Toronto, and, especially, Ryan Paterson of Toronto were very helpful with the illustrations.

Our only regret about this book is that Alan Phillips did not live to see it. He would have enjoyed the story and taken great pleasure in the fact that his son and daughter-in-law had written it. We dedicate it to his memory.

Cast of Principal Characters

Baldwin, Ona: daughter of Ed Baldwin
Bray, Attie: niece of Sarah Hurt; married Sampson Levins in 1906
Brooks, Charles: Creffield's second in command in 1903; former Salvation
   Army captain
Campbell, Lee: engaged at one point to Sophia Hartley
Creffield, Franz Edmund: sect leader; former Salvation Army officer
Creffield, Maud: see Maud Hurt
Hartley family: Cora and Sophia, wife and daughter of Louis
Hurt family: Sarah, née Starr, wife of O.V. Hurt, called "Mother Hurt" by
   Creffield; Ida Maud (Maud), eldest child of O.V. and Sarah Hurt who
   became Creffield's wife; Frank, second child of O.V. and Sarah Hurt,
   and the husband of Mollie, née Sandell; Eva Mae (May), the third child
   of O.V. and Sarah Hurt
Hurt, Mollie: née Sandell; wife of Frank Hurt
Levins, Sampson: later married Attie Bray
Mitchell, Donna: see Donna Starr
Mitchell, Esther: sister of Donna Starr and George Mitchell
Sandell, Mollie: see Mollie Hurt
Sandell, Olive: sister of Mollie Sandell Hurt
Seeley family: Edna, Florence, Rose, and Wesley
Starr, Clarence: brother of Burgess Starr and Sarah Hurt, husband of
   Hattie Starr

Starr, Donna: née Mitchell, older sister of Esther and George Mitchell, married to Burgess Starr

Starr, Hattie: wife of Clarence Starr, sister of Ed Baldwin

OTHER PRINCIPAL CHARACTERS

Baldwin, Ed: Corvallis resident and father of Ona; tried to kill Franz Creffield

Berry, James: Corvallis businessman, briefly a member of the sect in 1903 and at one time engaged to Maud Hurt

Frater, Archibald: superior court judge, King County; trial judge for the Mitchell trial and for the insanity hearings of Maud Creffield and Esther Mitchell

Gardner, William: superintendent of the Boys and Girls Aid Society Home in Portland

Hartley, Louis: leading Corvallis businessman; husband of Cora and father of Sophia

Hurt, Orlando Victor (O.V.): Corvallis resident, senior employee of Kline's department store; husband of Sarah and father of Frank, Maud, and May

Mackintosh, Kenneth: King County prosecuting attorney

Manning, John: district attorney of Multnomah County (Portland)

Miller, John: King County deputy prosecuting attorney

Mitchell, Charles: father of Esther, Perry, and George Mitchell, and of Donna Starr

Mitchell, Fred: brother of Esther, Perry, and George Mitchell

Mitchell, George: brother of Esther Mitchell and Donna Starr; killer of Franz Creffield

Mitchell, Perry: younger brother of George Mitchell

Morris, Will: lead defence attorney for George Mitchell

Sandell, Lewis: brother of Mollie Sandell Hurt and Olive Sandell

Shipley, Silas: second defence attorney for George Mitchell

Starr, Burgess: brother of Sarah Hurt and husband of Donna Starr

Thompson, Chester: Seattle man who killed George Emory on the last weekend of the Mitchell trial

Murdering
Holiness

I

Introduction

AT JUST AFTER 7 A.M. on Monday, May 7, 1906, Franz Edmund Creffield, an itinerant evangelist and self-proclaimed prophet and messiah, was shot to death at the corner of First and Cherry in downtown Seattle. His killer was George Washington Mitchell, a twenty-three-year-old mill worker from Portland. Creffield's death marked the end of his short-lived religious sect, which operated in Oregon, primarily in Corvallis, from 1903 to 1904 and briefly again in the early months of 1906. But it was just the beginning of a remarkable sequence of events that included Mitchell's trial for murder, his acquittal and almost immediate death in a revenge killing, and the proceedings against Mitchell's murderers.

The Creffield story was well known in the Pacific Northwest at the time and attained a considerable notoriety outside the region. Creffield's "spectacular career," said the *Seattle Times,* had "been read about from Maine to California"; a Salem, Oregon, newspaper similarly noted that Creffield's sect had "made the name of Corvallis famous from the Pacific to the Atlantic." It was probably an exaggeration for the *Corvallis Gazette* to claim that "there is no village, town, or city [in the United States] but that is familiar with the facts," but millions of people could have read about the sect's activities in their local newspapers.[1] One notorious episode, an alleged animal sacrifice in October 1903, even made it into the *Scotsman,* the major newspaper of Edinburgh, Scotland. Reflecting the tendency of rumours to inflate as they spread, that report also had the sect contemplating a human sacrifice.[2]

The Creffield story is immensely rich in human interest. Its principal characters are "ordinary people," men and women of little property and rudimentary education. Yet for a brief period they made and took part in extraordinary events, impelled in some cases by intense religious beliefs, in others by a conviction that they had both the right and the duty to take the law into their own hands. We are not the first to tell their story. Stewart Holbrook did so more than sixty years ago, and he repackaged his version a number of times.[3] Although Holbrook's accounts are poorly researched, sensationalistic, and lacking any explanation of context, his work has been relied on by most other writers. We have found more than two dozen renderings of the story, some in book chapters and journal articles,[4] most in short magazine and newspaper stories.[5] Like Holbrook's accounts almost all of these are also to some extent inaccurate, and they tend to stress the sensational aspects of the story. Rather better researched are three recent book-length studies, but none provides much in the way of context.[6]

This story of a small group of people and the world they tried to forge involves large historical processes played out in Oregon and Washington in the early years of the twentieth century. In this book we wish not only to tell a good story but to examine its wider contexts and probe its deeper meanings, to use Creffield's career as a window into many aspects of life and law in the Pacific Northwest at the turn of the twentieth century. The use of case studies – or "micro-history" or "history of everyday life," as it is sometimes termed – to reconstruct past lives and social processes has become increasingly popular in the past two decades. Natalie Davis' *The Return of Martin Guerre* was one of the earliest studies in the genre and remains perhaps the best-known example.[7] The case study's principal merit, as many historians have noted, is that it brings into view particular, non-elite individuals, casting a spotlight on how they lived their lives and thought about their world – on the *mentalité* of ordinary people, as Davis puts it.[8] Case studies provide insight into how individuals are affected by and, as importantly, contribute to larger historical events and movements. They are not simply about "the people" writ large, and thus they constitute a valuable addition to the social history that relies more on large-scale statistical studies or on tracing peoples, communities, or institutions over time. We do not see these two ways of doing social history as being in opposition; they are complementary, providing different sight angles for viewing the past.[9] Micro-history, Michael Grossberg aptly notes, "traces structural changes in a society through stories of the struggles in individual lives."[10] They stress individual agency and the contingency, rather than the inevitability, of the playing out of large-scale processes.

Many recent historical case studies of this type, including our own, uti-
lize legal records. Such records provide sources through which ordinary
people speak to us from the past; as Robert Finlay succinctly puts it, "the
personalities and perspectives of rural people usually were recorded only
when peasants ran into trouble with the law."[11] While these recordings
were always constructed and shaped by the legal process and thus must be
treated with some caution, they are nonetheless an immensely rich source
of information on everyday lives. They are also, of course, the best source
for studying how law and legal institutions worked in the past. Since
this book is part legal history, we also strive to explicate both criminal and
civil law and process in the early twentieth-century Pacific Northwest,
hoping to show, as another recent case study puts it, "how completely
interwoven are the legal and the cultural."[12] Legal cases are also often used
for micro-historical studies because they chronicle conflict. One can learn
much about a society from the clash between mainstream and aberrant
values and practices.[13] Oregon in the early twentieth century contained
thousands of ardent Christians, for example; by studying why a small
number were committed to the insane asylum as a result of their beliefs
we can uncover the boundaries of religious and social tolerance. As this
example suggests, the magnifying glass through which we view people,
places, and events in this book gives way at times to, or is employed simultaneously with, a wide-angled lens capable of focusing on broader dimen-
sions and larger historical movements. We cannot understand why a small
number of people were placed in an insane asylum for their religious
beliefs without understanding the ways in which asylums were generally
used and viewed in the early twentieth century. Nor can we appreciate
why many people in Seattle approved of George Mitchell's deliberate murder of Creffield without trying to understand, among other things, the
deep appeal to ideas about masculinity and family honour that his crime
evoked. In turn these particular events add to our existing store of knowledge about larger social and legal questions.

Among other things, our story illustrates the profound hopes that people could pin on the promise of salvation in a period of religious upheaval.
It shows also how that upheaval could produce intense conflict within
one community, conflict that produced various forms of repression. That
repression was both legal and extra-legal, and this book tells us how,
when, and why some Americans in the period turned to vigilantism when
they deemed the law inadequate for their needs. The manipulation of
law and legal systems – insanity commitment procedures and the defence
of insanity – is also crucial to our story, especially in the later stages.

Although some of the key figures in this story are men, many of the participants are women, and ultimately the narrative has a great deal to tell us about the lives of women in early twentieth-century Oregon. Indeed, gender is a common thread running through our analysis of all the large historical processes discussed here. This book is about women; the individual lives of the women of the Creffield sect, and society's expectations of them and other women. It is about what women could and could not do, and about what they tried to do despite strictures on their behaviour.

In a recent case study located in the same period as this one, Linda Gordon aptly notes that the case study offers, at the same time, "universal and local knowledge." All "rich narratives," she reminds us, "take on their meanings from the way in which universal motives interact with local contexts." Gordon expresses the hope that her story of orphan abduction in the Southwest "possesses great powers of revelation."[14] We have the same hope. And we should start our story with the central figure, Franz Edmund Creffield, a man who believed that he possessed the greatest of all powers of revelation.

FRANZ EDMUND CREFFIELD

We know very little about Franz Creffield's early years. He was of German origin, and probably born around 1873.[15] He likely came to the United States in 1884, as a child or young adult, and one press report from 1904 refers to his having a mother living in one of the eastern states; if he came as a young boy, it seems reasonable that at least one parent would have come with him.[16] He was not only literate in English but had good command of grammar and syntax, although he never became a US citizen. He was of a small build even for the period, standing no more than five feet three inches tall and weighing about 135 pounds, with fair hair and blue eyes.[17] A mild-looking man, his name was not originally Creffield, which was an anglicization of Crefeld.[18]

Beyond these few details nothing is known of Creffield prior to 1899.[19] In that year he became an officer in the Salvation Army in Portland, Oregon, although he may have previously been a "soldier" in the Army in Seattle.[20] The Army had been active in Portland since 1886, a few years after its establishment in the United States. During its early years there, not untypically, the Army had been derided and its members both assaulted by opponents and prosecuted for violating municipal ordinances, but by the mid- to late 1890s opposition had died down and the organization was flourishing.[21] In a 1904 interview two Portland area officers – Ensign Maud Bigney and Captain Bertha Holeman – claimed to have known Creffield well, although they were reluctant to speak about him, for by that time he was a notorious adulterer. A few years previously he had been a "common street listener," but "was led to see the light of Jesus" and "from that time on he was, an earnest worker in the Army."[22] Creffield preached at a variety of meetings, and while he was "never considered a clever man in a high degree," he was "above the average" and made a number of converts. Employment in the Army meant that he had rejected the religion he had been brought up in – Catholicism.[23] In 1899 he was promoted from cadet to lieutenant.[24]

In November 1899 the new Lieutenant Creffield was posted to Grant's Pass, in southern Oregon, where from January 1900 he worked with an officer named Garden.[25] He served in Grant's Pass until late May 1900, at which point he was transferred to Corvallis. Further postings followed – to The Dalles in August 1900, on the Columbia River some sixty miles east of Portland in Wasco County, and in November 1900 to Oregon City, just south of Portland. Possibly he lived briefly in Seattle between the Corvallis and The Dalles postings, for in June or July of that year he was captured on the census as a Seattle resident.[26] In February 1901 he was posted to McMinnville, Yamhill County, some thirty miles south and a little west of Portland. A few days later, on February 14, he was promoted to captain. His final posting, officially recorded as June 26, 1901, was to Heppner. Such short tours of duty were common in the Army of this period, officers frequently moving from place to place.[27] In October 1901 Creffield resigned from the Salvation Army in order to search for what he considered a more authentic way to follow God's word. As he put it later, "God called me to preach His will,"[28] and just before he left, he published in the Salvation Army newspaper the first of only two articles he is known to have written, a strident call to live a life of complete holiness.[29]

We cannot follow Creffield's movements precisely in the year or so after his resignation, but it appears that he moved from town to town as an itinerant preacher, presumably looking for converts. He went mostly to places he had worked as an Army officer, perhaps because he had contacts among the more fervently religious in those communities. He may have returned to McMinnville; a later story has him driven out of the town, presumably for his radicalism, but we are inclined to doubt this. McMinnville press stories about Creffield after he had become notorious do not refer to his earlier presence there.[30] He was in Portland for a time in July 1902 – it was there that his future wife Maud Hurt first heard him speak, and another follower, Esther Mitchell, may also have encountered him for the first time.[31] Creffield spent some time in 1902 in the state capital, Salem, in the Willamette Valley to the south of Portland, a place he had not visited with the Army. He was drawn to Salem because of his interest in the Apostolic Holiness Mission led by M.L. Ryan, a group that operated in the city from the turn of the century until at least late 1906, and that became one of the first Pentecostal churches in Oregon. It was in Salem, Creffield later said, that after months of prayer God first instructed him to take up his own brand of evangelism.[32] A Salem newspaper carried a story some four years later about him preaching in a tent and "making a big fuss and jumping up in the air."[33]

Creffield probably spent most of 1902, however, in The Dalles. He had some success there in persuading twenty or so people to leave their churches and join a mission – the Peniel Mission – headed by Creffield and, probably, two other evangelists, Frank Cooper and James van Zandt. His teachings in The Dalles bore a marked similarity to those he later enunciated in Corvallis, explained in the next chapter, and while there he published an article detailing his own version of radical Christianity. Creffield probably left The Dalles when his adherents made it clear that they found him extreme. His group engaged in noisy worship, and it was later suggested that he caused an "uproar."[34] Disillusioned with the Salvation Army and seeking and advocating a stricter approach to religion, late in 1902 the itinerant evangelist's travels took him to Corvallis, another community he had served in with the Salvation Army. It is to that period of his ministry that we now turn.

2

The Creffield Sect in
Corvallis, 1903

F RANZ CREFFIELD'S CORVALLIS CAREER was as dramatic and
sensational as it was brief. By early November of 1903 he was the
principal talking point of the community and well known throughout Oregon, with his fame, or more properly infamy, also carrying well
beyond the confines of the state. In this chapter we will examine the history of Creffield's sect in Corvallis in 1903 down to the late summer, looking at its origins, growth, and operations, its membership, the doctrines
Creffield taught, and the practices he encouraged. Those doctrines and
practices are linked to general developments in American religion in this
period, and to the holiness movement in particular. Before we embark on
this, however, it is necessary to introduce the setting – the college town of
Corvallis.

The Corvallis on which Creffield had such a profound effect was a
small town of some 2,500 to 3,000 people located at the confluence of the
Willamette and Mary's Rivers, on the west bank of the former.[1] Founded
in the mid-1840s as Marysville, it was renamed Corvallis in 1853 and when
incorporated in 1857 was just the fourth city in what was still the Territory of Oregon. The name was coined by J.C. Avery, the first man to file
a land claim in the region (in 1845), from the Latin for "heart of the valley." Situated in the Willamette Valley, a remarkably fertile agricultural
area that served as the principal magnet for those embarking on the
Oregon Trail mid-century, Corvallis' economy was based primarily on its
role as a market town for the region and as a transportation hub. Lumber
and agricultural produce – by 1900, mainly flour, fruit, hops, and dairy

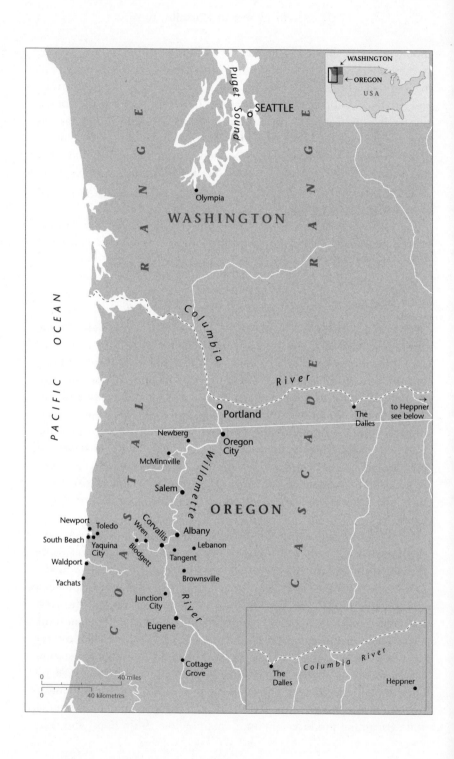

WASHINGTON
OREGON
USA

SEATTLE

R A N G E

R A N G E

Puget Sound

Olympia

WASHINGTON

PACIFIC OCEAN

Columbia

River

Portland

The
Dalles

to Heppner
see below

Newberg

Oregon
City

McMinnville

Salem

Willamette

OREGON

C A S C A D E

Newport
Toledo
South Beach
Yaquina
City
Waldport

Yachats

Corvallis
Wren
Blodgett

Albany

Lebanon

Tangent

Brownsville

C O A S T A L

Junction
City

River

Eugene

Cottage
Grove

The
Dalles

Columbia   River

Heppner

0   40 miles
0   40 kilometres

products – were shipped to markets in California and elsewhere, first by river steamer and, from the 1880s, by railroad. Basic industries – sawmilling, tanning, a brickyard, a brewery and a cider factory, a furniture factory, and the like – supplemented this, as did Corvallis' status as the county seat for Benton County. Corvallis was probably best known then (as it is now) as the location of the Oregon Agricultural College – now Oregon State University – established in 1868. Dominating the small and low-rise downtown was the striking Benton County Courthouse. Completed in 1888, the courthouse was a symbol of style and architectural achievement as well as of law and order.

Corvallis' population was a homogenous one; the vast majority of the people were first-, second-, or third-generation Anglo-Celtic white settlers, largely from the Midwest, and only a few Chinese residents provided anything of an ethnic mix.[2] In 1903 the community supported two newspapers – the *Gazette* and the *Times* – and a community centre and recreation facility known as the "Opera House" in which visiting theatrical companies performed regularly. Its citizens endorsed a wide-ranging set of "blue laws" against gambling, nude bathing in the rivers, and Sabbath entertainments, invariably voted for the Republican Party, and had little truck with demands for female suffrage or, indeed, for any substantial role for women outside the domestic world and the churches.[3] Although by this time it was clear that Corvallis was never going to rival Oregon's commercial metropolis, Portland, some sixty miles north at the head of the Willamette Valley, the first two decades of the new century were prosperous and comfortable ones for the town, in contrast to the region-wide depression of the 1890s. The renovation and reopening of the Hotel Corvallis in late 1902, which had lain empty for almost a decade, symbolized the optimism of the town at the time our story took place, as did the opening of the town's second bank.[4] Economically self-sufficient, taking pride in living in a college town, embracing symbols of modernism such as the telephone, electric light, and an albeit rather limited street railway, and filling its variety of Protestant churches every Sunday without taking their religion too seriously, the citizens of Corvallis were content with their lot and confident about the future. The year 1903 saw two new arrivals in the town – the motor car and Franz Creffield's version of Christian holiness. The former was yet another symbol of progress and prosperity; the latter would show how fragile modernism could be for some, and would pose a profound threat to the comfortable, male-dominated social order.

THE ORIGINS AND OPERATIONS OF THE
CREFFIELD SECT

Creffield arrived in Corvallis sometime in the later months of 1902.[5] The itinerant preacher attended meetings of the active local Salvation Army corps,[6] and by early December 1902 he had induced almost all the local "soldiers" in the Corvallis corps – essentially the Army "congregation" – to follow him and his teachings. "The Army is not of God," Creffield was later said to have announced, and many obviously agreed, for they went over "almost in a body" to the new sect.[7]

The principal corps members defecting to Creffield were members of one family – the Hurts. The matriarch of the family, whom Creffield called "Mother Hurt," was Sarah Matilda Hurt, née Starr. Born in Monroe, Oregon, in 1861 or 1862, she was from one of the first pioneer families in what is now Lincoln County, the coastal region west of Corvallis.[8] Her father George Starr had migrated from Ohio to Oregon, taking up land in the Alsea region. Sarah had a common school education and worked the family farm until, not yet twenty, she married Orlando Victor Hurt on April 11, 1880, at Lower Alsea. Hurt, invariably referred to as O.V. Hurt, was born in Indiana in 1857, emigrating to Oregon with his parents in 1877. Two years later he met and married Sarah. The young couple homesteaded on two farms, spent a winter in Indiana, then returned to Oregon and lived on the Siletz Indian reservation, where Victor was industrial teacher and Sarah matron. They likely obtained these positions through the influence of Sarah's father George, Indian agent for the region. They relocated in 1893 to Corvallis, where O.V. Hurt found employment at Kline's, the leading department store in the town and a fixture since 1864, and where he worked for thirteen years.[9] In the course of establishing himself as one of the town's best-known citizens, he rose to become a senior employee. While O.V. was never a rich man, nor particularly well educated,[10] he had an abundance of civic engagement and respectability: he was a county committeeman for the Republican Party between 1898 and 1902, and a member of the party's state central committee from 1902 until 1906. He did regular jury duty and served as an appraiser of estates for the county probate system. O.V. was consequently a "highly esteemed" resident, "one of the most highly respected citizens of Corvallis."[11]

O.V. Hurt had little enthusiasm for radical religion; he joined the sect only briefly in the fall of 1903, and without much real conviction. But his modest house just south of Corvallis, set in two acres of ground, became one of the sect's principal meeting places. Sarah Hurt had a long-standing interest in religion, and she had been a Salvation Army soldier.[12] She and her three eldest children were early converts to Creffield's sect. Ida Maud Hurt, usually referred to as Maud, twenty-two years old in early 1903, had long been ardently religious.[13] Her father later said that Maud was "always of a religious turn of mind and generally took up with every new creed that presented itself"; on other occasions he was less kind, saying she was "always a very peculiar girl and hard to understand" and somebody who refused to speak with those who differed with her on religious questions.[14] In an obituary written by "A Friend," Maud was described as "intensely religious" from a very young age and a keen proselytizer. At the age of eight she was already "an energetic worker in revival meetings, going among the congregation and pleading with friends and acquaintances to seek the salvation so freely offered." She combined her zeal with "an even temper and a good disposition," helping the sick whenever the opportunity presented itself.[15] By 1902 this "amiable and eminently respectable young woman, of more than ordinary intelligence" was devoting most of her energy and enthusiasm to the local Salvation Army corps, although there is evidence that her zeal made her at times critical of her superiors.[16]

Maud's younger brother, Frank Hurt, twenty-one years old and living at home at the beginning of 1903, was a mainstay of the sect. Indeed, he and Creffield worked together to bring about the defection of Army members, the two having become friends while Creffield had been stationed in Corvallis and Hurt was a soldier in the local corps. Variously a salesman and a shipping clerk, Frank had been educated in the Corvallis public schools and worked in Portland for a time. According to his father, he was "always very religious, becoming a member of the Methodist Church while a mere boy" and joining the Salvation Army when just eight or nine years old.[17] Eva Mae Hurt, invariably called May or Mae, was rather younger than her siblings, just sixteen years old when she joined the sect in 1903. She, too, had been a member of the Salvation Army before joining Creffield's sect.[18] The Hurts' two other children, both adopted, were too young to be involved; Roy Robinett Hurt was a boy of thirteen, and Martha Hurt, née Brown, was an infant taken in by the Hurts the previous September.

Other Creffield followers included, remarkably, Charles Brooks, the Salvation Army captain sent to Corvallis to reinvigorate the local corps after the defections, who went over sometime after late March 1903, probably in late May. He claimed some initial success in attracting new members to the Army, but when he attended one of Creffield's meetings in an attempt to win back others of his flock, he was converted.[19] The defection was a fatal blow to the local corps, with only Lieutenant Mannes soldiering on in June. At that point, the Salvation Army closed up shop in Corvallis and did not return permanently to the town until the 1990s.[20]

In the early months of 1903 Creffield's sect met in a rented hall on Main Street (now Second Street) and occasionally in the homes of members, especially the Hurt house and that of Cora Hartley, who is discussed in detail below.[21] Their meetings were animated and noisy and involved rolling about the floor, shouting, and going into trances. By late May or early June 1903 the group was sufficiently coherent and committed to set up a camp on a small spit of land in the Willamette River just south of Corvallis that was not quite an island, being reachable by a ford from the town most of the time. Referred to by contemporaries as the camp on "Kiger's Island," it was actually on neighbouring Smith Island.[22] There for at least two months, probably longer, Creffield and his followers lived in large and commodious wigwam-style tents.[23] Not all members camped out during that summer. Some returned to their homes in Corvallis at night, others stayed a few days, interspersing camp life with the comforts of home. This transience was probably necessary since the group was not self-sufficient beyond what its members contributed from their family economies – and what they could take from R.C. Kiger's orchards.[24] Rather, Creffield encouraged his followers to give to his church, and those comfortably off were able to do so.

It was at a meeting on the island that Brooks was converted, a "spectacular" event that involved him seeing "the devil approaching enwrapped in a network of snakes," at which he "tore off his Salvation Army cap and coat and hurled them into the fire."[25] While they were on the island the sect members posed with Creffield for a group portrait, bequeathing to posterity the only known picture of them together (see Plates), a picture that contrasts markedly with the image evoked by Brooks' conversion. Six men and sixteen women are ranged in two rows, with Creffield positioned just off centre in the front row. Formally dressed, they look like the archetype of sober and respectable citizens.[26]

For most of 1903 the group attracted no sustained opposition from the community, although they were talked about and to some extent complained about. They were known as the "Army of Holiness," the "Holiness Mission," or the "come-outers" (a term whose meaning will be explained later), and only occasionally by the more pejorative epithet of "Holy Rollers."[27] The few stories published in the local press about them observed variously that they were a "burlesque on religion," and that the members were "very devout" but that "their customs, rites, and formalities are so queer and unusual that the organization has been the subject of much comment."[28] When the sect had used the meeting hall on Main Street, they made enough noise with their "nightly incantations" that the neighbours complained.[29] Opposition from the community may have occasioned the move to the island, as some later claimed,[30] but we should be careful not to exaggerate the extent of this opposition. Press attention was minimal – only one story about the sect appeared in the Corvallis press before late October 1903 – and few people saw anything fundamentally wrong with the group. One noted that adverse comment came from "those who do not enter fully into the idea of allowing persons to worship God in the manner that seems to them best." Another worried that the group's eccentricities would cause the young to "scoff at religion in any form."[31] The island camp was only once mentioned in the local press, which otherwise recorded the most minute details of Corvallis life. This lacuna may have been partly because many of Corvallis' citizens who could afford to do so went to the coast for extensive periods during the height of the summer.[32] More importantly, the group operated well within the bounds of community toleration, attracting curiosity rather than antipathy.[33]

THE SECT MEMBERS

The Creffield sect had a core membership of only about twenty people in 1903. Not all members joined at the beginning, and some had left by the time the sect was persecuted by the community at the end of the year. If we add the less enthusiastic and less steadfast members to the core group the number rises to more than twenty-five.[34] Four features of the sect's membership stand out: many of the adherents were related; many had prior involvement in the Salvation Army; membership was predominantly female; and members were drawn from a variety of class backgrounds. Creffield's sect, unlike many such groups in this period, was not largely made up of people from the poorer classes of society.

As mentioned, the Hurt family (with the exception of O.V.) were core adherents, and a number of other sect members were closely connected to that family. Mollie (Sandell) Hurt was a twenty-four year old from Mercer Island, Seattle, who had moved to Corvallis as a captain in the Salvation Army in December 1900.[35] She met Frank Hurt through the Army, and the two were married in a civil ceremony in July 1903 at the Hurt house, with O.V. Hurt and Charles Brooks as witnesses.[36] Their courtship thus survived Mollie's postings to Salem, San Francisco, Boise, and Portland, where she spent her time between February 1901 and July 1902. She resigned from the Army in the latter month, and we suspect she did so to follow Creffield. Mollie's older sister, Olive Sandell, twenty-six years old, was another adherent, although we do not know what brought her to Corvallis beyond being able to live with her sister. She too had been an officer in the Army, stationed in Portland in 1901.[37] Attie Bray, seated on the extreme right in the group portrait (see Plates), was Sarah Hurt's niece, the first child of her older sister Georgianna, who had married Ira Bray, a well-known and successful pioneer of the Waldport area and originally from Indiana. Attie had come to Corvallis in 1896 because the schools were better there than on the coast, and had stayed. In 1903 she was twenty-two years old and working as a domestic in the Kline household, a position probably secured through the influence of her uncle, O.V. Hurt.[38]

One brother (Clarence Starr) and two sisters-in-law (Hattie Starr and Donna Starr) of Sarah Hurt also joined the sect. Clarence and Hattie (Harriet Adelia) Starr ran a farm five miles west of Philomath. Hattie was born Hattie Baldwin to yet another coast family (discussed in more detail below) and married Clarence in Corvallis in 1890. In 1903 the couple, she in her early thirties and he thirty-five, were raising five boys ranging from two to twelve years old.[39] Clarence was never an enthusiastic adherent to the sect and is not in the group portrait, though Hattie is. Both became disillusioned with aspects of Creffield's teaching and left either during the Smith Island period or shortly thereafter. When she did so, her image in one version of the group portrait was covered by bible verses. Donna Starr, née Mitchell, was the twenty-three-year-old wife of Burgess Ebenezer Starr, usually called Burt, the youngest sibling of Sarah Hurt, whom Donna had married in 1900. Burgess and Donna lived in Portland, the former working variously for Standard Oil and a meat market as a "helper," a driver, and a labourer. Both were Salvation Army supporters, and by 1903 they had two small girls. In 1903, on a visit to Corvallis, Donna committed herself to the sect.[40]

Three more sect members had a connection to the Hurt family. James Kemmer Berry was originally from Minnesota and a rising young Corvallis businessman; he ran a general hardware store and sold and repaired bicycles and other machinery, and was the first man in Corvallis to sell a motor car.[41] He was also for a time in 1903 Maud Hurt's fiancé. He liked Maud more than religion and had little or no involvement in the Smith Island camp. Berry was one of the first to leave the sect, doing so before the group picture was taken. That decision cost him his relationship with

Maud, but he soon found solace elsewhere, marrying Clara King of Salem in January 1904. Eunice Baldwin, usually called Ona or Una, twenty-two, was the oldest of the four daughters of Edwin (Ed) Baldwin. Second from the right of those standing in the portrait, her connection to the Hurts was a distant one – Ed Baldwin was the older brother of Hattie Starr, Sarah Hurt's sister-in-law. A Waldport sawmill owner, Baldwin had moved his family from the coast to Corvallis in 1900 for his children's schooling and had tried his hand at many occupations. He farmed and engaged in construction during his Corvallis years and spent part of the time back in Waldport.[42]

In the group portrait, Esther Mitchell, the final person connected to the Hurt family, is standing in the back row. Donna Starr's younger sister, Esther was born in January 1888 and thus was fifteen years old in 1903. Esther, her sister Donna, and her brother George play central roles in this book. The Mitchell family – Charles and Martha and three girls and four boys – had migrated to Oregon from Illinois in the late 1880s, probably in 1888, just after Esther was born.[43] They settled in Newberg, Yamhill County, likely because they were Quakers (Newberg was the principal Quaker settlement in the state) and because Charles Mitchell's brother, George W. Mitchell, lived there. Charles' wife Martha died of tuberculosis in December 1894, and he returned to the east shortly afterwards, leaving behind all seven of his children. Six-year-old Esther was farmed out to relatives.

Charles Mitchell stopped supporting his children a few years after he left Oregon, and by the turn of the century the three Mitchell girls – Phoebe, Donna, and Esther – were living in Portland and involved with the Salvation Army. Phoebe was the most committed, holding the rank of sergeant-major. In 1904 she married another Army officer, Peter Vanderkellen. But Esther and Donna were also committed soldiers before they joined the Creffield group. Donna probably defected during a visit to her sister-in-law, Sarah Hurt, in late 1902,[44] and she and Burgess moved to Corvallis in 1903. In early 1903 Esther was living in Oregon City and working in the woollen mills there, probably as a tailor. During a visit with Donna and the Hurts she too joined the sect. This was not the first time Esther Mitchell had met Creffield, however; she had previously heard him preach in Portland.[45]

In total, fourteen members of the sect had some connection to the family of O.V. and Sarah Hurt, and with the exceptions of O.V. Hurt, Clarence Starr, Hattie Starr, and Berry, they were deeply committed to the sect over time. All of the ten people we identify as close and consistent adherents were female, except Frank Hurt. Another mother-daughter combination, Cora and Sophia Hartley, had no connection to the Hurt family, and came from the highest strata of Corvallis society. They were the wife and only daughter of fifty-year-old Louis Hartley, who managed the Great Eastern Mining Company's interests in the Bohemia Mines near Cottage Grove, Oregon, in which Louis was also a major investor. Louis was frequently away from home on business trips, leaving Cora and Sophia plenty of time to devote themselves to religion. They lived on Smith Island for much of the summer of 1903. At age forty-four, Cora was a few years younger than her husband. Sophia was just twenty and a student at the Oregon Agricultural College (OAC), taking household science;[46] she was said, like many of the sect members, to be "an intelligent and amiable young woman" apart from "her delusion on religious matters."[47] Neither woman appears to have had prior experience with the more radical forms of Christianity; they were "reputable ladies and former members of the Methodist Episcopal Church."[48] The Hartleys also had a son, Warren, a mining engineering student at the OAC, but he had no interest in ardent religion.[49] The Hartleys likely joined the sect in the first couple of months of 1903, while Louis was in the Midwest on an extended business trip.

Another family group in the Creffield sect were the Seeleys. Three sisters – Rose (twenty-seven), Edna (twenty), and Florence (Urania) (fifteen) – and their brother, Wesley Seeley (nineteen), are in the back row of the portrait. Wesley, Rose, and Florence stayed with the sect throughout 1903, but Edna left sometime after the Smith Island period and went to live in Oregon City.[50] Little is known about the Seeleys' background, beyond the fact that they were a poor family from the Alsea region of Benton County. Their mother, Julia, died of tuberculosis in 1897, and the sources state both that their fisherman father Judson Seeley was also deceased and (more likely) that he had abandoned the family. Florence Seeley is described as "more than passing fair." Rose Seeley worked as a domestic servant in Corvallis in the same house (the Kline's) as Attie Bray, which may have provided the entree first of Rose and then of her sisters to the sect.[51] The Seeleys were not the only sect members who had had a difficult upbringing; Donna Starr and Esther Mitchell had lost their mother and seen their father walk out on them, while Attie Bray had lived many years away from her parents.

Four other men and another woman complete this listing of the sect members. The woman was likely Mrs Coral Worrell, of Portland, but we know little about her beyond her name, and do not know what brought her to Corvallis that summer. She is not mentioned as part of the group in Corvallis after Smith Island, and, as a Portland resident, she presumably returned there in the fall. We shall see later that she again became a follower of Creffield when he went to Portland in 1904.[52] The additional men include two who are in the photograph and who remained with the group throughout 1903 – Milton Lee Campbell and Sampson Levins, both "ardent followers."[53] Campbell was in his mid-forties and worked as a general labourer and in the logging industry.[54] Levins, variously referred to as Sanford and Samuel, was born in 1868. He was a private in the Oregon Light Artillery in the Spanish-American War, and a devout Methodist before joining the sect. One source says that he worked in Corvallis for a time, principally in logging; another describes him as "a very ordinary man of the working class" who came from Portland and had worked in The Dalles.[55] He "converted" to Creffield's version of holiness in the fall of 1902.[56]

Both Campbell and Levins stayed with the sect through 1903, but our final two men, about whom we know very little, did not. One Terry Mercer – a "fellow revivalist" – briefly shared the leadership of the group with Creffield, but the two had a falling out and Mercer left; he later became prominent in one of the larger holiness churches, the Church of the Nazarene.[57] He is not in the group portrait, nor is he mentioned in the 1903 sources. There is even less evidence of Ed Sharp, mentioned in one newspaper story as a youth briefly associated with the group while it was on the island.[58]

At most, therefore, the sect consisted of eleven men, including Creffield, and sixteen women. But the total of twenty-seven members is reached only by counting people who were involved either peripherally or temporarily, or about whom there is very little evidence. Sharp, Mercer, O.V. Hurt, and Berry should be excluded from any count of the group's effective strength during the Smith Island period, meaning that there were no more than twenty-three sect members during the summer of 1903. Although O.V. Hurt joined the sect for a few weeks in the fall of 1903, Worrell, Edna and Wesley Seeley, and Clarence and Hattie Starr were not in it at that time, reducing the number to nineteen. Other people went to a meeting or two early on but never effectively joined the group, and what we would term the "core followers," which excludes O.V. Hurt, consisted of just thirteen women and five men, including Creffield.[59] The truly committed followers were thus predominantly female, and many – including the Hurts, Sandells, and Mitchells – had been involved with the Salvation Army. This group was fairly evenly divided between the middle and lower-middle classes (the Hartleys, the Hurts, the Sandells, Attie Bray, and Ona Baldwin) and those from lower down the socioeconomic scale – Levins, Campbell, the Mitchell sisters, the Seeleys, and probably Brooks. In attracting middle and lower-middle class adherents, the Creffield sect was unusual; as we shall see, it was mostly the working classes who joined such groups during this period.

THE HOLINESS MOVEMENT

The Creffield sect was part of a larger movement in American religion in the period, usually referred to as the holiness movement, and an understanding of this particular group's beliefs and practices requires looking first at that movement. This in turn necessitates coming to terms with certain key doctrines in nineteenth-century Protestant theology and practice. What follows is a general survey, and by no means a complete one; a comprehensive understanding is probably impossible to achieve, because both contemporaries and historians used and use terms to mean different things. As one of the movement's leading historians, Melvin Dieter, has put it, variety and heterogeneity were its hallmarks.[60]

Broadly, Protestantism teaches two principal stages that Christians pass through on their way to salvation. The first is justification, in which God forgives sins, and guilt is removed from his followers; they are made righteous in his eyes and saved. The second is sanctification, in which God releases believers from the power of sin and enables them to live truly godly or holy lives. While the Lutheran and Calvinist traditions tend to stress the former, Methodism – the dominant Protestant tradition in the United States – has always placed more emphasis on the latter. John Wesley described the difference between the two as that between what God does for his followers (justification), and what he does in them (sanctification). Wesley believed that sanctification was a process that would occur gradually and culminate in a dramatic experience, a "second blessing" after conversion in which the believer would be filled with the perfect love of God – hence, the teaching that sanctification is possible is sometimes called perfectionism. Sanctification did not mean a complete lack of sin, but it did entail freedom from conscious or deliberate sin.

Throughout the nineteenth century there were differences of opinion over when and how one could achieve sanctification. One of the most influential evangelists, for example, Phoebe Palmer, attracted many adherents in the 1840s with her message that a person could achieve "entire" or "complete" sanctification as an instantaneous gift from God and do so well within the compass of one lifetime. Sanctification did not, as Wesley had believed, have to be a gradual process with perfection achieved only at or near the end of one's life. Palmer thus refined Wesleyanism by teaching that sanctification was "more the beginning of the Christian life rather than the goal."[61] Palmer's simple and optimistic message built on the enthusiasm for personal religion inculcated by the Second Great Awakening, and led in turn to what historians have dubbed the first, pre-Civil War phase of the holiness movement. It should be stressed here that "holiness" had, and has, more than one meaning. The term "holiness movement" simply describes a movement – a process in which thousands were convinced of the "possibility of a Christian believer's gaining complete freedom from sin in the present life."[62] But holiness also came to mean the desired state in which a sanctified person would live. In Frankiel's words, holiness adherents were evangelicals who were "inspired to seek a greater sense of Christian grace, purity and devotion within themselves."[63] Generally, an adherent to "holiness" in the second half of the nineteenth century believed that, once sanctified, a person lived, or at least was able to live, in a state of holiness. The second phase of the holiness movement, which began soon after the Civil War and is often dated from the formation of the National Holiness Association in the late 1860s, saw many thousands of new adherents from all classes and regions drawn to its message. Holiness reached out beyond its earlier urban and middle-class strongholds to rural areas and to all classes, drawing in as disparate segments of the community as the urban poor and the Van Rensselaers of New York. At the same time, schisms emerged within the movement, which were not rooted in basic theology but in differences of opinion about how those imbued with holiness should behave in the world. One strand of holiness became the social gospel movement, which emphasized "social holiness" and was dedicated to social and political change – temperance, sexual and racial equality, and pacifism, for example. The other principal strand was a pre-millennialist one, a belief not in social holiness but in personal holiness. Pre-millennialists believed that Christ would come again before the millennium – the thousand-year period of peace on earth – and judge each person. The world could not be made better before that event, for it was fundamentally corrupt, and thus holiness adherents should work to save individual souls – theirs and others.

In this phase holiness was still largely a movement within the established denominations, especially the Wesleyan Methodist Church. The differences between the pre-millennial holiness adherents and others became much more pronounced during the third phase of the movement, the beginnings of which are generally associated with the founding of the Church of God in Anderson, Indiana, in 1881. The creation of new institutions was the most significant feature of the third phase. During the last two decades of the nineteenth century and the first decade of the twentieth, thousands of pre-millennialists broke away as mainstream hierarchies became increasingly unsympathetic to holiness within the churches. Innumerable small congregations were formed throughout the United States, with the greatest growth in what was called "come-outism" in rural areas and the west. The term was derived from the second epistle of Paul to the Corinthians, in which true believers are told not to mix with unbelievers, to "come out from them, be separate from them."[64] By 1910 "come-outism" had "almost totally removed the holiness movement from the main denominations into independent holiness churches."[65] The best known of these, and certainly the most enduring, was Phineas Bresee's Church of the Nazarene, founded in 1908. In the newly industrializing cities these churches appealed particularly to the poorest classes; in rural areas their appeal seems generally to have been equally potent for all classes. Everywhere holiness churches attracted more women than men to their congregations, as did the Creffield sect, and women often occupied central roles in those churches because of the emphasis on lay involvement. But it is not clear that holiness movement congregations attracted women in greater numbers than all religious denominations and movements did throughout the nineteenth century. In particular, all churches that emphasized the personal nature of a relationship with God, unmediated by authority figures (invariably male), attracted substantial numbers of women.

The creation of new churches was much more than an institutional reordering; it represented an increasingly profound difference in doctrine and practices. By the late nineteenth century, the new churches had become known for enthusiastic and ecstatic practices – shouts of praise, waving of arms, and so on – which derived from stressing the power of the holy spirit within each individual. Holiness people also criticized the established churches, especially the Methodists, for their worldliness, their laxness in discipline and membership standards, their ecclesiastical bureaucracies, and their church-building programs, all of which they claimed were too often given priority over individual salvation. In contrast to the worldliness they saw around them, many holiness groups encouraged asceticism and plain living in all things. The gap between these two varieties of Christianity grew apace as members of the established churches weighed in with their own criticisms of followers of the holiness movement as "fanatics."

We will see shortly that Creffield was very much a part of the holiness movement. He joined it, however, only a few years before a crisis disrupted the already fragmented movement and a new direction was taken by many of its members. Some preachers in the first years of the new century saw speaking in tongues, a gift given by God to the apostles on the day of the Pentecost, as "the definitive sign that one had received Spirit baptism." For these people the presence of the Holy Spirit was manifested not just by an "inner witness" but also by outward "charisms" such as tongues, prophecy, and healing. The result was the Pentecostal movement, usually dated from William Seymour's Azusa Street Revival in Los Angeles in 1906 and which has become the principal legacy of the holiness movement in the century since then.[66]

THE CREFFIELD SECT: HOLINESS IN OREGON

Contemporary accounts of the sect's beliefs and practices, statements to the press by Creffield and others, and articles published by Creffield in 1901 and 1902 make it clear that the sect was an Oregon instantiation of the holiness movement. In one of those articles, "He'll Not Compromise," Creffield argued that true believers should not concern themselves with "charity" but with baptism with the fire of the Holy Ghost.[67] There were too many "soft" preachers in the holiness movement who were willing to compromise with the world. A person truly baptized with the fire of the Holy Ghost would not think that way: "When you get baptized with fire," he argued, "fear of man is burned out, and all you see is the soul plunging into an everlasting, burning, seething hell, and your cry becomes 'Holiness or hell.'" Preachers who looked for success in this world, who counted conversions or craved worldly recognition, had forgotten the essence of holiness. Our words cannot capture Creffield's own fire better than his:

> There are evangelists who were once all aglow, a flame of fire. Today they are a back number. What's the cause? Compromise, human sympathy, shrinking from persecutions, lowering God's standards a little, letting down the bars and giving carnality a chance to creep in, keeping silent when they should rebuke sin, grieving the Spirit, and getting so at last that they can not detect the devil creeping in.

"God save us from compromising preachers," he concluded. Creffield's earlier article, "Holiness," covered much the same ground. "'Be ye holy' is

just as much a command as 'Thou shalt not steal,'" he insisted, adding
that "without holiness no man shall see the Lord" and using a phrase he
would later cite in another piece – "it is either holiness or Hell."[68] He
brought the same kind of fire to his preaching, exhorting and exciting his
followers in much the same way that an eyewitness described him as acting when he had been in Salem earlier – "jumping up in the air and going
through all kinds of antics."[69]

Creffield brooked no compromise. He taught that the end of the world
would soon arrive, and a new world come, in which there would be no
sin, as in early Eden. But only the truly sanctified would be saved to enjoy
it, only those baptized with the fire. "If we ever expect to gain Heaven,
and see the King in his beauty," he wrote, "we must live holy lives here
on earth."[70] As one reporter put it, "he thinks no one can be saved unless
filled with the power of the Holy Ghost." When you were baptized with
fire, you could not sin. "We are told in the Bible that the Apostles lived
without sin," he told the reporter, because "they lived by faith"; he insisted, "I can live the same way." The alternative to true holiness was hell,
a concept in which Creffield believed deeply, scorning "the modern doctrine that there is no material hell and that Satan does not exist in form."
Creffield's conversion to this radical version of holiness came, according to
his own account, through many months of prayer, after which he received
the Holy Ghost, which told him to leave the Salvation Army "and follow
evangelistic work." It also instructed him to "live a life of pure faith," to
"do everything by faith."[71] Although there was some talk in the fall of 1903
about proselytization,[72] Creffield evinced no interest in doing good works
in the world, despite the prior Salvation Army connections of many of his
adherents.

Although Charles Brooks played a major role as a kind of second in
command, Creffield had a special status in the sect. Like other holiness
preachers, it did not matter that he had no formal theological training or
appointment from some authority. Sanctified preachers were "immediately
directed by the spirit" and considered themselves "the special instruments
of the Spirit," the men, and occasionally women, who could convey the
message of redemption.[73] Creffield, unusually, went further, claiming to
be a prophet and an apostle. He announced himself as "Joshua II" during
his time in Corvallis, and the designation remained a constant one until
his death in May 1906.[74] Creffield thus wished his followers to believe that
he was much more than a minister of the gospel – that he was the second
coming of the man who had led the Israelites into Canaan. Although not
equal to him in status, Joshua was Moses' successor and, most importantly,

was "filled by the Spirit of God."[75] God was in Joshua and worked through him, as he worked in and through the apostles who received the Holy Spirit on the day of the Pentecost, and by taking his name Creffield claimed a similar status and authority. In addition, he was said by his followers to be "an apostle endowed with the power of the apostles of Christ."[76] While the name of Joshua was used throughout his career, for a time Creffield also took on another prophetic guise, that of Elijah, and in 1906 he and his followers came to believe that he was in some way divine, that he could not be killed and would rise from the dead. However, there is no evidence of any such beliefs in 1903.

What Creffield did claim throughout, however, was that he received messages from God and had a duty to disseminate them. "God revealed himself to me ... in the form of messages," he told a reporter in 1904, "He spoke to me" and "I heard his voice." Creffield did nothing "without querying heaven and receiving direction from above." He read his Bible constantly, for "in the Bible God speaks to men, and we must search the Scriptures to know the will of God."[77] Like the apostles, he had been given the power to "intercede" between Heaven and those on the earth.[78] While Creffield no doubt did believe that he had received messages directly from God, he was also deeply influenced, and led to reject the Army, by the teachings of Martin Wells Knapp, a holiness preacher based in Cincinnati. Knapp was a one-time Methodist Episcopal Church pastor whose career was in many ways a microcosm of the holiness movement itself. He experienced sanctification in 1889 and organized a series of revival meetings in Cincinnati before establishing his own organization in 1897. Although Knapp died in 1901, his International Apostolic Holiness Union continued to operate. The Union later merged with others to form, in 1922, one of the largest holiness breakaway churches, the Pilgrim Holiness Church, which is now part of the Wesleyan Church.[79] It was Knapp's journal, published by God's Bible School in Cincinnati, in which Creffield published "He'll Not Compromise," and Creffield was a principal member of a small group of Knapp followers in The Dalles in 1902. Although others in the group at The Dalles later insisted that Creffield became too radical, he continued to look on Knapp as an inspiration and had his Corvallis followers sing hymns composed by Knapp.[80]

Sect members absorbed Creffield's teachings fully. Their theology stressed sanctification and living a life of holiness. Frank Hurt, for example, claimed that he "became sanctified" after he left the Salvation Army and joined Creffield, and he referred to the group as "the holiness people."[81] O.V. Hurt offered an impassioned defence of the group during his brief time as an active member, in which he sought to place it in the mainstream of holiness tradition. "They preach the faith of John Wesley," he insisted in an interview with the *Corvallis Times* in late 1903; the sect, he assured readers, was composed of men and women "sincere and honest in their belief" with views "but slightly in advance of what has been the foundation of many new sects."[82] Many members matched Creffield in their ardency. "We take the Bible in its entirety," Sampson Levins told a Portland *Evening Telegram* reporter, "and do not, like other Churches, admit a member because he pays the membership fee." The qualification for membership was simple – "one must be saved." That meant having received the Holy Spirit, and the person seeking admission would have to be sure that he or she had done so. "It is," Levins continued, "the old religion from the time when Christ was on earth."[83] Frank Hurt explained to the same reporter that he had left the Salvation Army "because I found it had compromised with the world." There would be no compromise with the Creffield sect: "To follow the Bible in its entirety is our object, to do as the book bids is our one purpose."[84]

While Creffield was Joshua from early on, his group of followers had no formal name. They referred to themselves as "come-outers" or "God's anointed," and Frank Hurt and Sampson Levins both said they preferred "Church of God."[85] They also called themselves "apostles," probably because like the original apostles they believed they were blessed with the Holy Spirit. In 1904 officials gave the name of the religion as "Creffieldism," among other things. But the name that was most commonly used, for them if not by them, after the fall of 1903, was "Holy Rollers," an epithet possibly derived from the practice of rolling on the ground, or, some claimed, because members were required to sign a document known as a "holy roll" once sanctified. The Creffield group did not care for the name, but it stuck.[86] Later, especially given the widespread notoriety of the Creffield sect, it became a general term of abuse for radical holiness groups.[87]

Many holiness people of the period were criticized for the wildness and "fanaticism" of their meetings, wherein nothing was allowed to "hinder the freedom and spontaneity of the message directly inspired by the spirit."[88] The Creffield sect was no exception. Meetings were held frequently and lasted many hours. When the group was at the Hurt house in the fall of 1903, these meetings took place at 6:00 a.m. and 7:30 p.m. and involved "testimony" and prayer, often for many hours on end.[89] But such bland words do not capture the enthusiasm of the participants. Members were exhorted to open themselves to receive the Holy Spirit, and they engaged in a variety of ecstatic and enthusiastic practices. They rolled on the ground, shouted about God and the spirit, and went into long trances. Contemporary accounts made much of these behaviours, especially the rolling on the floor. Adherents would "spend hours tumbling about the floor," they would "roll on the floor, groan, scream, pray, shout and otherwise give evidence of great bodily and mental agitation."[90] At other times they would "lie on the floor for hours" and while doing so "would pray continually" or "shout so that they could be heard half a mile away."[91] Esther Mitchell believed that she should spend every minute of her time in prayer, and Frank and Mollie Hurt were said to "often spend entire days and nights lying flat on the floor, face downward, praying to the Lord for further light."[92] This was in conformity with "teachings of the Bible, which say that one should fall on one's face to call for different things."[93] Such practices were not restricted to meetings; according to Burgess Starr, his wife, Donna, "took to rolling around the floor of their home all night,"[94] and a number of people continued their ecstatic practices after being institutionalized.

There are suggestions that the rolling on the floor was to atone for sins, and that may at times have been the case.[95] But it is more likely that the various ecstatic practices, some of which were not uncommon in the Salvation Army,[96] were for purposes standard to most holiness groups – they both facilitated the receipt of the Holy Spirit and were manifestations of that spirit's presence. As Ann Taves demonstrates, all Protestant groups whose members experienced "fits, trances, and visions" explained them by references to "the 'power' or 'presence' or 'indwelling' of God, or Christ, or the Spirit."[97] The spirit transformed Creffield's group, as it did the followers of Bresee's Church of the Nazarene, enlarging and strengthening their psyches and importing thereby a mystical element to Christian devotion.[98] There is no evidence, however, that Creffield or any of his followers claimed either the gift of healing or that of speaking in tongues, both, especially the latter, features of the Pentecostal movement.[99] In this sense the sect followed "mainstream" holiness, for most holiness groups disapproved of the idea of speaking in tongues.

Over time ecstatic practices meant more than inculcation with the Holy Spirit, as by the fall of 1903, and perhaps earlier, members came to believe that they, as well as Creffield, could have "direct communication with the almighty" while in trances.[100] Frank Hurt explained that "the Lord speaks to us as his children and reveals his will through the spirit that is in us." One can sense the thrill that went through him as he went on: "We can feel the very will of God."[101] O.V. Hurt later said he had witnessed his wife and daughters roll about the floor for hours and then "rise and claim to have received divine messages."[102] Frank Hurt stated in April 1904 that "at first messages were received from God by Creffield, ... [but] now all receive direct commands from the Lord."[103] The earliest reference to this direct communication can be dated to the period immediately prior to Smith Island, when James Berry was still engaged to Maud Creffield; Berry later claimed that she "did anything that came into her mind, saying that she had received a message from the Lord to do so."[104]

Other physical manifestations distressed contemporaries. When members of the sect were seen in public they looked haggard, hollow-eyed, and showed signs of "great mental or nervous excitement."[105] Lack of food likely accounted for some of this; on occasions sect members would fast for days at a time.[106] Lack of sleep no doubt contributed as well, for receipt of the Holy Spirit frequently kept people up all or most of the night. As for "mental or nervous excitement," it should not have been surprising to see it in people who believed they had received the Holy Spirit. Two aspects of the sect's refusal to compromise with the world and members' sense of being "God's anointed" require extended discussion because they were crucial to the community's reaction to the group. Like other holiness leaders, Creffield exhorted his followers to both abandon the worldly desire for material goods and to forsake relationships with those who were not in the sect. He apparently abhorred the Salvation Army's practice of soliciting for funds: "it is not right to hold ice cream socials and other social gatherings where money is taken," he told a reporter.[107] Frank Hurt offered a simple statement of the attitude to material wealth: "we do not believe that those saved and having their names inscribed in heaven should enjoy luxuries."[108] But over time this forbearance amounted to much more than denial of luxuries. As a former follower put it after she had left the group, "to follow Creffield's teachings to the letter ... [a person] must wear old clothes, no shoes and stockings ... eat only one thing at a meal ... sleep on the floor ... know what it is to feel cold and hunger."[109] Not only clothing but also food, dishes, and furniture should all be as simple as possible, and many household items were deemed unnecessary for people who wished to eschew the trappings of "civilized" life. Louis Hartley's complaints about the sect included the fact that his daughter Sophia had "destroyed her clothing" and that she and her mother had broken all the ornamental dishes, leaving him to eat off "the plainest" of them. In a 1906 petition for divorce from Cora, he complained that she had "burnt furniture, clothing, ornaments, watches, jewelry and generally everything necessary to the comfort of a well-regulated household."[110] Adherents even refused to sit in chairs, for man, not God, had made such things, and there is one suggestion that they eschewed artificial light.[111]

Although anti-materialism formed part of Creffield's teachings from early on,[112] it does not seem to have manifested itself strongly to outsiders until after Smith Island, and it became more extreme over time. By 1904 members were refusing to use any furniture at all.[113] By then also, although we think not initially, anti-materialism had been extended to include food taboos. Pork was not permitted and, according to one report, members were to eschew all meat and other cooked food.[114] From early on, not surprisingly, Creffield preached prohibitions against smoking and drinking, which Frank Hurt said were "filthiness of the flesh and in violation of the rules of the Bible."[115] Thus the Creffield sect members adhered closely to the popular holiness aphorism – "In the world, not of the world" – and in the process were heirs to a long tradition of asceticism and self-denial being used as "a transcendent method of attaining a higher level of spiritual connectedness with Christ."[116] Florence Seeley explained the link between true holiness and the rejection of material goods: "In time we will be restored to innocence and purity such as marked the condition of Adam and Eve, but in order to reach that state we must put away all that is sinful. To do this we must conquer our pride and everything that tends to make us proud, and this includes the destruction of clothing and ornaments."[117]

One aspect of the rejection of fine clothing became particularly controversial. O.V. Hurt claimed in 1906 that "Creffield made the women burn all their clothes as a sacrifice and wear nothing but thin wrappers."[118] These "wrappers" were simple shifts, covering the women neck to toe but not otherwise restricting their bodies or their movements. A woman who claimed to have seen the garments described them as "'Mother Hubbard' dresses which were ankle-length with full skirts gathered into narrow yokes with long sleeves and high necklines."[119] This particular aspect of anti-materialism – an attempt perhaps to dress as people had done in Jesus' day – would lead in time to broader concerns about accompanying immoral practices.

Anti-materialism was by no means uncommon within the holiness movement. Wesley had disapproved of adornment, and in many groups very strict codes emerged. Some holiness leaders were criticized for teaching that their members "should not sleep upon their beds, but make their couch on the ground ... eat crackers out of the dirt ... or go without food."[120] Such codes were often in part derived from the fact that holiness had its greatest appeal among the dispossessed, with adherents finding "virtue in the necessity of their condition."[121] But the codes were also fundamentally underpinned by strength of conviction. For people like the Hurts and the Hartleys, asceticism was a marker of true holiness rather than acceptance and valorization of a pre-existing socioeconomic condition.

Anti-materialism brought the sect much criticism. It was wasteful and destructive and, since it was accompanied by what more than one newspaper referred to sarcastically as "the Creffield plan that God will provide," it offended economic morality.[122] Creffield abhorred both money and the fact that most denominations solicited it, and he taught instead that God's chosen children should not work, that God would take care of them. This was fundamentally opposed to early twentieth-century liberal economic ideas, which stressed self-reliance and material accumulation. Not surprisingly, in practice God's provision meant living off those members who worked and using money and accommodation provided by O.V. Hurt. Some members did work and insisted on stressing that to the press,[123] but Creffield was often concerned about finances, especially early on, before he and others moved into the Hurt house. James Berry left the sect in part because a suggestion was made that he should sell his possessions and donate the proceeds to the group to build a "tabernacle."[124]

Along with rejection of material things went a second highly controversial teaching – rejection of relationships outside the group. In The Dalles in 1902 Creffield had taught that his followers should eschew relationships with non-believers, and in Corvallis he also wanted members to forsake all others, including their families, and devote themselves exclusively to the sect.[125] Members should not see their old friends. This philosophy was espoused in "He'll Not Compromise," Creffield asserting that "when you get baptized with fire, your friends become few." Isolation from the rest of the community was manifested early, with the group making every effort to exclude "the public" from the Smith Island camp and their services. Over time this isolation became more pronounced. As the *Corvallis Times* put it, "the members of the sect are withdrawn from the world, and must have nothing to do with those who remain in the world." Sophia Hartley did not believe that "there is a Christian in any of the other churches."[126]

This was not simply a matter of preference for people who shared one's beliefs; it was a rejection of all who did not, no matter what the relationship between the believer and the non-believer. As her brother Perry later put it, Esther Mitchell "refused to have anything to do with the members of her own family, believing them to be defiled and accursed of God."[127]

A similar statement was made by George Mitchell's defence lawyer after a visit to Oregon in May 1906; women were told that "their husbands were defiled and impure and that the family relationship should no longer be continued."[128] Donna Starr refused even to shake hands with her husband when he visited her in Corvallis in 1903, "because she had been taught to have nothing to do with him on account of his relations with the wicked world."[129] Sarah Hurt claimed in June 1904 that her husband was "not related to her" and that "Christ [was] her husband."[130] This was a consistent feature of Creffield's teaching from the beginning and became more pronounced over time, extending according to one rumour to a ban on even touching the hand of "an ordinary sinner."[131]

Separatism was often the corollary of holiness; Christians who achieved true holiness could not live among those who had not.[132] It was but a short step from separation from established churches to separation from family – although it was not a step that many holiness groups took in practice. The isolationism practised by Creffield's followers later contributed substantially to the community turning violently against the sect, for it also represented a rejection of that bedrock societal institution, marriage. Separatism encompassed matters as simple as a wife not cooking meals for her husband after a day's work and extended to the radical notion that husbands were not really husbands in the sight of God. Louis Hartley's divorce petition of 1906 complained, for example, that his wife "pronounces him unclean," and insisted that he was driven to divorce because she refused to "return to her marriage obligations."[133] As the *Corvallis Times* complained, "a bitter alternative was necessarily left to a husband whose wife was in the sect and he was not. She was out of the world, and he was of the earth earthy, and she would have nothing to do with him."[134] Sarah Hurt gave up caring for her adopted infant.[135] Fathers were not spared their children's contempt either; according to O.V. Hurt, his daughter Maud came to refer to him as "that old man Hurt."[136] Hurt summarized the overall effect of these teachings on Creffield's female followers: "They let their children, their husbands and their parents go uncared for and without a kind thought or word."[137]

In telling his followers that they must reject their families Creffield made very large demands on them, as he did in insisting on radical changes in behaviours in other areas of their lives. Such demands increased over time as Creffield's teachings became more extreme. That they were largely obeyed suggests that over time the sect members developed an ever-increasing emotional and psychological reliance on him, to the point that it was possible to depart from Christian ideals and to lose sight of what it was that had attracted members to "holiness" in the first place. We will see later that this replacement of the Christian message with a particular Christian leader may have led to extra-marital sexual relations and did lead to murder and suicide, all highly "un-Christian" acts.

The Creffield sect was an unusual phenomenon in 1903, not just in Corvallis but in Oregon generally. There were other holiness groups operating, including M.L. Ryan's followers in Salem and the Knapp group in The Dalles. But the Oregon holiness movement consisted of isolated groups, most of which operated outside the notice of even the small town press.[138] The Creffield sect likewise escaped attention for many months, but gradually knowledge of it grew, and that knowledge created in turn uncertainty, confusion, and, ultimately, substantial hostility. But that is a subject for another chapter. We will also defer discussion of what in 1906, after Creffield had been killed, dominated discussion of the sect – the supposed sexual activity that took place between Creffield and his female adherents. We do so because the purpose of this chapter is to catalogue what we feel confident that we know about the sect as it operated in 1903, and we have doubts about whether sex was an aspect of the group's activities and beliefs at that time. Moreover, explaining those doubts is better done after we have completed the narrative of Creffield's time in Corvallis.

THE APPEAL OF RADICAL HOLINESS:
WOMEN AND RELIGION IN CORVALLIS

Contemporaries struggled to account for Creffield's appeal to his followers. Most of the time they alluded to his having some kind of "occult" power, or an ability to hypnotize or exercise "mental telepathy."[139] They also explained his influence over the women in his group by reference to their being "weak-minded," reflecting both a long tradition of associating religious enthusiasm, especially among women, with weak-mindedness, and the more recent tendency of psychiatrists to draw a correlation between religious extremism and supposed female emotionalism.[140]

Along with such explanations went a tendency to deprecate Creffield by insisting on his lack of sincerity, which made his teachings "false" religion. Before he was tried for adultery, the *Corvallis Times* confidently announced that Creffield, "the rogue," would "play the crazy dodge and instead of his just desserts . . . be sent to the asylum."[141] This kind of assessment was wildly wrong. Creffield had an abundance of faith. He believed in his teachings, in holiness and the possibility of its attainment, and he was willing to risk and sacrifice much to achieve it. Some press reports conceded that he was indeed "a sincere, if extravagant, religious teacher." And even his critics acknowledged that Creffield was an impressive preacher. He had "a strong voice" and "a good flow of language"; he was "most forceful, convincing and magnetic."[142] He was also said to be well educated, at least in biblical matters, and in that area, according to O.V. Hurt, "few could hold their own with him in argumentation." Hurt also observed that he had a "wonderful power" over his followers.[143]

It is by no means surprising that Creffield's critics denied his sincerity and attributed his success to hypnotism and the weak-mindedness of his female followers. As the *Corvallis Times* put it, what else but hypnotism could allow "this insignificant man" to gain such "control over daughters as to cause them to deny their parents, and such power over wives as to induce them to forswear their own marital relations."[144] But if contemporaries evaded the hard questions, we cannot. The answers must lie in a combination of social context, individual predilection for religion, the power of Creffield's preaching, and the indefinable sense of freedom and power that holiness gave to its most ardent adherents.

To a certain extent Corvallis was a promising place for Creffield's religious outreach. It had a flourishing church community, and church members, including Sarah Hurt and her children, were sufficiently enthusiastic about their religion to support that ubiquitous feature of nineteenth- and early twentieth-century American life, the revival meeting.[145] Nor were Creffield's followers the only people in Corvallis who could be drawn to new religious ideas; both the Spiritualists and the Seventh-day Adventists established themselves in the town in this period and recruited local members.[146] But the general pervasiveness of Christian belief takes us a very small way in explaining Creffield's success. Despite the important role Methodist missionaries played in its early settlement, Oregon had no substantial tradition of radical movements, religious or secular.[147] Indeed, church membership in the state as a whole was low and, as we have seen, the holiness movement had little impact beyond Creffield's and Ryan's groups and the followers of Knapp in The Dalles.[148] Ironically, given the storm that was shortly to break, a *Corvallis Gazette* editorial in July 1903 lamented the lack of enthusiasm for religion in the community, attributing it to loss of the fear of hell.[149]

If Corvallis was not a hotbed of religious enthusiasm, the personalities of Creffield's followers must to a large degree explain his success there, especially given his relative failure elsewhere. Many in the group had a history of enthusiasm in religion through the Salvation Army. As the *Corvallis Gazette* recognized, they were "very conscientious" people who were "possessed of a sensitive religious nature"; such "well-meaning people," it lamented, were "apt to be led astray."[150] Moreover, the enthusiasm and ecstasy that characterized the sect's practices were not untypical of the Army, and members therefore did not make such a great leap when they went from one to the other in response to the obvious power of Creffield's promise of salvation.

If Creffield's success can be explained through individual factors – the coming together of willing minds and a persuasive leader – we must still ask why so many of those minds were female. Historians have had little to say about the history of women in Oregon, and much of what has been written concerns the struggle for suffrage, achieved in 1912 after six referenda.[151] While the state had relatively liberal divorce and married women's property laws and tough sanctions against wife-beating,[152] women's roles in Oregon society were principally defined, as elsewhere, by duties of home and family. To the extent that women engaged in public activities, those were limited to involvement in churches or temperance organizations or the women's club movement.[153] In short, what we know of women's status and gender roles in Oregon does not help explain why Oregon women were more attracted to the sect than men.

Throughout the nineteenth and early twentieth centuries, however, women were over-represented in church congregations of all kinds in the United States, and they seem to have been particularly attracted to evangelical religion and other radical movements, such as the breakaway holiness groups of the later nineteenth century.[154] The Creffield sect was thus not untypical. Historians have suggested a variety of explanations for these trends, some of which seem particularly well suited to explaining the female preponderance in this particular group. It has been argued, for example, that women's social roles required a level of submissiveness to authority, and of piety, morality, and self-denial, that fitted the attributes of enthusiastic churchgoers. As Marks argues, late nineteenth-century Protestantism was gendered, imbued with female imagery.[155] One can certainly see many of these characteristics in the Creffield sect women, and they form a clear contrast with men's cultural roles as competitive, self-reliant, and self-assertive. Maud Hurt's and James Berry's respective characters reflect these different world-views. It has been similarly suggested that religion provided for married women in particular a sense of importance within their own sphere, compensating in part for the loss of independence that marital submission to male authority entailed.

Other explanations are also persuasive in accounting for both the intensity of the beliefs of Creffield's followers and their willingness to flout social, economic, and gender conventions. First, the theology of more radical groups, including "come-outer" sects, was egalitarian, in the sense that it taught that the only real distinction between people was that between the saved and the unsaved. Divisions based on race, class, and gender were downplayed, which appealed to those who otherwise had lower status based on these grounds. As Haynes puts it, "religious ardor functioned as a common denominator in leveling sex and class differences."[156] Women in the Creffield sect, whether married or single, responded to the message that men and women were equal in the sight of God and equal in their capacity to know and love God, while working-class women, like the Seeleys, as well as men like Levins and Campbell, could hold their heads up in the company of their social "betters," even feel superior and self-righteous compared with the unsaved. Second, radical religion appealed to a set of values different from those stressed in mainstream culture. As with the Creffield sect, pre-millennialism was often accompanied by a critique of the market economy and acquisitiveness, which were men's spheres. At the same time, if women were expected to embrace emotional expression and value relationships, holiness offered them a legitimate outlet for the former and the best of all relationships – a direct, personal one with God.

Studies of women and religion also stress that holiness and similar movements gave women power, independence, and a freedom to act not found elsewhere in their lives. They were often expected to preach or testify, and in a group like the Salvation Army, they held important positions of authority. In the Creffield sect human authority rested in Creffield and, to a lesser extent, Brooks, and the only people who spoke extensively to the press were Frank and O.V. Hurt and Sampson Levins. But Sarah Hurt had a kind of spiritual authority and, more importantly, all the women could commune with God, were equal by his laws and equally valuable to him as adherents. And there is ample evidence that if following Creffield did not give the women status within the group itself, it freed them from pre-existing constraints. They defied and denied the authority of husbands, fathers, and employers, they participated equally with the men in the group other than Creffield, and they behaved in ways otherwise unthinkable. As Winston argues with reference to the Salvation Army, giving oneself to God "validated the emotional aspects of religion and justified female preaching by emphasizing the unfettered prompting of the Holy Spirit." Blauvelt makes a similar argument, that religion "gave women a new set of values often at odds with their husbands' . . . and imbued them with a self-confidence and sense of righteousness that enabled them to stand up to human authority."[157] In the Creffield sect working- and middle-class women alike found the freedom of adherence to God liberating from the bonds of social and gender convention. Whatever the cause, Rose Seeley certainly remembered her time spent camping on Smith Island as an intensely happy period.[158]

It is impossible to explain precisely why the women in the Creffield sect were so attracted to it and why they took up Creffield's teachings with such fervour, especially in the absence of their own testimony. But some combination of the power of his preaching, their personal affinity for radical religion, and the more general explanations explored above likely provide the answer. While membership entailed submission to God and Creffield, it also brought a feeling of power, worthiness, and agency. The women who followed Creffield received the enormous power of the Holy Spirit without a male authority figure acting as intermediary. They could also testify and seek to persuade others of its glory. Their sense of their place in the world ultimately derived not from Creffield, a male authority figure like a husband or father, but from the knowledge that they were sanctified and that whatever the world thought of them, they were at one with God. These women did not join political struggles for suffrage and temperance, and they did not follow the path of many lower-class girls and experience the new freedom that came from working in the expanding cities of the Gilded Age. But they differed little from the thousands of girls and women who joined the Salvation Army in part because it offered a degree of freedom and some excitement;[159] the excitement in their case was the thrill of sanctification, and the freedom was the hope of everlasting life.

3

Driving Out the Sect

THE TRIUMPH OF THE
WHITE CAPS, 1903-1904

The Bonfire of the Vanities

CORVALLIS TOLERATED THE Creffield sect for much of 1903, but in the last two months of the year the group went too far, and the community responded with threats and, ultimately, substantial violence, sufficient to drive the leaders out. Such an outcome would have been difficult to predict when the Smith Island camp was abandoned with the onset of fall, and many sect members moved into the Hurt residence. In addition to the Hurts, Creffield and Brooks lived there, as likely did Esther Mitchell, Donna Starr, Ona Baldwin, Attie Bray, and Florence and Rose Seeley. Frank Hurt and his wife and sister-in-law occupied their own small cottage nearby, while Levins and Campbell lived in a tent pitched in Frank's yard.[1] Cora and Sophia Hartley were frequent visitors and occasional residents, whenever Louis was away on business.[2] There the group continued their meetings, during the day when O.V. was at work and in the evenings as well. Until late October O.V. was still an outsider, tolerant of his family's religious enthusiasms but not a sect member.

The come-outers were not as tolerant of the agnosticism of the man they called the "Black Devil." They had tried for months to convert him,[3] and in the last week of October they succeeded. On Wednesday, October 28, O.V. handed in his resignation from Kline's department store, along with a message that "he had been living in sin and that hereafter he intended to devote himself to the work of God."[4] That same night, with his moderating influence gone, the members engaged in an orgy of destruction.

Kitchen utensils and other goods were "beaten to pieces and buried." Buried with them was the group portrait, perhaps because it represented vanity and worldliness. Many articles were broken up and burned – "guitars, mandolins, chairs, window curtains, clothing, carpets," all "without regard to value or cost." With Louis away at the mines, a "considerable quantity of goods," including some furniture, belonging to the Hartleys was burned after being taken to the Hurt house. Ona Baldwin packed a trunk of her effects to take them to the fire also, but her father prevented her from taking it, although he could not, or did not, stop Ona herself from going to the Hurt house.[5] "The reason assigned for the destruction," reported the *Corvallis Times*, "is that it is the will of God."

Like the Bonfire of the Vanities ordered by Savonarola,[6] this destruction of worldly goods was a spectacular affirmation of the rejection of the things of the world, done "in order to fully sanctify the Hurt house."[7] But there was also a sinister aspect to the fire – neighbours reported that into it had gone cats and dogs, making it a "sacrificial fire." There were likely no "sacrifices," of course, for such a practice was not part of holiness beliefs. Creffield may have been testing his followers' willingness to accept whatever came through him as the word of God, and Frank Hurt later insisted that God had "commanded their destruction because the animals were a nuisance."[8] Word of the bonfire and "sacrifices" electrified the townsfolk, but they barely had time to digest the news when, on the following morning, the sect found more corrupting influences to destroy. The wooden sidewalks around the Hurt house were torn up, as were flowerbeds and shrubberies, and the fruit trees in the yard were uprooted. All was done "on a theory that God wills it."

The town could talk of nothing else. And people wanted to see for themselves; by the afternoon of Thursday, October 29, 75 to 100 people were lining the walk in front of the Hurt house. According to the *Corvallis Times*, the fires demonstrated not just "religious fanaticism" but a state of mind "bordering insanity." Officialdom intervened, and late in the afternoon Deputy D.A. Edwin Bryson and Sheriff M.P. Burnett paid a visit to the house.[9] They found the front gate secured against them and had to clamber over a fence. Their knock was answered by Creffield, who both refused them entry and said that they could not see O.V. Hurt because he was "seeking God." A confrontation was avoided when the crowd spotted Hurt in the yard on the other side of the house and directed Bryson and Burnett there. If the officers were investigating whether there had been cruelty to animals, O.V. seems to have mollified them by saying that no cats had been burned and downplaying the dog accusations. A dog had indeed gone into the fire, but it was a stray that would not stay away from the house. It had first been killed "in a humane way." Hurt's explanation seemed to satisfy Bryson and Burnett, who left without taking further action, but the *Corvallis Times* did not believe it, noting that the story that more than one dog, and a few cats, had been burned "comes from the neighbours," some of whom "insist" that it was true.

THE COMMUNITY RESPONDS

That evening the streets outside the Hurt house became even more crowded as people finished work and wandered over. Many were there to see what the sect would do, but the members stayed inside and kept quiet. Some in the crowd believed that more action was needed, and that evening saw the first of a series of moves against the sect. The house was stoned, the barrage going on for some time and breaking many windows as "rocks rattled frequently on the roof or crashed through window panes, scattering broken glass right and left." Two men tried to gain access to the house, "knocking loudly at the door" and, when this failed, breaking the glass of the door. But those inside simply ignored it all, and eventually the crowd lost interest and left. Much as it disapproved of the sect, the *Corvallis Times* also condemned the "wanton, excuseless and brutal acts" of the townsfolk responsible for the stoning, asserting that they "should be sought out and punished."[10]

Bryson and Burnett must have given some thought to what they could, or should, do next. A deviant group was disrupting the town, both by its own actions and by the reactions it inflamed. Their answer was to use the civil insanity laws, the first of many occasions in this story on which resort would be had to them. On the complaint of any person, the county court judge was obliged to have the individual alleged to be insane brought in and examined by him and two doctors. In addition to potentially providing a way to get rid of Creffield and Brooks, an insanity proceeding was also a useful device to effect an entry into the Hurt house; Bryson and Burnett had wanted to enter the premises the day before but O.V. Hurt had invited them into only part of his home.

It was likely Bryson who made the allegations of insanity, and when Burnett and Deputy Henderson went to arrest the two men on Friday morning, October 30, they had a good look at the place. What they saw provided further grounds for concern. They found "most of the worshippers lying about on the floor on mats, blankets, and other places of rest."

In a room bare of furniture "a young girl" with "a cloth over her head apparently in a trance" was "at the moment receiving a message from on high" while the others wrote it down. Creffield's head "was close beside that of the youthful message-taker," resting on the same pillow, so perhaps he too was lying down with her. It was a disturbing scene, and suggested that there was more to worry about than strange religious ideas.

Creffield and Brooks were arrested and taken to the county courthouse where they were examined in a closed hearing for the whole of Friday afternoon before county court judge Virgil Watters.[11] The medical examinations were undertaken by Doctors Henry S. Pernot and B.A. Cathey,[12] with Bryson and Burnett in attendance. Sarah Hurt, Cora Hartley, Frank Hurt, and Ona Baldwin were all subpoenaed and testified. The process took some hours, but the two were eventually released that same evening. Although there is no record of the proceedings, the doctors must have concluded that they were dealing with eccentricity, rather than insanity. They would feel rather differently about the situation the following year. Ed Baldwin already felt it was time for more decisive action, for after Ona had given evidence he and others grabbed her and forcibly took her away, "screaming and wailing."[13] She had tried a day or two before to take her trunk and clothes to the Hurt house to burn them. In removing Ona, Baldwin was following the lead set by Louis Hartley, who on three separate occasions that fall had gone to the house and more or less forced Cora to return home.[14] Nonetheless Cora and Sophia were by now sufficiently emboldened to remain at the Hurts even though Louis had come home on Saturday, October 31.[15]

Since legal channels had proved ineffective, extra-legal ones were resorted to. As Creffield and Brooks were led out of the courthouse by Deputy Henderson he warned them "of the existence of a strong public sentiment against them" and advised them to leave town. Both men scoffed at the idea, insisting that "the Lord would take care of his own."[16] The details of what happened next are not available, but at noon on Saturday, October 31, O.V. and Frank Hurt went to Burnett's office to request protection. There were rumours that some kind of an assault was to be made that night – Halloween; there was "many a reference to tar and feathers, vigilance committees, and to proposals to find means for sending the apostles away." The Portland *Telegram* similarly noted that "a mob of citizens were preparing to present them with a coat of tar and feathers, and a pleasant ride out of town on a rail."[17] Burnett did spend the evening of the 31st in the Hurt house, leaving at midnight after the crowd that had gathered dispersed. There was one threatening moment when a crowd of young men from the OAC persuaded Creffield to come out and speak to them. When he emerged onto the porch the cry went up to duck him in the river, and he quickly withdrew into the house.[18]

While he provided the protection of the law, Burnett also told the Hurts that if Creffield and Brooks left there would be no cause for further trouble. This indication of where the sheriff's sympathies lay persuaded the two men to go, in the afternoon of Sunday, November 1. They had wanted to leave earlier but were afraid of the large crowd around the house. Not until it thinned as the afternoon wore on did they get away, Brooks leaving around 4 p.m. and Creffield an hour or so later. Brooks departed on foot; reflecting the greater danger he was in, Creffield was driven away in a buggy, probably by Frank Hurt. The Hartleys left also, persuaded by Louis to come home when he arrived from the south.

These events represented the first, and by no means the last, resort to extra-legal methods by the community. The idea of some kind of animal sacrifice was obviously deeply repellent, and people were starting to worry about the appearance of some sect members. They were "haggard of face and hollow of eye," and there was concern that the "peculiar faith" would "ultimately send some of them into the mad house."[19] There was also an element of civic embarrassment involved. The town had "received a black eye that will cling to her for years," for it was now known as "the place where the people make a practice of offering up cats and dogs as burnt offerings," complained the *Gazette*.[20] As importantly, by early November people were increasingly angry about the disruptive effect the sect had on families and were beginning to worry about moral questions. They "resented" the fact that "wives and daughters in the home joined the sect and other members of the family did not," and, even more, that the sect taught that its members should shun their families if they refused to join. Brooks had said as much at the sanity hearing. In addition, there were now suspicions about immoral activities. It was said that Creffield taught that "marriage was not necessary," and while nobody quite knew what it meant, the phrase "did as much as anything else in his system to bring him into public reproach." These concerns were likely linked to reports of the scene Burnett had witnessed when he took the two men into custody, that of a girl lying down and Creffield near her. That story had been "told and retold and always with indignation," with Creffield "set down as a mountebank."

The *Corvallis Times* reflected all these concerns in an editorial that both sought to justify community action and reaffirmed the constitutional right to practise religion, which, it insisted, extended even to a "holy roller."

Religious freedom meant that a person could destroy furniture if that was part of his or her faith – "provided his debts are paid and that the destruction of such articles is not to make of him or his a care upon the community." The same principle extended to the animals. A man could kill a cat, provided it was his cat. If he chose to burn the dead cat, that was not only acceptable but "wise," for "it is better sanitarily . . . that the carcass be reduced to ashes than to fester and decay either in or out of the ground." However, the editorial doubted that other aspects of the sect were protected by "religious privilege." That is, if "persons of moderate mental vigor are being led into false positions, that is not a proper worship." It was not right to use a "profession of superior godliness" to induce "delusion and folly," especially by "leading weak women into a state of mind where there is more frenzy than reason."

In keeping with its emphasis on the "weak-minded" female followers of Creffield, the editorial was most concerned that "home ties are wrecked and happiness driven away from firesides," which was a "great and irreparable wrong." It also noted that excess in religion could lead to insanity. Newspapers from other places reflected the same list of community concerns. The possible mental instability of the sect members was noted in the *Oregonian,*[21] while lengthy stories that appeared in the Portland *Evening Telegram* by a reporter sent down when the news of the bonfires first broke criticized ecstatic practices and family disunity.[22] The worship itself, with its wild shouts and screams, was "disgusting" and fanatical, but the major problem, what provoked a "genuine hatred," was the "disuniting" of families:

> The fact that so many women have been inveigled into the ranks is regarded with suspicion, as the sincerity of the leaders is generally doubted. Creffield is spoken of as a home-breaker. In more than one instance, it is said, he has persuaded women to desert their homes, and his orders are that when a wife becomes connected with the "Rollers" her husband must follow, or the family ties are severed, until such time as the obstinate family head accepts the spirit. This more than anything else, perhaps, has given rise to the ill feeling against the new sect.

Family destruction was especially troubling, the *Evening Telegram* later noted, because some of the women in the sect were "prominent in . . . social circles."[23]

The *Corvallis Times* clearly approved of the "deserved" threats that had compelled the men to leave, as did the *Gazette*. Although it hoped that in future the authorities, not a mob, would take any action required, the *Gazette* was not above predicting a little vigilantism: "It is but right . . . to warn these people that a single overt act on their part will be the signal for prompt and effective measures to rid Corvallis of a nuisance, and that will be a lesson to future Rollers and howlers."[24]

The first moves against Creffield ultimately had a very limited effect. On Wednesday, November 4, he and Brooks were again at the Hurt house, brought back by Frank Hurt.[25] Meetings were resumed, with the sounds of worship clearly heard from the street, and the members largely remained in seclusion. Some of the burned furniture was replaced, and renovations were started to "provide a comfortable room for religious worship" while most of the members' time was spent in Bible study.[26] Renovations were certainly needed. The house presented a "sorry appearance" according to one observer: "The ground is charred and barren and heaps of ashes mark the spots where some of the furnishings a few days ago were sent up in smoke. All the windows have been smashed and suspended sheets cut out a view of the interior."[27] In line with the general rejection of the world, O.V. Hurt had his phone disconnected at about this time.[28]

A serious confrontation had been avoided, but the crisis was far from over. The community kept a wary eye on the group, and the press warned that another "eruption" would bring retribution, and that "any day may bring forth an organized movement to drive them out of town by force."[29] Knowing the danger they were in, both Frank Hurt and his father engaged in some public relations exercises. Creffield would not be interviewed,[30] but Frank Hurt talked to the Portland *Evening Telegram* and O.V. to a *Corvallis Times* reporter. Frank was depicted as "affable" and "honest in his convictions" and "rather anxious that the world should know and understand" the sect.[31] He explained their beliefs and sought to refute published stories about their excesses. Only old pieces of furniture had been burned, to make room for worship. A few "trinkets" and goods "of no particular value" were also destroyed, because the group had no time for "luxuries." A dog and a cat had been killed, but they were animals the Hurts had wanted to be rid of for some time and had been unsuccessful in giving away. As the ground was hard, it was difficult to bury them, and the corpses were thrown on the fire "for sanitary reasons." Frank stressed that burning animals had "no connection with our religion," since "you find nothing like that in the Bible." He downplayed the practice of rolling on the ground, asserting that they more often lay on their faces in prayer, again "in accordance with the teachings of the Bible." Frank's public relations efforts were to good effect and a photograph of him in a subsequent issue of the *Telegram* had the caption: "This man appears sincere in his convictions."[32] But the reporter nonetheless believed the sect had something to hide. And he was unimpressed by the sight of O.V. Hurt, who was going about in old clothes with several days' growth of beard and an appearance of "heavy mental strain." Perhaps worse, O.V. was clearly under the control of his womenfolk.

Some ten days after Frank's interview, O.V. talked to one of the local newspapermen, to much the same effect.[33] He had not intended to resign from Kline's permanently, he explained, and indeed had now returned to his job. He defended his house guests. He himself had "not so much faith as have they," but they were entitled to their beliefs. (The reporter had the same impression of the extent of Hurt's convictions: "In all things Mr Hurt is as he was in former days, save that he is an adherent of the new faith, though less zealous than are others in the movement.") Like Frank, O.V. also sought to partly deny some of the stories about the sect's activities while, somewhat contradictorily, also evading responsibility for them. The household items burned were mostly rubbish, he said, "useless articles such as accumulate about all houses." He denied that any carpets had been burned, and said the sidewalks had not been destroyed but stored for future use. He also repeated his earlier claim that only one dog had been consigned to the flames. At the same time, he asserted that the fires had been lit while he was "occupied with other matters" and that "Brooks and Creffield were the leaders in the delivery of articles to the flames." According to the reporter, "It is apparent, from his conversation, that some things were burned without Mr Hurt's knowledge." It was an inconsistent performance, one in which his ambivalence comes through clearly. Regarding the animal burnings, O.V. was not entirely straight; there is other evidence that it was more than one dog, and he himself later testified that a number of animals were involved.[34]

Within a week of giving this interview, Hurt ordered Creffield, Brooks, and most other sect members out of his house.[35] Creffield and Brooks quietly left Corvallis in the afternoon of Thursday, November 19, and many others departed also. The press attributed O.V.'s action, taken just weeks after acceding to his family's entreaties to join and days after defending the group, both to a change of heart and to pressure from friends, especially James Berry, that he should no longer tolerate the group. It is also possible that on a visit to Portland made just before the expulsion O.V. learned more about the Smith Island camp, which caused him to turn against the prophet. Donna Starr had been forcibly taken back to Portland by Burgess sometime after the Smith Island camp,[36] and if Hurt visited them the latter may well have told him things. Possibly O.V. heard that Creffield "taught that marriage was not necessary," a story that was beginning to circulate and that almost certainly came from apostate Hattie Starr. Hurt himself attributed his decision to the animosity Creffield had aroused in Corvallis and insisted to a *Telegram* reporter that "nine-tenths of all the reports regarding the Rollers are false and the other tenth is greatly exaggerated."[37] Whatever the reason for it, Hurt's action was popular. The *Corvallis Times* was delighted and the *Gazette* confident that "the Holy Roller craze in this city is a closed incident."[38] The paper was wrong.

THE INCARCERATION OF ESTHER MITCHELL

Creffield's departure was accompanied by the first of what would be a number of instances of institutionalization of his followers. In mid-November, at about the same time that Creffield and Brooks left town, fifteen-year-old Esther Mitchell was taken to Portland and eventually placed in Oregon's Boys and Girls Aid Society (BGAS) Home there.[39] This was the work of her brothers, George and Perry, who at twenty and eighteen were only a few years older than Esther, and her sister Phoebe. After a period working in the Yamhill County lumber mills, by 1900 George Mitchell was following the same occupation in Portland.[40] Perry also lived in Portland, as did an older brother, Fred Mitchell.

The BGAS was a non-sectarian charity established in 1885 to look after children considered in need of care. A reflection of the period's discovery of the "child problem," it was one of a matrix of institutions established to care for delinquents and orphans, and to rescue "fallen" women. It performed a number of roles, its officers travelling throughout the state to investigate allegations of child abuse or neglect, but its most prominent one was running an institutional home in East Portland.[41] Although it was a private organization, it received state funding and carried out state functions.[42] It took children charged with, or convicted of, criminal offences, and was thus part of a series of piecemeal initiatives that served as precursors of a full-fledged juvenile delinquency system introduced not long after the time of this story.[43] Children not the subject of criminal proceedings could also be committed by the courts to its care for a variety of causes, including abuse, neglect, abandonment, and the immoral lives of parents.[44] The dominant figure in the BGAS in this period was Superintendent William Gardner. A sometime lawyer and businessman and former supervisor in a state asylum in Buffalo, New York, Gardner had been

superintendent since the early 1890s and would serve until 1913. Opinion-
ated, irascible, and an ardent defender of children in equal measure, he
was a classic exemplar of the middle-class "do-gooder" whose charity was
leavened with heavy doses of paternalistic self-righteousness.[45]

Esther Mitchell was initially removed from Corvallis and taken to
George's home in Portland, but she ran away and returned to Corvallis.
Phoebe Mitchell followed her and again took her to Portland. As home
restraint did not work, on November 18 Esther's siblings placed her with
the BGAS. Although some press stories suggest that she was placed in the
Society's home by court order, in fact she was simply confined at the
request of family members – "brought by her sister Phoebe Mitchell to
be cared for."[46] There is no record of a court order in the Society's records,
no commitment proceeding in either the Benton County Court or in the
Portland courts,[47] and no report of such a proceeding in the Portland
newspapers; given the interest that the *Telegram* in particular had taken in
the sect, it seems most unlikely that a court hearing would not have been
reported there at least. Moreover, it is not easy to see on what grounds a
court could have committed her. Gardner later claimed that she had been
examined by physicians and diagnosed with "acute religious mania," and
the Society's register describes her as having a "mind almost unhinged by
religious fanatics."[48] But insanity was not a statutory ground for committal to the Home, only to the asylum. The child protection legislation
covered abandonment and neglect, and one or both of these might have
covered Esther's case. Thus as far as we can tell, the Society took her in
and kept her under restraint at the request of the family, as it did on many
other occasions, although Gardner preferred that there be a court order
where possible.[49] Esther Mitchell's commitment was a further clear sign
that families were prepared to take measures to counteract the influence
of Creffield's teaching. The *Corvallis Times* applauded the action and had
no doubt that it was "religious agitation" that had "dethroned the mind of
one young woman of its reason."[50]

Esther Mitchell spent about three months in the Home, being released
on February 23, 1904. At some point, Gardner later alleged, she confessed
to him that she and Creffield had engaged in some sort of sexual activity,
but that allegation, which does not appear in the Society's records and
was almost certainly untrue, was not made publicly until much later.[51]
Throughout her stay Esther remained true to her religious convictions,
"carrying her bible with her at all times" and complaining that not enough
time was allowed her for prayer. Asserting that she still received messages
from God, she "refused to wear much clothing, would not associate with

the other inmates . . . and constantly read her bible until the officers had to take it away from her." She also, according to Perry Mitchell, "refused to recognize us [Perry and George] as her brothers, saying we were such in name only." Gardner told a reporter that in his view she was so deluded that she might have to be sent to the asylum.[52]

Esther Mitchell was released when her family decided to try a different disciplinary strategy – sending her back to her father in Illinois.[53] According to later accounts the move was partly motivated by fears that Creffield would try to effect her escape from the Home; by February 1904 he was in Portland. Esther was accompanied to Illinois by Perry and Phoebe, with the latter then returning to Oregon. It could not have been a pleasant sojourn with the man who had deserted her and her siblings in 1894, when Esther was just six years old. In Oregon Charles Mitchell had combined lack of worldly success with a difficult and disputatious, but unyieldingly self-righteous, personality, and despite a remarriage in 1903 none of this had changed.[54] A keen Salvation Army soldier and a prohibitionist, Charles was aggressively intolerant of the views of others.[55] He must have had little human sympathy for Esther, and none at all for her religious views. For her part Esther continued her holiness practices in Illinois and "refused to call her own father by that name, saying that her only father was God and that she had no father on earth."[56] After a few months, however, she became more complaisant and eventually returned to Oregon.

A COAT OF TAR AND FEATHERS

For the two to three weeks following the expulsion of Creffield and Brooks from the Hurt house the sect appeared to have been effectively broken up. Most members stayed in Corvallis, but, leaderless, they likely held few, if any, meetings. The sect's principal men – Creffield, Frank Hurt, and Brooks – all left town for a short while, and our knowledge of where they went is far from complete. The first two initially travelled west towards the coast, apparently with the idea of establishing the sect in the Yachats area. They passed through the Alsea Valley, but at one of the many river crossings to the west they had an accident, their buggy overturning and then breaking up in the stream.[57] Brooks had not gone with them, and the only story about his whereabouts was one told with much amusement. He visited a farm near Wren, some fifteen miles west of Corvallis, and told a woman that he was an apostle and should be fed. She summoned neighbours who threw him out still hungry. Creffield and others may have been in Eugene on December 10, when three people disrupted a Methodist service at the Humphrey Memorial Church there with their "vociferous" and "boisterous" worship. The press in Corvallis and Eugene speculated that the interlopers were members of the Creffield sect.

Some time after his watery misadventure Frank Hurt turned up in Portland, where he tried to contact Esther Mitchell at the BGAS Home. He was refused entry but was then seen hanging around the grounds, and he eventually intercepted her on her way to church on Sunday, December 6. He urged her to "Remember and keep on victory's side." That brief show of support enthused Esther such that she created a scene in the church, demanding to be allowed to "testify" to her beliefs.[58] Esther was also clandestinely visited by her sister Donna after Donna had several times been refused entry by the Home; she got in via the cellar and she and Esther were found "embracing and exclaiming 'Glory to God. Down with the devil. Victory. Victory.'"[59] Gardner later claimed that all this was engineered by Creffield, who planned to abduct her,[60] but there is no other evidence of that. Her fellow believers may indeed have wished to get her out, for they rightly thought that she had been institutionalized for her beliefs.

By sometime in mid-December the come-outers were back in the Corvallis area, setting up in a house just across the Willamette River in Linn County, invariably referred to as the "Beach house" after Anna Beach, whose land it was on.[61] Creffield himself arrived on December 18. The house was rented by one of the men – likely Frank Hurt, perhaps Wesley Seeley – and its occupants included Frank and Mollie Hurt, Creffield, Brooks, Levins, Campbell, Olive Sandell, Bray, and Wesley, Rose, and Florence Seeley. The group carried on their worship in a house without furniture but were careful not to make much noise. While the Hurt women did not move in, they visited often, the Beach house being only a few hundred yards from the ferry that linked Benton and Linn counties. Cora and Sophia Hartley also stayed at home, but the proximity of Creffield led to renewed worship in their house. He may have visited them there when Louis was away, for he did come into town on more than one occasion.

In returning to the area the group showed a dogged resistance to the community's efforts to suppress them. Indeed, they likely drew on those efforts to reinforce their beliefs. Creffield had long taught that one mark of true believers was that they would be persecuted. He had written in "He'll Not Compromise" that "consternation" would follow true holiness people, that members of other churches would "rise up in arms" against them and call them "fanatics," and, he predicted, "those of your own household may

fight you." No doubt he drummed this lesson into his followers throughout the latter months of 1903, and when the reaction came it likely served
only as further proof that he was right.

Despite the sect's attempt to keep a low profile, community intolerance
quickly manifested itself. The *Corvallis Gazette* was the first to issue a public warning of vigilante action:[62]

> Events are likely to occur in a few days, if the Rollers become in any way
> aggressive, that will put a stop to any further proceedings on their part. Mr.
> Creffield will be provided with a nice warm coat, that will fit him as closely
> as the paper on a wall, and that will contain more feathers than the wings
> he promises himself when he reaches the place where the holy roll is kept.
> He will also be given a walking pass out of this locality, and a warning about
> returning that he will do well to heed. This is the program outlined by some
> desperate and determined men in this vicinity, and there is no doubt that it
> will be carried out.

No specific reason was given for the threat, although when it was renewed
some ten days later the paper mentioned the problem of insanity among
the members: "We have no room in our county for men who murder
reason. Save your own neck, Parson Creffield, and the quicker you go
the better."[63]

These threats were made good on the evening of Monday, January 4,
1904. At about 9 p.m. some twenty men met on the Corvallis side of the
river, crossed on the ferry – there was no bridge across the Willamette until
1913[64] – and broke open the door of the Beach house.[65] As the women
sang, Creffield and Brooks were tied together and taken back across the
Willamette and marched down Main Street and through the town to a
bridge across the Mary's River about a quarter of a mile beyond the city
limits. There was no concealment; the vigilantes wore no masks and chose
a route that was as well lit as any. At the bridge the victims were made
to strip, covered with pine tar, and "bedecked with feathers galore," the
feathers provided by a woman of the town who had ripped up two pillows
for the purpose. Creffield proposed a prayer but was curtly told there
had already been too much praying. While Brooks was stoical, Creffield,
perhaps fearing that worse was to come, "trembled" and was "much fright-
ened" throughout the proceedings, according to one account giving way
to "tears and sobs repeatedly during the march to the bridge." Once the
treatment had been administered they were told to dress, to leave town
immediately, and not to return on pain of being hanged from a tree. They

did so, moving at full speed across the bridge and along the Albany Road. Campbell and Levins may also have been given a lesser form of the tar and feather treatment. Although the sources are inconsistent on this point,[66] it is probable that they were at least warned off if not also assaulted, for they left the Beach house forthwith.

The Corvallis newspapers refused to name any of the vigilantes, but did insist that most were known and that they were "men of standing and character" with "not a boy or hoodlum in the party."[67] All accounts agree that many of those involved were relatives of sect members. It seems probable that the vigilantes included Louis Hartley and his son Warren, Ed Baldwin, and Clarence Starr. Baldwin and Starr had apparently intended to attack Creffield just at the time that O.V. Hurt threw him out and were thus not averse to a little violence. The group might also have included Samuel Starr of Chehalis, another brother of Sarah Hurt. James Berry had joined with Clarence Starr and Baldwin in November, but he was probably not present, as January 4 was his wedding night.[68] His general forbearance throughout this story suggests that O.V. Hurt was probably not involved. Given the size of the group, others with no direct connection to the sect must have joined in as well.

The action was taken when it was for two principal reasons. The *Corvallis Gazette* attributed the timing to the fact that only in early January did a leader come forward to make good on the numerous threats that had filled the air for weeks: "Plenty of assistance could have been procured weeks ago had any one been willing to shoulder the responsibility of leadership," it asserted.[69] It seems reasonable that this was at least part of the explanation, and that the leader who stepped forward was the often-absent Louis Hartley. He had returned to Corvallis from an eastern trip in late December.[70]

But there was more. Commentary before and after the night of January 4 attributed public antipathy to the same causes that had been around for a couple of months – apparent insanity and the destruction of families. But a new issue also began to be spoken of in late December and was reiterated in later justifications of the vigilantism. The *Albany Democrat* was the first to give expression to this, predicting action in its Christmas Day issue because Creffield and Brooks were operating "a free love establishment" and "the people are tired of the disgraceful arrangement."[71] A group of men and women living in congregate fashion was viewed as inherently immoral, especially if that group included girls. The *Corvallis Times* expressed this concern more fully a few days after the tarring and feathering, stressing not just the impropriety but also the secrecy of it all:[72]

A system of religion was set up in which this pair of high priests and their followers worshipped behind barred doors and closely drawn blinds, behind which the public could neither pass nor see. Though a shock to the proprieties, it was alleged worship of Almighty God for these two huskies to live in the same locked house with a number of young girls, and do nothing in the world but be religious. Whether as fools or knaves, whether as fanatical zealots or as sinister hypocrites, it remains a fact that the acts of Creffield and Brooks, practised under any other name than that of religion would have led to violent scandals and an interference by the public on the grounds of common decency long ago.

Thus the sect's new accommodations provided the final straw. As an anonymous leader of the mob, perhaps Louis Hartley, put it, the citizens were determined to "rid the community of this blot upon Christianity, morality and citizenship, adding that "the public does not know an iota of what occurs at the so-called séances of those Holy Rollers."[73]

Creffield and Brooks were intercepted in their flight by Frank Hurt, who had crept out to see what was going to happen. He brought the two men back to the Beach house, and later that same night paid a visit to Henry Wortham's drugstore to get the turpentine needed to remove the tar. After much scrubbing, Brooks, but not Creffield, took the mob's advice and left the area. Creffield had one more surprise for the good folk of Corvallis. On the following morning, January 5, he and Maud, Frank, and Mollie Hurt drove the twelve miles to Albany, in a carriage hired by Frank, where a licence was quickly secured and Creffield and Maud Hurt were married. The ceremony was performed just before noon by county court judge H.M. Palmer, with Frank and Mollie as witnesses.[74] The press could not resist noting that Creffield's face and neck were "red from excessive scouring" and that "the odor of tar was noticeable."[75] Ignoring reporters' questions, the wedding party returned to the Beach house for a few hours and were then driven by Frank Hurt the seven or eight miles to Tangent, from where it was supposed that they took a train.[76] Creffield had earlier in the day stated that he would not allow "criminal methods" to drive him out, but he obviously quickly changed his mind.[77]

The wedding must have been a surprise, for there had been no hint of an understanding between the two. We would surmise that it was intended to protect Creffield from community wrath, in the hope that people would be less inclined to take more drastic action against the son-in-law of a respected and well-liked citizen. This was O.V. Hurt's view. He thought that the marriage plans "were formulated during the night when it became certain to Creffield that he would no longer be endured by the people" of Corvallis.[78] The *Lebanon Express Advance* also suggested something of this kind, arguing that as "free love" was one of the things the community objected to, Creffield was trying to nullify that concern.[79] Certainly it does not seem to have been a love match; as we will see in the next chapter, the two were together for a very short period before Maud returned to her father's house. The marriage was not well received by either O.V. Hurt or the community more generally,[80] nor did it work as a defence. Rumours that Creffield was still at the Beach house brought another visit from the vigilantes the evening of the wedding. This one was much more clandestine, the men crossing the Willamette in small boats rather than using the ferry, for this time they brought a rope and the police were watching for them. They did not find Creffield in the house, only six women.

The vigilantes did, though, later apprehend Frank Hurt in Corvallis after he had returned the rented carriage he had used to transport the newlyweds. He was confronted and warned, for by now the antipathy towards him was "almost as strong as against the leaders of the Holy Rollers,"[81] in part because it was he who had brought Creffield back in November. He may have been told to give up his religion on pain of tarring and feathering, but the threat, if made, was an empty one. People were unlikely to want to drive out a local and a member of O.V. Hurt's family – that sanction was reserved for disruptive outsiders. But Frank was issued some sort of threat, for while he vowed that he would "never give up his religion," he also agreed that "he would hereafter live within such regulations as would put an end to the Holy Roller troubles."

The Corvallis White Caps and the American Vigilante Tradition

While the tarring and feathering was obviously a significant event in the history of the Creffield sect, it also provides insight into the origins and use of extra-legal sanctions in the region in the early twentieth century. Reports of the incident immediately identified the men involved as "white caps" or "white cappers," and the process as "white capping." The reference was to an aspect of American vigilantism that, while it had antecedents in the long history of American popular violence against non-conformists, is usually dated from the late 1870s.[82] The name "white cappers" comes from the regalia of white hoods, robes, and masks, which were borrowed from the first Ku Klux Klan[83] – although the Corvallis vigilantes did not go about their work disguised. While there were significant regional differences in the methods and targets of white capping, it usually involved the moral regulation of social deviants by violent but non-lethal means.[84] This kind of white capping originated in the Midwest, beginning in southern Indiana in the 1870s and spreading first to Ohio and then south and west, so that by the late 1880s it was a near nationwide phenomenon. This was not "crime control" vigilantism, a supposed substitute for effective formal institutions of law enforcement, but focused instead on the enforcement of moral codes, usually codes that found no reflection in the criminal law of the jurisdiction. White caps targeted what communities considered to be moral transgressions – wife- and child-beating, neglect of family, adultery (whether or not it was criminal in a particular jurisdiction), immorality generally, laziness, and aberrant religious beliefs.[85] As a character in a turn-of-the-century novel about white caps in Indiana put it, "White-Caps are a vigilance committee going after rascalities the law doesn't reach, or won't reach."[86] The methods employed were primarily whipping and tarring and feathering, although beatings and mock hangings were also used on occasions. There is no study of white capping in the Pacific Northwest, but there was at least one other incident of violence by men identifying themselves as such, in eastern Washington in March 1904.[87]

In some times and places white-capping movements were organized semi-formally and operated for some time within a particular locality, but most incidents were "spontaneous, sporadic effort[s] to enforce standards . . . used on the spur of the moment, when local outrage exploded at one final transgression."[88] The events of January 1904 seem, at first glance, to constitute just such a spontaneous resort to extra-legal action. Yet the action was not quite so spur of the moment. The Corvallis citizens who took Creffield and Brooks out that clear and starry night in January 1904 were largely of Midwestern origin; they were therefore recreating a form of social regulation familiar to them through the oral history of family and community; white capping was a true "folk tradition," as the *Albany Herald* implicitly noted.[89] As Linda Gordon has commented, this kind of vigilantism is a cultural phenomenon, and often participants brought with them to the event memories, direct or indirect, of a previous one.[90]

White capping, therefore, was not a new idea, nor one that took a lot of persuasion to adopt, even if it was infrequently resorted to. Historians have discovered only one Oregon example of the kind of lasting vigilance committee that some authors see as the marker of American vigilantism,[91] but our story shows that Oregonians did not hesitate to take the law into their own hands when they deemed it necessary. And while tarring and feathering was probably not common in the region in this period, it was not an aberration either. There are examples of vigilante action being taken in other Oregon communities, ranging from the banishment from Pendleton of a child abuser to the Marshfield (now Coos Bay) lynching of a black man accused of raping a white woman, and including, in late 1906, the use of force to drive a Pentecostal group out of Corvallis' neighbour, Albany.[92] And by the 1920s Oregonians' willingness to sanction vigilantism against minorities was manifested in extensive support for the Ku Klux Klan. Indeed, the use of white capping in Oregon may have served to lay the ground for the success of the Klan in the state.[93]

Most Corvallis residents approved of what had been done to Creffield and Brooks. As the *Albany Herald* put it, "the peaceful little city in the valley" was "rejoicing." The *Corvallis Times* was confident that "no word of sympathy" had been expressed for the "disciplined apostles" in the community; there had been "many outspoken expressions of satisfaction" about it.[94] This reaction could not have surprised the vigilantes; that they expected approval was obvious from the fact that they wore no disguises and took their victims through the main streets of Corvallis before administering the tar and feathers. They were confident that nobody, including law enforcement officers conspicuous by their absence, would intervene. But while the resort to vigilantism may have been popular, it was also worrying to some, for the use of violence and the by-passing of proper legal process suggested a lawless society and was at odds with prior condemnations of lynching and mob rule elsewhere;[95] the city risked a reputation for lawlessness and intolerance. The press dealt with these concerns by reference to a well-developed set of justifications that were typical of the way such action was legitimated elsewhere.

Three themes were emphasized in the press defence. First, and most importantly, Creffield and Brooks had broken the law, albeit not state law. Rather, these "rankest of fanatics," while they enjoyed ordinary religious freedom, had gone too far and "encroach[ed] on the rights of others." The community in general and individual relatives of those in the sect had been injured by the immorality and evident insanity associated with Creffield's teaching, as well as by the breaking up of families. Creffield and Brooks "had committed offenses against the people of the vicinity that the laws could not reach."[96] Those affected were entitled to "justice" and "Justice is above law," asserted the *Gazette,* adding that "the common sentiment stamps it an act of justice."[97] Once this point had been established, the right to act against the two men was easy to assert, as it had been more than half a century earlier when Mormon leader Joseph Smith and another man were tarred and feathered in Ohio.[98] The idea that both communities and individuals could resort to self-help because of a natural law right of self-preservation was a mainstay of Americans' defence of vigilantism in the nineteenth and early twentieth centuries. Examples of such appeals are voluminous, the right of self-preservation often depicted as "the first law of nature."[99] Vigilantes, whether they were lynching blacks or tarring and feathering adulterers, appealed to "a pre-existing, immanent morality, inherent in nature."[100] In this instance the *Corvallis Gazette* was confident that a relative of one of Creffield's victims "has the undoubted right to claim reparation for this crime, even to the taking of life." Thus the ineffectiveness of state law could not be a bar to the delivery of justice according to some higher law. There was also an assertion that the principle of legality – that no one should be punished by retroactive law – had been adhered to. Creffield and Brooks had received plenty of warning in the two preceding months, and their failure to heed those warnings, to act in accordance with community will, made them ultimately responsible for the treatment they received.

A second theme in the defence of the vigilantes' action was that those involved acted on behalf of the community rather than their personal interests and were upright, decent, and respectable citizens. "Stalwart" the *Corvallis Times* called them; "determined and fearless citizens" said another newspaper.[101] Many of those involved were relatives of sect members, and it is likely that the leader was Louis Hartley. But Hartley, and those without such a direct connection, were acting for the community, not from personal motives. It was "not revenge" but "an effort to get Creffield and Brooks out of the community" and "thereby secure a rest from ... religious agitation."[102] It was common when vigilantism was debated to insist that it was the action of a better class of people, thereby resisting suggestions that it was dangerously lawless activity. Such justifications also frequently reflected the fact that vigilantism in rural areas and small towns was indeed more often than not the preserve of the middle and upper classes.[103]

Third, and this is a point related to both of the above, that the vigilantes were not an unruly mob was evident from the way they had carried out the tarring and feathering. It was public and open, which showed confidence in the rectitude of the action. It was carried out with solemnity and restraint, and no excessive force was used. Indeed, the *Albany Herald* suggested it was carried out in "the approved way."[104] The apostles had not been violated, they had been "disciplined." Participants even "sincerely regretted" being "compelled" to do what they did, but there was no other way to enforce the natural law of community self-defence.[105] Cool and dignified restraint showed that serious men were taking seriously a difficult problem, and showing respect as well for the forms of formal law, which of course were also marked by a due measure of gravitas.[106]

Although some newspapers in neighbouring communities offered outright approval of the tarring and feathering, others evinced concerns. It violated freedom of religion, would encourage mob violence, and represented an over-reaction.[107] The Corvallis press acknowledged and conceded some of these arguments and also expressed concern that the town had been made to look ridiculous and would develop a reputation for lawlessness. The *Corvallis Gazette* was "opposed to all mobs" and hoped that "we shall never have occasion to again chronicle any such breach of law in our county." The *Corvallis Times* took a similar line, calling the incident "an act of violence" and acknowledging that everyone who took part was guilty of a crime.[108] But while accepting that tarring and feathering was not the preferred method, the same newspapers insisted that in the circumstances it was the only way to rid their community of a blight. Creffield's departure "could only have been brought about by some violent measure and no easier method could have been adopted," insisted the *Gazette*. In regretting but insisting on the necessity of the action, the *Corvallis Times* replicated its views on mobs who lynched blacks accused of sexual assaults. Lynching was to be condemned as responses to the supposed escalating incidence of such crimes, but it was understandable, and would end only when "the black man ... ceases his assaults on white women and white girls."[109] Both newspapers also asserted, in an appeal to local self-determination, that their communities had the right to make the decision to resort to vigilantism, and that others should not judge when not offended against.

The tarring and feathering of Creffield and Brooks was therefore an action that came from deeply imbedded folk traditions and was understood and justified by reference to equally deeply and widely held values. Those values were obviously on the retreat in early twentieth-century Oregon, but they obviously continued to coexist with adherence to state law and legal process, and could come to the fore under pressure. They would perhaps have also worked to justify lynching in 1904, as was intended after Creffield's marriage to Maud Hurt, given the belief that a relative's reparation could extend "even to the taking of life."[110]

The Sect Fragments

The dramatic events of January 4 and 5 were followed by fragmentation of the sect. Creffield made his way to Portland; his activities there will be examined in the next chapter. Some members, such as Sarah and Mae Hurt and Cora and Sophia Hartley, stayed in their homes, no longer visiting and worshipping with the group. A small number continued to live in the Beach house – Frank and Mollie Hurt, Olive Sandell, Rose and Florence Seeley, and, perhaps, Wesley Seeley, and Attie Bray.[111] So close to Corvallis, they were careful to do what Frank Hurt had promised on the night of January 5 – keep a low profile and not excite further community animosity. The Seeley sisters and Attie Bray returned to their work as domestics in Corvallis homes, thereby bringing in a little money.[112] But the community must have largely subsisted on what Sarah Hurt brought over on visits. The group's faith remained strong. One female adherent gave an interview to a reporter from the Portland *Oregonian* the day after the tarring and feathering in which a defiant note was to the fore: "They killed Christ, killed the apostles and stoned the disciples to death; and we expect them to do anything with us." She added: "It is either Heaven or Hell, and I am for Heaven."[113]

Charles Brooks, Lee Campbell, and Sampson Levins all thought it best to leave the area, and they travelled together. For a few weeks they did not go far, staying in Linn County.[114] The press first reported their presence there in the middle of January, at which time they were in a cabin in the woods near Lebanon, some seventeen miles east of Corvallis. They may have been moved on, for reports of their presence brought suggestions that "the militia" be called out – meaning more vigilante action to move them on – and they were near Brownsville at one point and later discovered some miles to the north. They seem not to have had any particular plan in mind other than keeping body and soul together on what they could forage and perhaps waiting for instructions from Creffield about what to do next. Or they may have thought they could wait out community ire and return to Corvallis without Creffield. Brooks claimed they were "seeking a secluded spot where they could study and be prepared to enter the work when the Lord called them."[115]

The Linn County sojourn came to an end in late January. Reports that three men were camping in the woods in the northern part of the county, seven miles from Albany, brought out the sheriff and Albany Police Chief McClain, and a posse of armed farmers, who thought the men might be a gang of robbers wanted for a variety of crimes around the county. But

they found the three "humbly perusing their bibles." It was no advertise-
ment for the notion that God would provide. They had been there for a
week, "camped under the open sky, with no protection from the elements
other than a windbreak improvised with fur boughs." They made their
bed from "ferns and a ragged blanket," were "in a disgusting state of filth,
with matted hair and unkempt persons," and subsisted on "a few potatoes,
some dirty flour and a little whole wheat."[116] Sheriff Huston ordered them
to move on, but not before the posse asked where Creffield was. Brooks
refused to say – if indeed he knew – but apparently expressed no resentment at being moved on, other than that it meant they had to labour on
the Sabbath.[117] Beyond the fact that the three men went initially north to
Marion County, we know little more about them. There were later reports
that Brooks and Levins were in Seattle in mid-1904, and that Levins went
first to Oregon City and then to British Columbia, where he worked in a
logging camp and tried to re-establish the sect under his own leadership.[118]
But nothing is known for certain, except that by the late summer of 1906
Levins was in Seattle and married to Attie Bray.[119]

4

"Sensualist Practices Prescribed and Ordained as Coming from Heaven"

SEX AND THE CREFFIELD SECT

CORVALLIS HAD TAKEN STEPS to ensure that the Creffield sect would never operate again publicly in the town. But it had by no means rid itself of Creffield's influence, for he continued to be a focus of public discussion, concern, and action through much of 1904. This chapter and the next examine the events of that year. The following chapter will analyze the incarceration of many of the sect's core members, a process that occurred from the end of April to the end of June 1904. In this chapter we look at Creffield himself in 1904, beginning with the brief period he spent in Portland, where he continued his ministry until March 1904, when he was discovered to have committed adultery with Donna Starr. As we will see in the second half of this book, from the time of the adultery, and particularly in 1906, sex became the major issue when the Creffield sect was discussed, and it has consistently been the dominant theme in other accounts of the group. We have some doubts, however, that sex was anything like as significant as some contemporaries argued, and in the final section of this chapter we assess the evidence on its nature and prevalence.

CREFFIELD IN PORTLAND:
ADULTERY WITH DONNA STARR

Franz and Maud Creffield did not travel with Brooks and the others who went to Linn County, but we do not know where they went after they caught the train at Tangent on January 5, 1904. They may have gone to Brownsville, Linn County, just a few miles away.[1] As Tangent was on the line to Portland, they may have gone straight there. All we can be sure of is that by early February Maud Creffield was back in Corvallis living with her parents, and that by the middle of the same month Franz Creffield reached Portland, where he preached his holiness message and gathered about him a small group of adherents, mostly women. He resided with Mrs Coral Worrell and her husband, J.F. Worrell, of Carson Heights; the former was likely the "Mrs Wurrill" of the Smith Island group photograph. His followers included Donna Starr.[2]

While living with the Worrells, Creffield committed adultery with Donna Starr. Some reports say that he did so with other members of his flock – as many as "10 or 15" – but there is no real evidence of additional liaisons. The incident with Donna Starr took place on February 28 at the Worrell home, although it was not until March 16 that Burgess Starr discovered it – presumably by Donna telling him – and swore out a criminal complaint. At the same time Donna signed a statement that there had been "improper relations of a most revolting kind" between her and Creffield.[3] Adultery had been a crime in Oregon since 1858 and continued to be so until at least 1920. It could be committed by either a man or a woman, and carried a maximum sentence of two years in the penitentiary. At this time a prosecution could be initiated only on the complaint of a husband or wife.[4] Donna Starr was not charged, although she could have been, presumably because Burgess Starr chose not to make her the subject of a complaint as well. While there were some occasions on which a spouse complained about both the other spouse and his or her lover, we assume that it was more common to proceed only against the latter.[5]

THE PROPHET ON THE RUN

The news of the adultery electrified the press in both Portland and Corvallis. "The details of the case ... are revolting in the extreme," said the *Corvallis Gazette,* adding that a "good long" penitentiary sentence, where Creffield could "roll to his heart's content" was actually "too good for a varmint of his calibre."[6] It must have pleased his opponents that here at last was a chance for the law to deal with him. But it would be months before it could do so, because Creffield evaded police and most likely went immediately to Corvallis.[7] We do not know where else he obtained refuge, but at some point he lodged himself beneath the Hurt house, where he remained for many weeks, probably months, until his capture at the end of July. He made contact with at least some of his followers for, as we shall see in the next chapter, they began in late April to provide public displays of their faith sufficient to again bring down the ire of the community on them.

The authorities searched assiduously for Creffield. Portland detectives conducted house-to-house inquiries, and men were dispatched to eastern Oregon and the Corvallis area.[8] Maud Creffield was questioned by Sheriff Burnett and Police Chief W.G. Lane when she returned home after disappearing for a few days immediately following Creffield's rumoured arrival in the town; she gave away nothing although O.V. Hurt claimed that Creffield "came and stole Maude away" while he was out.[9] Some vacant houses as well as the Beach house were searched, but to no effect. At the initiative of Louis Hartley and O.V. Hurt, a reward was offered, growing over time as public and private contributions came in to augment it. By early June it was $400; later that month it was raised to $450 when S.L. Kline, O.V. Hurt's employer, kicked in another $50. At least one relative of a member of the sect joined the hunt – Ira Bray, Attie's father, who was seen in Corvallis "gunning" for Creffield,[10] while other men were encouraged by the reward to go bounty hunting.

The reward did not bring in any useful information, although there were numerous claimed sightings of Creffield – in Philomath, Oak Creek, and Toledo, among other places. Some thought he had never left Portland and a house there was searched, although earlier reports had him leaving that city by train on March 21. Some were convinced that Frank and Mollie Hurt knew where he was, others that it was advisable to watch Cora Hartley closely. At least some of his adherents knew where he was, but there was no Judas among them.[11] In May Florence Seeley was sent to the Boys and Girls Aid Society (BGAS), a matter discussed in detail in Chapter 5, and there questioned about Creffield, but she claimed to have no idea where he was.[12] We do not know how Creffield explained the adultery to his adherents, especially his wife, but they remained steadfast in their belief in him, as he did to his God: the description put out by the Benton County sheriff's office was careful to note that "he is sure to have a Bible under his arm or in his pocket."[13] By late June the authorities still had "no clue to his whereabouts."[14]

Creffield was finally apprehended on July 29, hiding under the Hurt house.[15] The house foundation was built up a little to avoid flood damage, and this enabled him to crawl under and scrape out a hole – six feet long, two feet wide, and eighteen inches deep – in which to live. He was discovered by the Hurt's fourteen-year-old adopted son, Roy Robinett. Roy ran to town and returned with his father and Chief of Police Lane, and a remarkable sight greeted them as the emaciated, filthy, and naked preacher with long, unkempt hair and a beard emerged from the earth. His nakedness was likely the result either of his clothing rotting or of his removing it in the summer heat. Creffield's physical condition was the result of lack of exercise and the recent loss of his food supply. In his hole were discovered two old quilts, some underclothing, and a few empty jars. Sarah Hurt had fed him until she was committed to the asylum at the end of June; Cora Hartley had taken over until she went with Louis to the mines in mid-July. It was later claimed that Creffield had come out regularly while O.V. Hurt was at work and conducted meetings inside the house, although it seems unlikely that he could have escaped public notice had he done so.[16] But Sarah Hurt spent a good deal of time sitting at the corner of the house nearest Creffield's hiding place and was heard apparently talking to herself. She was, of course, talking to Creffield. It is a testament to Creffield's own faith that he stayed where he was with his food supply gone; presumably he saw this as a test of his faith that God would look after his chosen. But he may have become sufficiently desperate to allow himself to be seen, and he made no attempt to escape when his discoverer left to get help.

Creffield was clothed and quickly and, as quietly as possible, removed to the county jail. Though weak from lack of food and exercise, he refused the aid of a doctor because his faith forbade it. He did accept some food – he asked for eggs – and was photographed and underwent a medical exam. He talked only of Jesus, according to the *Corvallis Times* reporter, saying "in whispers and disjointed sentences" – "I feel so good; Jesus is so near me; Jesus told me last night this would happen."[17] His apprehension quickly became the talk of the town, with crowds visiting the jail to try to catch a glimpse of the man or some more gossip.

The Corvallis authorities immediately wired to Portland for someone to collect Creffield and take him to the jurisdiction where he faced a criminal charge. There must undoubtedly have been some concern, given the previous tarring and feathering, that vigilante action would be taken. Something did happen, although the press accounts are contradictory as to what occurred; there was a war of words between the Portland *Oregonian* and the Corvallis mayor and press over whether a mob had had to be rebuffed with armed guards. It seems unlikely that this was true. But four men came from Portland on the 29th – including Burgess Starr – and sought to persuade O.V. Hurt and others to join them in settling with

Creffield. Starr was presumably interested, among other things, in avoiding the embarrassment of the forthcoming adultery trial and had threatened back in March that he would "have justice if he has to take the law into his own hands."[18] Hurt declined to participate, counselling against any such extra-legal action, and as a result the presence of the deputy sheriff in the jail was not needed. Events might have taken a different turn had Louis Hartley been in town, although even he might have been convinced that the law should take its course, given that Creffield was almost certain to be penitentiary bound.[19]

Rumours must have been in the air, however, for the next day Creffield was taken not to the train station but to a spot on Sixth Street where it had been arranged for the train to stop. Again, there may have been fears of a mob to be avoided, but the precaution was probably unnecessary.[20] Certainly, however, the event generated public interest. Crowds gathered at the jail and the station to see Creffield, and other passengers on the train "craned their necks for a sight of the dashing Elijah,"[21] while bystanders at the place where the train actually stopped hurled derisive comments at him. Creffield was accompanied to the train by Lou Hartman, the Portland detective sent down to collect him, as well as Police Chief Lane, a deputy sheriff, and O.V. Hurt – Creffield's great rival was given the honour of a triumphant march with his defeated enemy. Hurt refused, however, to allow Roy Robinett to accept the reward for Creffield's capture and the money was returned to donors.[22] The spectacle continued on the journey to Portland, as "great crowds" gathered at each station along the way to see Creffield.[23] The local press was ecstatic, rejoicing in the capture while heaping opprobrium on Creffield.[24]

THE ADULTERY TRIAL

Once lodged in the Multnomah County jail, Creffield was an object of considerable interest.[25] He was the subject of jibes of other prisoners, and a visiting group of clergymen tried to persuade him that he had "crazy" ideas. Creffield responded that he was Elijah, and not crazy. He was interviewed by at least two reporters. To one from the *Oregonian* he repeated the claim of being Elijah, and also said that he expected to be killed: "I am doing as the Lord ordered me to do. I know they tried to kill me; they will try it again. If the Lord wants me killed, I will die."[26] He similarly told a *Telegram* reporter that it was God who had ordered him to hide under the house, and added that while there he had been visited by God, who told him he was to "suffer for his people," to "die from hunger and from the cold." Creffield likened this to a crucifixion. He also insisted that he was not guilty, and "did not have any undue relations with her [Donna Starr] or any of the women."[27]

The reference to Elijah shows that Creffield's beliefs were evolving. Elijah was a major prophet in the tradition of Moses, a believer in only one God and in everyone being equal under that God. To many Christians he was an acknowledged precursor of the Messiah and on his death was taken up to Heaven in a whirlwind and was expected to return as forerunner of the Second Coming. In identifying himself as Elijah, Creffield was in a sense elevating himself in the hierarchy of prophets, for Joshua did not enjoy the same status. Elijah had been given food and kept alive by God after being cast out by Jezebel, just as Creffield had been succoured while on the run. God communicated with Elijah through "low muttering sounds," "soft whispers," and a "still small voice" – much as Creffield now described his own communication with God.[28]

By the time he gave a second interview to the *Oregonian* reporter Creffield was recovering physically and taking a little exercise. He was also reading a lot from a Bible supplied to him by O.V. Hurt, whose capacity for observing the common decencies seems at times to be almost beyond belief. Hurt, however, took pains to tell the press that the Bible was Creffield's, left under his house, and that he had no sympathy for the prophet.[29] In this second interview Creffield again claimed to be Elijah and gave a hint of what he would later say to defend himself. The Lord had come to him in a vision, he said, and told him to tell the truth about the crime he was charged with, and thereby to show men that he was "innocent" and acting in accordance with the commands of God. That is, God had told him to explain that "what men call sin is virtue, and what men call virtue is sin."[30] A little more than a week later he was feeling strong enough to defend himself and his adherents more vigorously, complaining that sending his adherents to the asylum, discussed in the next chapter, was "persecution."[31]

On August 1 Creffield was arraigned.[32] He was "staggering from great weakness" and when asked if he wanted to go through a preliminary hearing or to waive that part of the process he seemed not to understand. When asked about a lawyer he said that he did not need one and that God would plead his case. The court nonetheless appointed attorney J.A. Logan to talk to him. Creffield does not seem to have cooperated with Logan, but the lawyer was able to obtain an adjournment for three days on the ground that Creffield was not well enough to proceed. On Thursday,

August 4, the adjourned hearing came on; Creffield waived his right to a preliminary hearing and he was granted bail on a $2,000 bond, although of course there was no one to put up the money. His appearance was an event. The room "was crowded to the doors all forenoon by a staring, morbid crowd" who were there "bent on catching a glance of the religious crank."[33]

Although suggestions of other liaisons had been made in March, when Creffield went to trial it was on the single count of adultery with Donna Starr. He was prosecuted in the circuit court on an information filed by Multnomah County District Attorney John Manning, who will feature more prominently later in this story.[34] Creffield pleaded not guilty on Thursday, August 25, and refused an attorney when offered a court-appointed one. The trial took place on Friday, September 16, before circuit court judge Alfred F. Sears Jr. and a jury,[35] with Deputy D.A. Moser prosecuting. A number of witnesses testified for the prosecution, including Burgess Starr and Louis Hartley. Unfortunately the reports of their testimony are scanty. Hartley is only reported as saying that his wife and daughter had been in the sect in Corvallis and that Sophia was in the asylum, the relevance of which is difficult to discern. Starr gave evidence about when he first heard of the adultery. J.F. Worrell of Carson Heights and his wife, Coral, also testified, the latter to the effect that she and her husband had been followers of Creffield's church but had left when they discovered an "objectionable doctrine."[36] Coral also said that she had seen Creffield and Donna Starr kiss on one occasion, and that she had found them in a room together. This is an admittedly thin account of the testimony; the press were reticent about publishing details and may indeed have been instructed by Judge Sears not to do so. Sears was sufficiently concerned about the "indecent" nature of the evidence that he ordered the public removed from the courtroom, and the large crowd that had turned up had to wait in the hallway.[37]

The principal prosecution witness was Donna Starr, who appeared quite willingly; according to Burgess she still believed in Creffield. Sitting quietly with an infant in her lap, "in a smiling way," according to the *Corvallis Times*, she admitted adultery; she had acted without any duress and "knew she was right." Donna also explained why she had done it. She had been "inspired by God for the purging of her soul of devils" – she asserted that sex with Creffield was a way of purifying herself, cleansing away the taint of the world and the worldly, with Creffield serving as the vehicle through which the Holy Spirit achieved this.[38]

Creffield defended himself, and we have better accounts of what he said than of the prosecution testimony. He affirmed rather than swore on the Bible, which he must have thought an improper use of the Good Book. He also justified the adultery as divinely ordained, in what one newspaper called a "sensational and rambling speech."[39] He began with a general assertion that God was on his side and that "while you may lock me in my prison cell, I can still cry 'Glory to God' and rest secure in the knowledge that when the time comes God will plead my case."[40] He then argued that what he and Donna had done was a matter only for them, and presumably God, to judge: "Among my converts was this woman. It was all an individual matter, a matter of conscience as she has told you. God teaches us that we must have direct communication with him before we can be saved." Further statements expanded on the idea that sex would purge or purify Donna to enhance her communication with, and receipt of, the Holy Spirit. "Man was composed of the spirit, soul and body, and it was necessary to purge the body," he insisted, also asserting that "God called me to do all that I have done and I am obeying Him. The gospel He put on me was to purge the body and I have done so. Jesus Christ, I tell you, has chosen me to purge the flesh from sin of all those who are willing."

Judge and jury had a difficult time following the explanation, and Creffield quoted various biblical passages, which he also asked the jury to look up. Sears did look through the Bible he had with him, but not for long, interrupting Creffield to ask if he was admitting that he had committed what state law defined as a crime. The answer was predictable: "Yes, in the eyes of the world I am guilty, but God is on my side." When asked how he reconciled the two statements he made a further speech suggesting that his sense of his own place in God's scheme was growing increasingly greater:

> When Christ came on earth the first thing he did was to break the Sabbath in the eyes of the Jews and they crucified him. I have broken the law of the land, and I don't expect the jury to understand me any better than the Jews understood Christ. If I were a court in a case of this kind I would act just as you are about to act. I would convict. I don't expect to be freed. I know the prison cell is staring me in the face, but I am not ashamed of God's command and will do what he has told me to do.

By 11:15 a.m. the case was given to the jury, Sears instructing them that they could acquit only if they thought Creffield was insane. The jury was out for twenty-five minutes – they did indeed have a brief conversation about insanity – and returned a verdict of guilty. Creffield took it calmly, returning to his cell "murmuring 'Glory to Jesus, Glory to God.'"[41] At 2 p.m. he returned to court and was sentenced to the maximum term of two years in the penitentiary. He had nothing to say when given the opportunity, although he did say, "God Bless you" to the judge afterwards.

The conviction brought great satisfaction to many, especially in Corvallis. The *Corvallis Gazette* gave full rein to its delight: "The lecher Creffield, self-styled Elijah II, bogus prophet of God, religious hypnotist, imposter and all round dangerous individual" had been justly imprisoned. The only problem was that the sentence was "not commensurate" with "the enormity of the crime," for "the work of this dangerous man has been far more extensive and far-reaching in its results than most people allow themselves to think." The paper went on to talk of the "stigma of the insane asylum" and the "baleful . . . effect upon public morality" in Corvallis that Creffield had had.[42] The *Corvallis Times* was even more virulent, asserting that "in vileness, diabolism and all-round deviltry, Creffield is unmatched."[43]

SEX IN THE CREFFIELD SECT

In Donna Starr's case the sacred became profane. By 1904 contemporaries were also hinting that sex between Creffield and his followers had been rather more widespread when the group had operated in Corvallis, and by 1906 the idea that Creffield was a libertine who sexually exploited his Corvallis followers was firmly entrenched in the public mind. Sex dominated press stories about the sect after George Mitchell had killed Creffield, with Mitchell's defenders repeatedly referring to the "orgies" and "disgusting practices" of the sect when it had operated in Corvallis in 1903. A letter from "An Oregon Girl" published in the *Seattle Times* in May 1906, for example, stated that "free love was ever a theme he preached" and referred to "the awful orgies Creffield made them do."[44] Many more examples could be cited, and although the newspapers were reticent about printing details, the message was clear – Creffield's version of holiness was inextricably tied to less than holy practices.[45]

If all this was true – and as we shall see there is some reason to doubt the extent if not the fact of sexual activity within the sect – the people of Corvallis did not know about it in 1903 and early 1904. Indeed, the group's opponents admitted that sex was not initially involved. O.V. Hurt, for example, later acknowledged that when it began the sect was "as clean and respectable as any other."[46] There was, of course, increasing public criticism of the group in 1903-1904, including references to "free lovers" and to Creffield's teaching that "marriage was not necessary."[47] But for all the complaints about ecstatic practices, the destruction of goods, and the harm being done to family relations, there was no suggestion of sex. There were one or two references to "orgies" and to the group being "free lovers," but the former concerned wild religious practices and the latter were always linked to criticisms of the group's congregate living arrangements. Indeed, when the *Corvallis Gazette* used the term "free lovers" in early January 1904, the same issue carried a defence of the right of even the "rankest of fanatics" to religious freedom, and presumably sex would have put the group outside the scope of that principle.[48] As the *Corvallis Times* noted much later, the community knew nothing about any sexual shenanigans.[49]

The first hints of allegations of sexual relations between Creffield and his followers in Corvallis emerged after the warrant for his arrest had been issued in March 1904. According to the *Telegram* the Portland events would not now come as a surprise to the people of Corvallis, but would be a "verification" of what was "suspected to be his practices and teachings" in Corvallis.[50] A little later a few more hints emerged in testimony in a series of insanity commitment hearings for sect members, a process described in detail in the following chapter. Clarence Starr, for example, said that he and Hattie had left the sect when the "practices . . . became so bad," and he referred to "the unspeakable actions of some of the leaders."[51] Edna Seeley was said to be delighted that her sister Florence was being removed from "the vicious practices of the Holy Rollers."[52] But stories hinting at sex still played only a minor role in reports about the group's activities: while Creffield was often excoriated in the press, the concentration was on other aspects of his teachings. When he was captured at the end of July 1904 the *Corvallis Times* called Creffield a "diabolical influence," a "monumental humbug and viper," and a "devil incarnate." But there was no reference to sexual conduct; he deserved these designations, the paper said, because he broke up families and drove people insane.[53]

By the fall of 1904, with Creffield captured, references to sex became more common. The Portland *Oregonian,* for example, claimed that Donna Starr had told Burgess about "orgies in which she and others, including Creffield, had participated in the name of religion and under the cloak of sanctification, that would disgrace Hottentots."[54] There was talk of "acts of God's Elect [which] would hardly pass muster in respectable society," of "indecencies," and of the fact that Creffield "regularly taught the practice of adultery as a part of his doctrines."[55] Most of the evidence on which these accounts were based was supposedly supplied by adherents who had been placed in the asylum or the BGAS Home. Either in those institutions, or on their release from them, his followers told all, "confess[ing] to their husbands and fathers a revolting account of Creffield's practices."[56] By the time Creffield was convicted of adultery with Donna Starr, the Portland *Telegram* was confident that throughout his ministry he had committed "unmentionable crimes under the guise of religious leadership," professed "the most revolting sacrilege," and was a "moral pervert."[57]

By the time Creffield resurrected his sect after his release from prison, a matter discussed below in Chapter 6, there was therefore a widespread belief that he was a libertine who routinely debauched his followers. "Adultery and Holly [sic] Rollerism seem inseparable," declared the *Corvallis Gazette*, and the Portland *Oregonian* advocated "a treatment which would ... [prevent] him from carrying out a portion of the religious rite which he is accused of practising on his victims."[58] Hence his killer's defenders could fill the Seattle and Oregon newspapers with claims of "orgies" and "unspeakable practices." Indeed, in only one case, that of Ona Baldwin, did Creffield's opponents concede that there had been no sexual activity; Ona, said her father, had "not gone as far as some of his victims in indulgence in the unspeakable practices which he demanded as evidence of holiness."[59]

Sexual relations between Creffield and his followers was the result, apparently, of two distinct, although perhaps related, religious justifications. As we have seen, sex with Donna Starr was intended to purge her body of impure influences. Later this would be referred to as Creffield's "purification" doctrine.[60] But "purification" was not the only justification and indeed is mentioned much less frequently than the idea that the second Christ would come again, born of a virgin mother, chosen from among Creffield's followers. Creffield would fulfill the role of the Holy Ghost in impregnating the chosen woman. Like the purification doctrine, the "second Mary" idea was not derived from the Bible but came from God speaking to Creffield.[61] As a result, his movement was named "The Church of the Bride of Christ." This name first appeared in September 1904, at Creffield's adultery trial, as the name of the church he had operated in Portland earlier in the year;[62] later reports insisted that this was the name of the church in Corvallis in 1903, although no mention of it is found in the 1903 stories about the sect.

If sex did become a feature of the Creffield sect, it would certainly mark the group as unusual within the holiness movement generally. A few other sects in the period engaged in, or allegedly engaged in, sexual activities, and male Salvation Army officers occasionally exploited their positions to gain sexual access to young women, but such practices were rare.[63] There were, of course, groups and organizations in the nineteenth- and early twentieth-century United States that advocated that sexual relations be conducted on lines other than married monogamy. The Oneida community, with its concept of group marriage, and the polygamous Mormons, are perhaps the best known, but there were other forms of unorthodoxy, from the celibate Shakers to "free love" groups such as that of Francis White.[64] But with a few exceptions, unconventional sexual practices were not characteristic of the holiness movement. Nor, for that matter, was sexual radicalism a feature of Oregon's history generally.[65]

All prior accounts of the Creffield story have uncritically accepted that the sect was indeed exceptional in this regard; indeed, it is probably the sex angle that has made the story such a well-remembered and oft-written-about one in Oregon. When the evidence is examined carefully, however, it suggests the need for some caution. As already noted, most of it consists of vague and very general statements about "orgies" and "odious practices" and the like, and much comes from well after the period in which these events supposedly took place. Moreover, the vast majority of it emanates from the mouths and pens of Creffield's enemies. In addition, statements about what occurred are often contradictory, and in some instances we are confident that contemporary critics were gilding the lily. The remainder of this section will examine the evidence about sex. It does not come to a firm conclusion either about whether Creffield did have sex with other followers, or about its extent; the evidence is, we believe, too vague and contradictory for that. But we are confident both that the sect engaged in practices which contemporaries believed were deeply immoral and that at least some of the claims about what happened are wrong.

We begin with the specific allegations about sex with individuals. In addition to all the general statements of the kind we have already quoted, particular claims were made about sex with five adherents. Three of these allegations involved Creffield's youngest followers – Esther Mitchell, Mae Hurt, and Florence Seeley. All three spent time in the BGAS Home in Portland – the commitment of Hurt and Seeley will be discussed in the next chapter – and while there they all, according to Superintendent Gardner, admitted their "criminal relations" with Creffield. Gardner made this claim on a number of occasions in 1906; in May, for example, he wrote to George Mitchell, then in jail, that the three girls had all been "victims of Creffield's lust" and had confessed to him that "Creffield had criminal relations with them." In July he told a *Seattle Times* reporter that the girls had made "terrible confessions" and were "victims of the lust of the man who called himself God."[66]

We have grave doubts about Gardner's story. Gardner claimed that the girls had confessed to him while in the Boys and Girls Aid Society Home in 1904, but he did not go public with his accusations until May 1906, after Creffield was killed and they could be, and were, used in his killer's defence. There is no hint in the girls' case files kept by the Society, nor in the correspondence between its officials and family members, of the confessions, although the letters refer to many aspects of the sect's activities.[67] Moreover, if Gardner was correct, Creffield could have been tried for statutory rape of Esther Mitchell and, perhaps, of Florence Seeley, if she too was under sixteen when the alleged events occurred, but no such charge was preferred.[68] Indeed, Multnomah County D.A. John Manning later insisted that adultery was the only charge on which Creffield could be prosecuted.[69] There could have been other reasons for the failure to prefer a charge, but Gardner's explanation of that failure simply casts further doubts on his story and does little for his credibility. He said that the girls' fathers had told him that "they hesitated to prosecute the man because of the notoriety that would result."[70] That makes sense until one remembers that Florence Seeley's father was dead, and Esther's father, Charles Mitchell, was in Illinois. Hurt himself thought at one point that Mae would testify against Creffield in September 1904, presumably on a second prosecution,[71] and Gardner later asserted that Hurt did not prosecute Creffield because Mae's "confession was of such a disgusting nature";[72] but the fact is that she had been sixteen in 1903 and no charge could have been preferred.

A further problem with the claim about Creffield having sex with Esther Mitchell in particular is that Creffield's opponents changed the story when it suited their purposes. Gardner said that Esther Mitchell was seduced by Creffield under the pretence that she had been chosen as the mother of the second Christ, and George Mitchell made the same claim immediately after he killed Creffield. But Mitchell later changed his story. By the time of his trial he and his supporters all asserted that Esther had not yet been seduced, but that she would have been had Creffield not been killed. As we shall see, the danger to Esther's future sexual integrity, not revenge for past wrongs, was the linchpin of Mitchell's defence.[73] We do not believe that Creffield engaged in sexual activity with Esther Mitchell, and we are similarly unwilling to accept that sex occurred with either of the other two.

The other two cases in which specific suggestions of sex were made involved Sarah Hurt and Cora Hartley, and here the evidence seems somewhat stronger. In his testimony at the Mitchell trial O.V. Hurt recounted being told by his daughter Mae that he should not be "harsh" with her mother because "she had been among the last to bend to Creffield's will."

Sarah resisted when Creffield "gave her a command" (which O.V. could not repeat in court), but Creffield "told her if she refused he would drive her out of the church, and . . . God would smite her" – so she "submitted."[74] In context, Hurt appeared to be referring to sexual intercourse – this passage follows one in which Sarah Hurt is described as entirely disrobing.

There is no doubt about Louis Hartley's meaning in a 1906 divorce petition. He complained of Cora's neglect of him, her destruction of household goods, and her refusal to live with him. But in a document as remarkable for its fulsome descriptions as for its angry, rollicking style, he reserved most of his venom for what he called the "sensualist practices prescribed and ordained as coming from Heaven by and through the mediation of . . . Joshua." He went on to accuse his wife of having had sexual intercourse with Creffield, of "divesting herself of her under clothing for the purposes of conforming to the revelations . . . and consenting to certain acts and practices with the Joshua in conflict with the fundimental [sic] laws of the State of Oregon."[75]

It is a little strange that only the *Corvallis Times* printed the part of O.V. Hurt's testimony quoted here – none of the Portland or Seattle papers included it – but it seems unlikely that the *Corvallis Times* would have made it up. Both Hurt's and Hartley's accounts are believable, in the sense that both men probably believed that their wives had had sex with Creffield. But this is not the same as saying that they had indeed done so, and while Sarah Hurt and Cora Hartley are never quoted as denying the statements, neither did they admit that they had had sex. Of course most women would have preferred not to admit such a thing in that period, but these were not most women. To persuade an ardent, upright matron such as Sarah Hurt to have sex with him, a woman who had devoted her life to a set of moral and religious standards according to which adultery was anathema, Creffield would have had to convince her that it was not only right, but required by God. Her conviction in the rectitude of her action would have been only enhanced by the belief that she was a new Mary. Sarah Hurt was prepared to say that O.V. was not in a spiritual sense her husband, and Cora Hartley did likewise; they and others also acted in ways that attracted much ridicule. Why, in the heat of their passionate defences of Creffield – we shall see in the next chapter that Sarah Hurt was dragged screaming from her house and taken to the asylum in 1904 – did they not declare that they had willingly made the ultimate sacrifice?

The same point can be made with reference to others among Creffield's followers. We have already dismissed the suggestion of sex with Esther Mitchell, but it is worth noting both that she consistently refuted any suggestion of sex[76] and that she too had such faith in Creffield that it seems improbable that she would not be proud of it had it occurred. Frank and Mollie Hurt admitted all the evidence against them in their insanity hearing as it related to the destruction of personal property and the like, but "denied Creffield's immorality."[77] Indeed, other than Donna Starr none of the women publicly admitted to sex with Creffield, and she later denied the stories of widespread sexual activity told at George Mitchell's trial, insisting that the witnesses had lied to get Mitchell acquitted.[78]

The obvious rejoinder to this argument is that the women of the sect knew what they had done was wrong and were ashamed to admit it. But if that is true, if they were in some way coerced into sexual acts they knew were wrong, we have to ask why they remained loyal to Creffield for so long. We shall see that they stayed steadfast throughout the travails of 1904 and rejoined him in 1906 after he was released from the penitentiary. By mid-1904 they all knew about the adultery, and by later that year they would have heard stories that Creffield supposedly spread his sexual favours widely. Why retain their allegiance in such circumstances? The high-minded Maud Hurt Creffield was similarly unlikely to have married the preacher had she believed him to be the libertine he was later painted as, and equally unlikely to have been ignorant of his transgressions had they occurred on the scale many suggested. But Maud denied it all and, for what it is worth, her and Esther Mitchell's denials were believed by the hard-headed deputy prosecuting attorney of King County, John Miller.[79] Maud Creffield did later state that the faith she and others followed in 1906 was "revised" from earlier, that they had "found further light" and "view our practices three years ago as wrong." They had "discontinued the practices which . . . rendered" their faith "obnoxious to the communities in which it had been established."[80] This is certainly consistent with an admission of sex, but it is equally consistent as a reference to any number of the group's practices, up to and including substantial disrobing. Frank Hurt similarly in 1906 "denounced" some of the earlier practices of the group, but again it is unclear what he was denouncing.[81]

A further reason for perhaps finding contemporaries' assumptions about sex unconvincing concerns the supposed principal rationale for it all – that a follower was to give birth to the new Christ. If one of Creffield's followers was to be the mother of the second Christ, why call the church the Church of the *Bride* of Christ? The consistent use of the name suggests that Creffield likely used it and that critics seized on it as a link to sex, but it is as likely to have meant that the women should be spiritual brides of Christ rather than brides of men, as nuns are so designated in the Catholic

Church. Radical Protestant groups such as the Shakers had also earlier appropriated the term "bride of Christ," and even Mark Matthews, pastor of Seattle's First Presbyterian Church and the best-known clergyman in the region, used the phrase in referring to the church generally.[82] Also, if a virgin birth was sought, why choose three married women for sex? Why, for that matter, choose Cora Hartley and Sarah Hurt, who in their early to mid-40s were at least close to the end of their child-bearing years? No pregnancies resulted from any apparent liaisons designed to produce precisely that result.

Another problem is that of a serious lack of precision in critics' accusations about what we might term Creffield's mode of proceedings. References to "orgies" and the like made it appear that sex acts were conducted in the presence of other members, including the devout Frank Hurt and his wife, Mollie. Is it really likely that Frank would have watched his mother and his sisters and his wife have sex with Creffield? O.V. Hurt claimed later that during the period Creffield was hidden under the Hurt house he would emerge during the day, while Hurt was at work, "and hold his orgies in my home, where his followers would assemble."[83] It seems highly unlikely that this could have occurred for weeks on end and nobody have wind of it. And how are orgies to be reconciled with the careful selection of one person to be the mother of the new Christ? If orgies did not occur, but rather sex was clandestine, how did Creffield find the opportunity to seduce women and girls when the sect lived together so closely, on Smith Island, at the Hurt house, and in Linn County, without others knowing? In short, the willingness of critics to accuse Creffield of anything and everything takes away from the credibility of many of their statements. And the contemporary tendency to accuse Creffield of both clandestine seductions and mass orgies has resulted in other accounts of the Creffield sect being similarly inconsistent in their descriptions of what happened.[84]

Against all this, of course, is the fact that many contemporaries purported to believe the sex stories generally, that both O.V. Hurt and Louis Hartley stated publicly that their wives had been adulterous – a humiliating admission – and that Maud Creffield and Frank Hurt later admitted that, at the very least, practices immoral in contemporary eyes went on. How do we reconcile these things with what we have just described – evidence that is at best vague, sometimes a fabrication, and often contradictory? In fact, we cannot claim to know the answer, and accept that it is possible that what contemporaries said was true, and that the evidence that would give us confidence is lost in early twentieth-century sensibilities about saying and printing details that would convince the historian. But it is also possible – and we make no larger claim than that – that the reality was different, and that we can explain how the sect's practices became, in the imaginations of its critics, the worst of all offences to respectable society.

The first part of that explanation is that almost all the limited evidence available from the 1903 and early 1904 period about the sex-related teachings and practices of the sect is susceptible to more than one interpretation. For example, the fact that Creffield taught that "marriage was not necessary," first rumoured in November 1903, could of course mean "not necessary as a prerequisite for sex," but it is equally likely to have meant not necessary as a social and religious institution. As a matter of religious doctrine Creffield believed there was an unbridgeable gap between believers and non-believers, and marriage between them was not only "not necessary" but potentially harmful to the sect's unity and cohesion. Indeed, there is abundant evidence that Creffield taught his followers that they were spiritually married to him or to God rather than to their husbands. Marriage was not necessary for holiness and salvation. Here we should also note that the *Corvallis Times* argued in early November 1903, in the same issue containing the "marriage was not necessary" rumour, that the group had a right to religious freedom and were "probably as orthodox as are the acts of a distinguished Presbyterian preacher who certified that all his football players are bona fide students." It worried about some of the things that were going on – apparent insanity and home wrecking – but said nothing about sex.[85] In addition, when the group wanted to cement relationships within itself, its members married. Frank Hurt married Mollie Sandell in July 1903 and insisted in late 1903 that "as to marriages, we observe the same rules as other denominations."[86] Creffield himself married Maud Hurt, not once, but twice – they were divorced in 1905 and remarried in April 1906.

Other bits of evidence later used as indications of sex are similarly susceptible to more than one interpretation. The "marriage was not necessary" message was said to be responsible for the departure of Clarence and Hattie Starr during or shortly after the Smith Island sojourn, but if the Starrs left the group because they believed that illicit sex had happened or would happen, surely they would not have departed quietly without telling others in the community, and surely the community would not have allowed the sect to continue to operate for months afterwards with that knowledge. It may be that "wrappers" worn by the women were dispensed with on occasion,[87] but undressing does not amount to sexual intercourse.

We saw in the previous chapter that Corvallis became increasingly concerned in 1903 about the congregate living and ecstatic practices of the sect, as well as the effect on families. And while citizens do not seem to have had any evidence about sex at that time, it is easy to see that they were disturbed by the living arrangements and considered them immoral. As already noted, the references made from late 1903 about "free lovers" may also not have been to sex. The phrase began to be used after the group had moved to the Beach house and was always conjoined with references to the living arrangements. The community did not care for the group living in the Hurt house earlier, but they were under the eye of neighbours and of O.V. Hurt. Once outside the town, and away from O.V., congregate living escalated from eccentric and fanatical to "disgraceful." And, as we have seen, a large part of the problem was that it was all so secretive. The community's concern was as much rooted in what it did not know as in what it did.[88]

If by the time of the tarring and feathering the sect was seen as immoral and dangerous, and given the evidence of the liaison with Donna Starr and the stories about wrappers and their possible removal, which emerged through 1904 as a few of the adherents repented of their former beliefs (discussed in the next chapter), many may have come to believe the worst. To contemporaries the sect clearly engaged in deeply immoral practices – congregate living and rejection of families – even if those did not include sexual intercourse. They also included things that must have come very close to sex: women dressed in "wrappers" and wearing their hair unbraided had bodies unrestrained by the usual physical constrictions of modesty. Even if there was no nakedness such behaviour was appalling in the Corvallis of 1903, as much an "orgy" of "obnoxious practices" as sexual intercourse. Thus our uncertainty about what occurred does not extend to uncertainty about whether critics found Creffield's teachings and practices immoral. They clearly did. Female members of the Creffield sect offended contemporary morality in many different ways. They removed most, perhaps all, of their clothes; they rolled or lay on the floor in that state; they lived in congregate accommodations; they "denied" their husbands. Creffield and his followers may well have received some form of sexual thrill from it all – rationalized perhaps as the Holy Spirit – a thrill that Creffield's critics understood.

If this is a reasonable reading of events it would explain, for example, Louis Hartley's honest belief about Cora and Creffield as publicly proclaimed in his divorce petition. He had seen his wife and daughter leave the family home to join Creffield and had heard his wife deny that he was truly her husband – she considered herself "the bride of the . . . prophet."[89] He knew as well that the female members of the sect dressed in "wrappers" and engaged in various ecstatic practices, and that Creffield taught that "marriage was not necessary." Hartley testified at an insanity hearing in May 1904 to "the actions of the Holy Rollers in lying around on the floor indiscriminately, half dressed and praying for hours at a time" without at that time mentioning sex.[90] By 1906 it was but a short step to an assumption that Cora must have had sex with Creffield, even though Hartley did not sue for divorce on the ground of adultery but because of "cruel and inhuman treatment or personal indignities rendering life burdensome."[91] Others may easily have employed the same reasoning, especially after the liaison with Donna Starr was apparently proven conclusively. And of course the explanation for all the anti-Creffield sex propaganda in 1906 may be even simpler: people believed that even if Creffield was not a libertine he was an evil man who deserved to be killed, and whatever needed to be said in defence of his killer would be said.

If Hartley and others did believe the accusations, they likely did so not simply because of their personal experiences but also because professional and lay opinion drew connections between religion, sex, and insanity in women. In the late nineteenth century, women's emotions were seen as often controlled by their sexuality and reproductive systems, and an "abnormal" interest in sex was taken as a sign of insanity. As Marks notes, by the late nineteenth century, female insanity was often seen as the product of "the most negative feminine qualities of over-emotionalism and sexual lack of control."[92] Many contemporaries thought the members of the Creffield sect to be religious fanatics, and we will see that in 1904 a number of the women were committed to the insane asylum. Given that the stories about the adultery became public at roughly the same time, an assumption that illicit sex had taken place was easily made.

Looked at this way, it becomes possible – we put it no higher than that – to reconcile the idea that the beliefs and practices of the sect did not include sexual intercourse with the allegations of generalized carnality. Knowledge of dubious and dangerous practices, the one incident of adultery, the assumption that female insanity was associated in some measure with unrestrained sexuality – all could have combined to produce allegations born of a conviction that the sect functioned as a kind of harem for its leader. Whether or not Creffield had sex with any follower other than Donna Starr, a point about which we are ultimately agnostic, we are sure both that sex was not as widespread as contemporaries came to believe and that those contemporaries did indeed become convinced that it was.

5

Disciplining the Sect

INVOKING INSANITY LAW, 1904

CREFFIELD AND HIS FOLLOWERS were in trouble with the law for most of 1904. In November 1903 the community had tried unsuccessfully to use insanity law to deal with Creffield and Brooks, and the same device was now resorted to, with much greater success, against the local sect members. When persuasion, exhortation, threats, and in some cases effective incarceration at home failed to discipline all local adherents, these informal methods of social control were abandoned and state laws and incarceration invoked; both child protection and insanity legislation were brought to bear by the community as it augmented its efforts to rein in errant sect members. Between late April and late June 1904 seven local adult adherents were declared insane and committed to the asylum, while two minors suffered the earlier fate of Esther Mitchell, being placed in the Boys and Girls Aid Society Home.[1]

THE COURT PROCEEDINGS

When we left the sect members at the end of the last chapter, a number of them were still living together at the Beach house without inciting further reaction. The community could not have been pleased about the situation, but nobody was going to tar and feather local people, all but one of whom were women, and it was presumably hoped that in time they would abandon their eccentric beliefs. Creffield's return to the area, however, changed the situation, for either his presence alone or meetings between him and his adherents emboldened the latter to public demonstrations of their faith. Creffield's messages must have concentrated on rejection of the material things of the world, for when the members became noticeable again it was because of their mode of dress. In late April a number of them appeared on the streets of Corvallis barefoot, with the women also bare-headed and wearing their hair unkempt and unbraided. Frank Hurt went to the post office "clad only in a pair of overalls and jumper," and his mother went about "clad much as were the young women"; she "wore her hair loose and down her back." All this, the *Corvallis Gazette* confidently asserted, occurred as a result of receiving some sort of message from Creffield – or, as the *Gazette* sarcastically put it, "from Heaven ... through their prophet Creffield."[2]

The community response was swift and decisive. Within a week or so, six people – Frank and Mollie Hurt, Rose Seeley, Sophia Hartley, Maud Creffield, and Attie Bray – had all been pronounced insane and involuntarily committed. There was no need to use insanity law against a seventh person, sixteen-year-old Florence Seeley, for she was a minor and child protection legislation gave courts a series of broad and highly discretionary grounds to deal with obdurate minors. The first sect member to be committed, Florence was arrested on Thursday, April 28, on the complaint of her sister Edna, who had been in the sect but left; she now lived in Oregon City. Taken from the Beach house, Florence was brought to the Linn County seat, Albany, "bareheaded as she had destroyed her hat according to divine revelations." She was well dressed, but "her luxuriant hair hung down her back uncared for and unconfined." The next day she appeared before Linn County judge H.M. Palmer, the man who had married the Creffields.[3]

Edna's petition, prepared by a local deputy district attorney, did not cite the precise language of the child protection statute, but Florence's case came squarely within its ambit because her parents were dead. The petition had still to convince Palmer that Florence was in need of care and protection, and in lurid language it sought to do so. Florence, it said, was under Creffield's influence and living with the holy rollers, who were "demented, depraved, disreputable and unfair for a girl to associate with." At the "Holy Roller Headquarters," it continued, men and women "lie around on the floor indiscriminately" and "go barefooted and half-dressed." The fear was that further association with the group "will utterly degrade and ruin" her.[4] At the hearing Edna gave evidence about the sect, as did O.V. Hurt, Louis Hartley, and Clarence Starr. Florence said nothing during the proceedings, and Palmer took little persuasion in finding, in words

nearly identical to those used in the petition, that Florence had been "living and associating with a number of disreputable and demented people,"
and that it was "ruining" her. He also had adverse comments on the sect:
"this so-called set of Holy Rollers go about bare-foot, hatless and otherwise,
half-dressed, and the men and women lie about on the floor indiscriminately together for hours at a time in obedience to alleged divine commands of one Creffield, who is notoriously disreputable . . . the teaching
and influence of said Holy Rollers is harmful, degrading and demoraliz-
ing." He ordered Florence given to the custody of "some organization
which will give her healthful and respectable employment, counsel and
assistance."[5] This turned out to be the Boys and Girls Aid Society, from
which Esther Mitchell had not long since been released. Fixing on what
was obviously a bothersome issue for all concerned, Palmer ordered Edna
Seeley to buy her sister a hat.

Florence did not speak during her hearing, but she was drawn out
shortly afterwards, before being taken to Portland, by a reporter from
the *Albany Herald*. She gave him a defiant explanation of why she lived
as she did: [6]

> In time we will be restored to innocence and purity such as marked the con-
> dition of Adam and Eve, but in order to reach that state we must put away
> all that is sinful. To do this we must conquer our pride and everything that
> tends to make us proud, and this includes the destruction of clothing and
> ornaments. When the world is restored to its original condition of inno-
> cence we will be as were Adam and Eve, and there will be no use of cloth-
> ing or raiment of any kind. Then the world will once more be innocent and
> God will dwell with us here on earth and we shall be like him.

The local press were unanimous in approving Florence Seeley's treatment, the *Albany Herald* insisting that "the practices of the Holy Rollers"
had to be stopped, as they were "a menace to young women," and predicting that more was to come.[7] Adults could not be dealt with by the
same process, and without evidence that sect members had committed any
criminal offence the insanity laws were the obvious tool to employ. The
process for commitment for insanity was a simple one, easily and widely
accessible as it was in most states at this time,[8] and used by people of all
classes to deal with family and social problems of various kinds. Invoking a
hearing required just one person to make a written application to a county
court judge stating that any person "by reason of insanity or idiocy, as the
case may be, is suffering from neglect, exposure or otherwise, or is unsafe

to be at large, or is suffering under mental derangement."[9] On receipt of the petition the judge was required to hold a hearing and to have one or more physicians attend and examine the person in question. If both the judge and the doctor(s) found the person to be insane, he or she was to be committed to the asylum, unless friends or family were prepared to "provide for their safe-keeping and medical treatment." It was a scheme designed to leave decisions in local hands. The initiative was to be taken by individuals, not the state. The local district attorney had the right to attend a hearing if he wished, although an earlier law requiring that attendance had been repealed in 1887. Assigning the jurisdiction to the county court judge rather than to the circuit court, and to local physicians, meant that communities, rather than some more remote state authority, made decisions about asylum commitments. Communities – counties – also paid for the costs of incarceration, although those costs would actually be borne wherever possible by families. This was the process to which Frank and Mollie Hurt were now subjected. They could not be found at the Beach house, for the rest of the group deserted it after Florence Seeley had been taken. The Hurts were arrested on April 29, after briefly evading authorities, and brought before Palmer at 1 p.m. on Saturday, April 30. In their case the complaining party was James Berry, and he, Louis Hartley, and O.V. Hurt appeared as witnesses. The substance of the complaints differed from that of Seeley's case, for the Hurts were adults. It was alleged that they were insane and because of that insanity were suffering from "neglect and exposure."[10] Thus the religious practices of living the simple life and dressing improperly were depicted as posing danger to the sect members themselves.

The proceedings before Palmer must have taken some hours. Both Frank and Mollie were questioned extensively by the judge and by two local doctors whom he had ordered to appear,[11] and evidence of the sect's practices was given by O.V. Hurt, Hartley, and Berry. The hearing covered the gamut of issues – strange religious beliefs, property and animal destruction, and refusal to conform to dress and deportment codes. There was a harbinger of things to come when Frank first set foot in the courtroom. O.V. Hurt had fitted his son out with a pair of shoes and a hat, but Frank burned them in the jail stove before the hearing. Without them he must have appeared completely disreputable – barefoot, clad in blue overalls, and with two weeks' growth of beard. Nor did it help that both Frank and Mollie, according to one reporter, looked "emaciated, having fasted for days at a time."[12] The hearing was dominated by the courtroom confrontation of father and son. O.V. Hurt was the principal witness, and his testimony showed that "the parties refused to work and that they destroyed all their good clothing and other property by fire, neglected their persons and generally showed insanity." Hurt "spoke with much emotion of the downfall of his son," but the most damning evidence probably came at the end of his testimony, when he pleaded with Frank to return home, "change his ways of acting and thus avoid spending a period of uncertain duration in the insane asylum." Frank would not listen. He apparently said that "he would rather spend years in the insane asylum" than return to his "worldly ways." He acknowledged that he had burned his "good clothing" on God's orders and had destroyed a bicycle for the same reason. The use of such articles was "sinful." He also admitted the killing of the animals and destruction of property in 1903, and said he went barefooted and bare-headed because of commands from God. He quoted Scripture liberally and declared "unlimited confidence in Apostle Creffield." Asked if he would obey an order given him in a revelation that required him to kill someone, he denied that any such order would be given.[13]

Mollie Hurt was also questioned. She was "clad in a plain black dress devoid of collar or ornament" and with her hair "hung down her back in luxuriant waves, uncombed and unconfined."[14] Like Frank she acknowledged that she had destroyed some clothing but insisted she had burned nothing useful, only the ornamental. Despite the fact that both Frank and Mollie were said to be "intelligent and reasonable" on "other subjects,"[15] the evidence was sufficient to get them committed, and they were formally admitted to the asylum the following day, Sunday, May 1. Their form of insanity was given as "mania" for Frank and "chronic mania" for Mollie; in both cases the cause was said to be "religious excitement."[16] Both of their "personal and medical" histories in the asylum records – copies of the information in the physicians' certificates committing them – contain the same account of the practices that had landed them there: "[They] go upon the streets bare footed and bare headed clad in the thinnest of raiment; destroy clothing and valuable and useful property belonging to themselves, injuring their mind and health by continuation of these practices which they claim are the commandments of God."[17]

During the ensuing week four others were similarly committed to the asylum – Sophia Hartley and Maud Creffield on Tuesday, May 3, and Rose Seeley and Attie Bray on Friday, May 6. The venue for the hearings shifted just across the river to the Benton County Court in Corvallis because the inhabitants of the Beach house returned to Corvallis, but otherwise both the process and the court's conclusions were the same.[18] A month later, on June 10, Mae Hurt joined Florence Seeley in the Portland home, and a few weeks after that, on June 27, Sarah Hurt was sent to the asylum.[19] With the exception of Sarah Hurt all seem to have taken their arrests and commitments quietly enough; Sarah, according to O.V. Hurt's testimony two years later, refused to leave when the sheriff came for her and "fought with all her strength" as she was carried from the house.[20] We will not detail each one, but the commitments are worth discussing for what they, and the earlier ones from Albany, reveal about why the community took the action it did, about how easily commitment was effected, and about the role of insanity and the asylum more generally in Oregon in this period.

Religion, Insanity, and Gender

Nobody believed any of the sect were "insane" in the sense of constituting a physical danger to themselves or others or being incapable of taking care of themselves. The physicians who examined Frank Hurt, for example, stated specifically that he was "not destructive . . . not violent" and that he had "not been restrained."[21] Time and again contemporaries spoke of sect members' calmness and rationality on all subjects other than religion.[22] Why, then, was the asylum resorted to?

To some extent the incarceration strategy was the result of Creffield's reappearance and continued evasion of the authorities looking for him. Until late April the sect was left alone, and it was only the rumoured return of Creffield and the public displays of members' beliefs that caused the community to formally pursue them. Presumably they were no more and no less "insane" or in need of intervention than they had previously been. Moreover, neither O.V. Hurt nor any other community member saw it necessary to deal with Sarah and Mae Hurt in early May, probably because they were living at home and isolated from their fellow adherents. But as time went on and the authorities proved unable to track Creffield down, it was believed that he must be receiving support from somewhere. That support could only be from the Hurt women still at liberty, and thus their removal was as much about isolating Creffield as it was about disciplining them. Sarah Hurt was considered "temporarily deranged" at the time of Mae's committal weeks earlier,[23] but it was not until the end of the month, with Creffield still at large, that she was sent away. The need to isolate Creffield and to shield his supporters from him were, of course, related. As long as Creffield remained free his supporters took comfort from that fact; as the *Corvallis Times* put it just after Mae Hurt was sent to Portland, "the very success Creffield has in eluding the officers has an unfortunate effect upon the unbalanced minds of the members of the sect.[24]

Explaining the timing does not, however, altogether explain the method, in particular the decision to use the asylum, and so we must probe a little deeper. A second cause was surely that some of the sect's opponents genuinely believed its members suffered from a form of insanity. O.V. Hurt was probably sincere when he said that he had hoped his wife would "recover from her hallucination" when deprived of the company of other members of the sect. When that did not happen "he at last decided to . . . have her committed and . . . thus effect a cure."[25] Asylum officials and court-appointed physicians likewise believed it was important to record the religious practices that served as symptoms of insanity. Intake records for Frank and Mollie Hurt, for example, refer to the fact that they "lie upon their faces on the floor and pray day and night, claiming to receive messages from God"; similar things were said about others.[26] All those in the asylum were said to be suffering from a form of mania, and the cause was variously stated as "Religious Excitement," "Religion," "Religion Holy Roller," or "Religion (Creffieldism)," and the girls in the BGAS Home were similarly described as "temporarily deranged" and the like.[27]

Men like O.V. Hurt and the officials responsible for commitment did not hold their beliefs in a vacuum. While it was less common in the nineteenth and early twentieth centuries than it had been earlier to use the asylum for people with extreme religious beliefs, it was not unusual either, with religious enthusiasm or despair seen as both a cause and a manifestation of mental illness.[28] Religious beliefs that emphasized unusual rituals and mysticism were seen as particularly likely to induce mental disorder, and it was widely believed that too much religion, an excess of ardency, could cause insanity. As the leading medico-legal text of the time put it, "Abnormal religious excitement, or depressive orthodoxy taken too seriously, is doubtless responsible for much disorder of mind; . . . the supernatural in religion must bear its share of responsibility for the causation of insanity."[29] Locally, this view received support from the *Corvallis Times*, which at the height of the bonfire scandal the year before had noted that "many of the patients in the insane asylums become crazed on religion" and that "one of the easiest ways in the world for reason to be dethroned is . . . pursuit of religious fervor."[30]

Given these beliefs, it is not surprising that the Creffield sect members were not the only people put in the Oregon asylum for this cause at this time. But while eleven others suffered that fate in 1904, no other group was targeted. The others were all isolated individual cases from many different

communities and invariably involved people who were a danger to themselves or could not care for themselves as a result of their beliefs.[31] What
needs to be explained, therefore, is the use of insanity against an entire
religious sect, and one whose members were clearly generally rational and
capable of taking care of themselves. Crucial to the decisions to commit
were two inter-related factors: that the Creffield sect was predominantly
female and that these women defied male authority and refused to conform to expected gender roles. Although women were not committed to
asylums for religious insanity more often than men in this period, what
Marks has called a "cultural association" was made between women, who
were anyway more prone to irrationality and over-emotionalism than men,
and religious insanity. Ecstatic practices reinforced this belief, for they were
diagnosed as forms of hysteria, and hysteria in turn was a "predominantly
if not exclusively female disease."[32]

While the predominance of women in the sect made designating
members as insane easier, there was more to it than that. The women also
committed gross violations of codes of moral and economic behaviour,
acting far outside the bounds of convention and decency. The unacceptable social practices and values associated with their religious beliefs were
the real problem. That the community chose different processes to deal
with minors and adults is instructive here. Child protection legislation
gave the community tools to deal with minors who misbehaved – insanity laws were not necessary to discipline them. But unless adults committed a criminal offence, they could not be reached in the same way.
An expedient solution was necessary, and insanity law was the obvious,
perhaps the only, device able to provide that solution.

As noted, the flouting of economic morality played an important role.
Frank and Mollie Hurt destroyed clothing and other property and failed
to take "proper" care of themselves. They, as well as Rose Seeley and Attie
Bray, refused to work before incarceration, and Mae Hurt continued her
refusal in the BGAS Home, an obvious affront to prevailing values of
industry and self-reliance.[33] The destruction of personal property was also
noted for Sophia Hartley and Maud Creffield – they were likely not cited
for failure to work because they came from family and class backgrounds
in which work was not required.[34] Rose Seeley was scorned because during her hearing she remained standing, a result of "the fool notion in the
Creffield creed that a chair and other furniture is contaminating."[35] One
editorial stated with reference to Frank and Mollie Hurt that a spell in
the asylum would "make them conform to the habits of a decent civilization." Another talked of the treatment they would receive, rendering them

again "useful members of society."[36] While property destruction, the refusal to work, and strange attitudes to material goods were often cited
as evidence of peoples' inability to take proper care of themselves, the fact
is that the sect members did indeed manage to keep body and soul
together. For example, Maud Creffield's "habits" were said by the certifying physicians to be "good," except for her "peculiar views and habits."[37]
Sect members may not have lived well, but they lived better than many
in that society. The problem was that they could have done better, and
in refusing to embrace wealth accumulation, in rejecting the things of the
world, they acted so far outside the bounds of propriety as to be seen,
literally, as insane.

More important than breaches of economic morality was the rejection
of traditional male authority. As the *Corvallis Gazette* put it, the sect
showed a "reckless disregard for decency and the sanctity of the home."[38]
Official documents and press reports reiterated time and again the flouting of social conventions associated with gender roles, and it was this that
most aroused the ire of the community and officials. What was unacceptable about the way the sect lived varied according to which members were
being discussed. In Florence Seeley's case much was made of her living
"indiscriminately" with men. We have seen that uncovered heads and free-
flowing hair were a feature of both press commentary and official condemnation of Florence Seeley and Mollie Hurt, and the same practices excited
comment and disapproval for others. Press reports of Maud Creffield and
Sophia Hartley noted that both were bare-headed and that "their hair
hung down their backs in picturesque abandon," and Maud's certificate
of insanity noted her belief in the lack of a need for head covering. The
certifying physicians' history of Rose Seeley's case was largely concerned
with the fact that she "wears no covering upon her head, leaves the hair
hanging down over her shoulders and back, going upon the streets in same
manner," and they similarly commented that Bray "goes about with her
head uncovered and hair streaming down her back, as all the women of
this sect do." When a local paper reported Sarah Hurt being taken to the
asylum it had little to say beyond that she "wore her hair loose and down
her back,"[39] and Gardner's early reports on her daughter Mae lamented
that while she was improved in some respects she nonetheless "insists on
keeping her hair hanging."[40]

At this remove the concern with women's hair flowing free and uncovered by a hat may seem quaint, even amusing, but the constant references
to these practices in testimony, court documents, and asylum files show
they were taken very seriously indeed at the time. To some in the press,

loose hair may have been titillating. Certainly it all represented much more than idiosyncratic religious belief: it stood for rebellion, for a refusal to acknowledge a social convention that was an important symbol of female submissiveness and appropriate deportment. The women were letting their hair down metaphorically as well as literally, making a public statement that they could live as God advised them, paying no heed to the authority of husbands and fathers, and choosing in some cases to live entirely independently of proper male authority. Florence Seeley's hair was not simply "down," it was, in the words of Judge Palmer, "unconfined," and as a result she was also. In ordering her sister Edna to buy her a hat before she was taken to Portland, he hoped to confine Florence's spirit as much as his commitment order would confine her body. Letting down the hair was also, of course, something that women did in preparing for bed, and it thus may have represented sexual licentiousness. That the women were victims of Creffield was accepted, but it did not relieve them of the consequences of their actions.

Not all the sect members were put in the asylum or the Home, a fact that again helps to cast what was done as social discipline.[41] Ed Baldwin had his daughter Ona under lock and key. Donna Starr had been in Portland since Burgess had forcibly taken her there in the fall of 1903. Some two and a half years later Burgess said he believed her to have been insane at that time, and indeed, that she had undergone a sanity hearing in court. But she was not committed, after promising not to try to see Esther Mitchell, then in the BGAS Home, again. According to a later report, Cora Hartley, who was noted as likely insane in her daughter Sophia's inmate record, was "kept under constant surveillance" until mid-July 1904, presumably by Louis, and then, when he had to leave again for the mines, taken with him. She did a little cooking but was not considered safe to be left to her own devices. Her Bible was kept from her, but this had "no salutary effect on the victim of Creffieldism." Cora was as "insane" as anybody else, but in her case a husband and a son, and the isolation of the mining camp, supplied the discipline needed, not the asylum.[42]

One final point should be made about the reasons sect members were committed to institutions. For all the concern about the inappropriateness of the group's living arrangements, and for all that dress and deportment played so central a role, not a single mention was made in these proceedings, even obliquely, to sex. The commitment processes provided opportunities, in court and in press commentary, for the community to say exactly what was so awful about Creffield. They did so, explicitly and implicitly – but the reasons adduced did not include sex.

PUBLIC LAW AND PRIVATE ACTION:
THE SOCIAL USES OF THE ASYLUM

The asylum commitments allow us a glimpse at the social uses of civil insanity commitment in early twentieth-century Oregon. Deputy D.A. Bryson and Sheriff Burnett had laid the insanity complaints against Creffield and Brooks in the fall of 1903, but they played no role this time around. The lead was taken by private citizens – members of families and community worthies – with O.V. Hurt and Louis Hartley to the fore. Hurt was the principal witness against his son and daughter-in-law, the complainant and the only witness in the case of his daughter Mae, and a witness against his wife, Sarah. He also helped put Florence Seeley away, and it was he who took Sarah to the asylum, along with a sheriff's deputy. Louis Hartley testified against Florence Seeley and the Hurts, and he, rather than O.V. Hurt, was the complainant in the case against Maud Creffield. It was also Hartley who followed Rose Seeley and Attie Bray when, after not turning up for work and afraid to return to the Beach house, they went to the Farmers' Hotel, seeking food and lodgings. Hartley prevailed on the proprietor, W.J. Howell, to make the complaint against the two women.[43] The involvement of Howell shows that others took part as well, some of whom had a connection to the sect. Ed Baldwin signed the formal complaint against Sarah Hurt, and local businessman Samuel Bayne made the complaint against Sophia Hartley.[44] As noted above, it was James Berry who initiated proceedings against Frank and Mollie Hurt and gave evidence about them. The involvement of all these people – relatives and others – in a variety of cases shows that this was a concerted community effort, as much, if not more so, as the tarring and feathering of Creffield and Brooks had been.

Once the sect members got to the courtroom it proved extremely easy to invoke the state apparatus of insanity laws. None of the hearings lasted more than a few hours, and some were much shorter. And their conclusions were surely inevitable, for the decision about whether somebody was insane was given to local men who would have been well acquainted with everything that had happened and as opposed to the sect as the complainants. When the venue shifted to Corvallis and the Benton County Court, the examining physicians in the cases of Sophia Hartley and Maud Creffield were Louis Altman and George Farra. Doctors Pernot and Cathey, the men who had failed to certify Creffield and Brooks as insane in the fall of 1903, were not invited to participate. Altman was a homeopathic physician and there is no evidence that he had any experience with mental illness, but he had been in Corvallis since 1891 and as a staunch supporter of the Presbyterian church he likely brought a religious conservatism to his adjudications, as well as a desire to assist established families he knew well. Farra, a resident of Corvallis for almost thirty years, was not only a successful doctor but one of the county's leading businessmen, a member of the city council, and the owner of the finest house in town. His allegiances were also sure to be with men such as Hartley and, if not O.V. Hurt, then his employer, S.L. Kline.[45] Farra also certified the insanity of Attie Bray and Rose Seeley, this time with Cathey, who by now was more willing to cooperate, while Altman was the only physician present for Sarah Hurt's case. Perhaps Cathey was also influenced by his own deep attachment to mainstream Methodism – in the 1890s he had been a lay preacher in the Methodist Episcopal Church at Woodburn. His economic ties to Louis Hartley may also have had an influence – he was an investor in the Bohemia Mines managed by Hartley, as were a good many Corvallis residents.[46] It is interesting – we say no more than that – that Pernot, the one doctor in town with experience of mental illness, at the Bellevue Hospital in New York, did not participate in any of the 1904 hearings.[47]

The third man with decision-making power, Judge Virgil Watters, was also likely to be ill disposed towards these religious radicals. In addition to being the principal county commissioner, a status his role as county court judge conferred upon him, he was president of the Board of Trustees of the Corvallis Methodist Episcopal Church and superintendent of its Sunday school.[48] In discussing the backgrounds of Watters and the other decision makers we are not suggesting some kind of overt conspiracy. Rather, these men surely shared, with each other and the community of which they were a part, a set of ideas about the acceptable bounds of religious beliefs and appropriate social behaviour, which, combined with the ties they had to many of the complainants, made it very easy for them to agree that the adults were insane and the children needed institutional correction. They performed their official duties in the shadow of those beliefs and connections. For Watters this is perhaps best exemplified by the case of Mae Hurt, for it is difficult to see how her situation came within any of the criteria for placing her in the Society's custody, discussed in the previous chapter. Unlike Florence Seeley she had a parent quite capable of looking after her, and the ground given for her commitment – that she was "temporarily deranged" – was not one listed in the statute that gave the court jurisdiction.[49] It was, of course, a ground for commitment to the asylum, but asylum legislation did not allow for incarceration in the Portland home. BGAS Superintendent William Gardner had no doubt that getting a commitment order would be easy; when O.V. Hurt asked him about sending Mae to the Portland home, he replied succinctly that "the better way would be for you to go and see your County Judge and have her committed."[50] The technicalities of the law were not important; what mattered was that the Creffield sect members had to be brought to their senses.

The ways in which the asylum was used in this case are consistent with arguments made recently for this period by historians of the American asylum generally. An historiography emphasizing benevolence and humanitarianism has long given way to viewing the asylum as an exercise in social control, part of the broader enterprise of restraining non-conformity and imposing the new values of the industrial socioeconomic order.[51] Tolerance for deviant behaviour was reduced, and those who could not or would not adapt were targeted in various ways, including being labelled as insane. Rates of incarceration went up as the net of insanity widened and as family members who traditionally cared for the insane were no longer able to do so because they were increasingly employed outside the home.[52] More recently this view of the asylum has undergone further modification, with a number of authors variously rehabilitating the theory of benevolent original intent and suggesting that the definition of insanity and the use of the asylum were manipulated not just by elite groups but by a broad cross-section of the community, in response to the inadequacy of social services or some other imperative.[53] Thus ordinary people "perceived the state asylum ... as their own community institution"; they "made selective use of the custodial function of an asylum ... and manipulated its therapeutic purposes to fit their needs."[54] It was not difficult to do so, for, as in Oregon, the commitment laws were administered "in a loose and informal manner" and decisions were based on "human rather than strictly legal terms." Generally "families did not find commitment a difficult undertaking or one that involved ... protracted conflict."[55]

It seems likely that the Oregon asylum's operation in this period accorded with this general characterization of the asylum function,[56] for people were sent there at the initiative of families and communities for a wide variety of reasons. Taking just one year of the Benton County Court's proceedings, for example, the year beginning on the day on which Attie Bray and Rose Seeley were committed, we find one man who threatened to harm children, an opium user, a non-violent man who acted "queerly" and loitered around houses, a man made suicidal by the belief that he was not properly providing for his family, and two others who had delusions of various kinds – one thought the phone company was charging his house with electricity so that he could not sleep.[57] Community newspapers throughout the state frequently reported insanity hearings, and it is clear that this summary was not exceptional in its variety. Some people were sent to the asylum because they were dangerous to themselves and others, but many were sent because they could not be cared for by their families or communities or some public institution. Indeed, asylum superintendents and others were wont to complain that too many people not really insane were sent there. As one newspaper quipped in 1902, "when a man gets to be a nuisance in Oregon he is sent to the Asylum," so that it contained a variety of people from "the worst ones in the violent wards to the harmless old people who have no other place to go."[58]

To this list of functions that the asylum served we can add another – community coercion of deviance, not just of deviant individuals. The classification of the behaviour of Creffield's followers as unacceptable was not made by a distant and faceless state bureaucracy, but was a local and popular form of coercion, similar to and perhaps an extension of the tarring and feathering meted out earlier. Asylum commitment might be seen as a modernization of this older, and ultimately unsuccessful, form of community control. But perhaps more importantly, it was also a form of control adapted to the fact that the Creffield sect members were locals, not outsiders, and mostly women. The failure to conform to established gender roles surely contributed to the judgment that Creffield's followers were insane, as it may have done elsewhere. While it was increasingly acceptable for women to complain of specific abuse within a marriage, to challenge the institution of marriage more generally, or the fundamental division of labour and social roles between men and women, was so irrational as to support the conclusion that the person must be mad.[59] As the women had broken no law and were, for the most part, of age, there was only one process and one institution available to be used against them – civil commitment for insanity. Whatever other purposes they may have thought it served, the people of Corvallis saw the Salem asylum as a place to discipline a small group of their fellow citizens.[60]

The community members responsible included the doctors and judges, men who were quite prepared to accept the need to use whatever means possible for the shared social purpose of eradicating "Creffieldism." This was a public-private partnership. Friends and family members invoked the process, provided testimony, and in some cases conveyed the committed person to the institution. They also paid for the upkeep of those in the asylum. But they could not by themselves obtain the legal authorization for institutionalization; nor could they provide the walls behind which the objects of their regulatory desires were to be kept. Those had to come, respectively, from the courts and the institutional authorities. Having failed to rid their community of Creffield's influence by running him out of town, Corvallisites turned to state authorities and the power and authority of the law to assist – and found them more than willing to do so.

THE SECT IN THE ASYLUM

We know very little about what kind of regime the sect members were subjected to in the asylum. The Oregon State Hospital was invariably overcrowded in this period, holding between 1,350 and 1,375 patients in the spring and summer of 1904.[61] Most patients lived in large wards and did little each day beyond taking some exercise in the yard. There were religious services on Sundays, which the sect members probably did not much care for, and the occasional entertainment laid on, which they would surely have found too worldly.[62] The sect members were kept apart from each other, including Frank and Mollie Hurt. Frank was so angered by this that he "prayed loudly for the destruction of the asylum."[63] The sect members gave little trouble, and the asylum authorities did not seek to dissuade them from their beliefs, hoping that in time they would see the error of their ways and that news of Creffield's capture in particular would lessen their faith in him. There was, however, an exception to this laissez-faire approach – when discussion of beliefs was "necessary" as an aspect of "compelling them to dress and wear their hair as other people do."[64] This exception demonstrates yet again the overriding importance of adhering to convention in the community response to Creffield's supporters.

It took time for all the sect members to at least pretend to give up their beliefs. Most still adhered to Creffield's teachings in August 1904, their motto being "Stick fast to the faith." The news of Creffield's capture was seen by them as evidence not of his fallibility but of God rescuing him from starvation.[65] Maud Creffield may have had the roughest time of it, on occasions being placed in a straitjacket or tied to a bed or chair – presumably because she insisted on continuing to pray and engage in ecstatic practices.[66] Maud must indeed have found it extremely difficult, for she was wrestling not just with incarceration but with betrayal by her adulterous husband and spiritual leader and, from late September 1904, with the knowledge that Creffield had been sent to the penitentiary. She became seriously ill at one point and seems to have been the slowest to give up active demonstrations of her beliefs, although she was one of the first to be released. More than six weeks after incarceration Rose Seeley still referred to the time spent on Smith Island as a very happy period for her and insisted, "I would like to camp there again," but shortly afterwards she apparently had come to the conclusion that "she was deceived" by Creffield.[67] Attie Bray also clung to her beliefs and kept her spirit, so much so that she escaped after a month or so and walked the thirty miles from the asylum farm to Corvallis. But she had nowhere to go but the Hurt house, and from there she was retaken. While at the house she refused to use a chair and prayed a good deal.[68] Sarah Hurt was reported by the asylum superintendent to be still "hopelessly insane" in mid-August 1904, so she too found it difficult to give up her beliefs.[69] She was allowed home on three months' "leave" in September, just after Creffield had been convicted in a Portland court, but was returned at the end of the month, as she was not sufficiently "improved"; she "still wears her hair down, Holy Roller style."[70]

Whether or not they were ever convinced of it themselves, the sect members in the asylum were able over time to convince asylum officials that they were abandoning their beliefs. Obviously they realized that freedom would be hastened by giving up ecstatic practices, and officials' statements that, for example, Sophia Hartley was likely to "regain her mental balance" reflected these changes in behaviour.[71] None of the sect members stayed incarcerated past the end of the year. Rose Seeley was said to have "had enough of Creffield's religion" by early July, and she was the first to be released, on July 9; she went to live with sister Edna in Oregon City.[72] Maud Creffield was released on November 24, Frank and Mollie Hurt in early December, Sarah Hurt on the 4th, Attie Bray on the 8th, and Sophia Hartley on the 17th; all returned to Corvallis. They were all said in asylum records to be "cured" or "recovered."[73] Sophia Hartley, the last to leave, renounced her beliefs following a visit from Maud Creffield; she was taken home by her father shortly afterwards, attired "in a new outfit of clothing in the latest style."[74]

As for the girls in the Portland home, Florence Seeley was released on June 30, after just two months. She went to live with her sister, Mrs Lily Wilson, in British Columbia.[75] Although she stuck fast to her faith initially, she was said to have "gotten ... over" her belief in Creffield by early June. Later that month she refused to reply to a letter from Rose that talked fondly of their time on Smith Island, and was "practically cured of her trouble" by the time she was released. She was, said matron Mary Graham, "quite herself again and ... a very nice girl."[76] By mid-August she was referring to her belief in Creffield as "that horrid delusion" and as "disgraceful."[77]

Mae Hurt also clung to her beliefs for some weeks, refusing work, taking off her shoes when she could, letting her hair hang loose, and refusing to write to her father.[78] O.V. Hurt was steadfast in his expressions of love and support for "my little girl" who he "could hardly get out of my mind," and from mid-July Mae seemed to change, so much so that by the end of the month Gardner thought she was "all right" and "will remain so, provided you [O.V. Hurt] do not allow any counter influence to come in." He was especially concerned about Maud and Frank. When asked if she was "still a Holy Roller," Mae had "laughed and said 'of course not, and never will be again.'"[79] O.V. Hurt said he was "so rejoiced I hardly know what to do" when he learned that she would be released, "as I need her so much."[80] Mae was returned to Corvallis on August 1, just after Creffield was captured – the timing reinforces the idea that she and Sarah were taken away only to prevent their assisting him. Mae was said to have "recovered from her delusion" and to be "completely restored."[81] "You never saw a more happy girl to return to her own home with her father," Mary Graham told Florence Seeley a little later.[82]

This account of the fate of those placed in the asylum reinforces our understanding of the causes of incarceration. The "insanity" of this group was short-lived, ameliorated by keeping them away from Creffield and each other for a few months. While there was generally a great deal of flexibility in discharge policies and practices in asylums during this period, with superintendents able to decide whether a person should stay or be released,[83] the cases of Maud Creffield and Sarah Hurt suggest that control was also vested in the hands of families and the community as, indeed, it often was elsewhere.[84] For these two, and perhaps others, discharge from the institution was as variable and discretionary, and as subject to private preference, as commitment. As one author has argued, the high "cure" rate for "religious insanity" in this period bolsters the proposition that insanity charges of this nature were used to discipline deviance.[85]

DECEMBER 1904: THE END OF THE AFFAIR?

When the *Corvallis Gazette* reported the release of Frank and Mollie Hurt from the asylum in December 1904 it noted that they were expected "to take up housekeeping in Corvallis." The innocuous domestic image was in marked contrast to the havoc the Creffield sect had wreaked in Corvallis and reflected a broader confidence that the town had surely seen the last of the troubles that had so disrupted and embarrassed it. As the

Times also noted, with all the members of the Hurt family "again at the fireside, fully restored in mind," the town had seen "the end of the unfortunate chapter."[86] Creffield was in the penitentiary and likely to remain there for some time, and the principal sect members either had not been heard of for many months, as was the case with Charles Brooks, or had been dealt with through institutionalization and were back home resuming normal lives – or would be shortly. As we shall see, the community had certainly not heard the last of Creffield or radical holiness. And perhaps O.V. Hurt knew this and did not share the press' optimism. He may have thought Mae and Frank were "recovered," but it was evident that his oldest child was not. When Maud returned home she refused to eat meat, had "melancholy weeping spells," still destroyed fine clothing, and from time to time announced that "God will protect me."[87] It took more than an adulterous husband and a few months in an insane asylum to convince the ardent Maud Hurt Creffield to abandon her beliefs. The same was true for a good many other members of the sect.

6

Revival and Revenge,
January to May 1906

1905 WAS A QUIET YEAR for Corvallis, and for Franz Creffield. Number 4941 spent it in the Oregon State Penitentiary at Salem, with some 300 other prisoners. His penitentiary photograph shows a sad-eyed and doleful man. He worked in the tin shop and laboured on the roads, earning from the latter statutory remission of 277 days. He was a quiet and well-behaved prisoner, and stuck to his religious convictions. Although he made little attempt to convert others and was reluctant to discuss his beliefs with the occasional visitor from the press, he did make one speech to his fellow inmates at an "evangelistic service," in which he gave a "conservative portrayal of his Holy Roller doctrines."[1] When he was released on December 13, 1905, he was again single. Maud had divorced him on account of the adultery, the decree granted on July 6, 1905, by the circuit court for Benton County, Judge Lawrence T. Harris presiding.[2] Maud later stated that she was forced into this action by her parents,[3] which seems likely given her continued commitment to Creffield in 1904 after the adultery and, as we shall see, her joining him again after his release. Maud stayed in Corvallis through 1905 and early 1906, living at home. O.V. Hurt saw life return to what must have seemed a blissful ordinariness. Being asked to judge wool for the Benton County exhibit at the Lewis and Clark fair in May 1905 was probably enough excitement for him after the events of the previous two years.[4]

The tranquility was rudely shattered in the spring of 1906 by a remarkable and dramatic series of events. Creffield was able to reinvigorate the sect, enticing back into the fold all three of O.V. Hurt's children, among others. That Creffield was able to bring his adherents together again to establish a colony on the coast of Oregon demonstrates both his own and his followers depth of conviction. Tar and feathers, the prison cell and the insane ward, family pressure and community contempt and ridicule – none of these was able to destroy the faith of either Creffield or most of his followers. Both the prophet and his apostles now recreated one of the classic themes of the Bible, which they so literally tried to follow – the casting out of true believers into the wilderness. Rejected and reviled, they did not despair but looked to their God and his earthly representative, Creffield, to sustain and save them. By now Creffield was well up to the task, for he had been transformed from a prophet to the Messiah himself, his release from prison a resurrection. As remarkable as all this was, it had a parallel in community reaction to the sect. As the apostles sought to return to their own version of a state of nature, so too did some of their relatives. Throwing off the shackles of civilization and law, at least three men picked up weapons and started their own personal manhunts in pursuit of Creffield, determined to exact their form of justice on a man who continued to entice away their women. The resort to deadly force by Louis Hartley, Ed Baldwin, and George Mitchell was a development in community response as remarkable as the trek into the wilderness was for their relatives. Hartley and Baldwin failed, but Mitchell succeeded, gunning down Creffield in downtown Seattle on May 7, 1906.

REVIVAL: THE LINCOLN COUNTY COLONY

On his release, with just the $5 given to ex-convicts, Creffield went first to California and then to Seattle.[5] He had lost none of his ardency; indeed he seems to have considered his time in the penitentiary as a test of his faith by God. He preached in San Francisco and Sacramento, but with little success, and may have visited Los Angeles. Creffield's return to the Pacific Northwest and Seattle resulted from his conviction that he was called to again lead his followers to salvation.[6] We do not know exactly when he got to Seattle, but it was probably in February 1906. He reestablished contact with Frank and Mollie Hurt, who had moved there in 1905, Frank taking a job with the Anderson Steamship Company as an engineer on a ship that plied the waters of Lake Washington.[7] In early February Sarah and Maud Hurt visited Frank, and we assume they met up with Creffield, who lived with the Hurts for at least part of this time.

Later the same month Esther Mitchell visited the Hurts in Corvallis.[8]

Although her family had plenty of evidence that she had not given up her beliefs, Esther had been allowed to return to Oregon late in 1904, after Creffield was safely in the penitentiary, and by early 1906 she was living in Oregon City and working in the town's woollen mills.[9] She may have been one of several women who, according to Mollie Hurt's brother, Louis Sandell, sent Creffield money during the winter.[10] A clandestine correspondence was also begun with other followers; it was clandestine because, with Creffield out of prison, the Hurt and Hartley mail was watched by the men of the households. It is likely that Esther Mitchell acted as go-between, receiving and passing on Creffield's letters, although one or both of the Seeley girls were also resident in Oregon City and may have performed that task.[11] As an extra precaution Creffield's followers addressed their letters to him to "E. Sandel, Seattle, General Delivery."[12] There are one or two suggestions that Creffield travelled to Oregon himself; we think that improbable in the circumstances, although he would likely have gone through the state earlier on his way from California to Seattle.

A dramatic symbol that Creffield was back in business was his remarriage to Maud Hurt, which took place in Seattle on April 3, 1906. Justice George of the superior court cemented the alliance, with Frank and Mollie Hurt again acting as witnesses, as they had done in 1904.[13] But long before that, people in Benton County suspected that something was afoot. In February there had been "slight manifestations of Rollerism" observed among sect members, and soon after that it was discovered that some of them had been corresponding with Creffield.[14] Maud's willingness to remarry Creffield is, at first sight, somewhat puzzling, given his betrayal. But later comments by Maud suggest that she convinced herself that the adultery had not really happened – Donna Starr had not told the truth at the trial – and, somewhat contradictorily, that Creffield had "discontinued the practices which ... rendered their faith obnoxious to the communities in which they have been established."[15]

Reviving adherents' interest was one thing, finding a place to operate was quite another. As a report from Corvallis in a Portland newspaper made clear, "the practice of the religion in this city will not be tolerated for a moment by the authorities."[16] Creffield instead decided to take the group to the Waldport area of the Oregon coast, west of Corvallis. Frank Hurt and Maud Creffield knew this area well; the Hurts and the Starrs had lived on the coast for a number of years before their move to Corvallis, and Attie Bray's parents, Frank's aunt and uncle, still lived there.[17] Its remoteness would also, of course, have made it attractive, in two senses. It might be far enough away that people from Corvallis would be unable to organize resistance to a colony, and it probably evoked a biblical sense of going out into the wilderness. There seems to have been little in the way of planning for the colony. No land was purchased, even though Frank Hurt sold his Seattle house to finance the venture and one or two sources mention a scheme to take up homestead land at what is now Yachats.[18] Someone may have scouted the region, but probably they relied on Frank's knowledge. It is likely that as late as mid-March no plan to go the coast had been made, for at that time Frank Hurt accepted an appointment as a deputy assessor for King County.[19] A month or so later the Hurts and Creffields left Seattle, probably on April 18 or 19, en route to Corvallis, from where they could take the train to the coast.

The sect went west in more than one party.[20] Frank and Mollie Hurt, with their five-month-old baby, Ruth, and two other women, took the Corvallis and Eastern Railroad to the end of the track at Yaquina City on Friday, April 20. One of the two women was surely Olive Sandell. Another party left the Corvallis station the next day, Saturday, April 21; it definitely included Maud Creffield and Cora and Sophia Hartley. At some point, perhaps also on the 21st, Esther Mitchell, Mae Hurt, Attie Bray, and Rose and Florence Seeley all travelled to the coast as well; one of them must have been the second woman with the Frank Hurt party.[21] Esther Mitchell walked from Corvallis to the camp near Waldport, a difficult journey of more than eighty miles through hilly country.[22] Although Creffield travelled from Seattle with Maud, he knew enough to avoid Corvallis. He got off the train from Portland at Airlie, Polk County, and journeyed in a rented rig to Wren, some twelve miles west of Corvallis, where he rejoined the train. The journey cost him $6 rather than the $3 the train ride alone would have cost, and he may also have disguised himself, but he must have known that he was perhaps buying his life.

Not all of Creffield's former adherents followed him to the coast. Sarah Hurt did not, although she remained a believer, telling O.V. Hurt at this time that she had "faith in his [Creffield's] perfection."[23] Perhaps, like Ona Baldwin, she was physically prevented from doing so; Ona's father proudly proclaimed that he had been able to "use force to keep her from going to him [Creffield]."[24] By now only Frank Hurt remained of the male adherents from 1903 to 1904. Whether Creffield tried to contact the others and failed, or made no such effort, is unknown.

The Hartleys' journey west was far from straightforward. Louis Hartley followed his wife and daughter when they left the house, boarding the same train.[25] When they discovered his presence the Hartley women disembarked at Blodgett without Louis realizing it. Cora and Sophia spent the night at a farmhouse and then walked the rest of the way to the coast, a distance of some fifty miles. Unable to find his wife and daughter in Yaquina City, Hartley tried other tactics. He took the ferry to Newport and asked the authorities to issue a warrant for Creffield's arrest but could not convince anyone that an offence had been committed. He then bought a revolver, determined to deal with Creffield once and for all. As he colourfully put it in the divorce petition he wrote out a week or two later, "in order to avoid further annoyance" he "deem[ed] it proper to assist the said Creffield to leave this mortal earth in a speedy manner."[26] His ferry back to Yaquina City reached the terminus just before the ferry that took Creffield and the others across Yaquina Bay to South Beach departed. Hartley raced to the other boat landing, aimed at Creffield, a few yards away, and pulled the trigger five times. But he had been sold the wrong kind of cartridge for the gun, and nothing happened. Creffield had survived Hartley's wrath once again, and he likely used this incident as further evidence of his invincibility.

From the South Beach landing Creffield and his followers travelled south, on Sunday, April 22. They probably boarded a wagon and took the wagon road to Seal Rock, the terminus, from there walking to Alsea Bay, a total distance of some fifteen miles. They stopped and set up camp at that point, on a piece of land near the beach owned by a farmer called Hosford.[27] Creffield may have initially intended to go farther; the reference noted above to homesteading in the Yachats area, a further fifteen miles south, suggests this, as does other evidence.[28] If so, the probable cause of his change of mind was the realization, following the Hartley assault, that he was not safe anywhere in Oregon.

There were "ten or a dozen" in the camp.[29] That total consisted of the Creffields, the Hurts, Olive Sandell, Mae Hurt, Attie Bray, Esther Mitchell, and, probably, the Seeley sisters, plus, of course, the baby.[30] The Hartleys were also there, although they cannot have travelled with the main party from Yaquina City.[31] That makes twelve, and Donna Starr joined them later. She journeyed to the coast independently, not leaving Portland until Saturday, April 28. In dramatic fashion, she crept out of the house in the small hours of the morning, taking just $3.50 with her, and travelled by train to Corvallis. Having exhausted her resources, she walked from there to the Waldport area, across the coastal range and through country populated with cougars and bears.[32]

Donna Starr may have travelled the farthest physical distance, and experienced the most difficulty, but all the women who went to Waldport journeyed a very long way spiritually. In 1903, when they first made their personal commitment to the holiness life, they had largely remained in their homes and communities. Now they were prepared to abandon everything – homes, husbands, children, material comforts – to follow their prophet. In many cases they did so without having had any direct contact with Creffield for two or more years, and following a period in which the adultery had taken place and immense pressure had been exerted to persuade them of how wrong-headed they had been. In the view of the *Corvallis Gazette,* it "passes human understanding" that people would rejoin "such a creature as Creffield";[33] but the establishment of the Waldport camp is a remarkable illustration of both the strength of belief in Creffield and the power of his followers' religious convictions. By now Creffield was claiming near-divine status, perhaps even that he was the second Messiah.[34] His followers accepted this, and their acceptance can be seen as both cause and effect of their willingness to follow him literally into the wilderness. Esther Mitchell, for example, asserted that "Creffield is Christ," and that he was "holy."[35]

Creffield's ability to convince his followers of his new divinity was likely augmented by his telling them he had cursed and called down God's wrath on the places where people had not listened to him or had treated him badly, including San Francisco. He was then able to exploit the San Francisco earthquake and fire of April 17, 1906, as a demonstration of his power.[36] This story, which circulated at the time the Waldport camp was operating, would undoubtedly have augmented his followers' faith in him, and they might also have seen the disaster as a harbinger of the coming of the end of the world. But we do not think he needed the coincidence; indeed it was only useful if people were prepared to believe in him in the first place. Most of the sect members had believed totally in Creffield in 1903, and their convictions remained strong thereafter. The difficulties they and Creffield had experienced since the heady days of late 1903 were probably taken as proof that they were right. Of course God's chosen were persecuted; God tested all true prophets and their apostles in such ways.

CREFFIELD'S DEPARTURE AND THE DISCIPLES IN THE WILDERNESS

We know nothing about what happened at the camp near Alsea Bay, but it effectively lasted less than a week. By the time Donna Starr arrived in early May, Creffield had gone; one source suggests he stayed only two or three days, another, citing Maud Creffield, that he stayed a week.[37] Others, including Maud Creffield and Esther Mitchell, left at more or less the same time. The camp was probably finally abandoned on Sunday, April 29.[38] The Seeleys must have departed as well, if they were ever there, for they were not among the small group who stayed in the area until mid-May. Frank Hurt may also have left quickly, or he may have stayed a little longer – the sources are inconsistent on the point.[39] Although Creffield and Maud went more or less immediately away from the region, some members must have tarried elsewhere on the coast, probably in the Toledo area, for a report in the second week of May had "a couple of Holy Rollers" going "valleyward" on May 10.[40]

Creffield's departure was undoubtedly caused by continued fears for his life, which also perhaps made him change his mind about taking the party farther south. Louis Hartley had already made one attempt on Creffield's life, and he did not give up. On Monday, April 23, Hartley replaced his useless revolver with a Winchester rifle and went down the coast to look for the camp. By the time he arrived Creffield had left, suggesting that the prophet stayed a very short time.[41] Hartley contented himself with forcing his wife – and presumably Sophia – to leave with him.[42] Ed Baldwin also travelled to the coast, again too late to find his quarry, but armed and with a purpose similar to Hartley's. George Mitchell went to Waldport as well, but he too was late.[43] One account has half a dozen men intent on murder looking for Creffield.[44] We do not know the extent to which Creffield was aware of this pursuit, but he knew well enough that he had tried to kill him and must have had a good idea that he would not give up easily. Maud obviously shared his fears; at some point she began carrying a revolver.[45]

Opposition to the group also arose locally, people from Waldport and vicinity proving "hostile to the undertaking."[46] Threats of violence no doubt contributed to the rapid failure of the colony, but so too did the difficulty of sustaining life. The sect had little and had made no plans for survival. Food needed to be obtained locally, but the people of Waldport refused to help. As the *Oregonian* put it, when Creffield had operated in Corvallis, "there were larders in well-supplied houses to be drawn on"; there were none now.[47] The fear and revulsion that the name of Creffield and the "Holy Rollers" evoked in the people of this coastal community show just how far stories of the sect had spread and, more importantly, just how deeply into people's psyches the idea that the sect represented evil had penetrated.

By the end of April the sect had fragmented. Five women and a baby remained on the coast – Mollie Hurt and child, Mae Hurt, Attie Bray,

Olive Sandell, and Donna Starr. They were not treated kindly by the people of Waldport, who gave them no help and probably insisted they move on.[48] Looking to find shelter and sustenance with Attie Bray's parents, who lived on a ranch some fifteen miles south of Waldport at Ten-Mile Creek, they crossed Alsea Bay on the ferry, passed through Waldport, and walked along the beach for part of the way, crossing from Lincoln to Lane County. They then had to go inland at times because of high tides and had to ford what is now the Yachats River; this was early May, and the not insubstantial river must have been swollen and fast moving with the spring run-off. Once past the river they had to negotiate a high cliff, Cape Perpetua, on a narrow trail a thousand feet above the rock-strewn sea. The trail had been built a few years before by locals, one of whom was Clarence Starr.[49] When the six finally reached the Bray homestead, Ira Bray refused help, even though his daughter was in the group. He was, recounts a local history, known as a "harsh" man with his children, and his action on this occasion certainly bears out that assessment.[50] In these circumstances, "without money, without food, having scant clothing and three or four cotton blankets only," they turned north again, walking for a mile or so before setting up a camp on a rocky, exposed beach at Cummins Creek.

When the five women and the baby were found on May 12, they were "emaciated, worn out and haggard, and with hardly enough clothing to cover themselves," and living in two thin tents.[51] Locals had again offered only a cold shoulder; they "would rather have let the unfortunates starve than do anything to encourage the male Rollers to return to that part of the country."[52] The women had lived on crabs and mussels for some days, and were in "a pitiful plight." Found by George Hodges as he took his river boat – a "timber cruiser" – to where the creek emptied out into the Pacific Ocean, they told their rescuers that "they had been sent out in the wilderness by Second Messiah Creffield, and while they had heard that he had been killed in Seattle they said they knew that such was not the case, for no one but the Lord could have the power to take his life."[53] Perhaps only that belief could have sustained them on the journey, and fuelled their determination to stay where they were, in a totally inadequate camp. They initially refused the food that Hodges provided, presumably on the grounds that Creffield or God would provide, but quickly reconsidered that decision.

It took a day or two to get the women off the beach, for when Hodges reached Toledo with the news, the people there also refused to help.[54] When the news reached Corvallis, O.V. Hurt, a better man in every respect than Ira Bray, contracted with William McMillan, a Waldport farmer, to bring them out. They were taken first to Waldport and then by boat to the head of Alsea Bay. From there Milt Beem's wagons conveyed them to Corvallis, which they reached on May 16 after an overnight stay in Alsea, and where O.V. Hurt accommodated them.[55] On the trip back they had, to their rescuers' surprise, not discussed religion at all, just "general topics" and "the enjoyable time they had in camp on Cummings Creek." Despite their condition and their getting soaked on the journey, "no complaint was heard from the thinly clad women." Altogether less cheerful was Burgess Starr; when asked by an *Oregonian* reporter for his reaction to the news of the rescue, he was so "incensed" at what Donna had done that he would "make no attempt to rescue his wife unless she is willing to return to her home and give up her fanatical religion."

GEORGE MITCHELL AND THE DEATH OF CREFFIELD

When Creffield and his wife left Waldport they journeyed back to Seattle, but by rather different routes. Creffield had to avoid the beaten path and, in particular, a route that would take him anywhere close to Corvallis. He went on foot through the coastal mountains to Eugene, a journey of about sixty miles, mostly to the east and a little south, away from his destination. From there he caught the train to Portland and on to Seattle.[56] It was a tactic that confounded his enemies, including Ed Baldwin, who searched in the Alsea region between Yaquina Bay and Corvallis for the last thee days of April. Burgess Starr, according to his own later statements, was now carrying a revolver and would have killed Creffield had he surfaced in Portland. Burgess had made similar threats in 1904, after the adultery was discovered.[57] Creffield met up with Maud in Seattle, probably on May 3; she arrived that day, having taken the more conventional route of a train journey from Yaquina City to Corvallis and on from there to the north.[58] They rented a small attic room at 1116 Fifth Avenue, near Pike Street, furnished with "just 2 two chairs, a small table, and a camp cot to sleep on."[59] They had only the clothes they stood up in and very few other possessions.[60] Their intention, Maud Creffield said a few months later, was to make their home in Seattle and continue to worship in the way they thought was right, in time gathering together a small band of followers.[61]

On her journey to Seattle Maud had encountered George Mitchell, and we need to divert slightly from the main story to examine how he came to be waiting at the Albany depot on May 1, hoping to find Creffield. In April 1906 Mitchell was living in Portland, but off work and a resident of the Good Samaritan Hospital, suffering with a bout of the measles.[62] While there he heard about Creffield's re-entry onto the scene. According to extensive testimony from O.V. Hurt at Mitchell's trial later that year, it was Hurt who visited Mitchell and first told him about the Creffield sect and its practices.[63] Whether this was true or not – and we shall see later that there is some reason to doubt it – Mitchell at some point became aware of the camp and Esther's presence there. He must have also known about the adultery with Donna Starr, although he could not have known about Donna going to the coast, because she did not do so until the end of April. It was time, he decided, to kill Creffield. His brother Perry's later trial testimony provides a melodramatic account of what George did: he "started out, weak from his confinement in the hospital, without money or other means, but with the determination to work, and walk from place to place until he had found Creffield and delivered him to God."[64]

As we have seen, Mitchell went to Waldport but arrived too late. He returned to the Corvallis area, hoping to pick up the trail.[65] He was in Corvallis on Tuesday, May 1, and that same day he encountered Maud Creffield at the Albany train depot. She had a wait of several hours, and informed the police that Mitchell, whom she knew, was shadowing her. Mitchell was interviewed but no action was taken. It was during his wait there that Mitchell met Ed Baldwin, returned from his fruitless search for Creffield, and had a conversation with him that would prove important in Mitchell's trial. When the train arrived, Mitchell and Baldwin searched it for Creffield, and Mitchell alone then rode the train to Portland, spending part of the journey looking through the carriages for Creffield. In Portland he either followed Maud or found out that she had gone on to Seattle, and so went north himself, arriving on the morning train from Portland on Wednesday, May 2. He spent the next few days living in a rooming house and walking the streets looking for Creffield; he also contacted Louis Sandell for information on Creffield's whereabouts and hung around the train depot in the hope of catching Creffield coming in.

Mitchell hit the jackpot in the early morning of Monday, May 7, catching sight of Creffield walking along First Avenue arm in arm with Maud.[66] They were out early to shop for a skirt for Maud, stopping at one point so that she could weigh herself at the Quaker drugstore. They then crossed the street, and by about 7:10 a.m. were near the junction of First and Cherry, directly in front of the Quick Drug Company's store. By then Mitchell was up against the building, possibly in the doorway. He let the Creffields pass, then stepped out, pulled out his 32-calibre revolver, and shot Creffield in the back of the neck. The bullet broke the spine at the base of the neck and entered the brain, coming to rest in the right side of Creffield's jaw. Death was instantaneous.

There were a few witnesses to the crime, people walking along First Avenue, and Mitchell made no attempt to escape. Maud flew at him, asking why he had done it and putting her arms around him to prevent an escape that Mitchell was not trying to effect. The next day Maud told her father that she regretted that she did not have her revolver with her that morning, else "she would have shot Mitchell in his tracks."[67] Maud quickly turned her attention to the body of her husband. She "dropped on her knees beside the corpse of her husband" and "pressed her lips to his as she threw one arm around his neck." When she looked up after a few minutes, she stated, "He can't die. He can never die."[68]

Mitchell surrendered himself as soon as the police arrived, handing over his gun. According to some reports he told the officers, "I have only done my duty" and "I came here to kill that man, as he ruined the lives of my two sisters, and I have completed my work."[69] He would have much more to say at the police station. The officers took Mitchell and Creffield's body into the drugstore. Doctor Emil Bories, the medical examiner, was summoned, and he pronounced Creffield officially dead. The body was then removed to the morgue, where Bories carried out the autopsy.[70] In the circumstances there was no need for an inquest. Mitchell was taken to the police station and made a full confession. He also sent a telegram to O.V. Hurt stating simply, "I've got my man. I'm in jail here." Later that day, or the next day, he was removed to the county jail, the usual place where those awaiting trial were held. Maud Creffield was also taken away, in the company of detectives Adams and Corbett, but to the prosecuting attorney's office, and there she told her story. She was then placed in the custody of Mrs Kelly, the "police matron," to be detained as a material witness.

7

Seattle Prepares for Trial, May and June 1906

THE TRIAL OF GEORGE MITCHELL for Creffield's murder began on June 25. In the seven weeks between the murder and the trial the case garnered enormous attention throughout the city. It appeared consistently on the front pages of the city's newspapers – the *Post-Intelligencer,* the *Times,* and the *Star* – and all three also ran substantial articles on the background to the killing and on Creffield's interment, the pre-trial legal proceedings, and the preparations of prosecution and defence lawyers. At the same time, a heated debate took place, in the press and among a wider public, about whether the homicide was justified. The debate was fuelled by a steady stream of revelations about Creffield and the events of 1903-1904 in Oregon. We will deal with that debate in the next chapter. Here we will begin by saying something about the city of Seattle, thrust so unwittingly and unwillingly into the spotlight of the Creffield saga.

The early years of the twentieth century were ones of considerable transition and turmoil in Seattle. While the Mitchell case was shaped by the particularities of Seattle politics, in a number of respects it also acted as a lightning rod for existing anxieties and debates. At the turn of the century Seattle was reaping the benefits of two significant events of the 1890s.[1] In 1893 the Great Northern Railway came to the city, giving it a transcontinental link previously enjoyed by its rival for Puget Sound supremacy, Tacoma. The benefits were not immediate, for the 1893-96 period was one of recession across the United States. But in 1897, when the Klondike Gold Rush began, Seattle found itself ideally positioned to benefit, and it became the principal entrepôt for migrating miners and, more importantly, for providing the goods and services they needed. Aided also by the spin-off benefits from the Spanish-American War and consequent Philippine insurrection, in the decade and a half between the mid-1890s and 1910 Seattle was transformed, developing a highly diversified commercial and manufacturing economy; its commercial activity increased eightfold between 1895 and 1900 alone. It relied principally on its role as a commercial entrepôt – shipping goods to and from Alaska and Asia; supplying the eastern United States with lumber, salmon, and Asian goods; and sitting at the centre of a vibrant Puget Sound and Pacific Northwest trading system. Seattle had never been a major manufacturing centre but, in this period, resource-based industries such as lumber prospered, as did shipbuilding and a variety of other industrial enterprises. Manufacturing growth was steady if unspectacular, the number of businesses engaged in it tripling between 1899 and 1914.

Economic development brought substantial and rapid population growth. The number of permanent residents tripled in the first decade of the twentieth century, from around 80,000 in 1900 to over 237,000 in 1910, due both to inward migration and the annexation of a number of outlying towns. These figures for permanent residents need to be augmented by taking transients into account; there were perhaps 20,000 in 1900 when the permanent population was 80,000, and a transient group of men, going to and from Alaska or working in seasonal resource industries such as fishing, mining, and lumbering, had long been a feature of the city.

The rapid development meant that migrants to the city necessarily came from outside the state of Washington; about a third of the new arrivals had been born outside the United States and most of the rest came from regions to the east – the Midwest being the principal place of origin. Seattle's immigration history, and consequently its social structure, thus continued a tradition of drawing on the Midwest that had marked migration to the Pacific Northwest region since the Civil War. Immigration did not, however, make the city a particularly multi-ethnic one, although there were small minorities of Chinese, Japanese, African-American, and other groups. The American immigrants were overwhelmingly white, and foreigners tended to come from northern and western Europe, especially Sweden, Norway, and the British Isles. Seattle's demographic profile was also unusual in that it included a large pool of single males under the age of forty. The sex ratio was about three men to every two women in 1906, and most of the male immigrants in the first decade of the century were between the ages of eighteen and forty-five.

Perhaps characteristic of male-dominated boom towns on the frontier with substantial transient populations, Seattle's downtown was full of saloons and gambling dens, and its streets and boarding houses provided much business for prostitutes.[2] The volatile mix of young men with easy access to gambling and alcohol meant it was also a violent city, with a homicide rate higher than that of other large cities in the period.[3] The issue of whether Seattle should be an "open" or "closed" town – of whether it should accept the vice trade and seek to limit it to a "restricted district" or crack down on it – was a constant in city politics. It featured in every mayoral election, provoked regular investigations, and was the issue on which the city's first recall mayoral election was fought in 1911, when the pro-restricted district Hiram Gill was forced from office.

The vice trade also kept the city police force in the public eye, as a combination of shortage of manpower, inefficient organization, and corruption meant that the police never gained control of the trade, even when the politicians tried to either eliminate the restricted district or contain vice within it. The relationship of the city's police with the vice trade had led to the killing of a former police chief by a vice-trade businessman in 1901[4] and is well illustrated by Charles Wappenstein, the man who was chief in May 1906 when George Mitchell killed Creffield. In 1901 a council committee recommended that Wappenstein, then a detective on the force, be dismissed for taking bribes, but he survived and became chief in 1906. His unsavoury reputation led to his dismissal by Mayor John Miller in 1908, but he was reinstated by Hiram Gill in 1910. After Gill was forced from office in 1911 a grand jury investigation revealed that Wappenstein had an agreement with the two principal vice-trade operators that the police be paid $10 for every prostitute operating in the restricted district. This time he did not escape the law; he was convicted and served a penitentiary sentence.

What to do about vice was not the only divisive issue in city politics. Seattle experienced both the corporate concentration and business dominance of political party "machines" that were prevalent in many parts of the country. Railways, especially James J. Hill's Great Northern, played a crucial role in making the city what it was, but their monopolistic practices, which lead to control of the transportation and utilities sectors, created substantial resentment. Often unable to effectively regulate absentee-owned corporations, for many, the answer at the local level was municipal ownership of public utilities, and the first decade of the twentieth century saw the creation of city-owned water, electricity, and street transportation companies, and partially successful attempts both to improve the franchise terms under which private corporations operated and to enforce those conditions when they did exist. Municipal ownership was the major issue in the election of 1906, which returned independent candidate William Hickman Moore to the mayor's office. This period also saw efforts to refine the city's image by enhancing its cultural life. Emblematic of such attempts was the opening of the Moore Theatre in 1907.[5]

The vice and municipal ownership questions were also part of a wider concern about the quality of public life and government, a concern that embraced the overt corruption of police and other officials and the covert domination of city council by politicians with ties to both the businessmen who profited from the vice trade and those with close links to the Great Northern Railway. But while the issues that formed the substance of city politics in this period are clear enough, understanding the personalities and twists and turns of political fortunes is made difficult by the fact that in Seattle, and in Washington in general, the Republican Party held power for much of the period between the Civil War and the New Deal.[6] Political conflict was thus as often within the Republican Party as it was between it and other parties.

Broadly, we can discern three principal groupings in Seattle's political economy in the first decade of the twentieth century. First, there were the older, established business interests, including the men with interests in the vice trade or at least with no desire to suppress it, and those with ties to the transportation companies. All Republicans, they controlled the city in the 1890s and the early years of the new century, but found themselves increasingly under attack as the decade wore on. Second, there was a loose coalition of new business and professional men, also generally Republicans, who wanted a place at the table and who often supported municipal ownership because they saw that any competition drove down rates. Their voice was frequently heard in the pages of the *Argus,* an independent Republican weekly owned and edited by the outspoken Henry Chadwick, and over time it was also given expression in one of the two major daily newspapers, the *Post-Intelligencer,* especially after Erastus Brainerd consolidated his hold on the editorship. Third were the moral reformers, advocates of cleaning up both the city and its politics and of introducing those staples of progressivism, the initiative and recall.[7] There was at times substantial overlap between these second and third groups, and the reformers also included in their ranks many women's clubs and organizations, campaigning also for the vote they would win in 1910.[8] In the broad reform coalition were also most of the city's Protestant clergy, and no figure was more prominent than the Reverend Mark Matthews, pastor of the First Presbyterian Church, who built his congregation into the largest church in the country and campaigned actively and aggressively for social and moral reform on a variety of fronts.[9]

These were not the only players. A nascent organized labour movement played a role in local politics as well, invariably in favour of municipal ownership, as did other reform groups and the city's outspoken press, including most notably the maverick figure of Alden J. Blethen, owner and editor of one of the city's principal newspapers, the *Seattle Times*.[10] We will have rather more to say about Blethen later in this chapter, but for now it is sufficient to note that he at various times supported both the Democrats and the Republicans, was for and against municipal ownership, and disapproved of vice but thought it an inevitable and necessary evil that should be controlled and regulated. Indeed, he was part owner of the Morrison Hotel, a well-known gambling spot.

This necessarily brief sketch of Seattle in the first decade of the twentieth century allows us to set the city's response to the Mitchell case in its contemporary context. The case offered opportunities and challenges to many of those vying for influence in the city. Blethen could exploit it both for its sensationalist value as newspaper copy and for the potential it had to garner him working-class support. Moral reformers could view suggestions that Mitchell was justified as symptomatic of the values they were seeking to displace. Workers could see Mitchell as a kind of working-class hero, asserting his right to revenge with as much legitimacy as a wealthy person. And civic boosters could worry about what kind of image the city presented to the outside world if a man could gun down another in so public a fashion and not be firmly and effectively prosecuted.

CREFFIELD'S INTERMENT AND THE
HOLY ROLLERS IN SEATTLE

On Wednesday, May 9, just two days after he was shot, Creffield was buried in Seattle's Lakeview Cemetery. Fittingly, he received a pauper's funeral, the coffin being provided by King County, although Maud Creffield (likely O.V. Hurt, in fact) paid for the grave.[11] The only mourners present were Maud Creffield, Mrs Mary Jane Kelly (the police "matron" in whose custody Maud was now residing),[12] and the undertaker's employees. Others who might have mourned him – Frank Hurt and Esther

Mitchell, for example – were all still in Oregon.[13] It was a very simple funeral. Creffield was covered with a white robe, and his coffin displayed only the words "At Rest." On Maud's instructions no religious services were performed, and after interment a plain wooden board was placed at the head of the grave with only his name, age, and death date written on it. Later that year he was exhumed and re-interred, with a stone marker, next to his wife, who died in November 1906.[14]

There was a good reason for the lack of ceremony and for Maud being "calm and immovable," showing "little sorrow" at the grave side. She believed that Creffield would rise from the dead in four days, a belief shared by other members of the sect, who wrote to her from Oregon to that effect. She was reputed to have said at the interment that "my husband, though dead in body now, will rise again as Jesus did."[15] The press heaped scorn on such views. "No guard has been placed at Creffield's grave," noted the *Seattle Times,* and nothing unusual had been done to prepare for the event. George Mitchell was likewise "not much concerned over the proposed return of the man he found it necessary . . . to kill," and "smiles quietly" when asked about it.[16] But Maud's faith was unshakeable, and she asked to be allowed to spend the night before the resurrection in the cemetery so as to be sure to see it happen. When the request was refused she "became hysterical" and started "groveling on the floor . . . and begging hysterically." She kept this up, refusing to eat or drink, and her cries were "like those of a wild animal." Prosecuting attorney Kenneth Mackintosh did allow her to visit the grave in the morning, hoping it might placate her. Maud visited the grave on more than one occasion in the weeks to follow, and it was some time before she abandoned her belief in her husband's resurrection. She decided that "his reappearance will be spiritual instead of corporeal" and that because he did not know she was detained by the police, Creffield's spirit "has been delayed in locating her." After a few weeks she finally gave up hope that Creffield would be resurrected.[17]

Maud Creffield was not the only member of the sect in Seattle in the period between the killing of Creffield and Mitchell's trial. Esther Mitchell hurried there from Corvallis when she heard about the murder, arriving on Sunday, May 13. She was met at the train station by George's lawyer, Will Morris, but it quickly became clear that she still believed in Creffield and was unwilling to help her brother. Esther too was placed in the custody of police matron Kelly once the prosecution had spoken with her, and with Maud she visited Creffield's grave on more than one occasion.[18] Frank Hurt also made his way to Seattle in mid-May and attended some of George Mitchell's trial in late June. Although named in some press reports as Creffield's successor, he seems to have lost faith with the creed by early July. Mollie stayed in Corvallis until late May, but then joined her husband.[19]

Preliminary Legal Proceedings and Trial Preparation: Testing the Unwritten Law

Prosecutorial authorities never entertained any doubt that Mitchell should be tried for killing Creffield. Indeed, the charge would clearly be first-degree murder, defined as when a person killed "purposely" and with "deliberate and premeditated malice."[20] Deputy prosecuting attorney John Franklin Miller announced the charge on the day Creffield was shot, noting also that Mitchell would be prosecuted by information rather than by indictment by a grand jury.[21] He formally did so on behalf of his superior, the elected prosecuting attorney Kenneth Mackintosh,[22] but it is possible that Miller made this and many other decisions in the case. Mackintosh was much less experienced in criminal prosecution than his deputy. Seattle born, a 1900 graduate of Columbia law school, and a member of the New York bar, Mackintosh was only twenty-nine years old and had been practising law for only five years when elected prosecuting attorney in late 1904.[23] Although he was a Republican his party had not been enthusiastic about his candidacy because of his youth. Mackintosh was highly regarded as a lawyer and went on to a distinguished career on the bench in later years.[24] The Mitchell case was exactly the kind of serious crime he thought public prosecutors should concern themselves with, rather than indulging in moral "clean-up" campaigns or other publicity-generating activities.[25] Indeed, he is considered to have professionalized the prosecuting attorney's office, and he easily won re-election later in the year.[26] He chose his cases well and fought them hard, winning over 90 percent of all indictments brought, but he was no courtroom orator and for this reason, and because of his lack of experience trying criminal cases, it was Miller who did much of the courtroom work on the Mitchell case.

John Franklin Miller was something of a contrast to his superior. At forty-four, he was almost fifteen years older; like so many of the characters in this story, he was born in the Midwest, on a farm near South Bend, Indiana.[27] The family was a comfortably prosperous one and Miller spent time at West Point before graduating from Valparaiso University in law in 1887. The following year he moved to Seattle, where he established a practice. He served two terms as the elected prosecuting attorney for King

County between 1890 and 1894, the first to hold the position after statehood was obtained; ironically, Miller had been even less experienced when elected in 1890 than Mackintosh was in 1905. We do not know what specifically made him take the deputy's job in 1905 in an office where he had once been the head man, but it may have been at Mackintosh's request, for the two were friends and fellow Republicans.[28] Although he had failed in a bid to join the superior court in 1902, Miller ultimately had the more successful political career of the two, elected mayor of Seattle for one term (1908-10) and serving as a Washington representative in the US Congress for fourteen years (1917-31). Miller was also a more visible public figure than his boss. He had a reputation for dressing well[29] and was considered to be a lawyer with excellent intuition who nonetheless prepared his cases thoroughly.

Matched against Mackintosh and Miller were two of Seattle's best criminal defence lawyers – William H. (Will) Morris and Silas Shipley of Morris, Southard and Shipley. Morris seems to have been engaged on May 7, although it is unclear how this was done, for the man who made the arrangements, O.V. Hurt, did not get to Seattle until the 8th. Summoned by the telegram from Mitchell, Hurt had rushed to Seattle as soon as he got the news, "for the purpose," he said, "of taking care of his daughter, but mainly to make arrangements for the defence of George Mitchell," to "hire a good criminal lawyer."[30] Either Hurt contacted him from Portland, where he spent the evening of May 7 en route from Corvallis, or Morris had seen the publicity opportunity and volunteered his services to Mitchell himself. In any event, his partner Shipley quickly joined him, and together they made a formidable team. Something of a self-made man, the forty-four-year-old Morris had joined the Ohio bar in 1890, having studied law in his own time, and immediately went west, entering practice with Isaac Hall, a judge in the territorial period.[31] After Hall died in 1893 Morris served for a short time as a deputy prosecuting attorney and then formed his own practice with Shipley and Southard, in which he enjoyed enviable courtroom success. A handsome man who had been a renowned athlete in his youth and was still referred to in 1906 as "Big Bill" Morris, he had a compelling courtroom presence. Although he practised in all areas, he had a sterling, and apparently deserved, reputation as a criminal defence lawyer. Of the eleven defendants charged with first-degree murder he had represented before the Mitchell case, all had been acquitted.[32] He was, said the *Corvallis Times,* "the most renowned criminal lawyer perhaps in Washington."[33]

Shipley had been raised in Oregon from the age of fourteen, although he was also a Midwesterner, born in Wisconsin. A graduate of Pacific University in Forest Grove and, in law, of the University of Oregon (1888), he moved to Seattle on graduation, started his own practice in association with Alfred Battle, and served on the first city council. He had been with Morris since 1900, and while he did not have his partner's courtroom flair, he was rated an excellent lawyer nonetheless – "one of the finest advocates in the country," crowed the partisan *Corvallis Times*.[34]

Neither defence lawyer took the case for the money, for they must have known that Mitchell had very little. But it was the kind of case that garnered publicity and they must have quickly intuited that it would bring them popularity and enhance their reputations. As it turned out, they received a modest fee of some $650, collected by subscription in Oregon.[35] Had these two not stepped forward, Mitchell would have had a court-appointed attorney, although no provision was made for public payment of such an attorney's fees until 1909.[36]

The information charging Mitchell with first-degree murder was filed in the Superior Court of King County on Thursday, May 10, making the case Number 3652.[37] Established with statehood in 1889, the superior court, whose judges were elected for four-year terms, was the highest level of trial court in Washington, with jurisdiction over all serious crimes.[38] The case was assigned to Judge Archibald Wanless Frater, one of six superior court judges presiding in King County,[39] and the arraignment – the formal appearance of the prisoner to hear the charge and to plead to it – was set for Saturday, May 12. When Mitchell was arraigned, Morris asked for and received an adjournment of one week to enter a plea.[40]

As important to the ensuing proceedings as the lawyers was, of course, the trial judge, and in Frater the prosecution had drawn a somewhat unpredictable character. Another Midwesterner, Frater had practised law in Minnesota and Kansas before moving to Washington in 1888.[41] A prominent Republican and Mason, he was elected to the superior court in 1904 after campaigning aggressively for the job, and was best known in legal circles for his advocacy of a juvenile court. Although one newspaper called him "a man of calm, careful judgement" whose decisions "are invariably the result of thought – not impulse," he could be irascible and excitable.[42] He also seems to have been deeply attached to maintenance of the traditional family, as his advocacy of parental responsibility for delinquents and stricter divorce laws attests.

Morris and Shipley may well have been pleased to have drawn Frater, for in a recent case he had shown considerable sympathy for a man who took violent action against one deemed to be interfering with his marriage.

In November 1905 George Beede had shot Roy MacDonald in the back for consorting with his wife. MacDonald survived, although for some weeks it was not clear that he would do so, and when he recovered said he did not wish to press charges. As a result the case against Beede, who had been bailed on a $1,500 bond a few days after the shooting, was not pursued by Mackintosh. Frater, in the course of formally dismissing the charge in April 1906, "delivered a scathing denunciation of MacDonald," in the process "declaring he instead of Beede ought to have been put on trial."

Such statements from the bench not surprisingly "created a sensation among attorneys at the time."[43] More importantly, they reflected a belief in the "unwritten law," a nineteenth-century doctrine that was to play a large role in the legal proceedings against Mitchell and in the public debate over his action.[44] Broadly speaking, the term refers to the idea that a man was justified in killing another who had been sexually intimate with his wife or an unmarried member of his family. The Sickles case in Washington, D.C., in 1859 and the McFarland case a decade later in New York are well-known examples in which the defence was successfully employed, and there were many others.[45] Some small differences exist among historians as to exactly what the term "unwritten law" meant to contemporaries, and how inviolate a rule it was, but those do not concern us here.[46] What matters is that although not generally a formal part of the law,[47] in practice the doctrine had allowed dozens of men to escape conviction, defence lawyers successfully appealing to a divine or natural law right to kill in such circumstances. It was certainly known about in the Pacific Northwest; Portland's *Evening Telegram* defined it as "a doctrine that a crime committed against women folk of a household is punishable by death at the hands of the ablest male relative."[48] We will have more to say about this doctrine in the next chapter.

The parallels between the Mitchell and Beede-MacDonald cases were obviously close and must have given the defence team hope that Frater would be sympathetic to its arguments, especially as Morris had been Beede's lawyer and the case had gone to court so recently. There were, nonetheless, two related differences: Creffield had died, whereas MacDonald had recovered from his wound and lived; and neither MacDonald nor the prosecuting attorney's office wanted prosecution in the Beede case. These distinctions between the cases turned out to be crucial, for Frater, despite admitting to "a deep interest in the case,"[49] was decidedly not partial to the defence.

The first test of Frater's attitude came with George Mitchell's arraignment on May 12, when the defence applied for bail.[50] The Washington law on bail was that all persons charged with an offence "may be bailed" if sufficient sureties were given and if the person "has offered to go to trial in good faith"; in essence, bail was granted if there was no danger of the accused fleeing the court's jurisdiction or tampering with witnesses. But there was one specific exception to this presumption in favour of bail: where the charge was first-degree murder and "the proof is evident or the presumption great," or, in other words, where there was direct evidence of guilt or strong circumstantial evidence, and where therefore the accused was most likely to flee the jurisdiction. In such circumstances, which clearly pertained here, the rule was that bail would not be granted.[51]

Given this law, the defence had an uphill battle. Clearly the "proof was evident" – it had been furnished by Mitchell himself, who freely admitted to the killing. In this regard Mitchell's case was clearly different to those of the Considines, whom Morris had successfully helped to defend in 1901. Morris probably cited this case, among others, but although the Considines had been charged with first-degree murder, the case against them was not strong; the judge also had doubts about whether the murder had been a premeditated one.[52] Despite the unlikelihood that they would succeed, defence arguments on the bail application lasted an hour or so, with both Shipley and Morris speaking.[53] Those arguments make it clear that, although they never used the phrase, Morris and Shipley had decided to invoke the unwritten law. Shipley told the court that bail should be granted because it was very unlikely that Mitchell would be convicted of first-degree murder. The facts in the Mitchell case, he said, showed ample "provocation and justification"; anybody familiar with the case would have an appreciation of "the impulse which prompted Mitchell" and realize that a jury would not convict of first-degree murder.

The key phrase here was "provocation and justification." The former, also referred to implicitly in Shipley's use of the word "impulse," was not, and is not, a full defence to a murder charge, but would reduce first-degree murder to manslaughter, and that was what mattered for the purposes of the bail application. The circumstances, however, did not make for a provocation defence. The law required the provoking circumstance to be immediate to the killing, whereas Mitchell had stalked his victim across a state line and lain in wait for him. It was well established that if a husband killed his wife's lover, having caught the two in *flagrante delicto,* that would constitute provocation sufficient to reduce a murder charge to manslaughter,[54] and while the principle might extend to a brother avenging the seduction of his sister, those were not the circumstances here. The second reason offered for Mitchell not being convicted – justification –

was, and is, a full defence, leading to acquittal. But justifiable homicides are those committed in self-defence, or in the defence of another in real and imminent danger of violent attack, and the like; nothing about the Creffield story could make this a justifiable homicide in law.

Unless, that is, the informal, unwritten law could serve as a justification, and Morris openly suggested this when he addressed the court. He accepted that the bail law "in so far as proof or presumption were concerned" was against him, but chose instead, at least superficially, to discuss flight risk. Morris must have known that it was formally pointless to discuss whether Mitchell would turn up for trial, because the law clearly stated that that consideration did not apply to people charged with first-degree murder in circumstances where the "proof was evident." But here it was not evident, he argued, because there was so much public sympathy for Mitchell that he would not be convicted. Under the guise of explaining why that public sympathy existed Morris recounted the essentials of the Creffield story, including the accusation that Creffield had had sex with Esther Mitchell, and argued that a jury would find this sufficient "justification." In a clear reference to the unwritten law he asserted that there was, in addition to man's law, "a divine law and a human law which admits beyond all cavil the right of a man to protect the honor of his family." Mitchell "had seen his sisters debauched by the man whom he killed." He also knew that Donna Starr had deserted her husband and children, and as a result he had "acted in the full knowledge that unless he acted as he did there was no salvation for the misguided woman." As lawyers generally had done in arguing unwritten law cases, Morris employed all his condemnatory eloquence against Creffield: "He has slain a human leper, one of the basest men who ever walked the earth and so thoroughly does he feel that he was justified that I believe upon my honor as a member of this court that if he was released upon his own recognizance he would make no effort to escape a trial before any twelve men who might be selected to act as a jury."[55]

Cleverly structuring their arguments around the bail law provisions, Morris and Shipley were testing Frater. Given his comments on the Beede-MacDonald case, they wanted to see how he would react to the unwritten law in their case. In addition, making these arguments in court was part of their wider strategy of trying their case – by trying Creffield – in the press, before it reached the courtroom. They were using every opportunity to talk about the iniquities of Creffield, and the bail hearing provided as good a chance as any.

In contrast to the defence, the prosecution had little to say that interested

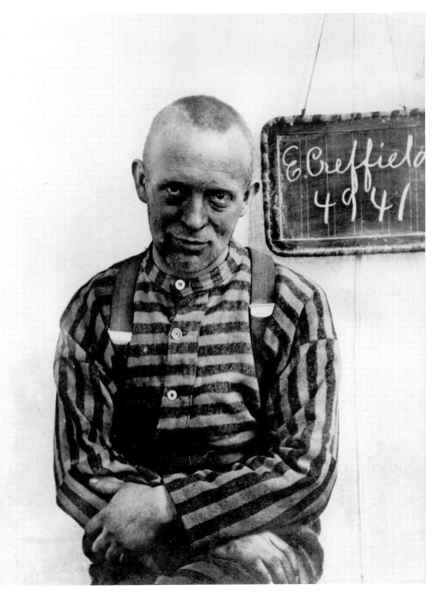

Franz Creffield in the Oregon State Penitentiary
(Oregon State Archives, Penitentiary Records, Case File 4941)

DEAD LEADER OF HOLY ROLLERS.

Franz Creffield when captured by Corvallis authorities in July 1904. He was naked and unkempt after months of hiding under O.V. Hurt's house, and dressed in a plain suit for the photograph. This photograph was reproduced many times; this version appeared just after George Mitchell was acquitted of Creffield's murder.

(Portland *Oregonian,* 13 July 1906)

Artist's depiction of Franz Creffield
(*Seattle Post-Intelligencer*, 9 May 1906)

Sarah Hurt, wife of O.V. Hurt and one of
Creffield's principal followers, in Salvation Army uniform

(Benton County Historical Museum and Society,
Philomath, Oregon, Print No. 1999-108-0051)

O.V. Hurt and Family. *From left:* Mae Hurt, Maud Hurt (Creffield),
Roy Robinett Hurt, O.V. Hurt, Frank Hurt, Sarah Hurt

(Benton County Historical Museum and Society, Philomath, Oregon,
Print No. 1999-108-0053)

Attie Bray and Mae Hurt, cousins and two of Creffield's younger followers

(Benton County Historical Museum and Society, Philomath, Oregon,
Print No. 1999-108-0092)

Creffield sect group portrait, Smith Island, 1903, including Hattie Starr.
Standing, from left: Sampson Levins, Charles Brooks, Hattie Starr, Esther Mitchell,
Rose Seeley, Florence Seeley, Wesley Seeley, Mollie Hurt, Frank Hurt, Edna Seeley,
Ona Baldwin, Lee Campbell. *Sitting, from left:* Cora Hartley, Olive Sandell,
Donna Starr, Coral Worrell (probably), Mae Hurt, Maud Hurt (later Creffield),
Franz Creffield, Sarah Hurt, Sophia Hartley, Attie Bray.

(Portland *Oregon Journal*, 16 May 1906)

Another version of the Creffield sect group portrait, with Hattie Starr
obscured by bible verses. The sect did this when she left and denounced them
within the community.

(Portland *Evening Telegram*, 2 November 1903)

"HE RUINED MY TWO SISTERS AND I
TOOK HIS LIFE"--GEO. MITCHELL

George Mitchell, "Slayer of Frank Edmund Creffield." In the weeks following the murder Mitchell's case was the talk of Seattle.

(*Seattle Star*, 7 May 1906)

THE SLAYER OF "JOSHUA" CREFFIELD
AND THE WIDOW OF HIS VICTIM

George Mitchell and Maud Creffield. Although this version is from the *Post-Intelligencer*, the *Times* frequently used this picture of Mitchell in his flat cap to emphasize his working-class roots.

(*Seattle Post-Intelligencer*, 8 May 1906)

Superior court judge – and Mitchell trial judge – Archibald Frater: "Judge Frater has made a great many friends and added to his reputation as a clear and logical thinker during his present term as judge of the superior court."

(*Seattle Mail and Herald,* 3 June 1905)

Caricature of Will Morris, lead defence lawyer for George Mitchell, with original caption: "Morris is familiarly called 'Big Bill' by his friends ... He has an enviable reputation as a criminal lawyer, dabbles considerably in politics, and is prominent in all lines of amateur sport."

(H.A. Chadwick, "Men Behind the Seattle Spirit," *The Argus,* Seattle, 1906, p. 12)

Caricature of Kenneth Mackintosh, King County prosecuting attorney. The original caption reflects his reputation as an effective prosecutor: "Mr. Mackintosh is prosecuting attorney of King County, and he is doing the best he can to build up the city by making it necessary to have a new jail."

(H.A. Chadwick, "Men Behind the Seattle Spirit," *The Argus,* Seattle, 1906, p. 107)

John Miller, deputy prosecuting attorney. This photograph was taken when he was mayor of Seattle in 1908. Miller had a reputation as both an elegant dresser and a highly effective lawyer.

(Seattle Municipal Archives)

Sketch of Prosecuting Attorney Kenneth Mackintosh
in court during the Mitchell trial

(*Seattle Times*, 27 June 1906)

MITCHELL IS AT LAST ON TRIAL

ury That Will Decide Whether the Killing of Creffield Was Justified

Mitchell trial jurors walking from court. It took almost four days to
select the twelve men who would decide the fate of Franz Creffield's killer.
(*Seattle Times,* 29 June 1906)

George Mitchell Leaving the Courthouse a Free Man

George Mitchell, his brother Perry Mitchell, and Silas Shipley, one of
George's lawyers, pose for the camera after George's acquittal.
(*Seattle Post-Intelligencer,* 11 July 1906)

Exterior of Union Station, Seattle. Esther Mitchell shot her brother
George here as he was preparing to take the Portland train.

(Seattle Museum of History and Industry, 1911, neg. 83.10.9337)

Gravestone of George Mitchell, Friends
Cemetery, Newberg, Oregon. The
inscription is the well-known passage
from John 15:13: "Greater love hath no
man than this, that a man lays down his
life for his friends."

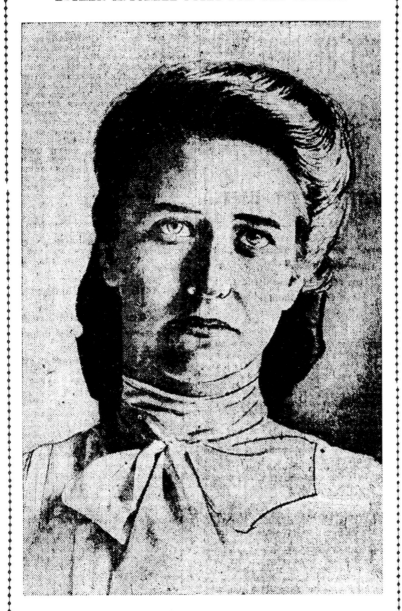

ESTHER MITCHELL POSES FOR THE CAMERA

GIRL WHO KILLED HER BROTHER HAS NO AVERSION TO BEING PHO-
TOGRAPHED.

Esther Mitchell poses for the camera shortly after murdering her brother.
(Clipping from the *Oregonian,* 16 July 1906)

WHICH IS THE CRAZY MAN?

Editorial cartoon "Which Is the Crazy Man," attacking the insanity defence
and the report of the "insanity commission," which found Esther Mitchell and
Maud Creffield not fit to stand trial in September 1906

(*Seattle Times,* 21 September 1906)

the newspapers. Mackintosh simply "made his formal objection and cited the law." And Frater went with that law, denying bail on the grounds that the statute was clear. His comments in doing so must nonetheless have given the defence some heart. He did refer to the statements he had made in Beede-MacDonald but insisted that the fact that a man might "expect to receive death or injury at the hands of the injured" did not "justify" murder, and, perhaps protesting too much given the embarrassment that case was now causing him, also confirmed that "this court does not want it understood that any such killing is condoned." In addition, and perhaps more importantly, Frater seemed to distinguish between what the law required him to do and what he might have done as a juror, and perhaps what he would not object to others doing as jurors:

> I take it from the statements which have been made that this is a case where, even though it is murder under the law, the defendant may be acquitted. As a judge, however, I cannot allow myself to be governed by my opinions as a man and must deal with the question at issue as a proposition of law. The law seems clear and is not questioned even by the attorneys for the defendant.

Frater knew he was to some extent on trial, given his comments in Beede-MacDonald, and according to the *Star* he was guarded and made sure that what he said was accurately recorded by a court reporter. The same newspaper also reported Frater as saying, "If my own feelings were consulted, I admit that my decision might be different."[56]

Although Morris professed to be disappointed by the result, and although the refusal of bail drew some adverse press comment in Oregon, the defence lawyers likely took solace from the day.[57] They cannot seriously have thought bail would be granted, and they had had an opportunity both to assess Frater's views and to advance a campaign, discussed at length in the next chapter, to persuade the public that Mitchell's action was justified. The final part of the pre-trial proceedings was Mitchell's plea, and the following Saturday, May 19, he stood before Judge Frater in a packed courtroom and declared himself not guilty. The trial was set for June 25, a little more than a month away.[58] Unusually, there was a large number of women at the brief hearing, presaging what would become a feature of the trial the following month – support for Mitchell from at least some representatives of Seattle womanhood.

In the meantime, both sides made their preparations, with most of the activity on the defence side. The prosecution saw this as a straightforward case and intended to rely principally on eyewitness testimony of the murder.[59] Maud Creffield was its key witness, and on Mackintosh's advice she did not talk to the press.[60] In what would turn out to be a tactical error, the prosecutors seem to have done nothing to counter a defence of temporary insanity. Mackintosh knew just a few days after the killing that this would, or at least might be, the defence offered, probably because, as discussed in more detail below, it was the standard tactic by which defence lawyers in unwritten law cases brought in the evidence about a victim's sexual transgressions.[61] But at no time did he have Mitchell examined by doctors. Indeed, beyond interviewing Esther Mitchell when she arrived in Seattle in mid-May, and later subpoenaing her as well as Maud Creffield,[62] the prosecutors, perhaps beguiled by what seemed to be the simplicity of their case or consumed with other work, did not attempt to find Oregon witnesses to counteract what they knew would be a defence barrage until a week or so before the trial began. John Miller travelled to Oregon for about five days, between June 18 and 23, but he was received "coldly" and apparently found nobody willing to assist.[63] Nonetheless, the prosecutor's office geared up for the case as it drew near, putting aside all other business in the week before the trial.[64]

The defence was much busier. Morris and Shipley quickly decided to argue that Mitchell had been insane at the time he killed Creffield, although he no longer was, and, as discussed in more detail below, to rely on evidence that knowledge of Creffield's supposed sexual practices had driven Mitchell insane. Thus whether or not they had seriously contemplated using provocation or arguing justifiable homicide when they sought bail, and despite the fact that they used the pages of the *Times* to assert that "Mitchell's act was justified" and they would "prove it by the usual methods of the law,"[65] they realized that their best chance lay with the unwritten law defence. Integral to the defence strategy was the securing of witnesses to testify both to Mitchell's temporary insanity and to its cause – Creffield's history. And here Morris in particular was busy. With O.V. Hurt acting as his consultant, and perhaps with the assistance of John Manning's deputy, G.C. Moser, as well, Morris assembled a list of likely witnesses and then, in the last week or ten days of May, travelled to Corvallis and Portland to interview them, spending a lot of time with Boys and Girls Aid Society superintendent Gardner in particular.[66] The defence issued witness subpoenas to thirty Oregon residents, most of whom did testify.[67]

The defence also researched George Mitchell's family background and contacted family members. The lawyers' appeals on his behalf relied on the theme of protection of family, but the family was not that willing to play along. Perry Mitchell, George's younger brother, was the most helpful. He came west from Illinois, arriving on June 22, and put up at the Stevens Hotel. From the second day of the trial he sat in court with George, providing tangible evidence of support to go along with his statements to the press. Fred Mitchell, George's older brother by five years and a "motorman" in Portland, also journeyed to Seattle, on May 18. A Salvation Army supporter like his sisters, his loyalties were said to be both with his brother and divided, and he kept a low profile, although he lived with Perry at the Stevens. He did, it turned out, fulfill a useful role for Morris and Shipley, for he had tried to commit suicide in 1903 when despondent over a love affair. This would be used to show mental imbalance in the Mitchell family.[68] Donna Starr, it was hoped, would also aid the defence. As we have seen, she was on the Oregon coast until mid-May, and from there went to Corvallis, where she lived with Cora Hartley, and then to Portland. She came to Seattle around June 23 or 24, and also took up residence in the Stevens Hotel. Donna came at the behest of Burgess, who believed she would help her brother, and, indeed, she was on the list of defence witnesses.[69] But Donna Starr proved a disappointment in this regard. And while Phoebe Vanderkellen, George's older sister, was on the defence's witness list, she was never called. We have no idea what she might have said.

Positively unhelpful was George's father Charles. Charles had left his seven children in Oregon when his wife died; he was both a failure economically and something of a religious zealot. Like Perry, he travelled west from Illinois, but Charles did not arrive until near the end of the first week of the trial, dallying a few days in Newberg to visit relatives. When he finally reached Seattle he had a five-minute meeting with George in the jail, and rarely attended the proceedings.[70] Charles was present in Seattle against the wishes of Morris. His father did not approve of what George had done and would not testify to Morris' liking; as Charles put it later, after the trial, he "love[d] truth and righteousness" and thus disapproved of "the simulation of insanity," which he thought a "monstrous practice," and he did not wish George to "perjure himself." He would not even contribute towards the attorneys' fees if they were to be used to support an insanity defence. He stated later that he would "gladly have died" for George, but of course that was not required. Perhaps the best thing Charles Mitchell did for his son was not to say any of this before or during the trial.

Charles was problem enough, but Esther's attitude must have caused

Morris and Shipley some sleepless nights. She consulted frequently with Mackintosh and offered no help to Morris when he interviewed her in mid-May. Worse, Esther publicly asserted that "Creffield is Christ" and would "rise again," and that her brother "lies" when he said that Creffield had harmed her. Indeed, she went so far as to say, "I hope my brother will have time to repent of his sins before they hang him . . . I believe he should be hanged after he is given a chance to repent."[71] Esther's attitude must have been worrying, but she would not decide her brother's fate at trial. The final stage of defence preparations involved influencing the minds of the Seattle citizenry who would form the jury pool, but that is a subject best dealt with in the following chapter, in which we examine the debate that took place before the trial began.

8

Justifiable Homicide
and the Unwritten Law

IN THE IMMEDIATE AFTERMATH of Creffield's death Seattle was witness to an impassioned debate about whether the homicide was justified. Mitchell, his family, the lawyers for both sides, the press, and others all contributed to that debate. The success of the pro-Mitchell campaign had much to do with the efforts of the *Seattle Times,* which was able both to tap into a well of public sentiment and to convince many in the city that Mitchell was the representative of the manly defence of family values and virtues. Mitchell's acquittal owed much, obviously, to the skill of his lawyers and the doctrines of criminal responsibility they were able to exploit in the course of the trial. But it owed an at least equal debt to the groundwork laid by his supporters in the weeks beforehand.

There were three closely related elements to the public defence of Mitchell. Generally it followed the same lines as all contemporary justifications of vigilantism – an individual or a community had the right to take the law, in this case natural law, into its own hands when the exigencies of the circumstances required it. To this general idea were added two others, related to each other and specific to the circumstances. First, the natural law involved here was the unwritten law that permitted a man to avenge the seducer of his wife or other family member. Second, true manliness, authentic masculinity, required men to act in this way when confronted with the antithesis of manly chivalry – the evil seducer. The debate over the killing of Creffield was thus not simply one about the acceptability of taking the law into one's own hands; it was infused by a set of understandings about both gender relations and gender identities.

George Mitchell's act was, his supporters urged, truly manly, impelled by a man's duty to protect the weaker sex.

George Mitchell's Oregon Defenders

The first contribution to the debate came from George Mitchell himself. He was allowed to speak to at least one reporter, Louis Sefrit of the *Seattle Times*, on May 7, from the police cells. After giving an account of the morning's events, and ignoring a warning that any statements could be used against him, he provided Sefrit with a simple and unadorned defence of his actions:[1]

> I killed Creffield because I believed it was right for me to do so. I have not the least regrets and am prepared to take the consequences whatever they may be. Creffield influenced my sister[s], Mrs Starr and Esther, until they joined his holy roller crowd at Corvallis. He had them under his spell and I could do nothing with them. I begged them to quit the shameful life being led by the Rollers, but they would not heed me. But that was not all. This brute of a man who declared he was appointed Joshua by God, ruined both those girls. I swore that I would be avenged and my time came this morning.
>
> I am, of course, sorry that I have been called upon to take another man's life, but there is no one among you who can appreciate my feelings. No brother could love his sisters any more than I. To have a man of the stripe of Creffield to take them away from me and ruin their lives under the guise of a frenzied religion, was too much to bear. The more I thought of it, the more angry I got and I resolved at the first opportunity to meet Creffield and secure my revenge. It was willed that I met him today and Creffield suffered the end that he was entitled to.

Mitchell also claimed, "I do not fear the outcome," for he had "done what any brother should have done." If he lost his life, "there will be no whimper from me."

Thus George himself justified his extra-legal act by the familial and chivalrous duty of a brother to avenge the harm done to his sisters, and this invocation of the unwritten law became the centrepiece of the case expounded by his defenders. Indeed, we have already seen it invoked by Morris and Shipley in the various pre-trial proceedings. Interestingly, however, by the time the case got to trial Mitchell's statements about Esther had changed. It was no longer claimed that Creffield had seduced her but that he intended to do so and would carry out his evil designs unless stopped. In either case, Mitchell could claim that he was justified by invoking the unwritten law or something very similar. There is no point in the pre-trial period that we can pinpoint as marking this transition, but it may well have come quite late; just a few days before the trial the *Times* reported that Mitchell continued to claim that Creffield and his younger sister had had sex.[2]

Mitchell quickly received support from Oregon. O.V. Hurt, apart from arranging for a defence lawyer, also left money with the jail authorities for Mitchell's needs, tried to persuade Mackintosh not to prosecute, and set about defending Mitchell in the press. "I am glad Creffield is dead," he said, "glad that he was murdered like a dog," adding that Mitchell had done "what any man would have done" and that he, Hurt, would do all he could to save him, "to the extent of all my possessions."[3] He still loved his daughter, he insisted, who "loved Creffield devotedly and thought his actions right and proper." Like all Creffield's followers, she was "sincere and honest."[4] Archie J. Johnson, mayor of Corvallis, in Seattle on business, weighed in by telling reporters that Creffield had committed "outrages," had "broken up dozens of families," and that "Mitchell was not the only man looking for him on account of his conduct."[5] Burgess Starr, interviewed in Portland, declared that the death of Creffield made it "a happy day," and insisted that George was justified and should not be prosecuted.[6] Louis Sandell demonstrated his support by visiting Mitchell in jail.

The most newsworthy intervention, however, came from John Manning, district attorney for Multnomah County. In an open letter to Mackintosh he asserted that he would not have prosecuted Mitchell if the offence had taken place in his jurisdiction, and he offered himself as a defence witness.[7] The letter told of "the outrageous crimes committed by this brute ... on simple-minded girls and women," of the adultery charge and conviction, and of the breaking up of families. Most importantly, this was a case in which "the taking of the law into one's own hands ... to mete out summary justice is almost excusable." Manning's opinion was an unusual one for a man in his position, especially given his apparently deserved reputation as an unshakeable advocate for law and order and moral probity, and his complaint a few years earlier, following a Portland jury acquittal of a man who admitted firing a shot that killed another, that "murder seems to be treated very lightly in this community."[8] But he seems to have been in tune with opinion in Oregon generally. Newspapers approved, or at least sympathized with, Mitchell; individuals asserted their belief that he was justified;[9] money was raised for his defence; and there was even talk in Corvallis of striking a medal for him.[10] As the Portland *Evening Telegram* noted, many believed that "Mitchell was justified by unwritten law."[11]

Whatever the people of Oregon thought, the murder had taken place in Seattle, and Manning's letter quickly drew responses from both Mackintosh and Miller. Miller told reporters bluntly that "the boy is a murderer plain and simple" and was "entitled to no sympathy." He was "indignant" and declared that the killing was "the worst murder that has been committed since I have been in Seattle." Miller was also the first to sound a theme that was to become increasingly prevalent as time went on: it was to be regretted that Oregonians "could not have done their killing down there, without picking one of the most prominent corners in Seattle as the washline of their dirty linen."[12] Mackintosh, who knew all about the unwritten law,[13] also reacted to Manning's letter. It was, he said, "the most remarkable thing I ever heard" from a public prosecutor,[14] and he published a reply.[15] It argued that the courts must enforce the law and asserted that "lynch and mob law and anarchy are the natural and only results of the efforts of individuals to personally avenge real or fancied injuries." Allowing people to take the law into their own hands threatened the "security of life or property." What Mitchell had done was murder, whether or not the stories about Creffield were true, and Mackintosh intended to do his duty and prosecute, and to do so "fearlessly and vigorously." He professed confidence that a jury would abide by their oaths and convict.

Vigilantism, the Unwritten Law, and Masculinity

Oregonians' opinions would have counted for little had not their arguments struck a chord in Seattle. There the key factor was the stance taken by Blethen and his *Seattle Times*. An editorial published the day after the killing, entitled "Should He Be Punished?" provided a vigorous defence of Mitchell:[16]

> According to legal bookworms the killing of "Joshua" Creffield by George Mitchell yesterday morning was murder in the first degree. According to fathers with families and to brothers with defenseless sisters it comes within the same category of the law as the killing of a mad dog. It is perhaps proper,

that in cases where human life is at stake there should be some such difference of opinion in order to discourage too hasty judgment by individuals.

If this man who was instantly killed on one of the most prominent street
corners of the city was the debased brute, clothed in a cloak of religion, he
is said to be, George Mitchell deserves immediate freedom that he may
display the gold medal his old neighbors in Oregon wish him to wear. If
the statements made by this young man and others in any way approach the
truth, he has merely gone straight at a task for which his duty to his family
and to the community made him the proper instrument.

In accomplishing it he seems to have shown straightforwardness of
purpose and a high disregard for selfish fears about the consequences. His
work was to take a life for the removal of which the law did not provide
the means. It was not lynch law – that is usurpation of the functions of the
courts. In such cases as this, the courts are powerless. The old, primitive,
animal law holds, and this was its fulfillment.

It is dangerous, perhaps, to say that every man whose women-folk are
injured in such a manner should take the life of the man responsible, yet it
is a law which has held good and true in the main all through the ages since
the doctrine of "Free-Love," which this man is declared to have taught, was
confined to the minds of hypocritical libertines, who still use it for their
own purposes in the guise of religious or sociological teachings. Yet when a
case is fully established, the crime of the man and the helplessness of the
woman proven, the inability of the courts to measure out any adequate
punishment is usually made only too clear.

Consider, then, a weapon in the hands of the man whom society expects
to lay down his life, if necessary, to protect his helpless ones. There is not
much to be said on the side of a law which places his act in killing the
destroyer of his home alongside the miscreant who shoots down a traveler
to rob him of his purse. It may not be technically correct to take the life of
such a scoundrel – but if there were more men like George Mitchell there
would be fewer human beasts and still fewer broken, ruined women in
insane asylums and on the streets.

George Mitchell is in the county jail. There has been no denial that the
man whom he killed was all that Mitchell says he was. If the Oregon stories are true the issue is plain. The verdict will be largely a matter of public
opinion.

This defence incorporated the three themes identified in the introduction to this chapter. First, there was much that fit the standard defence
of vigilantism of the period. The appeal to a "natural law" – "the old,

primitive, animal law" – was the centrepiece of the argument, with that natural law contrasted to the "technically correct" law preferred by "legal bookworms." This was a common theme of those who defended vigilantism – that "justice" or the right of the people to enforce their law to protect themselves could take precedence over state law and legal process.[17] The conviction that vigilantism was justified when it fills a gap in the law had animated the citizens of Corvallis to tar and feather Creffield; the same rationalization was now employed to excuse his murder.

The editorial also dealt with the relationship between natural law and man's law, or state law, acknowledging that there ought to be a line separating one from the other, for otherwise the door was open for any man or group of men to act like Southern lynch mobs, whose activities were frequently reported and castigated in the *Times* itself. The difference was that lynch mobs took the law into their own hands – "usurpation of the functions of the courts" – whereas Mitchell had provided a remedy the law could not – "the courts are powerless." Similar sentiments had been uttered two decades earlier by a prominent Washingtonian and Seattle's first major historian, Clarence Bagley. So long as people were adequately protected in their lives and property by the police and the criminal justice system, he asserted, extra-legal violence was wrong. But when the system failed, citizens had the right to protect themselves. Commenting on recent killings of alleged criminals by vigilantes, Bagley "unhesitatingly" declared his "belief in the justice and expediency" of such acts.[18] In this Bagley echoed similar ideological defences of Washington lynchings of the late nineteenth and early twentieth centuries.[19]

Second, the particular variant of natural law operating here was not, as in Corvallis in 1903-1904, the right of a community to defend itself, but the unwritten law – the right of a man to avenge sexual dishonour when his wife, daughter, or sister was seduced. The *Times* did not use the term nor refer to other cases, but it implicitly invoked the idea that there was such a law, and in so doing anticipated by just a few days Morris' use of it in the bail hearing. In line with the way the defence had been justified for decades, by biblical invocations to kill seducers, the *Times* insisted that the law that allowed Mitchell to do what he did was "a law which has held good and true . . . all through the ages."[20] There is evidence that the defence was used less often towards the end of the nineteenth century, but it was a sufficiently common perception that men could literally get away with the murder of seducers of wives and other family members for it to be listed as one of the "fundamental rules of lawlessness" in a famous 1906 critique of vigilantism.[21]

Although women occasionally invoked the unwritten law to defend their own honour, such cases were rare and women tended to be less successful than men in the courts.[22] It was a gendered defence, as exemplified by the third theme in the *Times'* editorial – that Mitchell's act was the embodiment of the best of masculine virtue, representative of how men should act, whatever their class or background. In this period the Victorian construct of manliness was still a powerful one, combining strength of character, a powerful will, and self-restraint with the idea that a real man was also a "Christian gentleman," capable of self-denial and selflessness.[23] Mitchell's killing of Creffield was an expression of all these traits. His strength of character and willingness to sacrifice his interests for others were shown by carrying out a task for which "his duty to his family and the community made him the proper instrument." The method embodied manly virtue also. He had "gone straight at" that task, shown "straightforwardness of purpose," and had done what he did with "a high disregard for selfish fears about the consequences." Mitchell was simultaneously a representative of a newer complex of ideas about what it meant to be a man, dubbed "masculinity" by historians, and which emphasized men's physical and aggressive attributes, their "primal masculinity."[24] The reasons these new ideas came to the fore in the late nineteenth and early twentieth centuries are not important for our purposes;[25] what matters is that we can clearly see their influence both in the *Times'* general approval of the killing – it represented the "old, primitive, animal law" – and in its stress on Mitchell's lack of fear, which no doubt drew on his own statement that "there will be no whimper from me" if he was hanged. All this not only justified his course of action but made it the only one open to a true man.

This editorial contained the most explicit press or public defence of a man's right to kill another in the appropriate circumstances. In the weeks that followed, the *Times* was relentless in defending Mitchell. It continued to characterize his actions as those of a man of conviction and seriousness of purpose,[26] it provided extensive coverage of all that had supposedly gone on within the Creffield sect, and it never wasted an opportunity to tell its readers that Oregon opinion was wholly for Mitchell. The tone of its reporting meant that every story was a closet editorial. Reports about the sect abounded with exaggerations and sensational depictions and were replete with pejorative epithets for Creffield and his teachings. Phrases such as "disgraceful scenes," "orgies," and "holy roller fanatics" reappeared time and again in news reports, either as quotations from witnesses or as reporters' apparently neutral descriptions.[27] When bail was discussed the paper insisted that Mitchell should not be confined with "criminals and other men with whom he has nothing in common" and urged readers to provide sureties if such were needed.[28] A common theme was the superiority of the natural or unwritten law over state law, expressed through references to prosecutors as "technical jugglers of the law" and the contrast between them and Mitchell, "a young man who believes he has done right and is willing to take whatever punishment" came to him. The forthcoming trial, the *Times* asserted in mid-May, would be "littered with many technicalities of the law."[29] The same theme was expressed in a letter to the editor, lamenting that "for the betrayal of women there seems no sure punishment," for "upon these matters the written laws are little else than sounding brass or tinkling cymbals."[30]

Some of the descriptions of Creffield were also clearly intended to paint him as exactly the opposite of Mitchell, as decidedly un-masculine. Morris was quoted calling him "a human leper, one of the basest men who ever walked the earth."[31] A letter from "An Oregon Girl," which was likely a plant by Morris, thanked the *Times* for its earlier editorial and purported to tell one family's story of being "broken up and ruined by Creffield." He was a man who deserved to be killed, a "dirty low dog," and a "vile wretch." Mitchell was not guilty of murder but merely of killing "a dirty, low-lived preacher of a false gospel," and should be "set entirely free."[32] Painting the "libertine" as a "noxious reptile," a "serpent" who invaded the Eden of the home, was a common tactic in unwritten law cases.[33] In the discourse of the unwritten law, the libertine was always excoriated; decades earlier he had been the "satanic embodiment" of conduct that "threatened ... sexual ideals,"[34] and the new ideas about masculinity emerging in the later nineteenth century did nothing to lessen that perception. Indeed, the sexual "deviant" was routinely excoriated as un-masculine and his excesses used to sharply delineate the boundaries between real men and others.[35]

As the letter from "An Oregon Girl" suggests, the *Times* also acted as a conduit for Mitchell's lawyers to make their points. Morris proved adroit at arguing his case in the press, hitting repeatedly at the themes of natural law and manly duty. After bail was denied, for example, he was quoted by the *Times* to the effect that he expected "a hard fight" to "free his client from the clutch of laws which make no provision for sentiment or the drastic necessities caused by the very existence of such men as this 'Joshua.'"[36] He also asserted that "Mitchell's act was justifiable and we will prove it."[37] A little later, after his trip to Oregon to gather evidence and interview witnesses, Morris re-ignited a debate that had moved out of the spotlight for a few days. Under the headline "RID WORLD OF A FIEND," the story was told of Morris – "the attorney for the man who killed the fiend who had ruined his sisters" – having discovered that "the half of the wrongs which prompted young George Mitchell to take the law into his own hands ... has not been told."[38] The trial would show "the horrible effects upon everyone who came within his influence." Families were broken up when respectable women succumbed to the evil influence, and people "throughout every section of Oregon" approved of Mitchell's action. Morris claimed that "it was the unanimous expression of all persons with whom I came in contact, including lawyers, doctors, ministers of the gospel, merchants, peace officers and public officials, that Mitchell's act has relieved the whole Northwest of the most dangerous brute who ever existed in human form." Thus, and echoing the *Times'* earlier editorial, this was one case where somebody was permitted to take the law into his own hands, because Mitchell's act was "for the protection of humanity" and was "prompted by a necessity from as high a source as the law, namely, the preservation of human society."

Many more examples of similar *Times* coverage could be given. The paper adopted its position out of conviction and expediency; the personality and ambitions of its owner-editor and an ongoing newspaper war between it and its chief rival, the *Post-Intelligencer,* influenced it as much as did the merits of Mitchell's case. As already noted, the *Times* was the personal fiefdom of one of early twentieth-century Seattle's most notorious figures, Alden J. Blethen.[39] A sometime lawyer and teacher, Blethen had run newspapers in Kansas City and Minneapolis before moving to Seattle in 1896, where he acquired the *Times,* initially in partnership with another, but from 1897 as sole owner. Blethen had found success elsewhere in the "new journalism" of the late nineteenth century – cheaper newspapers because of new technology, lively content and style, immediacy of news because of the telegraph and the telephone, and the development of mass readership. He had also been an exponent of "yellow journalism" – sensationalist and muckraking content – with the *Penny Press* that he founded in Minneapolis. Described by his biographers as "coarse and intemperate and harsh and hasty and unreliable," but also as a "great newspaperman," he transformed the *Times.* Blethen emphasized "hot news, sports, local crimes and politics, humor, entertainment and the theater" and carried a fiercely patriotic message that bordered on the jingoistic, especially during the Spanish-American War. By the early years of the century Blethen and the *Times* had become Seattle institutions, the latter more popular than the former, whose drunken binges, foul language, and vicious temper made him few friends, especially among the elite, who also deprecated his supposed connections with the vice trade and corrupt municipal politicians.

Politically the *Times* was by 1906 an independent, although Blethen had previously supported populist political movements and various reform agendas and continued to follow many of William Randolph Hearst's populist campaigns. But Blethen was more concerned with self-promotion than with politics, and by 1906 his real enemy had become Erastus Brainerd, editor of the *Post-Intelligencer*. A Harvard graduate (1874) and career newspaperman who worked for papers in New York, Philadelphia, and Atlanta, Brainerd moved to Seattle in 1890, working as an editor with the *Seattle Press*, as a government official, and as the publicist for the chamber of commerce. A staunch Republican, he was appointed editor of the *Post-Intelligencer* in 1904, a post he held until 1911. He was a conservative reformer, and although not an advocate of municipal ownership, Brainerd was a fierce opponent of the municipal corruption that Blethen was often associated with.[40]

In his war with Brainerd and the *Post-Intelligencer* Blethen sought to position his paper as the voice of the common people and of recent immigrants, as distinct from the staid middle-class reform Republican organ run by Brainerd. Circulation mattered more to Blethen than convictions, and he was winning the circulation war in 1906.[41] He attracted not only working-class readers but the middle classes as well with his readable and provocative, often sensationalistic, style. His paper was often referred to as the "Seattle Crimes" for the lurid accounts of cases splashed across the front page. The *Times*' treatment of the Mitchell case was clearly derived from Blethen's more general ambitions and approach to journalism. If ever there was sensationalist fodder with which to sell newspapers, this was it. The facts themselves, however, needed to be spiced with provocative views, and defending Mitchell was infinitely more sensational than demanding that he be tried and hanged for murder.

We are not suggesting that Blethen entirely lacked convictions. The stance adopted by the *Times* fit his own rough and ready approach to dealing with conflict, and he sincerely believed in the vision of true masculinity that he so publicly supported. Blethen's position would also, he likely surmised, both appeal to his working-class readers and ruffle the comfortable middle-class sensibilities of men like Brainerd. Urban vigilantism of this period tended in any event to draw more support from the working classes than from more respectable sectors of society, and the *Times*' portrait of Mitchell was carefully crafted to draw a link between manliness and the working classes. Mitchell was a representative of the manly virtues of the respectable working classes: ordinary and decent, a simple and straight-forward young fellow, the boy next door.[42] He had an "honest look" on his face, he understood the seriousness of what he had done but was "manly, quiet and unperturbed" when he appeared in court. He showed emotion when talking of his poor, wronged sisters. In appealing for somebody to put up bail money for him, the *Times* stressed that his family was re-spectable and hard working but had little money. They were "not the class of persons who own stocks and bonds"; he was a "poor young man."[43] This portrayal was also used to reinforce the iniquities of Creffield, who "did not find his victims among the wealthy or among those whom the world classes as our 'best citizens,'" but among the "poorer residents" of the "little Oregon towns."[44] This was not entirely true, but it suited the *Times'* appeal to the working class. Depicting Mitchell this way not only made the appeal to masculinity relevant to the working classes, it also shored up the unwritten law defence. That defence tended in the nineteenth century to be invoked by men of wealth and influence, with those of lower socio-economic status less able to invoke it. In turn, the apparent favouritism of the defence became one of the criticisms aimed at it. In insisting that the Mitchell case was not about the sexual peccadilloes of the effete elite, the *Times* sought to allay at least some of the criticism of the defence.[45]

The *Times* took the lead, along with the defence attorneys, in defend-ing George Mitchell, but others in the press and among the public offered similar if not always such explicit support. Two other newspapers rallied behind Mitchell. The *Republican,* a weekly run by Seattle's best-known African-American, Horace Cayton, and with a readership rather wider than the small black community, announced a few days after the murder that a "human monster" had been disposed of and that killing was "too good" for a man "who will lead to ruin young girls of tender years." It expressed confidence that no Seattle jury would convict Mitchell.[46] A week later it asked rhetorically, "Under the circumstances who would not have done just what he [Mitchell] did?"[47] For the *Republican* to take such a view is surprising, both because it naturally consistently deprecated vigilantism as manifested by lynchings of blacks, and because it otherwise had no time for Blethen. Its position testifies to the strength of the appeal to the un-written law and the masculine avenger, which in this instance overcame any reservations about condoning vigilante killing.

While it did not make quite the same explicit defence of Mitchell as the *Times* and the *Republican,* the Seattle *Star,* the city's third daily, was none-theless clearly sympathetic. It ran a number of stories referring to Creffield as a "brute," a "destroyer of homes," and as the man who had "ruined"

Mitchell's sisters, and it gave ample space to those who approved of Mitchell, including Louis Sandell, who asserted in its pages that "if he was placed in the same condition [as Mitchell] he would have done the same."[48] This argument was a staple of the defenders of the unwritten law – all men needed to place themselves in the position of the man who had taken the law into his own hands, and then judge the act. The *Star*'s only editorial comment on the case also made clear its view that Mitchell should not be prosecuted, through a comparison with Mackintosh's attitude in the Beede case. Mackintosh, the *Star* noted, was "the man who permitted George Beede to go forth without punishment for a crime equal in intent to that of Mitchell's" but who was now intent on convicting Mitchell. "Why this sudden desire to enforce the law?" it demanded, and attributed the difference to the fact that Beede had intercessors in the city while Mitchell has "no influential friends in Seattle."[49] The *Star*'s support for Mitchell grew much stronger once the trial was under way, due as much as anything to it being an avowedly pro-working-class paper and thus very much a rival to the *Times* in the battle for that readership.[50]

Expressions of support for Mitchell also came from others; we assume that they derived from the kinds of ideas the *Times* promulgated, although there is no evidence of that. William H. Paulhamus, one of the state's leading farmers and farm lobbyists and sometime Speaker of the State Senate, offered to put up $5,000 for bail, to give Mitchell a job on his farm "until [he] . . . is acquitted," and to provide him with a permanent position thereafter.[51] According to Will Morris, other prominent citizens were prepared to come forward with bail money.[52] Another supporter of Mitchell was Seattle Chief of Police Charles Wappenstein. He said nothing before the trial but would later assert that he would probably "have voted to free Mitchell," as "I think Creffield ought to have been killed."[53] The *Times* and Mitchell's lawyers clearly had fertile ground in which to sow their defence; the unwritten law had been invoked in other contemporary but less notorious cases, and one of the Corvallis newspapers went so far as to claim that nobody had ever been convicted in Seattle "for murdering the seducer of his wife and daughter" and that "Mitchell's case is stronger than that of the men already liberated for shooting down libertines."[54]

DEFENDING THE RULE OF LAW

The *Times* and Mitchell's other supporters did not have it all their own way in the debate over Creffield's killing. The remainder of the press, and others whose opinions we have evidence of, were deeply concerned about the idea that vigilante killings could be justified by an unwritten law. Some also seem to have offered a rather different understanding of masculinity, one that stressed the virtue of obedience to state law rather than adherence to a primitive code. The *Seattle Post-Intelligencer,* organ of the Republican establishment and reflective of the views of many in the respectable and middle classes, adopted a position of careful neutrality. It said much less about the Mitchell case and its background than did other papers, and while it offered the occasional jibe at Creffield and his followers,[55] it eschewed the pejorative epithets that dominated the *Times'* coverage. Although it said very little in its editorial columns, the *Post-Intelligencer* was critical of the *Times'* May 8 editorial, offering a short but pointed response: "It may be fairly presumed that the courts of King County will see that the ends of justice are met without hysterical outcry or the clamorous advice of paranoiacs."[56] Beyond this implicit and muted suggestion that Mitchell ought to be convicted, the *Post-Intelligencer* did not comment on the merits of the case. This reticence may have reflected a belief that the courts, not the pages of newspapers, were where alleged murderers should be judged, but more likely it demonstrated a reluctance to take the wrong side of the issue in the battle for circulation. Support for Mitchell was widespread, and in this atmosphere Brainerd, who could not condone vigilantism, preferred to say nothing.

Other Seattle newspapers and magazines, however, all less important and many of them weeklies with relatively small circulations, were not afraid to launch a counterattack against the *Times.* They were careful to show their contempt for Creffield, and to that extent shared with Mitchell's supporters the conviction that Creffield was not truly masculine. But they joined this contempt for the victim to concerns about the larger consequences of permitting individuals to take the law into their own hands. The *Argus,* a weekly that voiced the ideas and aspirations of the emerging professional and new business classes and was run by another Blethen enemy, Henry Chadwick,[57] insisted that murder to avenge apparent wrongs could never be justified. There was "no excuse for such murders as the one of Creffield in a civilized community," and Chadwick marvelled at a public prosecutor offering the views Manning had expressed. He was also worried that Frater was part of the problem the city now had, and argued that his comments in the Beede-MacDonald case would make it difficult for Mitchell to be tried "fairly and impartially."[58]

Another weekly, the *Mail and Herald,* also expressed amazement at Manning's intervention, suggesting it made him "little better than an anarchist." It asked what was to now stop Maud Creffield from shooting Mitchell, as he had wronged her, and then a friend of Mitchell shooting her? Once the city went down this road, the "foundations of government" were gone. The next issue continued with the same theme in an editorial entitled "Law versus Anarchy," insisting that "the dignity and majesty of the law must be upheld," with the alternative being "anarchy." Creffield obviously deserved severe punishment, but it must be applied within, not outside, the law: "society cannot allow such a bold, public and vindictive infringement of law as that of the Creffield murder without prompt and adequate punishment, unless it is prepared to have the very foundations of law and order undermined by a pernicious and sickening sentimentalism." The *Mail and Herald* was still on the same theme when Mitchell's trial started, linking the case to presidential assassinations, for all had their origin in "a studied disregard of laws." In the same issue it complained of "the nauseating apologies for this high-handed crime on the part of some of the daily newspapers of this city," which "linger as a stench in the nostrils of all who respect law and order."[59] The *Argus* and the *Mail and Herald* were joined in these sentiments by other papers and magazines, including the monthly *Pessimist,* which insisted that "the spirit that prompted Mitchell to ignore the law and mete out summary and undeserved punishment to Creffield is the same spirit that incites the hot-blooded Southerner to lynch the Negro, or the Russian Christian to kill the Jew."[60]

The concerns about vigilantism were likely expressed with an awareness that Seattle in particular and the state in general had something of a history of it. Half a dozen self-proclaimed vigilante movements had operated in the state in the nineteenth century, including the Seattle Vigilance Committee of 1882.[61] On other occasions Washington residents had lynched alleged criminals when the law was deemed inadequate to deal with them.[62] The most recent outburst prior to 1906 involved a threat of violent raids on an anarchist commune in the wake of President McKinley's 1901 assassination, widely laid at the door of anarchist groups.[63] The existence of support for vigilantism in Seattle in 1906 is clearly demonstrated by the brief emergence later in the year of a group calling itself "The Seattle Vigilantes," in response to a series of murders and attempted murders – including Creffield's – which the self-proclaimed vigilantes thought were being inadequately dealt with. The *Times'* response to this group is instructive. At one and the same time it urged that the proper recourse was law reform to make conviction more certain and proclaimed that should the state legislature fail to respond, then "let the Vigilantes, as openly and completely as their predecessors of Old California, go down to Olympia and hang the Judiciary Committee."[64] Recourse to extra-legal violence was thus never as far from the surface as many middle-class residents of the city would have wished.

Some critics of Mitchell did not concern themselves solely with vigilantism. They also offered a different view of masculinity from that endorsed by the *Times*. Why should "a hero" be made of Mitchell, a man who had shot another in the back? His act was hardly that of an impassioned and provoked defender of family; in stalking his victim and shooting him without warning he had committed a cowardly act, hardly the kind of thing that fit the straightforward and manly image the *Times* sought to create. There were also related suggestions that women needed less protection and more moral fibre; those who engaged in "low debaucheries" with Creffield knew what they were doing and were responsible for the consequences. The *Times* therefore did not have a monopoly on what constituted appropriate masculine behaviour. That issue was heavily contested terrain, for Blethen's opponents could not agree either. For some, as we have seen, the problem was the cowardly way Mitchell had killed his victim. For the virulently anti-feminist *Patriarch,* which came out most strongly against the killing being justified, the problem was the simple fact that women were determining a man's actions. In joining the sect and doing whatever they may or may not have done, Mitchell's sisters had rejected male authority, and no man should have to risk life or liberty to rescue or avenge them.[65]

But the most important alternative view of manliness was that which equated it with the "civilized" virtues of respectability and adherence to law rather than the "primitive" resort to force. This view was expressed in the pages of the *Mail and Herald* by Rev. Myron W. Haynes, pastor of the First Baptist Church. From the outset Haynes campaigned against Blethen's view of the case, telephoning Mackintosh with "assurances of support" and using his pulpit to denounce vigilantism, "begging his congregation to stem the tide of public opinion in his [Mitchell's] favor."[66] In mid-May he published a long article refuting all aspects of the *Times'* defence of Mitchell.[67] He was willing to assume that all that had been said about Creffield was true but insisted that even then the murder could not be justified. If the killing was a benefit to the community, as many claimed, Mitchell should be employed as a "sort of public shooter," for "there are several men in the states of Oregon and Washington whose departure would be unmourned." If the killing avenged the wrongs to his sisters, "many another man would be justified on similar grounds."

The problem that Haynes saw, however, went beyond fears that others would be encouraged to follow Mitchell's example; two other principles were at stake, both engaging notions of citizenship and masculine virtue. First, Creffield as much as any other man was entitled to a trial before punishment, and in depriving him of that Mitchell "violated a fundamental principle of our civilization as well as broke a law of our land." Second, to approve just one vigilante killing would strike a blow against the whole constellation of modernizing and reform ideas. Haynes put it this way:

> The man who decries law and clamors for the acquittal of a murderer, forgets that he is sadly out of harmony with the spirit of the age. We are now living in an age when, more than for many years, the people are demanding an enforcement of the law, and high officials are responding to that demand. Men in high estate, as well as in low estate, are facing the law and brave men are enforcing it . . . strong men all over the land, are determined to maintain the majesty and supremacy of the law, [and] it is high time that we joined and kept pace with that noble procession.

Haynes thus linked the debate over George Mitchell to much broader issues, issues very much at the forefront of Seattle's hotly contested politics in the early years of the century. The "spirit of the age" he referred to incorporated not just adherence to law and legal process but also the anti-corruption and anti-vice campaigns that Haynes and other reformers were consumed with. The Mitchell case symbolized a much wider debate about the kind of place Seattle was to be, a point Haynes made explicitly in his conclusion: "Every man who is seeking a higher type of citizenship, who advocates civic reform and law enforcement, finds his hands tied by sentiments of approval for crimes such as we have heard of late." Although many other ministers shied away from the issue,[68] Haynes was probably not alone. The city's best-known clergyman, Rev. Mark Matthews of the First Presbyterian Church, had feuded publicly with Blethen on other issues and attempted to convince men that religion and masculinity could go together, and it is very likely that he used his pulpit to castigate both Mitchell and Creffield, although the only evidence we have of him doing so comes at the end of the year.[69]

The case also raised the question of what kind of men Seattle's citizens ought to be. For Haynes the authenticity of a man was not to be measured by his willingness to resort to force or his physical strength. He was to be judged, at least in part, by the more traditional values of self-restraint, by the extent to which he could put aside the lust for revenge. Haynes was perhaps also invoking, in his reference to "civilization," another feature of the intellectual climate of the times – the belief that races and civilizations could be placed on an evolutionary hierarchy, with Anglo-Saxons at the top. One measure of the superiority of "white civilization," and simultaneously an aspect of the standards that real men should attain, was adherence to law and legal process.[70]

PUBLIC OPINION

It is easier to chart the broad parameters of the debate in the press and among those whose words or actions were reported in newspapers than it is to assess public opinion more generally, or to say whether it was influenced by the press salvoes. People took an intense interest in the case; the courtroom was packed when Mitchell made his appearances,[71] and many wrote to their friends about the case and discussed it in fora as august as the chamber of commerce.[72] We can surely assume that it was also talked about on the streets and in drawing rooms, clubs, and saloons. As former Washington governor John H. McGraw put it at a meeting of the Seattle chamber of commerce, it was "a case that every man present ... has in his mind."[73]

The evidence about the content of public opinion is limited, and we would venture just three general comments. First, the Mitchell case seems to have split the Seattle elite, a fact discernible from the newspaper war alone. We have seen that men such as Paulhamus spoke out publicly for Mitchell, while other men sent messages of support to the prosecutors.[74] In addition, there are indications, albeit from a slightly later period, that Blethen's stance was not appreciated by many members of the middle class. Referring to Mitchell's case and others, one Ross Parker, a lawyer, considered that Blethen, "more than any other person, is responsible" for the "maelstrom of homicide" in Seattle, while Milo Root, a judge of the Washington Supreme Court, deprecated the attempt to "make heros [sic] of" people like Mitchell.[75] The Seattle correspondent of the Portland *Oregonian* probably got it right when, just before Mitchell's trial began, he suggested that while there was support for Mitchell and some sympathy for him, there were many who "cannot reconcile their sympathy ... with the idea of personal assassination, who believe that no man has the right to take the law into his own hands."[76]

There is no better indication of this split than a debate on the case in the Seattle chamber of commerce in mid-May. One Ebenezer Shorrock, the president and general manager of Northwest Trust and Safe Deposit

Company, asked the chamber to "go on record as deploring the stand taken by the daily press of Seattle as condoning murder as the proper method of righting family wrongs in the attitude it has maintained towards the future vindication of George Mitchell."[77] The motion was ultimately tabled, apparently on the ground that the chamber should not comment on an ongoing legal proceeding. Its introduction, however, reveals that a body of Seattle opinion was very concerned about the idea that a killing like Mitchell's could ever be justified. At the same time, the failure to pass the motion also demonstrates that this was an issue that split the city's respectable classes. And in the course of the debate on Shorrock's motion to censure the *Times* for its stance, no less a person than John H. McGraw, a former state governor, a leading Seattle businessman, at that time president of the chamber, and a man who as sheriff of King County in 1886 had organized the city's middle-class resistance to those who wished to expel the Asian community,[78] voiced his difficulties with the case:

> I have always stood for the defense of the law and order, and presently and as president of the chamber of commerce, I deprecate all forms of lawlessness, but I can conceive of cases where a man's duty to his family is paramount . . . I must say that I would not be eligible to sit upon a jury in trial of this man, for the reason that I would be unable to truthfully answer questions touching my competency as a juror.

Such views, from such a source, demonstrate the power of the pro-Mitchell arguments in support of the unwritten law and its accompanying vision of masculine behaviour, even among those with most to lose by encouraging lack of respect for the law. Mitchell's supporters included many members of Rev. Haynes' congregation, who took issue with him over the killing.[79] Perhaps representative of an equivocal attitude was Marion Baxter, president of the Wayside Emergency Hospital, who, while not directly supporting Mitchell, was highly critical of Creffield. For men like Creffield, who betrayed and led women astray, Baxter's solution was "the surgeon's knife," which we take to mean castration; he neither condemned nor endorsed vigilante killing in the absence of what he thought would be laws effective against seducers.[80]

Our second point about public opinion concerns those who did not give sermons, publish articles in newspapers, or attend chamber of commerce meetings. Partisan newspapers – the *Times* in Seattle and many Oregon papers – insisted that public sympathy for Mitchell was widespread and that an acquittal was certain, and went so far as to claim that police and jailers shared this view.[81] And they were probably right, for even the *Argus* acknowledged widespread public sympathy for him: "Mitchell thought he was ridding the world of a great scoundrel, and nearly everybody agreed with him."[82] Sheriff Burnett of Benton County was one of a number of admittedly partisan witnesses who also believed the Seattle public was pro-Mitchell; he had not heard "a single person in Seattle say Mitchell ought to be convicted," he told the *Corvallis Times* after a visit to the city, adding that he had "heard hundreds express the hope that he would be promptly acquitted."[83] Subsequent events also suggest a widespread degree of support for Mitchell among the less well-educated and affluent, even if that support was by no means complete. As we shall see in the next chapter, it proved difficult to select a jury for Mitchell's trial because many potential jurors had already formed an opinion in Mitchell's favour. Thus, to this extent at least, the *Times,* obviously not a neutral commentator on the point, was correct to argue, a week after the killing, that "throughout the States of Oregon and Washington there is an intense feeling of sympathy for and indorsements [sic] of" Mitchell's act.[84] Whether this was due to the influence of the *Times,* which had the widest circulation in the city, or whether the *Times* simply reflected the public mood, is ultimately impossible to say, but we think it likely that the paper turned many minds.

Our third point about public opinion is that this debate about a man's right to invoke the unwritten law and about the right way for men to behave was one conducted, at least in public, by men only. Women, of course, did not own newspapers or hold public office, but many were active in public life through the women's club movement, suffrage campaigns, and the temperance movement, and working-class women contributed to the increasingly strong and aggressive labour movement.[85] Yet the press coverage contains no comments from any women's organization nor any individual woman, and we have not located any evidence that the case was discussed within women's organizations.[86] Their views would not have been welcomed by men who asserted the man's duty to obey the unwritten law, for the woman central to that law was a domesticated and passionless being with no public role other than that of recipient of chivalry. Women were invariably ciphers in unwritten law trials; as we have seen, they rarely invoked the doctrine themselves. Many women in the emerging feminist movement of the late nineteenth century had been understandably critical of the unwritten law, and we assume Seattle women active in public life would have taken the same position.[87] However, we have no evidence for this. The only women who featured at all in the debate, Maud Creffield and Esther Mitchell, sent the wrong message entirely for Mitchell's supporters when they insisted that Creffield was a good and righteous man. They were equally unhelpful to the opponents of the unwritten law, for while those opponents deprecated extra-legal violence, they also bought into the depiction of Creffield as a base libertine.

Whatever women might have had to say, Mitchell's defenders ultimately won the battle for public opinion. It was a complex struggle, one that pitted deeply held ideas about sex and honour against concerns about lawlessness, which were given special salience in a city trying to shake its rough-and-tumble frontier image and its reputation for corruption. It was a debate mediated by class and strongly influenced by contested views of appropriate masculinity. Religion played a limited role. Creffield's alleged sexual excesses prevented Mitchell's detractors from making this a case about religious freedom, and if anything the debate exemplified the dangers of religious extremism in a state with no real tradition of religious radicalism and generally unenthusiastic about religion.[88] It may be that Mitchell's defenders won in part because Seattle in particular and Washington in general had something of a tradition of turning to vigilante action when circumstances were thought to warrant it. But that is very speculative, and we would be loath to place emphasis on so diffuse a tradition. In the particular circumstances of the Mitchell case in 1906 it was the unwritten law that counted most. If there were people who could contemplate approving vigilantism in the appropriate case, a man's right to avenge sexual dishonour made the Mitchell case an eminently suitable one.

9

The Trial of George Mitchell, Part 1

JURY SELECTION AND THE CASE FOR THE PROSECUTION

"GEORGE MITCHELL ON TRIAL FOR HIS LIFE" screamed the front-page headline of the *Seattle Times* on Monday, June 25, the day that Case Number 3652 began. The *Post-Intelligencer* headline the next day was smaller and less dramatic: "Select Jurors in Mitchell Trial." Nonetheless, like the *Times* and the *Star,* the *Post-Intelligencer* had the trial on its front page for much of the next two weeks, testament to the intense public interest in the case. It was the fourth prosecution for murder of the year in King County, although only the second to go to trial, guilty pleas having been entered for two of the three previous cases.[1] Proceedings lasted a total of twelve days: four days were taken up with jury selection, only one with the prosecution case, and seven with the presentation of defence evidence and arguments. Judge Frater delivered his instructions to the jury on Tuesday, July 10, and it took the case and rendered its verdict the same afternoon. Criminal trials in early twentieth-century America, even capital trials, were generally short affairs of a few days, a week at the most, and thus the Mitchell trial was unusually long.[2]

This chapter and the next provide a detailed account of the trial, taken largely from newspaper reports. In this chapter we will examine the first two stages: the selection of the jury, a statutory requirement in a capital case,[3] and the presentation of the prosecution case. Chapter 10 looks at the case for the defence and the concluding proceedings: speeches and instructions to the jury, and the verdict. Our analysis of the Mitchell trial will demonstrate what numerous other historical studies of trials have shown – that while the substantive law that defined crime and the procedural rules governing trials shaped the process, neither entirely determined the outcome. As Rosenberg among many others has noted, it is a "commensensical observation" that "the circumstances of a particular case had ordinarily as much to do with its disposition as the precise injunctions of rules of law," but it is nonetheless one worth repeating.[4] The Mitchell case was not determined by a simple and objective application of rules of law; the result was reached through the interaction of those rules, the arguments of the lawyers, the persuasiveness of witnesses, and the values, predilections, and prejudices of the jurors. Within this complex interaction the lawyers played a crucial role, for it is they who shaped the case, they who sought to structure their arguments as persuasive narratives. Morris, Shipley, Mackintosh, and Miller were not seeking the "truth" of the case, whatever that might be, although of course they would have said they were. They wanted a verdict, and verdicts are the product of getting the jurors to see the case in a particular way. Thus the lawyers wanted to mix law and rhetoric to tell a version of the story, a version that would appeal to the "common sense" view of the world, what we might term the popular consciousness, likely to be shared by the jurors. The stories we are most ready to believe are the ones that best resonate with our own experience and the way we want to see the world, and prosecution and defence lawyers alternately cast the Mitchell case as a simple story of cold-blooded murder and as an equally straightforward tale of love, betrayal, honour, and justice. Legal rules mattered in the process of telling those stories; indeed, we will see that much time was spent arguing about those rules. But we cannot attribute the outcome to those rules.[5]

High-profile trials, those that "touch a cultural nerve,"[6] are also great drama, and the Mitchell trial was no exception. Public interest was sustained throughout the proceedings. Despite the at-times intense summer heat, the courtroom was crowded every day with people who toiled up "Profanity Hill" to the imposing King County Courthouse.[7] The crowds included Mitchell's supporters from Oregon as well as Seattle residents keen to get a taste of the sensational event. People not only turned up, they participated, cheering and applauding in ways that infuriated the irascible Frater.

JURY SELECTION

The courtroom was crowded by 10 a.m. on Monday, June 25, when the proceedings began – as many as 150 people were present according to one report.[8] There was a substantial group of some twenty people from Oregon, some subpoenaed and others having voluntarily travelled north; O.V. Hurt and Burgess Starr were the most prominent, sitting at the back of the courtroom every day.[9] Most spectators, however, were local. The *Times* expressed surprise that only nine or ten women showed up and noted that the majority of the spectators "were men of affairs, lawyers and business men deeply interested in the ethical questions at issue."[10] There was also a strong representation of elderly people, members of local church congregations, and more women attended on subsequent days. George Mitchell sat calmly in the middle of it all, mostly silent and thoughtful. From the second day he was joined by brother Perry, who received permission to sit at his table. Although George showed emotion, perhaps contrived, when tales of Creffield's iniquities were recounted by his lawyers, he was also relaxed enough by the end of the week to laugh and chat with his Oregon friends. Despite what the press often referred to as the tedium of the jury selection, the room continued to be packed with spectators throughout that process. There were few demonstrations during this initial phase, although there was at least one show of support for Mitchell during the morning recess of Tuesday, June 26. A number of women – reports differ, but somewhere between four and fifteen – approached him "to shake his hand and express their sympathy"; they were not "young women or seekers of morbid sensation," insisted the *Times,* but "ranged from middle aged to white-haired venerability."[11]

The opening of the trial gave the *Times* an opportunity to renew its cheerleading for George Mitchell, and its report of the first day elaborated the same themes that had marked its earlier coverage of the case. Mitchell had "done his part"; he had "killed the man who ruined his sisters and broke up their home."[12] And, of course, "most" men think that "Mitchell was right." But he had a hard road ahead to deal with the law's "manipulations" and with "legal technicalities," which threatened to get in the way of "the red-blooded judgment of twelve men who, all unprejudiced, must review the pitiful tragedy." Mitchell was "like a man who has leaped beneath a swaying rock, hung low on a derrick, to throw his sister out of danger, and finds himself prostrate, helpless, able only to wonder whether the rock in its fall will crush him, maim him, or fall to one side." This wonderful metaphor captured the "unwritten law" interpretation of the story: the shooting of Creffield was not just right or acceptable, it was brave and noble, the only action a true man could have taken. The law, lawyers, and jurymen did not represent justice or righteousness, but an abstract law of nature – gravity, the cruel caprice of a falling rock. And Mitchell's fate under the rock – crushing, maiming, or escape – was clearly intended to refer the reader back to an earlier passage in the article, where the writer noted that the trial would decide "whether he shall go free and return to his family, or to the penitentiary, or – the gallows."

Similar comments laced the reports of jury selection on subsequent days and continued throughout the trial.[13] Consistently with their earlier positions, the *Star* and the *Republican* also supported Mitchell, the latter insisting that "public sentiment is all with" him, and that "it is the consensus of opinion that he will be acquitted."[14] The *Times* conveyed its views largely through its reporting style, not via its editorial pages. A rare editorial on the second day was typically short and guarded: "The Mitchell trial is on. In a few days we will know what a jury thinks about a young man taking the law in his hands to revenge the injuries done to his family."[15] In the result it would take more than a few days to find out what a jury thought – it took a few days simply to choose one, and it was not long before the press began to complain that the much-anticipated trial was rather a bore.

When court opened on the 25th, the jury panel, the group of men – known as talesmen – from which the twelve jurors would be selected, was present. The panel itself had been chosen by lot by two jury commissioners. Jurors had to be electors in the state of Washington (meaning they had to be males and citizens of the United States), a "male inhabitant" of King County for the year preceding selection, between twenty-one and sixty years old, literate in English, not a felon, and either a freeholder or householder (the head of a household).[16] This last provision and the residency requirement excluded the poorest segments of society, and women were also ineligible,[17] but jurors could nonetheless represent a broad spectrum of the county's male population. Immigrants would likely have been under-represented as a result of the citizenship and literacy requirements, and this in turn would have worked particularly against the likelihood of ethnic minorities serving on juries. But minorities were not formally barred from service and at least two members of ethnic minority groups were among those examined in the Mitchell case.[18]

The jury commissioners had chosen two groups of talesmen. A panel, or venire, of as many men as the judge thought necessary for the upcoming session was drawn monthly for the beginning of every court session, and those men were present. Forty names had been chosen on May 12 to serve in Department No. 1, Frater's criminal court, and they had been at work already, sitting on various trials in the week beginning June 18. But Frater knew that Mitchell's case would be a difficult one, and he had ordered the calling of a special panel of an additional sixty men, which had been drawn on Saturday, June 16.[19]

After each man was chosen by lot from the array, there were two further stages to the jury selection process. Potential jurors were first "examined for cause." That is, they were questioned by the lawyers and/or the judge to ascertain if there was some good reason for them not to serve. In a few instances this reason might be entirely unrelated to the case – a juror was not qualified, had served previously in the year, was sick, or had a compelling reason to be excused from jury duty, such as serious illness in the family.[20] But for the most part this stage was designed to exclude people who, for some reason or another, could not try the case impartially. Those who survived this test were said to be "passed for cause." The second stage of the process would then begin, with both sides exercising their peremptory challenges, excluding jurors they did not like without needing to show cause. In a capital case the state had six peremptories, the defence twelve.[21] As each peremptory was used, another round of questioning for cause to fill the vacancy was required.

Jury selection occupied the whole of the first four days of the trial, from Monday, June 25, until Thursday, June 28. About sixty men were examined for cause,[22] thirteen of the potential eighteen peremptory challenges were used, and a substantial number of talesmen had excuses not to serve or were found unqualified.[23] As a result both the regular panel of forty and the special venire of sixty were exhausted by the end of the third day, and more men had to be found, drawn from members of the regular panel who had initially been assigned to civil cases in other courtrooms and from a new special venire of thirty men chosen that day.[24] Although none of these thirty was selected, at the time "deputy sheriffs scurried all over the county in search of" them.[25] Given the length and complexity of the process, we cannot provide a detailed and day-by-day account of it. But we should look closely at the examinations of potential jurors, for they tell us a good deal about each side's tactics and concerns at this stage and about the knowledge and attitudes brought by the talesmen to court. We can also acquire a sense, albeit a tentative one, of the stance taken by Judge Frater.

The law on challenges for cause was straightforward, although at the end of the day it left much to the judgment of the presiding judge. If a man had an objection to capital punishment that would prevent him from finding guilty any defendant charged with a capital offence, he was to be excluded.[26] Second, and rather less clearly, a judge could disqualify a man "for such cause as the court may, in its discretion, deem sufficient, having reference to the causes of challenge prescribed for civil cases, as far as they may be applicable, and to the substantial rights of the defendants." The civil procedure rules referred to in this section divided bias into two kinds. A juror had an "implied bias" if he was related to one of the parties, or in some kind of business relationship with one of them, or had an interest in the outcome of the case. Much more important was "actual bias," and here the statute laid down a rather vague standard. A juror would be disqualified if his "state of mind" was such that he could not "try the issue impartially." This would encompass personal bias against or for the defendant or his victim, or it might mean, for example, that a juror in a case in which the defence was insanity believed generally that all insanity claims were subterfuges, or that no one should ever be acquitted on that ground. In practice, however, the issue was invariably whether the potential juror had formed an opinion on the case before the trial from, for example, reading the newspapers or talking to friends.[27]

The law thus gave the trial judge broad discretion on what constituted a "state of mind" sufficient to say that the talesman was not impartial, albeit a discretion reviewable by a higher court.[28] But it was limited by extensive guidance from the state supreme court. In a long line of cases through the 1890s and early twentieth century, the court had consistently held, in the words of the most recent of those cases, that "if a juror has an opinion as to the guilt or innocence of the defendant" and that opinion was "so far fixed that evidence would be required to remove it," he was to be disqualified. This rule applied "notwithstanding [the juror] may answer that he can, or believes he can, disregard such opinion and try the case according to the law and the evidence that is given upon the trial."[29] Thus mere knowledge of a case before being called for jury service would not disqualify. But the cases show that it was often difficult to distinguish between an "opinion" as to guilt or innocence and an "impression" about the case, although the niceties of that distinction do not concern us here.[30] What matters is the general principle – those who went into court and said they had a decided view as to whether Mitchell should be convicted or acquitted would be disqualified.

Against this background the lawyers set to work. All four men participated, although press reports suggest that Morris and Miller did more of the questioning than Shipley and Mackintosh. Obviously a central issue was whether a talesman had formed an opinion on the case, and the lawyers, and in some cases Frater, questioned them all on this point. Not surprisingly, almost all had read about the case and discussed it with others. But there were other issues covered in the lawyers' questions, for

two reasons. First, as we have seen, having an opinion about guilt or innocence was not the only form of actual bias. An opinion adverse to capital punishment would also disqualify, and attitudes to insanity, religious
zealotry, or a man's duty to his family might do so as well, if the judge
could be persuaded that the talesman would not be impartial. Everyone
was asked what states he had lived in, because it seems generally to have
been agreed that no former resident of Oregon should be on the jury. But
eliciting jurors' attitudes on a range of matters served a second purpose.
Even if Frater rejected the challenge, the talesman could later be removed
with a peremptory. The challenge for cause process was thus also about
gathering information about which jurors to challenge peremptorily when
it came time for that.

Although the press did not tend to report questions and answers relating to actual opinions on guilt or innocence, it had a lot to say about
the less direct questioning of jurors, and from this we can see what kind
of men each side wanted and which they wished to exclude. Defence questions covered four related issues. The first was whether or not potential
jurors would be willing to believe that a man whose sister had been seduced
by Creffield might be driven temporarily insane as a result. The questions
on this issue were "thorough and minute."[31] Second, they investigated
whether or not talesmen were generally willing to accept the defence of
insanity; a question about this was asked of every potential juror.[32] Third,
they did not want anyone disposed towards a religious leader.

The fourth concern was more complicated: Would someone disposed
to be sympathetic to a person's anguish at knowing that his sister had been
seduced become less so if it was then revealed that the seducer had served
time in the penitentiary for the offence? That is, would they feel differently about the likelihood of Mitchell being driven insane if the law
had already dealt with Creffield? This question represented an impromptu
defence response to prosecution questions probing jurors' attitudes not
just to the right of a man to take the law into his own hands but to his
right to do so if the law had already dealt with the victim. From Wednesday on, the defence also began more often to invoke the name of Esther
Mitchell, rather than Donna Starr, and to introduce the idea that it was to
protect Esther, rather than avenge a wrong done to her, that Mitchell had
acted. Thus the trial was under way before Morris and Shipley signalled the
demise of Mitchell's original claim that Esther had been "ruined," and a new
tack – that she would have been had not George Mitchell prevented it.

This shift probably occurred for two reasons. First, making Esther, not
Donna, the focus suggests that the defence feared that the prosecution's

stress on the time Creffield spent in the penitentiary might reduce the potency of their implicit unwritten law defence. One of the justifications for self-help in adultery cases was that state law did not provide a remedy. But it had done so for Donna Starr, whereas it had not, and could not, for Esther. Second, the move from Esther as ruined girl to sister in danger of debauchery had become necessary since it was by now abundantly clear that Esther was not going to play along. If called to testify – and the defence did call her – she would simply deny any seduction, and Mitchell would thus appear to have acted without good cause. Esther would also, of course, deny that Creffield had designs on her, but that was much less damaging to the defence case, for she could easily be depicted as his dupe.

All this questioning took a long time, for the questions needed to be preceded by an explanation of the background. In the process, of course, the defence was able to tell its side of the story, not just to the men being questioned but to those who had already been passed for cause and who were then placed in the jury box. The *Times* referred to Morris' questions as often being "addresses to the jury," as he "outlined much of the charges of disgraceful orgies practised by the Holy Rollers."[33]

The prosecution in its turn concentrated on questions that essentially represented the reverse of these defence concerns. It frequently asked jurors about whether they believed there were ever circumstances in which a man had the right to kill another, other than in self-defence. The prosecution wanted a jury, said the *Oregonian,* of men who believed that "retribution is a matter to be left entirely in the hands of the law." Miller was "especially anxious" to test views on "justifiable assassination," for "the state will accept no man that professes to uphold the right of one individual to kill another, regardless of legal remedies." As noted, the defence also wanted to know whether the fact that Creffield had been convicted of adultery made a difference to those views. Mackintosh frequently asked a "long and involved" question as to whether a juror would be influenced by the evidence, "if it should develop in the course of the trial that this deceased Creffield committed adultery with ... the sister of this defendant." The prosecutors were also interested in attitudes to the insanity defence; they wanted to "secure men who would explicitly follow the court's ... instructions that a man is to be believed sane until he has established his insanity." Thus they probed for indications of scepticism about insanity, asking whether jurors would "endeavor to distinguish between the actual insanity of the defendant and a pretense of insanity put up as a means of escaping punishment for a crime."[34]

Given the need for background explanations preceding questions, the questioning of some jurors took a long time. For others the time spent being scrutinized must have been quite short, for the court got through at least twenty men on each the first two days and at least ten and eight respectively on the third and fourth days. We suspect that many of those disqualified because they had a fixed opinion admitted to it quite quickly; the time was taken up with those who did not immediately make the admission. It took Morris and Shipley two hours on the 26th, for example, to get one H.R. Compton, a streetcar conductor, to admit that he had an opinion on the case based on his prejudice against the insanity defence.[35] In line with the law delineated above, Shipley spent much of that time trying to ascertain from Compton whether he had an "opinion" or an "impression" about the case from reading newspapers.[36]

Not all of the court time was used for questioning; dealing with the talesmen was often interrupted by objections from one side or the other to the questions asked. By the end of the second day the record was "already cluttered with objections and exceptions," mostly from the defence, and mostly in the form of objections to the prosecution's references to Creffield's adultery conviction.[37] The prosecutors in turn objected to Morris' questions becoming speeches about Creffield's iniquities. On the first two days Frater appears to have overruled almost all these objections and in the process to have allowed both sides a wide degree of latitude. As long as the lawyers made their statements as preludes to questions that were relevant to the case, they were allowed to proceed. For example, after Morris had outlined at length the alleged practices of the Creffield sect, he would ask whether such stories "as tending to explain Mitchell's mental attitude towards the Holy Roller leader, would create any prejudice against the defendant in the talesman's mind should he be accepted as a juror."[38] The third day also saw much "legal quibbling," with each side accusing the other of trying to influence the jurymen already in the box with "statements of the case adroitly presented in the guise of questions on examination."[39] Miller also objected to epithets used by Shipley about Creffield, such as "brute," and this was sustained; when Frater did allow an objection it was usually the prosecution's protests that were upheld.[40] At one stage he called a halt and held a private conference with the lawyers, asking them to shorten their questions and reduce the rancour. The sources are inconsistent on whether this had an effect, but on the whole it would seem that questioning did not become any briefer.[41]

A good many of the talesmen knew about the case and had an opinion on it. The newspapers report more than thirty men being disqualified. Some objected to capital punishment,[42] and as already noted at least one man was prejudiced against the defence of insanity. One man initially passed for cause was removed simply because he was part Indian, although he had served on juries for trials of lesser offences the previous week.[43] But most of those removed were disqualified because they had decided opinions on what Mitchell had done. Many thought Mitchell had done the right thing. The *Star* thought it remarkable that "so many men believe that circumstances can arise in which a man is justified in taking the law into his own hands."[44] On Monday, June 25, for example, six men were excused because they thought Mitchell had been right to kill Creffield, and two others because they thought that "a man was at times justified in taking the law into his own hands."[45]

Those who were retained tended to be like P.E. Fisher, a Seattle druggist who thought that people should never be allowed to take the law into their own hands. Similarly, John Dore was passed for cause, having asserted his impartiality in a way that could not have pleased the defence lawyers; he was reported to have said that "if he were to trade places with Mitchell he would rather have a more partial juror than he himself was likely to prove."[46] The Harvard-educated newspaperman and son of a well-known Seattle lawyer was later quickly removed by the defence when it came time for peremptory challenges. When the defence objected to men like Fisher, they were invariably passed by Frater, who was of course right to do so, for their views were precisely in accordance with the law. A further ten men were excused on Tuesday, June 26, for having an opinion, and others were likely excluded on the final two days as well, although the press reports are not as full for the later stages as they had been earlier. Most of these were men who thought Mitchell was justified and were therefore challenged by the prosecution, although some were equally convinced that Mitchell should be found guilty.[47] Of those who were excused, two said their wives had told them "to be sure and acquit Mitchell," and another said he was afraid to serve because his friends "told him that he ought to be tarred and feathered if he came home without acquitting Mitchell."[48] The jury selection process shows both that the debate over Mitchell's case in the weeks after May 7 had indeed engaged the populace generally, and that Mitchell's supporters had won that debate.

The prosecution did not always get its way. We have seen that the defence was successful with Compton, the man who did not care for the insanity defence, and Frater refused to disqualify C.G. Swanson, of Vashon Island, who rather confusingly said that if what he had heard about Creffield was true he deserved to die, but that he could not say whether Mitchell was justified in killing him, and that he would abide by the court's instructions to decide on the evidence. Swanson was later the first man to be peremptorily challenged by the prosecution. According to the *Oregonian*, Miller thought Swanson had "strong convictions" that Mitchell was innocent and had "quickly modified" his views under questioning in order not to be disqualified.[49] The prosecution also failed in a challenge of M.F. White, a former police magistrate who "declared unequivocally that under like circumstances he would probably have shot Creffield."[50] But this happened at the end of Wednesday's session, at the point that the special venire had been exhausted and men were being brought in from other courtrooms, and Frater was probably getting tired of all the wrangling. One way to speed up the process was to force the parties to exercise their peremptories, and Mackintosh immediately did so on White.

One unusual aspect of this jury selection was noted by the *Post-Intelligencer* – each side had the reverse of what it normally wanted in jury selection. Generally the prosecution liked people who had already formed an opinion, presumably because that opinion was likely to be that the defendant was guilty. Here it wanted men with no views. Conversely, while the defence usually wanted people who knew nothing of the case, here it wanted well-informed jurors.[51]

The process of questioning talesmen for cause went on throughout the four days of jury selection, but from the afternoon of the second day, Tuesday, it was joined by peremptory challenges, Frater having by then passed twelve men for cause. The prosecution had the first peremptory, the defence then had two, the prosecution another one, and so on. When a juror was removed by peremptory, a further round of questioning for cause began as the vacated spot was filled. Sometimes the first new talesman was accepted, on other occasions it took much longer. When the prosecution started by getting rid of Swanson, for example, six men were questioned before his place was filled; four had opinions on the case, one objected to capital punishment, and the one passed for cause had "talked of the case" but had no opinion.[52]

In all, the defence used just eight peremptories, the prosecution five. The former tended to dismiss men who had strongly voiced views against taking the law into one's own hands, such as Fisher, or men from outside the city, such as G.W. French, an Enumclaw "dairyman," and Thomas Olin, a civil engineer from Preston. As already noted, they also removed the best-educated juror, Dore, who had fiercely asserted his impartiality, and one Simpson, a barber from Kent, according to the *Times* because of a "cold-blooded indifference in his demeanour"; it did not want anybody without "much capability of emotion." The prosecution, of course, eliminated people who had shown sympathy for Mitchell but nonetheless claimed they could decide the case on the evidence, such as Swanson. It also got rid of White, who had so clearly shown sympathy to Mitchell, and one W.I. Evans, perhaps because as a real family man – he had five sons and seven daughters – he would favour the defence of family argument, or perhaps because he had confessed in his examination that he was "not anxious to be here."[53]

Jury selection, expected to take at least a week, unexpectedly ended on Thursday, June 28, "at a moment when all hope of securing a jury had been abandoned."[54] This was especially surprising because the Wednesday had seen the use of five peremptories – four by the defence and one by the prosecution to add to the one it had used at the end of Tuesday – and a lot of slogging to replace the men removed, interspersed with much argument between the lawyers. Twelve peremptories were left, and the prospect of more argument beckoned. But things moved much more quickly on Thursday. The defence used four more peremptories, the prosecution three, and each time either the first or second man questioned in an attempt to fill the space was accepted for cause. At 4:30 p.m., when everyone expected a peremptory challenge, Morris announced that he and Shipley were happy with what they had, and Miller immediately concurred, giving up one remaining peremptory. The result was that seven of the twelve who finally served were selected on the last day. It was really the defence that decided to settle for what it had, for it had four peremptories left, the prosecution only one. It may have been, of course, that Morris and Shipley were simply content with the twelve, and that was their public posture. However, although this is only speculation, the defence likely also made a tactical decision. By this time Frater, the press, and the jurors in the box must have been getting tired of it all, and it was time to move on. The more avid "law and order" types had been removed, and Morris was no doubt confident, given his past record, the clear evidence of public sympathy for his client, and his courtroom skills, that he could deliver an acquittal if the jurymen were willing to be swayed by him.

The jurymen chosen varied in age, occupation, and social status. Two had been passed on the first day of selection and made it all the way through. Melville H. Ring, who was elected foreman, was a mail collector with the Seattle Post Office; the *Times* thought him "middle-aged, intelligent and business-like."[55] Unfortunately he was one of the men about which little was reported during the questioning, presumably because he said nothing of interest, which was why he was not challenged. Francis M.

Townsend was a foreman with the Seattle water department; like Ring he was "middle-aged" and was also noted to be "black moustached, stern and quiet." Three were selected on the Tuesday. L.F. Jones was a farmer or rancher from Enumclaw, a rural community east of Seattle, who was beginning to go grey. Fred Clinton was a cook who lived at Chautauqua on Vashon Island and generally worked the steamers that plied Puget Sound; he was "short, swarthy and firm." William Howard kept a saloon "in the lower part of the city"; since it doubled as a hotel he may well have been involved in more than one aspect of the vice trade.

As noted above, the other seven all came from those examined on the last day. Walter S. Perkins was a "farmer and mill hand" from Brighton Beach. George W. Arnold was a painter and grocer, and he was joined by another tradesman, John W. Bovee, a paperhanger. James R. Hall worked as a "finisher" for Fritch and Company, paving and concrete contractors. Milo O. Rex was referred to as a restaurateur in the newspapers, but the city directory lists him as a waiter. Rex was the only juror identified as married, although many others must have been as well. The final two members were H.E. Start, a rancher from Vashon Island, and Clyde Wetmore of Bothell, described both as a "street car man" and as a clerk.

It was therefore in most respects a homogenous group of men, which was perhaps fortunate for them given that they were immediately sequestered in a hotel. They were, of course, all men, all Caucasian, and Anglo-Saxon names were predominant. They seem to have been largely tradesmen, small businessmen, and farmers, representative of the respectable upper-working and lower-middle classes. There were no professionals,[56] and assessment records show no obviously wealthy men. Even the "rancher" Jones had stock worth only $120 in 1909, while foreman Ring's personal property was assessed at just $20.[57] Indeed, all those we know about were men of modest means, with the possible exception of Howard.[58] While only Ring, Townsend, and Jones were identified as being in their forties, many of the others were probably middle-aged also. Half the members hailed from within the then limits of Seattle proper, with two from Vashon Island in Puget Sound and three others from suburban towns that would shortly be incorporated into the city. Only Jones was a rural representative, from the farming community of Enumclaw, across Lake Washington. Mitchell's jurors almost all had some courtroom experience. Ironically given the trouble taken to get extra men in, eleven of the twelve came from the men drawn in the regular way in May for the June session; only one came from the special venire of sixty men.[59] This meant they had been in court the whole of the previous week, and in that time all eleven of them had sat. Ring, Jones, Townsend, and Clinton had sat on four cases, Bovee on two, and the rest on one each. The only "rookie" was the saloonkeeper Howard.

THE PROSECUTION CASE

Nobody expected the prosecution case to take long, and it did not.[60] The opening address, the examination and cross-examination of eleven witnesses, the presentation of three exhibits, and some legal arguments were all completed on Friday, June 29. There were no surprises for the spectators in the packed courtroom or for the many who could not get a seat but stayed and thronged the courthouse hall.[61] But the day was certainly not without drama, for it featured the public's first glance of the grieving widow, and it also saw the first skirmishes between the lawyers over what kind of evidence could be introduced.

The trial proper began with a ten-minute opening address by Miller, which simply recounted the events of May 7. It was a "prosaic presentation of the facts of the killing," though of course the *Times* saw the low-key, unemotional statement, which deliberately avoided any reference to Mitchell's motive, as evidence of Miller "prosecuting this case in his most savage manner."[62] There followed six witnesses. Dr Emil Bories, the physician who was called to the scene and performed the autopsy, mostly testified about the medical details relating to the cause of death, as did Dr Francis M. Carroll, the King County coroner.[63] John Tuchten, a jeweller; John Whalley, an insurance broker; Dr W.G. Capp; and boot black Peter Wooley all gave evidence as well. None of these people had seen the shot fired but all had responded more or less immediately to hearing it. Between them they filled in the story of what had happened in the few minutes between the shooting and the arrest of Mitchell. The prosecution also presented two exhibits – the bullet and the gun. All these witnesses were cross-examined by defence lawyers, but only to bring out two points – that Creffield had died instantly and that Mitchell had neither been agitated nor made any attempt to escape.

The most interesting testimony in the morning was Tuchten's. He said that when he got to the scene – he was the first there, having been walking on the other side of the street to the Creffields – George Mitchell was "looking at the body with a cigar in his mouth." No doubt the prosecution wanted to elicit this piece of evidence to show the cool, calm, and even cold-blooded demeanour of the killer. Its effect was somewhat diminished by the confusion Tuchten showed on cross-examination; he had to explain that he was very excited at the time. More importantly, at one point during his testimony, Maud Creffield was brought into court so that he could identify her as the woman who had been with Creffield. Why the prosecutors thought this necessary is not clear, for nobody was going to deny her presence. Perhaps they wanted to show the jury the consequences of Mitchell's act – widowhood. Maud made a dramatic entrance, emerging from Frater's chambers in widow's weeds and standing defiantly in the courtroom. The *Times*, of course, could not resist the opportunity: her eyes, it said, were "blazing with the fire which seems to burn in the look of every one of the women who believed and still believe that . . . Creffield was . . . Joshua."[64]

These six witnesses took up the morning. There was much more drama in the afternoon, when Maud Creffield took the stand for an hour and a quarter. At Miller's request she identified Mitchell as the shooter and recounted the few minutes after the shooting. When she identified Mitchell she was almost overcome with emotion, although there was nonetheless "fire" in her voice, and on another occasion she "swayed dizzily in the witness chair." When asked to get out of the box and demonstrate how she had seized Mitchell she "practically fell in to Mr Miller's arms and almost sank to her knees from weakness." The contrast between her demeanour and Mitchell's was marked; the defendant sat "stolidly" beside his lawyers, staring at Maud, the only sign of emotion his restless fingers.[65]

The prosecution goal was to have Maud Creffield present an account of the killing of her husband that was straightforward in tone if dramatic in effect, but the defence cross-examination made it clear that its principal tactic would be to get evidence before the jury about the background to the case. For those in the know, the defence had already done this in the morning, in questioning Bories and Whalley. Bories was asked if he had seen Maud Creffield remove any letters from her dead husband's pockets, and although he did not know for sure his answers seemed to indicate that she had likely done so. These were presumably the letters written to Creffield from his Oregon adherents in the early months of 1906, the ones for which the empty envelopes had been discovered. It was an oblique reference to the Oregon background, but this was all that Bories could have known about it. Whalley had testified that he found Maud Creffield talking to the dead body of her husband, and on cross-examination Morris asked him what she was saying. Again, the purpose was to introduce evidence about the Creffield sect, in this case presumably about her belief in Creffield's immortality and divinity. The prosecution objected to the question, likely on the ground that it was irrelevant, and Frater sustained the objection.

When he cross-examined Maud Creffield, Morris was rather more direct in going after testimony about the events preceding May 7, 1906. He first asked her when she had married Creffield, and when she referred to the April 1906 marriage in Seattle he asked her if she had been married to him before. Frater sustained an objection to the question on the ground that it was irrelevant and because it had not been touched on in direct examination. Morris tried another tack, eliciting from Maud an admission that she had known Mitchell for several years, and then asking if anything had happened to make her think he posed a danger to Creffield. When she answered "Not in Seattle," Morris, with "a triumphant ring" in his voice, asked about any time "previous to Seattle." Miller was out of his chair in a flash, and Frater again sustained his objection. Morris' final attempt to bring in the background had an air of slapstick about it. He asked Maud if her husband was "ever known by the name of Joshua." Miller was up again, saying that Morris ought "to know better than to act that way." When Morris replied that he was not as smart as Miller, the riposte was quick: "You wouldn't ask such a question as that if you were."[66] Shortly thereafter Morris gave up, having tried for an hour and a half, and Maud was dismissed. Although none of the reports mentioned what they were, Shipley had asked some questions also, which were objected to and drew a warning from Frater about asking questions known to be improper and then withdrawing them as soon as an objection was made.

The *Times* reported little of this and claimed that Morris had been lenient with Maud and that his forbearance was a good tactic, for "he would have prejudiced the jury had he pressed her."[67] But clearly Morris forbore because Frater made him; he later admitted that his feelings towards Maud that day were far from gentle. He and Shipley were concerned that some attempt at revenge would be made by Creffield's adherents, and they watched her very closely as she walked from the witness stand, concerned lest she had a revolver.[68] Most importantly, Frater had prevented any discussion of events prior to May 7, 1906, other than the marriage. He did so on the ground that they were irrelevant, and in that he was right. All that mattered was whether Mitchell had fired the shot that day, unprovoked and in no danger from Creffield. Questions about the background went to motive, and motive was irrelevant. It might help the prosecution in a different case to establish motive, but here it had no need of such help.

The rest of the day was taken up largely with police witnesses. Arresting Officer LeCount, Detective Sergeant Charles Tennant, Inspector D.F. Willard, and Captain John Sullivan all testified, as did Louis Sefrit, the *Times* journalist who had interviewed Mitchell at the police station. LeCount said that Mitchell had been cool and collected when arrested and had said, "I have only done my duty."[69] Tennant and Willard reported on the statements they had taken from Mitchell at the police station; Sullivan did likewise and also introduced the state's final exhibit, the telegram sent to Victor Hurt. All these witnesses were cross-examined, although very briefly so, and we do not know on what lines. Sefrit gave testimony similar to LeCount's – that Mitchell had said that "he had only done what was right, what duty had called him to do."[70] Morris tried again to bring up the past, asking Sefrit what his next question had been. Presumably he hoped that it had been a request for Mitchell to explain why it was his duty, and the next question would have been about Mitchell's reply. But Miller objected immediately, and another avenue was closed down.

It was a good day for the prosecutors, who had done what Mackintosh told the press the evening before they would do: "prove that the act of George Mitchell in killing Creffield was premeditated murder."[71] The prosecution had prevented any suggestion that Mitchell might have been justified from being implicitly aired through discussion of the Oregon background to the killing. The defence would have to try to get that in through its own case. "It remains to be seen whether a jury, sworn to see that men are punished who violate the laws, will prove faithful to their trust," noted one weekly.[72]

IO

The Trial of George Mitchell, Part 2

THE UNWRITTEN LAW

THE DEFENCE CASE BEGAN on Monday, July 2, and lasted a total of six days, until Monday, July 9 (the court did not sit on the Fourth of July or Sunday, July 8).[1] Closing speeches were made and the verdict delivered on July 10. Thirty witnesses took the stand,[2] although a number of them left it very quickly because they were not allowed to give the testimony that Morris and Shipley wanted. With the courtroom packed and overflowing every day, some spectators standing jammed against the walls until Frater stopped this practice, and with the searing summer heat making for short tempers, the proceedings were at times filled with tension. That tension was no doubt increased by the continued inflammatory reporting of the *Times* and, to a slightly lesser extent, the *Star*. Typical of the former was its issue of July 1, which contained a long article on the forthcoming defence case, in which Creffield – the "masquerading libertine" – was yet again excoriated.[3]

To be successful with the unwritten law the defence had to convince the jury that this was not a simple case about one man who cold-bloodedly shot another – the prosecution's version of the story. Rather, it was a case about duty to family, about the natural, understandable, and, most of all, justifiable, instinct to avenge or protect a woman. At the same time, as we noted in the previous chapter, a trial is a legal proceeding, governed by procedural rules and constrained by the limits set by substantive legal doctrines. Thus to fully understand the defence case we need to set the narrative of the proceedings against both the version of the story that the defence wanted the jury to accept and the limits that the law set on how that story could be told. To know why certain witnesses were brought forward, why they said what they did, and why the lawyers engaged in numerous arguments about the admissibility of evidence, we need first to understand the legal strategy of the defence, which employed the unwritten law under the guise of the defence of insanity.

THE INSANITY DEFENCE AND THE UNWRITTEN LAW

There were two, intimately related, defence strategies. Overtly, the defence sought to make out a valid insanity defence; the elements of that case will be discussed shortly. The more important, covert, strategy was to convince the jurors that Mitchell had been justified in removing from the earth a man whose "crimes" against morality and the families of Mitchell and others were so heinous that he deserved to die. Where the two strategies intersected, and where the latter relied crucially on the former, was in getting before the jury evidence about Creffield's teachings and activities. The history of the Creffield sect was irrelevant as direct evidence. All it did was show that Creffield was an evil man, and it was no defence to murder to say that the victim deserved to die. The defence argument was that it was knowledge of Creffield's activities and their consequences, and particularly knowledge about what had happened to Donna Starr and what would happen to Esther Mitchell, that had led to Mitchell's insanity. Awareness of the danger that Esther faced had driven Mitchell to his delusion that God ordered him to kill Creffield. The defence attempted to get before the jury evidence of the insanity of Creffield's followers, of family destruction, and of alleged sex by having witnesses say what they had supposedly told Mitchell about all these. Thus the insanity defence was necessary as the device by which evidence in support of justifiable homicide was admitted. As the *Star* writer perceptively observed, the trial would see "a studied, skillful and persistent effort on the part of the attorneys for Mitchell" to get the jury to "consider" evidence about Creffield's character.[4] As the *Star* also noted after the trial, Morris and Shipley did not think anybody would take the insanity defence seriously; they hoped rather "to give to the jurors some excuse for acquitting their client."[5] Pleading temporary insanity was what one historian has termed the "classic method" of "opening the door for proof of sexual misconduct" in unwritten law cases. As here, the door was typically opened through an argument that knowledge of the adultery or seduction had driven the defendant temporarily insane.[6] Morris and Shipley undoubtedly knew all this; by June 1, if not much earlier, they had decided that "temporary insanity, superinduced by continual worry over the humiliation and ruin of his sisters, will be the defense."[7]

The unwritten law claim had thus to be made under the cloak of the defence of insanity. As in most other states during this period, the defence was part of the common law, not statute law, and like all states but one it was based on what are known as the *McNaughtan* rules, laid down in an 1843 English case,[8] which states that "to establish a defence on the ground of insanity it must be clearly proved that, at the time of committing the act, the accused was labouring under such a defect of reason, from disease of the mind, as not to know the nature and quality of the act he was doing, or, if he did know it, that he did not know he was doing what was wrong." This was not a test for whether somebody was "insane" or "mentally unbalanced" or anything of that ilk; it was, and is, a test of criminal responsibility, an exercise in drawing the line between those people who will be held culpable for their actions, whether or not they are "insane," and those who will not be made culpable because they lack the requisite mental element, the *mens rea*. Many people could be considered mentally ill by the medical profession and still be capable of knowing what they were doing was wrong. Similarly, others might seem rational on a wide range of matters but be insane in the context of the particular criminal act; the law did not, as it had once done, require a person to be totally impaired.[9] The *McNaughtan* test, because it was a doctrine about criminal responsibility, was also not concerned with degrees of culpability; a defendant was either guilty or insane at the time of the crime. There was no middle ground.

Three further points about the insanity defence should be noted. First, whether or not a defendant had a disease of the mind such that he or she did not know right from wrong was always a question of fact left to the jury, like all other significant determinations in a criminal trial. It was not a matter for experts.[10] Second, another aspect of the *McNaughtan* rules was that everybody was presumed to be sane, and thus the onus was on the defence to raise the issue of insanity and prove it to the satisfaction of the jury. There were some differences among the states, but in Washington the rule was clear: the defence had to prove insanity by the preponderance of the evidence, not merely raise a doubt as to the defendant's sanity.

Third, and finally, there was at this time only a slowly emerging sense that there were experts in the field whose views should carry more weight than those of other witnesses. Doctors with no claim to specialized training or experience were just as much "experts" as asylum superintendents or other "alienists." Moreover, although those with medical training were accorded more weight than those lacking such training, any witness could give evidence about insanity. There was, however, a distinction between the lay and the medical witness. The former had to provide a foundation for any opinion offered from his or her own experience of the defendant. That witness had to say what he or she had observed the person doing or heard him or her saying; in appropriate circumstances the witness could then be asked his or her opinion as to sanity. Those qualified as experts could likewise give an opinion as to sanity if he or she had examined the defendant. But the expert could also provide opinion testimony based on hypothetical questions posed by counsel, without any experience of the defendant. The hypothetical questions, of course, always mirrored the facts of the particular case, facts counsel wanted the jury to accept.[11]

The defence of insanity was a subject of considerable controversy throughout the nineteenth and early twentieth centuries, controversy that engaged different camps within the medical profession, saw science and religion virulently opposed at times, and that often pitted doctors against lawyers in the courtroom.[12] Those controversies do not, for the most part, concern us, largely because the Mitchell trial saw no debates between medical experts about the meaning and causes of insanity. But three aspects of the nineteenth-century social, legal, and medical history of the defence are relevant. First, by 1900 it was accepted in almost all states, including Washington, that an insane delusion could constitute a disease of the mind sufficient to acquit provided the defendant was driven to act by force of that delusion. This was a more expansive view of delusions than had been accepted in *McNaughtan* and meant that people rational on a whole range of issues could be found insane with reference to the particular act, provided they were impelled to act by the delusion. That delusion had to be such that it "controll[ed] his will and judgment," overwhelmed the defendant, prevented him from knowing right from wrong.[13] As we shall see, this was the central pillar of Mitchell's insanity defence.

Second, while there were disagreements on a host of issues, by the turn of the century all specialists in the field (the word psychiatrist was not then employed, terms such as neurologist or alienist being the ones used) shared certain beliefs about the causes of mental illness. They agreed that it was a disease of the brain, and as such a physical phenomenon. They also agreed that external environmental factors, such as grief or great anxiety, could either make the disease worse or cause it in the first place. Outside causes brought on insanity by acting on the body and thereby injuring the brain. People could also have a hereditary predisposition to the degenerate weakness that caused mental illness, and these environmental factors would be more likely to cause damage to the brain in them than to those not so predisposed. The belief in heredity, greatly strengthened following the Guiteau case, meant that judges were generally willing to accept evidence about the insanity of relatives, and not just parents and siblings but also uncles and cousins.[14]

Third, by the close of the nineteenth century the insanity defence was the frequent target of criticism by those who saw it as a manipulable device by which murderers in particular avoided their just desserts. By the 1880s it was popularly known as the "insanity dodge," a technique often used as "a formal justification for the acquittal of obviously culpable yet sympathetic defendants."[15] Worse for many critics was that these cases involved temporary insanity, so that the acquitted avoided any form of incarceration at all, even committal to an asylum. Of course, many of those "culpable yet sympathetic defendants" were men who invoked the unwritten law, who killed their wives' lovers, or their unmarried female relatives' seducers. The unwritten law was under attack from the late nineteenth century, but it was still alive, as this case and a contemporaneous one from New York, the trial of Harry Thaw for the murder of society architect Stanford White, demonstrate.[16] The insanity defence was also seen as favouring those classes which could afford the expensive medical testimony and legal representation required to make it effective. There is evidence of the increasing suspicion accorded the defence in Washington; some twenty years before the Mitchell case, Washington Supreme Court justice Orange Jacobs declared: "The world has had quite enough of that kind of insanity which commences just as the sight of the slayer ranging along the barrel of a pistol marks a vital spot on the body of the victim and ends as soon as the bullet has sped on its fatal mission."[17] Such sentiments grew stronger over time.

OPENING ARGUMENTS

The defence case began with an opening address to the jury delivered by Silas Shipley. The choice of Shipley certainly indicates that while Morris had the greater reputation, his partner was a formidable advocate also. He may have been chosen because the address dealt at length with the insanity defence, and Shipley seems to have taken on the responsibility for mastering the technicalities of that law – it was he who conducted the examinations of insanity experts. In a speech of about three hours, which took up the whole of the morning and part of the afternoon session on Monday, July 2, Shipley made clear the structure of the defence argument. He began bluntly enough by not denying that Mitchell had fired the shot, stating that his actions were not "controlled by a mind in the possession of its reasoning faculties to such an extent as to apprehend the true relation which he bore to his surroundings."[18] The defence would show that when Mitchell shot Creffield he believed that "he was performing an act for which he had been especially selected by God." He had had the belief for months and had expressed it to a number of people who had tried to dissuade him of it. Mitchell's insanity claim was therefore exactly the same as that put forward, unsuccessfully, by the assassin of President Garfield a quarter of a century earlier.[19] Shipley insisted that Mitchell had not been generally insane but the victim of this one insane delusion. In keeping with the law delineated above, this delusion was the "disease of the mind" from which he suffered, and it was also responsible for his not knowing that it was wrong for him to kill Creffield. Shipley used the evidence that the state had emphasized about Mitchell's cool demeanour: the defence would show that not only was he not agitated but also that "he was dead to any fear of punishment" because "he failed to apprehend that he was amenable to man's laws, believing . . . that he had only done what was right, what duty called him to do and that he could not be punished." Only an insane delusion "could account for Mitchell's strange composure and fearlessness after he killed Creffield and [had] been taken into custody."[20]

Shipley delineated three aspects of the insane delusion claim. First, there was Mitchell's belief that Creffield posed a real danger to Esther's sexual integrity. Knowledge of Creffield's general licentiousness, of the adultery with Donna Starr, and of his supposed designs on Esther "blunted" Mitchell's mind "to aught else except his married sister's fate and the moral doom which hovered over Esther." This was not consistent with the story Mitchell had first told the press – that Creffield had already seduced Esther. The story was changed, we think, for two reasons. First, the prosecution could bring a witness – Esther herself – to deny any seduction. Second, the defence probably decided that a defendant who sought to save his sister would garner more sympathy than one who had revenged her.

The second leg of the argument was that with Mitchell's mind so affected, he became convinced that he had received a message from God to kill Creffield. Many witnesses would testify to this, and to the visitation from God would be added Mitchell's belief that he had also been visited by the spirit of his mother, who warned him of the "influence" that Creffield would exert over his sisters. This claim was made the more credible by George being said to have a belief in spiritualism, which in turn showed that he, like other members of his family, had a capacity for religious extremism.

The third and final piece of the argument was that there was some tendency to insanity in the Mitchell family, that George's mind was "tainted by an inherited blight." By the end of May Morris had been confident that the defence could show insanity in the Mitchell family,[21] and Shipley now signalled that this card would be an important one. Although such evidence was admissible, in line with the general belief in hereditary insanity, not all courts allowed it. Knowing this, and fearing that such evidence might not be allowed in, Shipley devoted a good deal of time to the Mitchell family history. He detailed the religiosity and eccentricity of Charles Mitchell and said that this would be shown to be a "family characteristic." Fred Mitchell was said to be similar to his father, religious and stubborn, and to have once attempted suicide, and of course the sisters all showed the same tendencies. In this part of his speech Shipley had to be careful, for he was mounting a defence of temporary, not permanent or continuing, insanity. Thus while George was generally different – had "never professed religion" – he was nonetheless susceptible to the same kind of delusions given the extreme stimuli provided by Creffield. The strategy was well thought out, for it dovetailed with the general backdrop to the whole Creffield story – religious extremism. If his sisters could fall prey to religious lunacy, so too, briefly, could George Mitchell. As the *Post-Intelligencer* put it, the defence intended to show that "this action of Mitchell was by no means simply one of revenge." Rather, "it was a result of the same religious frenzy which . . . has characterized his sisters and his father to a degree."[22]

Shipley did much more than delineate the structure of the insanity argument. He also laid the groundwork for the real defence appeal: that the jury should acquit because Mitchell had done right. This covert defence required full knowledge of the Creffield story, and here the lawyers had a problem, for they knew that attempts to introduce that story would be resisted by the prosecution lawyers and that Frater would side with them;[23] on a number of occasions during jury selection he had said that evidence simply going to Creffield's character would be excluded unless it could be shown to have affected Mitchell's mind. The evidence would have to be brought in through the back door, through the recounting of supposed conversations with Mitchell, but that meant that not all the witnesses would be able to testify; those who had not talked to Mitchell would likely not be allowed to say anything about Creffield. Thus when he dealt with the first leg of the insane delusion argument – Mitchell's knowledge about the relationship between Creffield and his sisters – Shipley went into great detail about what the *Times* called "the awful revelation of baseness." As one Oregon newspaper noted perceptively, "nothing that could possibly sway the emotion of the jury . . . [was] omitted."[24] It was not evidence, of course, that a jury ought to have paid attention to, for it did not come from sworn witnesses testifying from their personal knowledge, but it was better than nothing. Jurymen and spectators, especially the "many women and girls of tender years who struggled for a point of vantage in the sweltering crowd which jammed the courtroom," listened intently to it all.

Mitchell's defence was both similar to and different from most unwritten law cases. It was similar in that a largely sham insanity defence was set up both to introduce otherwise inadmissible evidence and to give jurors a formal reason to acquit.[25] It was different in that Shipley made no overt mention of the notion that Creffield deserved to be killed. Earlier trial judges had "tolerated discussion of the unwritten law" by defence counsel, even as they repudiated it in their own jury instructions.[26] It seems reasonable, and consistent with the idea that the unwritten law defence was used less frequently through the late nineteenth century, to assume that overt mention of it became less acceptable over time, and that by 1906 judges such as Frater simply would not have allowed any such appeal to the jury at any stage of the trial. Indeed, Frater had said as much at the earlier bail hearing.

DEFENCE WITNESSES: TELLING THE CREFFIELD STORY

Following Shipley's address, the rest of the afternoon of July 2 saw some of the major players in the drama – Esther Mitchell, Donna Starr, and O.V. Hurt – give evidence, along with Alpheus Mills of Newberg. Donna Starr was supposed to testify first, but she was not found when called. She had been reluctant to go to court in the morning and had to be brought in by a sheriff's deputy. Having returned to her hotel during the lunch recess, she stayed there. Frater issued a bench warrant for her, and two deputies brought her from the hotel this time.[27] She had come to Seattle shortly before the trial, with Burgess and the defence team confident that she would do what she could to help George. But one meeting with Esther was all it took to reconfirm Donna's faith; as the lawyers were busy selecting jurors on June 26, the sisters "went through some of the forms of Creffield's teachings at the Stevens Hotel."[28] Donna no longer wished to testify.

In her absence Esther Mitchell took the stand. She was clearly an unwilling, albeit compliant, witness, but said little beyond acknowledging that George was her brother and stating that she had first met Creffield in Portland some six years previously. Most of the questions seem to have been about Fred Mitchell, and after some prompting she told the court that he had attempted suicide in 1903. It is surprising that she was allowed to answer the questions about Fred, for, as we shall see shortly, the prosecution consistently and successfully objected to questions going to hereditary insanity. However, it may not have seen Esther's testimony as evidence on insanity at all. What is most important about Esther's appearance is not what she was asked, but what she was not asked. The defence did not question her about her relations with Creffield, sexual or otherwise. Morris had had a meeting with her in Frater's chambers the previous Friday,[29] and that may well have decided him to steer clear of the subject and switch the defence line to George wishing to protect Esther from future harm. In any event, when he and Shipley did not ask about sex with Creffield, Esther was deprived of the opportunity to deny any seduction. And since the matter had not been covered by the examination-in-chief, the prosecutors could not ask her about it on cross-examination.

Esther's brief and innocuous appearance was a disappointment for those looking for sensation. Yet the fact that she was there at all, with her brother in the dock, was great theatre, and the cheerleading *Times* made much of it. It described George Mitchell listening to his sister's evidence, "nervously interlacing his toil-knotted fingers and biting his lips until they showed white, in a vain effort to repress the volcano of feeling which surged in his breast." And it reminded readers of why George should feel that way: "It was to save his sister from being totally ruined by the man who held her in the hollow of his hand ... that the young farmer boy took the law into his own hands and placed himself in jeopardy because he loved her." The terrible tragedy, of course, was that Esther did not care at all. She had "no appreciation of the great love" George had for her, and "for all she cares her brother may pay the penalty which the law exacts for the crime of murder." She would not mourn him, although she did mourn the death of Creffield. Despite the prosaic nature of her evidence, people "hung upon every word which Esther Mitchell spoke" and also "turned and craned their necks to better see this child who ... would see her brother punished for what he has done in her behalf."[30]

The next witness was Alpheus Mills, a Newberg fruit merchant who had known the Mitchell family when they lived in Yamhill County. He was called out of turn to cover the gap created by Donna Starr's failure to appear. He was asked one question about whether he had noticed any odd or eccentric behaviour in Charles Mitchell but never got the chance to answer it. The prosecution immediately objected and, after a long argument in the absence of the jury, Frater sustained the objection and Mills was dismissed. Unfortunately, the press reports reproduce very little of the substance of the argument, but they do suggest that Miller's objection was to questions about oddities or eccentricities. He conceded that evidence showing actual insanity in the family might be acceptable, but not something so vague as "oddities."

By the time these arguments were disposed of Donna Starr had arrived. She said more than Esther Mitchell, but not much more. She was asked to identify three letters which the defence entered as exhibits; they included a letter she had written to Clarence and Hattie Starr in 1905 recanting her belief in Creffield, and the one she had left for Burgess when she went to Waldport in the middle of the night. She also testified about Fred's attempted suicide. Donna was sullen and hesitant, but it was conceded that she also carried herself with pride, despite the fact that all knew of the "disgrace" she had endured. The *Times* made much of an incident involving her two oldest children, whom she brought to court. One of them saw her uncle George, "ran to him and threw her tiny arms about his neck and shoulder," and then sat on his lap for a few seconds before the sheriff led her back to her mother in the judge's chambers.[31] The point, one assumes, was to contrast this idyllic family picture with the attitudes of the two sisters towards their brother on trial for his life.

The decision to have Esther and Donna testify at all requires some explanation, given how little they were asked and their known allegiance to Creffield. The defence probably had three reasons for doing so. First, they could both testify to brother Fred's attempted suicide, and thus begin to fix in the jury's mind the idea that George Mitchell might be susceptible to some degree of insanity. Second, not to have called the sisters might have seemed strange to the jury. They were at the centre of the defence case, and the jury would have expected to hear from them. Third, the sisters' reluctant appearance, and their refusal to help their brother, was implicit evidence of Creffield's evil influence. In this the *Times* was, as ever, willing to assist in making the case at the bar of public opinion. The day before it had run a long story on Creffield's adherents in general, and Esther in particular. They had been taught to regard non-believers as outcasts and thus were hostile to George Mitchell. Esther in particular was not to be judged by ordinary standards; she was "one of the few persons on earth whom the naturally prevailing rule of blood kinship" should persuade to help her brother, but she would not. The *Times* also added a new perspective on the affair that highlighted gender differences. It was women who had joined Creffield, and almost exclusively women who had remained faithful. Creffield's followers generally "are not mental heavyweights," and the women fared worse because "as in all religious teachings, particularly those which have to do with the emotions," women were more susceptible. Thus the *Times* bolstered the notion that a man had a duty to defend his family while depicting the women being defended as unable to take care of themselves.[32]

After Donna Starr came the man whose evidence would prove decisive – O.V. Hurt. His testimony absorbed the remainder of the afternoon and most of the following morning. It was a potent mixture, we believe, of truth, exaggerated truth, and fabrication. He told the story of his family's relationship with Creffield, much of which was probably accurate enough – although he testified to telling Mitchell that not only were there animal sacrifices but that there had been some discussion of sacrificing a little girl as well. This was nonsense, but it likely had a strong effect on the jury. He also strongly implied that his wife and daughter Mae had engaged in sex with Creffield. Hurt was allowed to say all this under the guise of recounting a long conversation he had with George Mitchell in Portland in late March. This conversation was supposedly the first full account Mitchell had received about the iniquities of the holy rollers, and its horror contributed to unbalancing his mind. It is with regard to this conversation that we think Hurt was tailoring his evidence to fit the law, for reasons we will soon explain.

Hurt did more than recount a harrowing tale of family breakdown, insanity, and immorality; he was also prepared to assist with other aspects of Mitchell's defence. He said that Mitchell "told me of his conversations with the spirits and of his conviction that he was selected by God to remove Creffield to a place where he could do no more harm." And to drive the point home for the slower jurors, he added that he had told Mitchell not to kill Creffield but that Mitchell did not listen, for he was "as crazy as his sisters." As the *Times* commented, Hurt "hewed closely to" the line sketched out by Shipley in his opening address.[33]

We have three reasons for thinking that Hurt's evidence contained some significant inventions. Neither the claim that he had recounted all the Creffield history to Mitchell nor the statement that Mitchell had talked about being ordered by God or the spirits to kill Creffield ring true. First, the latter is quite inconsistent with Mitchell's own statements to police and press in the days immediately after the murder; at that time he justified the killing in terms of simple revenge for what had happened to his sisters. If he had believed in a command from God he would surely have said so immediately afterwards, for the delusion must still have had him in its grip at that point. It is probably for this reason that the defence did not put George Mitchell on the stand. Had it done so Mackintosh and Miller would have been able to impeach his credibility by bringing in these prior inconsistent statements.[34]

Second, we doubt Hurt's suggestion that his conversation had a particular force, because it was the first time Mitchell had heard the full story of Creffield's doings. Such a meeting may have taken place, and Hurt may have given Mitchell an update on what Creffield had recently been doing – contacting followers and reviving the sect. But Mitchell had long known generally about Creffield. In November 1903 he went to Corvallis to take Esther away from the sect. He visited her in the BGAS Home and knew enough in early 1904 to send Esther east. And he knew plenty about the events of 1904 from his brother-in-law Burgess Starr.

Our third reason is a more impressionistic one. The story of the conversation is simply too pat, too well tailored to what the defence needed – to get the Creffield story into evidence and show that Mitchell was suffering from a delusion. It also dovetails too well with the testimony of other people keenly interested in securing an acquittal – Burgess Starr, Louis Hartley, and Ed Baldwin, among others, all testified to remarkably similar conversations with Mitchell. The similarity of what so many of the defence witnesses said was sufficiently obvious for some of the newspapers to comment on it, expressing in some cases a distinct touch of scepticism. The *Post-Intelligencer* noted that the phrase "'I told George Mitchell' is one of the commonest of the . . . trial," and "the readiness with which the witnesses use it testifies to their willingness to do what they can to save the prisoner from conviction." Contrived or not, it was effective, for it "quiets the objections of . . . Miller and allows the witness to continue his story without interruption."[35]

Hurt was not able to give his evidence uninterrupted, his appearance marked by constant and at times bitter battles between the lawyers. At one point the jury was sent out. At another Miller objected to the testimony about animal and child sacrifice, and Frater sustained the objection. The newspaper reports give us very little sense of what these arguments were about, but they probably concerned the relevance of questions that sought to have Hurt talk about Creffield and the sect outside the parameters of his supposed conversation with George Mitchell.[36] Whatever the cause, Morris became heated at one point, complaining of Frater's "obvious partiality and unfairness in his rulings" and talking about Mitchell's constitutional right to a fair trial.[37] Frater's sympathies were entirely with the prosecution, for he announced at another trial less than a week after Mitchell's had concluded that Mitchell was "clearly guilty of murder."[38] But he was likely not "antagonistic" towards the defence, as the *Times* claimed,[39] except in the sense that he applied the law correctly, refusing to allow the introduction of character evidence against the victim.

Despite all this, Hurt was able to say a good deal, and it was arresting testimony. The presentation was melodramatic and effective in equal measure. As he told the story, "the tears ... welled up in his sad old eyes" and at times he "halted and begged to be relieved from going into further details." The *Times* played this for all it was worth, throwing in references to the "horror" of the "human vampire" that was Creffield, to "conditions which would appall a Zola," and to the "immoral maelstrom" of involvement with the sect.[40] A common tactic in unwritten law trials was to appeal to the jurors' concerns about the integrity of their domestic life, and this is what Morris, through Hurt, did. If the family life of this solid, upright citizen could be so affected by an interloping religious fanatic, nobody's domestic idyll was safe.

Hurt's testimony was crucial. Several of the jurors were apparently obviously irritated by the interventions of the prosecution lawyers, and according to the *Corvallis Gazette,* "the jury was visibly affected by the recital of Hurt's domestic wrongs." One juror supposedly told the *Star* after the trial that from the time of Hurt's testimony, "there was never any doubt as to what the verdict would be." One of the state's lawyers admitted later that they had "been beaten ever since Hurt's testimony was given the jury" because it had exposed "Creffield's hideous crimes" and "turn[ed the] scale in [the] avenger's favor."[41]

Whether or not Hurt's evidence was as effective as these claims suggest, it had been a torrid few hours while he was on the stand. His emotionally told story, the bickering between the lawyers, a summer heat wave, and the crowded courtroom all made for tension, and at the end of the morning session on Tuesday, July 3, Frater began to show signs of it, declaring that after the noon recess only those who could find seats would be allowed in court for the afternoon. Those standing in the back aisle and perching on the windowsills reduced the air circulation too much. One result of this edict was that many spectators did not leave their seats at the recess, while others queued in the corridor to get the first available seat, staying there throughout the afternoon.

O.V. Hurt's testimony took up most of the morning of July 3, although there was time before the recess for a brief appearance by one of Mitchell's former employers to attest to his good character.[42] The afternoon session was taken up with testimony from Burgess Starr. Although his appearance was brief, the evidence he gave was very similar to Hurt's, in both presentation and content. Under the guise of a conversation with Mitchell he talked about his own and his family's relationship to Creffield, and about Mitchell claiming that he had received a divine command to kill Creffield, backed up by a request from his mother's spirit to do likewise. Starr insisted that Mitchell seemed "crazy" to him.[43] There were "wordy skirmishes" over some of Starr's evidence, most notably about his telling of a conversation he had supposedly had with Sarah Hurt in which the latter had told Starr that Creffield had "importuned" her "to procure Esther Mitchell for him" from the Portland home "for the purpose of bringing forth a second Christ." Not surprisingly, the prosecution fought bitterly against the admission of this testimony, and it is a puzzle why it was allowed in, unless it was also one of the things that Starr told George Mitchell. Like some of Hurt's evidence, it was also a somewhat unlikely tale; if Sarah Hurt would not talk to her husband, why would she tell such a story to Burgess Starr? Like Hurt, Starr was an emotional witness. As he was called on to "lay bare his family shame," he "wept during the telling," his tears falling "unreservedly." And Mitchell, who had to that point sat through the proceedings stoically, broke down and "laid his head on his arms and his shoulders shook with sobs."[44] Again, there was a clear appeal to domesticity or, rather, to the threat that hovered over it if men like Creffield were allowed to run rampant.

Miller's cross-examination of Starr elicited the fact that Mitchell had had the measles and been in hospital when their conversation occurred, and that he was "feverish and delirious." Miller also got Starr to admit that while Mitchell had said he would kill Creffield, he had said nothing about how he intended to do so. Miller asked Starr whether it was "commonplace" for him to hear death threats, and why, if he really believed Mitchell was "insane and dangerous," he did not inform the authorities. This was an obvious trap, and Starr tried to wriggle out of it, saying he did not believe that Mitchell would really do it, because "the latter had told him there would be no trouble, as he was commanded by God to remove Creffield." He must have been primed to give that rather convoluted answer, and it was a good one, both avoiding the trap of seeming to support the idea of killing Creffield, while driving home again the point about Mitchell's insanity.[45]

Starr's appearance concluded Tuesday's session, a tense and emotional one from which all participants would have the July 4 holiday to recover. The proceedings to this point had been marked by plenty of demonstrations of support for Mitchell, mostly from among the large group of women whose presence was frequently noted by both the *Times* and the *Star,* presumably because it indicated that Seattle womanhood was behind the man who was willing to risk all to protect his family. As Mitchell was brought into and taken out of the courtroom, the women crowded around him "to get close to the boy and impress upon him that they are his friends and support him in what he did." Mitchell also received daily "floral tributes" in his cell from different women, as well as flowers in the courtroom from a girl of about twenty, "well dressed and good to look upon." At the end of each session she approached Mitchell, shook his hand, said a few words, and gave him a bunch of roses. Mitchell seemed to enjoy the attention, in the afternoon wearing in the lapel of his coat one of the roses he had been given at the conclusion of the morning session. Adding to the mystery was that the young woman was clearly alone – no one knew who she was, and she refused to give a name. By July 9 the roses had changed to sweet peas, and on that date the *Times* could also report that her name was believed to be Corbett.[46]

Pro-Mitchell demonstrations were augmented by attacks on the prosecuting lawyers who were heckled on their way in and out of court. A "gray-haired lady" told Miller that he should be "ashamed of himself" for trying so hard to convict "a boy who only did a brother's duty in trying to defend his sisters against a reptile." Another "gray-haired mother" "hissed" at Miller: "Is it by convicting innocent boys who fight for the honor of their sisters that you get all your fine clothes?" Miller apparently responded that if he were the judge he would "clear all that rabble out of the courtroom."[47] Mitchell himself, no doubt under instruction, never said anything. The only spectator mentioned in the press who was known not to be a Mitchell supporter was Frank Hurt, who was seen several times in the courthouse corridors during the week.[48]

The rest day was used by the jurors to get out and about; accompanied by bailiffs, they took a trip to Lake Washington. The insanity issue was front and centre when the court reconvened on Thursday, July 5. Having laid the groundwork for why Mitchell, or any other man, might have been driven insane, and having presented testimony that suggested that Mitchell was suffering from a delusion, the defence now had to make the case that

Mitchell was likely to have had a disease of the mind and was susceptible to insanity, and for that it needed expert witnesses. Dr Arthur Crookall was called to the stand, a Seattle physician whose lack of specialized training in psychiatry was not a bar to giving evidence as an expert.[49] Morris wanted an opinion on whether Mitchell was likely to have been susceptible to hereditary insanity and asked a hypothetical question about whether somebody might be so susceptible if his family members had shown symptoms of insanity – the symptoms were those alleged to have been revealed by the conduct of Fred and Esther Mitchell and Donna Starr. It had to be a hypothetical question, for Crookall could not give an opinion about George Mitchell when he had not examined him. But Miller immediately objected that there was no evidence about those symptoms. Frater sustained the objection after a long argument between Miller and Shipley with the jury out. Unable to ask hypothetical questions related to the case he was defending, Morris had to be content with having Crookall answer general questions about the different forms of insanity and about the kinds of things that were known to drive a person insane.

The only other witness to testify on the morning of July 5 was another of Creffield's would-be assassins, Ed Baldwin, who gave his evidence in chief before lunch and was cross-examined afterwards. His testimony was not about the ruin of his family by Creffield, as told to George Mitchell, but directly about Mitchell. This time the conversation was supposed to have taken place on May 1, at the Corvallis train depot, when both were looking for Creffield to kill him. Mitchell told Baldwin to give it up, because it was Mitchell who had been selected by God for that duty. Baldwin tried hard to convince Mitchell that it was better for the older man, with fewer years to live, to do the deed, but to no avail. He also dutifully offered his opinion that "Mitchell was crazy at the time, as he would talk only on one subject, that of the harm done his sisters and the necessity of losing no time in carrying out what he believed was a divine injunction to kill Creffield."[50] Miller's cross-examination sought to undermine the assertion that Baldwin thought Mitchell crazy by asking him why he had not disarmed the young man.

Eight other people took the stand on Thursday afternoon,[51] including another employer testifying to Mitchell's general good character,[52] and two men from Newberg – J.J. Woods, a deputy sheriff, and Henry Morris, mayor. The latter two gave Mitchell a good character even though they had not seen him for several years, but the defence had really called them to talk about Charles Mitchell. This they were not able to do, Frater quickly sustaining Miller's objection. Two men who had seen Mitchell at the Albany train depot – John Catlin, a deputy sheriff, and George Van Drandt, an Albany hotelkeeper – testified that he had acted strangely on that occasion. Catlin said Mitchell had told him about God's command and that as a result he classified Mitchell as "crazy but harmless." When asked by Miller on cross-examination why, as an officer of the law, he had not done something about a crazy, armed man who said he was going to kill somebody, Catlin's response was that his twenty-five years of experience had taught him that "it does not do to arrest or search every man who acts kind of crazy."[53]

The most important witness of the afternoon was Louis Hartley, who, like Hurt and Starr, testified that he had told Mitchell about Creffield's history and the ruin of his family. Thus another example was presented to the jury of how Creffield was the serpent who invaded the Eden of the domestic hearth. Hartley also testified he had told Mitchell of his own failed attempts to kill Creffield, and that in turn Mitchell had asserted that God had ordered him to kill Creffield and therefore Hartley could not. Hartley, of course, had advised Mitchell, who he thought "utterly out of his mind," not to try to kill Creffield. Spelling it out for the jury, as Hurt had done, he said he told Mitchell that "he was as looney as my wife and daughter." The *Corvallis Times* thought the evidence of Hartley, and of Baldwin who preceded him, extremely important. Coming as it did from "elderly men of reserved and conservative aspect and manner," it "had a profound effect upon the jury." It was remarkable that "neither witness seemed to regard the shooting of Creffield as any greater offense than the killing of a mad dog."[54]

After Hartley, Mary Graham and William Gardner were called, but they were allowed to say little after prosecution objections. Gardner had wanted to offer his view of Mitchell's insanity, but this was not permitted. Probably encouraged by the defence team, he nonetheless spoke to the *Seattle Times* that evening, insisting that Mitchell was insane when he shot Creffield, the knowledge of what Creffield had done to his sisters being "enough to drive any man crazy." Mitchell "worried so much about the terrible thing that his mind was on nothing else. Upon that subject he was as insane as it was possible to be." Gardner had worked in a New York state asylum before moving to Oregon, and he claimed to draw on that experience for his assessment. But the intemperate Gardner rather gave it all away by insisting that Mitchell should not only be acquitted but "given a bouquet" for "removing one of the vilest creatures who ever lived."[55] In this he was repeating sentiments he had privately expressed to O.V. Hurt in mid-May; he had argued then that Mitchell "was simply exterminating an animal in human form whose prey was innocent young girls."[56]

By now the defence had spent two full days making its case, and the *Post-Intelligencer* acknowledged that the lawyers had been able to reveal much of the Creffield story.[57] The partisan *Corvallis Times* opined that it was "generally believed" that "the jury is prepared at this moment to acquit Mitchell."[58] The *Star* was convinced that the testimony of Hurt, Hartley, and Baldwin had been highly effective:

> Sane or insane, laboring under what he believed to be a God given command or in full possession of all his mental powers when he committed the deed, there seems to be everywhere, even at the table of the prosecuting attorneys, a feeling that it is all a farce – that all the wrangling and bickering about the introduction of that or this bit of evidence is purely a waste of time and energy – that the twelve good men and true who sit in the jury box, if they don't believe George Mitchell to be insane, are going to perjure themselves – it's a strong word but it fits – in order to free the boy.

And the paper went on to make it clear that it agreed with such sentiments. Anybody who would "listen every day to all of the testimony" would make Mitchell a "hero," a man who "single handed and at the risk of execution or imprisonment, undertakes to remove a pestilence whose blighting influence has wrecked homes and broken hearts, ruined women and driven strong men to despair."[59]

The suggestion that the defence had done a good job to this point is supported by what we know about the courtroom atmosphere. The courtroom was still crowded, with a great many women present who "listened eagerly to the revolting testimony adduced." On Thursday, July 5, Frater had to quieten spectators who hissed and laughed at Miller's objections, and on Friday an elderly female spectator stepped forward at the end of the morning session and subjected Miller to a "tirade of abuse" about his attempt to convict Mitchell. She said he should be "ashamed of himself," and that "the motives impelling him to such a vigorous handling of his case were not altogether creditable." Miller paid her no attention other than to tell her to keep her opinions to herself.[60] Frater also wanted the spectators to keep quiet. There were several occasions on the Friday when a defence win on a legal argument was followed by cheering and clapping, and Frater threatened more than once to clear the courtroom because of these demonstrations.[61]

The morning of Friday, July 6, saw six witnesses from Oregon – employers, friends, and acquaintances of Mitchell – all testify that they had spoken to him in April 1906 and that he had told them he was commanded by God and his mother's spirit to remove Creffield. Some also said that Mitchell was a believer in spiritualism, which would, of course, have bolstered the evidence about the spirit of his mother. On cross-examinations Miller established in each case that the witness was not an expert in insanity. In the afternoon James Berry and Lewis Sandell gave evidence, following the by now familiar script: they had had conversations with Mitchell in which they recounted their experiences of the Creffield sect, and Mitchell in turn had acted, in Sandell's words, "as crazy as a loon."[62]

The final witness of the day was Perry Mitchell. The reports of his testimony are confusing, for they seem to suggest that Perry was able to say a good deal about the events of 1903-1904, which should have been irrelevant. There are no specific reports of prosecution objections to Perry's evidence, only a reference, which might be germane, to the defence winning some of the legal arguments that day. In any event, Perry was able to recount his and George's 1903 "rescue" of Esther, her condition at that time, and the time she spent in Illinois. In the process he talked about George, in particular about George's concern for Esther and his worries about Creffield's influence over her once she returned to Oregon. Perry could not have had a conversation with George in 1906, because he was in Illinois, but he contributed to the evidence about George's visions, claiming that George had written him about them, the letter stating: "I am God's agent. I am chosen by God to hunt Crefeld down, and I am going to do it."[63] He was not, of course, able to produce the letter, which we do not believe existed. But it was one more piece of evidence for George's delusion.

Perry was also able to get before the jury, for the first time, evidence about Charles Mitchell's eccentricities. He talked about his father's changeability in religion and his tendency to fall out with people he disagreed with. Rather inconsistently, Perry was not allowed to talk about his brother Fred's attempted suicide; he did mention it but it was ruled inadmissible. This seems inconsistent with allowing Perry to discuss his father, but the explanation may be that by this time suicide was not generally considered an indicator of mental disorder but as an extreme version of the "depression" that anybody could suffer from and as often the result of social or environmental factors.

By the end of the day the defence was pleased with what it had accomplished in the week. Shipley told the press that "the greater part of the evidence, which the defense wished to get before the jury, was in," and that it might well rest its case by the end of the next day. If the evidence of Sheriff Burnett of Corvallis is to be relied on, the defence was right to be optimistic. As discussed below, Burnett did appear briefly on the witness stand the next day, having spent a couple of days in Seattle before that. When he returned he told the *Corvallis Times* that he "did not hear a single person in Seattle say Mitchell ought to be convicted, but heard hundreds express the hope that he would be promptly acquitted." He thought a verdict would be "quickly reached" unless "one or two men held out." Indeed, he thought "all the jurors have their minds already made up," for "they spend most of their time looking out of the window and pay no attention whatever to the wrangling of the lawyers."[64]

EXPERT TESTIMONY ON INSANITY

The proceedings of Saturday, July 7, were largely dominated by extensive arguments over the admissibility of testimony about the insanity of George Mitchell and members of his family, and by the examination of the trial's first expert witness, so that only four witnesses testified. The day began, however, with a brief appearance by John Manning. It was brief because almost all the questions put to him were ruled inadmissible, Frater sustaining prosecution objections without hearing argument from the defence lawyers. The defence principally wanted Manning to talk about the evidence in the Starr adultery case, but it surely knew there would be objections, as such testimony was simply aimed at attacking Creffield's character and was thus irrelevant. It also knew that those objections would be sustained.[65] Our sense is that Manning's presence was little more than a publicity stunt. He was a public prosecutor who had, it was well known, come out in support of Mitchell. Morris and Shipley probably thought it was good public relations – for the jury and the wider audience – to see Manning prepared to repeat these sentiments in court. That he was not allowed to do so was immaterial. As it was, Manning created a stir when he shook Mitchell warmly by the hand and chatted with him for a few minutes in the courtroom prior to his appearance.

Manning was followed by Sheriff Burnett, who was also allowed to testify about his official dealings with Donna Starr. But, as with Manning, when the defence asked questions about her mental condition, obviously still pursuing the hereditary insanity point, Miller objected. Frater sustained the objection, and went further. He was by now tired of Morris' "persistence in this particular line of questioning which had been ruled upon adversely several times since the trial began," and he took "radical action."[66] The jury was excused and a twenty-minute argument took place in Frater's chambers. There is some inconsistency in the press reports about the result of this argument, but the accounts that best tally with what happened later are those stating that Frater ruled that no evidence would be heard from lay witnesses about insanity in the Mitchell family until expert testimony had been introduced to lay a foundation for it – until an expert had testified that the degeneracy that could lead to insanity might be present in the family.[67]

The defence immediately brought on its expert, Dr Donald A. Nicholson. A native of Prince Edward Island and a graduate of the University of Minnesota, he had been in Seattle only since 1905, having spent the five years prior to that as the head of the Minnesota State Asylum. Nicholson was one of the few doctors in the region who specialized in mental disease, and he later became president of the Washington State Medical Association.[68] Following the usual procedure Shipley asked him a hypothetical question: "Mr. Shipley recited what he considered a statement of facts regarding Mitchell's actions, and the mental conditions to which he had been subjected, and asked the physician if he thought a man who acted in such a manner, and under such conditions, would be insane."[69] Nicholson said yes, of course, that Mitchell's acts as described indicated an "insane delusion." An "insane delusion," he said, was one "which had gained such a strong control over the patient as to compel him to act in a manner contrary to reason." In Mitchell's case the delusion would have been worry from knowing the "danger" he believed Esther to be in. It was widely accepted among specialists in mental diseases that brooding on a subject could make it more likely that a person would become insane,[70] and thus Nicholson's opinion was very much in line with contemporary understandings. Nicholson also spent a good deal of time on the distinctions between different kinds of mental illness, particularly that between delusions and insane delusions.

This was perfect for the defence, and Shipley followed with another hypothetical, about "the probable mental condition of such a man's brothers and sisters and antecedents." Nicholson stated that the mental condition of ancestors or siblings "always had a bearing in determining" a person's sanity, and that he would expect to find "similar mental conditions, or 'dispositions,'" although not necessarily similar actions, in other family members. This, again, was exactly what the defence needed the jury to hear, and the morning ended with Nicholson's examination-in-chief making his evidence uppermost in the jurors' minds as they went off to enjoy their lunch.

Most of the afternoon session was given over to Miller's cross-examination of Nicholson, and he laboured mightily to repair the damage, although we know little of the details. In an answer to a hypothetical question posed by Miller, Nicholson restated his belief in Mitchell's delusion. Belief in God instructing a person to do certain things, said Nicholson, "is pretty generally agreed among authorities not to be the working of a normal mind." All the press reports state that Miller was unable to shake Nicholson's opinion or undermine the effectiveness of his testimony. The *Post-Intelligencer* called the afternoon "the climax in the Mitchell defence." It was indeed a crucial session, although not because the defence had somehow convinced anybody that Mitchell really had been insane. But it had made the insanity argument plausible and respectable. The jury would decide the case based on their view of the legitimacy of the unwritten law; but they could now reasonably conceal that view behind the cloak of a valid insanity argument.

There was not much of the day left after Nicholson departed, but the defence sought to press home its advantage before the rest day. Edwin Bryson was summoned next, called by Morris and Shipley to talk about his knowledge of Esther Mitchell's insanity. But Frater refused to allow Bryson to answer the question, and the day ended with further legal argument with the jury out. Morris insisted that he could prove Esther Mitchell's and Donna Starr's insanity through a number of witnesses,[71] all of whom had been on the stand before, and he also wanted to have another (unnamed, possibly Phoebe) Mitchell testify that Fred Mitchell was insane when he tried to kill himself. Frater would allow none of it, however, perhaps because he thought the expert testimony insufficient to lay a foundation for the other evidence. As noted earlier, it was not insanity that was considered hereditary but the physical weakness that made it more likely in some than others. Esther Mitchell's and Donna Starr's form of insanity was, Frater might have thought, the result of religion, and female weak-mindedness, rather than a family trait. All this is speculative, however, and in any event the disgusted defence attorneys could do nothing but demand the court's ruling be made a matter of record. They also dismissed most of their remaining witnesses.

While obviously displeased over their continuing failure to get in the testimony about the Mitchell family, Morris and Shipley could not have been unhappy when they left court on July 7 at the end of a long week. They had got the full details of Creffield's sect before the jury, as well as plenty of evidence about Mitchell's delusion and the opinion of an expert that it was reasonable for their client to have had that delusion. They planned to call more experts to back that up. Asked if the next week would see the drama of Mitchell himself on the witness stand, Morris said it was not necessary, "because we have proven that the man was insane," have established "a legal excuse for the act."[72] The fact was, of course, that putting Mitchell on the stand could only undermine the defence, for as we have seen the prosecution could have used his prior statements, in which nothing was said about delusions, against him. But nothing threatened the defence case as much as another shooting by another young man, in one of Seattle's best neighbourhoods, on the Saturday evening, and we need to divert briefly from the Mitchell trial to examine the circumstances surrounding the death of George Meade Emory.

THE EMORY MURDER

At about 9 p.m. on Saturday, July 7, Chester Thompson, the twenty-year-old son of prominent local lawyer William S. Thompson, tried to visit Charlotte Whittesley, a young woman with whom he was infatuated.[73] Charlotte's father was Charles F. Whittesley, a former county treasurer. Although Thompson was from a good family, and although he and Charlotte were childhood friends, Charlotte's family considered him unsuitable, and he had been told to stay away from her by both her father and her uncle, George Meade Emory, a prominent Seattle attorney and former superior court judge.[74] Charlotte was not keen on his attentions either, preferring another young man. Despite all this, Thompson had written to Charlotte frequently while he was at the University of Washington and she was being educated in the east, and this was not the first time he had tried to find a way to see her after she had returned home.

On that Saturday evening Thompson believed Charlotte was at the house of her uncle, Emory, and went there to find her. When he arrived the family was sitting on the portico. He rushed into the house, and when Emory called out to him to stop, Thompson delayed only long enough to fire his revolver three times at Emory. One bullet missed, one went through the body near the hip, and one entered Emory near the top of one lung and did damage to his heart, spine, and lungs. Emory survived the shooting in the short term but died on the evening of Sunday, July 8. Thompson was arrested after a delay of a couple of hours, during which time he barricaded himself in the bedroom of the Emorys' two young children. By that time an angry crowd had gathered in the street, and the police had to take him out down the back stairway. He was charged with first-degree murder when Emory died.

The shooting of Emory was sensational news, forcing the Mitchell case off the front page of the *Times* for the first time since it had begun, and similarly relegating it to an inside page of the *Post-Intelligencer*. The city now had another spectacular murder on its hands. "Whole City Cries for Vengeance" and "Cold-Blooded Crime Must Be Punished" announced the *Times* headlines, with the *Post-Intelligencer* choosing the more sober "Judge Emory Shot Down by Mad Youth." It would have been troubling enough for the Mitchell defence team that an eminent man had been gunned down in his own home; that by itself might have changed public and jurors' attitudes towards whether the deliberate killing of another could ever be condoned. But much worse was that Thompson, it was quickly revealed, would plead insanity.[75] It had become, said the *Times* as it made a 180-degree turn, "the popular and modern way of defending murderers."[76] The *Times'* refutation of an insanity defence for Thompson could easily have been adapted to Mitchell:

> Thompson was sane enough to get a gun – and load it! Thompson was sane enough to choose a time of night when he expected to find the young woman with her chosen company! ... Every act which Thompson performed touching this murder was as sane as the conduct of any man can be when he starts out to commit murder! It may be that this young man was eccentric ... But these eccentricities ... are all of a kind that if they can be excused on the grounds of insanity ... about 25 per cent of the population [would be] insane.

The *Times* explicitly made the connection to the Mitchell case. The city had seen several recent murders, and in one case a "deliberate murder" had been done "after long consideration" and "because of alleged injuries done to members of the family, according to the murderer's opinion." It was a far cry indeed from the assurance with which its earlier coverage had talked about the real wrongs – not "alleged" ones – to the Mitchell sisters, and where it had been confident that Mitchell would not, and should not, be convicted. Now Blethen declared that "the time has come when it is going to be necessary to make an example of a few insane persons." If not, "murder will run riot in our city." It will occur "every time some tempery young man ... happens to get his back up toward some other person." Blethen, as we have seen, was always willing to adopt the sensationalist position; in this case he drew criticism from many other newspapers for his demand for "vengeance" rather than "the calm, unflinching administration of the law."[77]

The *Post-Intelligencer* also drew the connection between the two cases. Having said nothing about the Mitchell case for weeks, an editorial that Sunday morning decried "the attempt to create public sentiment in favor of a murderer" and condemned the idea that men could be tried "by newspaper" or by "the higher law."[78] The latter phrase in particular "ought to be abhorred by all good citizens when used in the sense that there is any human law higher than that of the courts." If Mitchell were acquitted because of some higher law, others, such as Thompson, could make the same claim. The *Argus* joined in, calling the killing of Emory "contemptible" but no different to Creffield's. Like Thompson, Mitchell was unmanly, a "coward" and a "cur," a man who "lacked the physical courage to step around and meet Creffield face to face." The insanity defence was "the barrier behind which men crouch in an effort to save their own miserable necks from the gallows months after their innocent victims have been laid to rest."[79] For those who had been concerned in May about the broader dangers that support for Mitchell would bring, as well as the *Times,* which had so strongly trumpeted the validity of the unwritten law, the Thompson case was an object lesson. Once the vigilantism genie was let loose, there was no getting it back in the lamp. State law, and only state law, should govern men's actions.

RUSH TO JUDGMENT:
THE CLOSING OF THE DEFENCE CASE

Mitchell's defence lawyers immediately realized the damage the Emory murder could do to their case, although Mitchell himself later claimed he was oblivious to it. He had read about Emory's death but thought it "so different to my case" that it did not concern him.[80] But when the trial resumed on Monday, Morris, in the jury's absence, told Frater that he was concerned that knowledge of Thompson's crime "might have a certain moral influence on the jury." He wanted the jurors taken to and from their hotel by a route that did not let them see the courthouse flag flying at half mast, and generally he wanted the bailiffs to use "extreme precautions" against knowledge of the murder reaching the jury.[81] Frater acceded to these requests. It was now very much in the interests of the defence to get the case to the jury as soon as possible, for the more time passed, the greater the chance that they would come to hear of the Emory murder. Morris pared his witnesses to just two more medical experts. He told Frater he did so to speed up the proceedings and have the trial over by Emory's funeral, but this was surely window dressing.

There was a thinner than usual crowd in court when the trial resumed on Monday, July 9, although the usual number of women were present. Perhaps people preferred to talk about the Thompson case, or perhaps they now felt much more ambivalently about Mitchell. In any event, the proceedings were short, as the defence hurried to conclude its case. It called only two witnesses, both "experts" on insanity although ordinary physicians. Dr John Wotherspoon went first, being asked a number of hypothetical questions by Shipley that assumed as fact the testimony given by the Oregon witnesses. To each Wotherspoon dutifully replied that "in his opinion any man so affected was insane."[82] He was also asked the crucial question of whether a man could have a delusion on one subject and be entirely rational on all others; he replied that that could happen. The process of getting through the examination was long, for many of the questions were objected to and some of those objections were sustained. Wotherspoon was given a "severe cross-examination" by Miller, but the *Times* thought he emerged unscathed. The cross-examination was not over by the noon recess, and thus took up part of the afternoon as well.

Later in the afternoon another doctor, William T. Miles, testified, to more or less the same effect.[83] He too was stringently cross-examined by Miller, and this time the press reports give an all too rare glimpse of the substance of the confrontation. Miller asked Miles whether, if the founder of the Mormon Church said that he had received a revelation from God and been directed by divine inspiration, he would have "an insane delusion." Miles' answer was that he would have such a delusion "if he actually believed it."[84] Miller pushed his point, saying that some people believed prayers were answered and illness cured by prayer – were such beliefs insane delusions? Miles said yes, "if adhered to beyond the point of reason." That is, everybody was entitled to their beliefs, "and so long as they did not carry them to the point of absurdity the 'divine' healers could not be classed as demented." Miller kept at it, pointing out that some Christian sects believed Christ had not yet appeared, while others thought he had come as Jesus: "The attorney asked Dr. Miles to pick the insane delusion, but the physician held there was none." In using these religious examples Miller was, of course, reminding the jurors of some of their own beliefs, and he was also probably drawing on the leading text, Wharton and Stille's *Medical Jurisprudence,* which uses the Mormon example as a case of "shrewd sane men" who choose to believe in, for example, polygamy, but must nonetheless "be held responsible for their delusions."[85] It was clever stuff, and at this distance Miles' answers do not seem convincing, but it was irrelevant because it was the unwritten law that counted.

At just after 4 p.m. Miles left the witness stand, and the defence closed its case. When asked about rebuttal witnesses, Miller and Mackintosh indicated they had not expected so sudden an end and had not decided whether to call any. The prosecution took the evening to discuss rebuttal testimony but decided not to offer any expert medical evidence. This is rather puzzling, given that Miller had hinted a couple of days before that it might do so, and given that the prosecution had at its disposal Washington's foremost figure in the field of insanity, Dr John B. Loughary. The first man in the Pacific Northwest to have an exclusive practice in psychiatry, Loughary was then in private practice, but he had been the medical superintendent of the Western State Hospital (asylum) at Steilacoom, and would hold the position again.[86] The rumour was that the defence had consulted with him, but not called him because he believed that Mitchell was sane at the time he killed Creffield.[87] Loughary had presumably been a member of the Association of Medical Superintendents of American Institutions for the Insane, a conservative body which in the late nineteenth century resisted new approaches to explaining mental illness that seemed to its members to substantially undermine doctrines of individual responsibility and therefore to pose a real threat to social order.[88] He would thus have been a good witness, but he was not called.

Whether the prosecutors secretly sympathized with Mitchell – which we think highly unlikely – or whether they either thought the case hopeless or did not want to dignify the insanity argument with rebuttals, or whether Loughary himself was unwilling to proffer unpopular testimony and harm his practice, is unclear; but the fact is that like many prosecutors in prior unwritten law cases, Mackintosh and Miller did nothing to combat the insanity defence.[89] The press mostly took the view that the prosecution had given up; the *Oregonian* even claimed to have this firsthand from one of the lawyers, who had been resigned to defeat since O.V. Hurt had testified. It was "the general discrediting of 'Joshua' Creffield by the 'I-told-George-Mitchell' witnesses for the defence," of which Hurt had been the principal, that had decided the case. Rebuttal witnesses could not prove a negative – that Mitchell had not been driven insane by the stories about Creffield – nor could they contradict what had been said about Creffield. In addition, the prosecution knew perfectly well that insanity was not the issue anyway. It was, said the *Oregonian,* "merely offered as an excuse to the jury for a verdict of acquittal."[90]

SPEECHES TO THE JURY

As in most American states, in Washington the prosecution addressed the jury first, followed by the defence and then the prosecution was given an opportunity for rebuttal.[91] No time limits were set beyond those imposed by an attorney's tactical sense of how long he ought to try to hold the jury's attention without incurring their resentment. Both sides had told Frater the day before that closing arguments would take no longer than a day. When court resumed on Tuesday, July 10, the defence began a series of stratagems. First, it offered to waive closing argument if the prosecution would do so as well. Ostensibly, Morris cited the inconvenience of a long trial, but he was, of course, concerned much less about convenience than about the increased chance, as more time passed, that the jury would hear about the Emory murder. If his offer was accepted, the twelve men would have the case before the lunch recess. Morris likely thought they were immune from hearing about Emory in the courtroom and while deliberating; the danger periods were recesses and, most of all, the evenings in the hotel. His tactic would ensure that even if the jury did not get the case until the afternoon there would not be another night to worry about. Miller, however, was having none of it, and insisted that "doing our duty by the state" required the prosecution to address the jurors.[92] Shipley then proposed a two-hour time limit for each side. There was some discussion of Frater enforcing this, which he would not do. That did not matter, for the prosecutors were willing to accept the limit, presumably because they knew it made no sense to speak to the jury for any longer than two hours.

The agreement between the parties having been secured, Mackintosh made his speech to the jury. It lasted only half an hour, and he played by the rules, saying nothing that could be construed as a reference to the Emory murder, although there was press speculation that he would try this as a last, desperate measure.[93] He began by reviewing the basic facts of the killing, in doing so casting Mitchell as unmanly, for he had fired a "cowardly shot."[94] He then adverted to three ways in which a killing of one person by another might be defended. One was self-defence, another was by alibi, and the third, "as in this case when the man is caught in the act" was to "set up" a plea of insanity. The phrase "set up" was employed to suggest concocted testimony, and Mackintosh expanded on the point, telling the jury that all the evidence about insanity had the air of being contrived. It was "of such a nature to indicate that it was prepared beforehand," and prepared "with a view" to "securing the acquittal" of Mitchell. Getting to what everybody knew was the real issue in the case, Mackintosh accepted that there might indeed be a benefit to society in Creffield's death, but this "did not justify any man in taking the law into his own hands." Moreover, if one man could make this claim, "any man might consider himself sufficiently wronged to, in his mind, justify taking the life of the man who had wronged him." Here Mackintosh must have wished he could refer to Chester Thompson. All he could do was distinguish insanity from the anger that anybody could be prone to: "No man . . . commits a crime of this nature in his normal mind. But are we to consider such insanity as a justification for taking a human life? If so, there is scarcely a man in this community who could not secure immunity from punishment after he had committed a murder, on a plea of insanity."

On the substance of Mitchell's insanity, Mackintosh poured scorn on the contrived nature of the defence case. There was "too great correspondence in the testimony of the witnesses," he said, "too many told the same identical story." To back up his assertion that it was all contrived, he used – apparently from memory – the quotation from Judge Orange Jacobs cited earlier about insanity that begins when the trigger is pulled and ends when the bullet is on its way. Finally, Mackintosh made a plea for law, not emotion, to govern the verdict. The jurors had sworn to try the case "in cold blood" and "not to allow sympathy to influence them." As for the unwritten law, Mackintosh pointed out that Donna Starr was "the only sister of the defendant who had been seduced by Creffield," and argued that she was an adult "capable of reasoning for herself." Moreover, the seduction did not justify murder. He finished by repeating points he had already made. The jury was not to be influenced by "expert evidence prompted by the pocketbook" and was to consider "whether a man is law in himself, and whether a man who goes out and kills another man and then comes in to plead insanity should not be punished."

It was an excellent speech, delivered not histrionically but in measured tones. Each part was carefully weighed, and it is difficult at this distance to say that he was wrong about anything. The law did not permit Mitchell to be judge, jury, and executioner, and the insanity defence was clearly as contrived as Mackintosh claimed it was. This speech, however, likely had no effect whatsoever on the jury.

The defence now tried its next stratagem. After a brief whispered consultation with Shipley, Morris announced that he would simply waive his closing argument. He and Shipley must not have thought that Mackintosh had damaged their case, and the press had the same impression. But there was more to the defence decision than that, for the question then arose as to whether there could be a rebuttal. This was a key issue because Miller was slated to give it, and it was intended as the principal prosecution address. As the *Oregonian* put it, Mackintosh had deliberately made a short speech and "left the critical study of the case to his assistant."[95] The defence argued that, as there was nothing to rebut, Miller could not speak. Miller protested, arguing that he had a right to make his speech whether or not the defence had done so. He presumably said that the prosecution's preparations had been made with the assumption that there would be a rebuttal, and that some points had been reserved for that. The defence tactic was a trick to deprive the prosecutors of the chance to make their best case. It was, said a Portland newspaper, a "brilliant" strategy because "Miller is regarded as a dangerous man to address a jury" and on this occasion had "prepared himself for an extended argument that it was believed would shatter Mitchell's case."[96] He was prepared, said another Portland paper, "to tear the defence's arguments to shreds."[97]

Morris had known what he was going to attempt and cited a number of cases for his position. Miller tried to argue, but had done no research, and Frater was forced to rule for the defence. But he also called an adjournment until 1:30, at which point the issue could be argued more fully. He gave an additional, more prosaic, reason for adjourning – he did not have his jury instructions ready yet. He had expected to deliver them in the afternoon, at the earliest, and they were still with his stenographer. The court adjourned an hour earlier than usual, at 11:00 am. When it resumed in the afternoon, with many local lawyers present, an hour or more of legal argument over Miller's right to speak ensued. With Miller having done his research and able to give him some support, Frater, as he had so often done, ruled for the prosecution, allowing Miller another speech.

The defence now turned to its third tactical ploy, threatening to speak for a long time. "Mr Shipley was prepared for a speech of several hours, and Mr Morris proposed, if necessary, to read the testimony"; Morris threatened to keep the trial going until Thursday.[98] This was, of course, a violation of the agreement that each side would limit itself to two hours. Why Morris and Shipley thought this a good tactic is unclear. Not only would they run the risk of annoying the jury, a jury they professed to believe was champing at the bit to acquit Mitchell, but, having tried to hurry the case along ever since George Emory was murdered, they were now asking the prosecution to take seriously a threat to delay it. But while the defence threat does not seem very real, it was enough for Miller. He gave up his demand to speak, asking only that Frater instruct the jury that both sides had waived any further argument. Morris was happy to agree to that.

JURY INSTRUCTIONS AND VERDICT

There remained only for Frater to instruct the jury before they withdrew to deliberate. The instructions took about half an hour to deliver. The press reported little of what was said, but we know something about this stage of the trial from a set of written "requests for instructions" submitted by the defence, which contain indications of which of the requested instructions were given and which refused.[99] The instructions requested were of three kinds. First, there was a series of straightforward and standard instructions about basic principles of criminal procedure, such as the meaning of reasonable doubt and the burden of proof being on the prosecution. Second, there was a longer and more complicated set of instructions in which Frater explained the insanity laws to the jury. In accordance with the law laid out at the beginning of our account of the defence case, Frater told the jurors that a man was not criminally liable if he had a mental disease that resulted either in his not appreciating the "nature and consequences" of his act or his not knowing the difference between right and wrong in the particular case at issue. He also expanded on this, to the effect that mental disease could include "an insane delusion impelling his act," and that the defendant did not need to be generally unable to distinguish right from wrong but only so incapable with reference to "the act charged."

All the above was duly conveyed by Frater to the jurors. But the defence attorneys also wanted other instructions, which Frater would not give. They asked him to tell the jury that a "common instance" of the kind of delusion that prevented somebody from knowing right from wrong was a belief that his act was the result of a command from God. Indeed, the defence asked for this in three separate requests, but none was granted – not surprisingly, for it was effectively an instruction to acquit. Frater refused for this reason, we assume, and also because it did not matter whether this was a "common instance" of a delusion. All that mattered was whether Mitchell had that delusion and that it prevented him from knowing right from wrong. The defence also tried to persuade Frater to tell the jury that they could acquit if they had a reasonable doubt that

Mitchell "had sufficient mind and intellect at the time of the homicide to premeditate or deliberate the act," but the judge did not accede to what was effectively a shift in the burden of proof regarding insanity. Instead he told the jury that the defence had to make its case "on the preponderance of the evidence." This was the accepted standard in Washington, and the defence lawyers must have known this and so could not seriously have been disappointed. This instruction was one of only two that the newspapers reported.

The third area covered by the defence requests was that of justifiable homicide – the unwritten law – and here Frater resisted all attempts to put that defence explicitly before the jury. Three of the requested instructions referred to it, two of them implicitly and one as explicitly as possible. The defence asked Frater to say: "If, on the whole evidence presented in this case, there is any rational hypothesis consistent with the conclusion that the homicide was justifiable or excusable, the defendant cannot be convicted, . . . it would be your duty to acquit." In refusing to include this instruction and the other implicit references to justifiable homicide, Frater acted consistently with his rulings at the bail hearing and throughout the trial, not contemplating any overt appeal to the idea that Creffield's killing could be excused. According to the press reports he also told the jury that no compromise verdict in the form of a conviction for manslaughter was available to them. It was acquittal or conviction for murder, although Frater did accept that it might be either first- or second-degree murder, depending presumably on whether there had been premeditation and deliberation.

The jury got the case at 3:14 p.m. The courtroom audience stayed put, "nervously and in low tones discussing the possibilities."[100] Mitchell was taken back to the county jail, where he waited in his cell with Charles and Perry Mitchell. Nobody had to wait long, although the hour and twenty-five minutes the jurors spent deliberating was more than some people predicted.[101] When the news came in that the jury was back, courthouse staff left their posts to hear the verdict read. Frater warned against any demonstrations, no matter what the result, and at 4:45 precisely foreman Ring read it out: not guilty. As often happened in unwritten law trials, many in the crowded courtroom ignored Frater's order about demonstrations by shouting their approval and clapping, and some "shoved and struggled to get within hand clasp distance." According to the *Corvallis Times,* "a flock of women . . . insisted upon giving him hysterical congratulations."[102] In vain did the bailiff demand silence, and the uproar continued for a full minute.

When order was restored there was still one more dramatic episode. Frater ordered Mitchell remanded to the custody of the sheriff. Morris immediately protested, threatening *habeas corpus* proceedings, and Frater relented almost immediately. It is not clear what Frater was thinking. He could not have been surprised at the verdict, although he certainly disapproved of it.[103] His explanation was that he wanted the courtroom demonstrations stopped and the room cleared, and thought he could achieve that by remanding Mitchell. Although such a tactic would be more likely to inflame than to quell a crowd, it might have seemed reasonable to Frater. There is, however, another explanation of his action, albeit one for which there is no direct evidence. Washington, like much of the common-law world, had a rule that if a jury found a person not guilty by reason of insanity it should state that fact when delivering its verdict – that is, it should provide what is usually called a special verdict.[104] The jury had not done so; the verdict form simply says "not guilty."[105] The jury might have not added the rider because no one had told them they should do so. However, it seems highly improbable that Frater would not have known about and mentioned this part of the law to the jury in charging them, even though none of the press reports of his instructions to the jury refers to his doing so. If he did charge them to this effect, the jury's failure to mention insanity can only mean that their verdict did not rely on the defence but on the unwritten law – on a conviction that Mitchell's action was justified.

This brings us back to Frater. Assuming that he charged the jury correctly, we can surmise that he was startled by the lack of a rider in their verdict, which he might nonetheless have assumed to have been based on insanity. And if he thought that, his order to remand Mitchell makes sense, for the same statutory provision that required the rider also stipulated that if the presiding judge thought the defendant "manifestly dangerous to the peace and safety of the community," he could commit the person to prison, or condition his release in various ways. Frater may have been expecting either a guilty verdict or one of not guilty by reason of insanity, and in either event he was ready to keep Mitchell under lock and key.[106]

All this is speculative, but it is supported by press commentary on the failure to have Mitchell incarcerated as insane.[107] More importantly, if we are right about why there was no rider, it tells us that the jurors felt they could simply acquit Mitchell, without pretending that that acquittal was based on the insanity defence. We do not know that they did that, but the assumption of most newspapers after the trial was that the acquittal had not been on the ground of insanity.[108] All this might also explain why a jury that everybody believed was champing at the bit to acquit Mitchell took ninety minutes to do so. They might, that is, have been debating whether to find him not guilty by reason of insanity. By its verdict the jury was making a bold statement not simply about their own values but about the law. The law, as Herrup and others have reminded us, "is made and used in every application," and here twelve men "made" a law about justifiable homicide in the circumstances of the case. Whether we think it right or wrong does not matter. What matters is that we understand the cultural meaning of the verdict in turn-of-the-century Seattle for, as Herrup has noted, "despite its superficial constancy, law draws its meaning from contemporary ideologies, not transhistorical categorizations."[109] Seattle opinion soon came to regret the law made in the Mitchell case, but that does not alter the importance of the moment.

It possibly never occurred to George Mitchell to worry about the niceties of why he had been acquitted. He just wanted to leave. He did not forget to shake hands with each of the twelve jurors as they filed out, and then he "elbowed his way through the mob, which was trying to congratulate him, into the corridors of the court house."[110] He immediately went to the jail to pick up his things, followed by a crowd that included many women. He said his goodbyes to jailers and fellow prisoners, the latter giving him a "parting cheer." A crowd still followed him, and everybody turned to look at him as, surrounded by his lawyers, father and brother, and Gardner, he walked to the offices of Morris, Southard and Shipley. A reception was laid on there, which provided an opportunity for the lawyers to bask in the congratulations showered on them. George talked briefly to the press, insisting both that he had been confident in the verdict and that he had no regrets about killing Creffield. That night he slept at the Stevens hotel – no doubt the best sleep he had had for some time.

II

"And the Evil That Men Do
Lives After Them"

THE DEATH OF GEORGE MITCHELL

SEATTLE RESPONDS TO THE VERDICT

ALTHOUGH THE VERDICT was front-page news in all the Seattle newspapers, the pall cast by the murder of George Emory meant that celebrations were distinctly muted. The offices of Morris Southard and Shipley received telegrams of congratulations, but most came from Oregon.[1] There was some cheering and clapping as Mitchell walked free from the courthouse, but no sustained celebrations. And while one person apparently offered Mitchell an education, most of the previous promises of employment and other assistance evaporated. Indeed, nothing testifies more strongly to the equivocal response to Mitchell's acquittal in the wake of Emory's murder than George, Perry, and Fred Mitchell's intention to leave the city as soon as possible and rebuild their lives in Portland. Peter View of Portland, who had been a character witness at the trial, had offered Mitchell his old lath mill job back, and Perry was going to stay and work side by side with his brother. It was all quite different from the reaction that had greeted acquittals in other unwritten law cases, some of which had even seen formal banquets in honour of the freed killer.[2] The response in Corvallis and other Oregon towns was more celebratory; there was a "joyous mood" in Corvallis, and the *Corvallis Times* was especially ebullient, providing an extensive justification of vigilantism in necessary cases.[3] Portland's *Evening Telegram* also thought the verdict correct, "all things considered."[4]

Two of Mitchell's long-time supporters in the Seattle press were more

192

or less unfazed by the Emory murder. The *Republican* heaped praise on Morris and Shipley for their "masterly" handling of the defence and maintained that while Mitchell had "technically speaking . . . committed murder," nonetheless "twelve men has [sic] never yet been found that would convict a father or a brother that killed the traducer of his daughter or his sister of any crime." Horace Cayton's sentiments were shared by the *Star*, which reported the acquittal enthusiastically and, a few days later, implicitly approved of Mitchell's act in the same kind of language it had consistently used to describe his motives. The *Star* was certain that the jury shared its own view: it was the "firm belief" of all those who had observed the trial that the jury "didn't believe that George Mitchell was insane"; they had acquitted him because they approved his action.[5]

Though it had previously been Mitchell's chief supporter, the *Times* shifted ground dramatically. It did not even give the verdict its main headline on July 11, reserving that for the news that Chester Thompson would be defended by his father, and a series of short comments on the inside editorial page that day reflected the paper's reservations. One said that Mitchell was found "not guilty" by reason of "insanity," the quotation marks presumably intended to indicate the dubious nature of the decision. On the same page it asked, "When a man becomes violently angry is he insane?" – a question that applied to both the Thompson and Mitchell cases. For the first time the *Times* also heaped praise on the prosecution; Mackintosh "had been a living exemplar of the stern dignity of the law which forbids the slaying of one man by another." The task had been difficult, especially as it went against public opinion in many respects, but society needed such tasks to be performed, and needed fearless men, unafraid of the consequences and of public opinion, to perform them. This new stance was quite a contrast to earlier references to the technicalities of the law, to the hard, solid, remorseless workings of the state's agents.

The following day the *Times* noted, among other things, that Mitchell was going to leave Washington "just as quickly as steam would carry him after the gracious verdict of a Seattle jury," and suggested that the Oregon courts confine him in an asylum.[6] A longer item again compared Thompson and Mitchell, noting that some thought Thompson should be "treated with kid gloves" because the murder was "done in a heat of temper." "Perhaps," the *Times* sarcastically suggested, "the young man will enter a plea of 'not guilty because of madness'" which would be "quite as sensible as the plea of insanity which has become so popular that it would seem to be sufficient for the defense of any crime."

The rest of the Seattle press was either neutral or hostile to Mitchell. The *Post-Intelligencer* did nothing more than report the verdict. The *Patriarch*, which had always disapproved of the defence of family argument, noted that "Mitchell the Assassin is free," and compared him unfavourably to Chester Thompson, who had at least shot in passion. The *Argus* called the verdict a "disgrace to Seattle." The *Daily Bulletin* thought the unwritten law argument was not applicable when a man's sisters had chosen their own "fate," and complained that verdicts like that rendered for Mitchell "were incentives for men laboring under emotional or other forms of alleged insanity to commit atrocious murders," including the likes of Chester Thompson. Indeed, the paper went further, asking presciently why, if Mitchell had been justified, Maud Creffield did not have an equal right to kill him? The *Bulletin* was also the first to sound a theme that would become increasingly prevalent – that Seattle was reaping the fruits of Oregon's problems. If Mitchell wanted to kill Creffield, he should have done it at home: "Is human life cheaper in Oregon, that men prefer to do their butchering here instead of there?"[7] In short, editorialists were largely united in their condemnation of the verdict.

THE MITCHELL FAMILY:
RECONCILIATION TURNS TO REVENGE

The days immediately following the acquittal saw much activity by members of the Mitchell family. Donna Starr had already left Seattle, returning with Burgess to her Portland home on the previous Friday or Saturday. She still believed in Creffield, asserting that she would keep the faith and telling Burgess that her brother George was on no account to be brought to their house when he returned to Portland.[8] She also told the Portland press her view that George "is no better than any other criminal who commits murder, and he should have been punished just like any other man."[9] The other family members remained in Seattle, with George, Perry, Fred, and Charles all convinced that Esther had to be removed from the region and the religious influences that so guided her, and taken back to Illinois with Charles. Charles devoted considerable time to this task while the trial was still in progress.[10] He enlisted James Berry as intermediary, perhaps because of Berry's prior association with Maud Creffield, but Esther Mitchell insisted she would return to Portland. Charles also tried to have the authorities intervene, appealing to the mayor, the King County sheriff, and the Seattle police, but as Esther was of age they refused to help.

Shipley advised Charles to get her on a train for the east by force, assuring
him that Miller for one would not do anything to interfere with such a
plan. To Esther's "bitter resentment," her father conducted his campaign
in the press as well, arguing that she was "not right in her mind" and
needed to be removed from the "influence of Holy Rollerism."[11] Charles
and other members of the family were afraid that she and Maud Creffield
would join the colony that Sampson Levins had supposedly established in
British Columbia.[12] After initially refusing to see her father, Esther talked
with him on the evening of July 10 and met with him on July 11, but
adamantly refused to return to Illinois with him. He left without her that
same evening, taking the train first to Dayton, Washington, to visit his
eldest son Perley, en route to Illinois.

Esther seems to have had more time for Fred Mitchell, who wanted
not so much to force her to go east as to achieve a reconciliation within
the family.[13] But Esther had her own agenda. Esther and Maud left the
custody of the police matron on July 9 or 10. They had only the money
paid to them as witness fees, a total of $14.20 each.[14] They rented room 27
in the Pretoria Boarding House near Sixth Avenue and Pike Street, and
moved in with their meagre possessions, which in Maud Creffield's case
included her dead husband's clothing. It was there, on the afternoon of
July 11, that Fred Mitchell called on his sister and asked her to see George
before he left. She refused, insisting that George had done wrong and
should have been punished – although she also apparently said, in con-
tradiction with earlier statements, that she did not wish to see him hang.
Fred called again later in the afternoon, this time persuading Esther to
go with him to the depot to see her father off. The next day he visited
Esther in the morning and again at 2:00 in the afternoon, "to effect a
reconciliation," in his words. George and Perry had decided to take the
4:30 p.m. train to Portland, George having spent most of the day saying
his goodbyes to Louis Sandell and his former jailers. Esther received the
news that George and Perry were leaving that afternoon "with apparent
interest."[15]

Esther's interest was very real. From the moment the verdict was announced she and Maud Creffield had talked of revenge. Maud had had a
gun when Creffield was killed, but it had been taken away by police. At
some point thereafter she had obtained another one; that too was taken
away, by Mrs Kelly. When Maud Creffield left custody she asked Mrs
Kelly for the guns but was refused. But the next day she went out early,
when few people were about, and bought a $6 gun and a 60-cent box
of cartridges at Herman Spangenburg's hardware store. Then she began to

look for George Mitchell but could not find him. It also quickly became apparent that even if she did, the Mitchells would be too suspicious to let her get close. If there was killing to be done, Esther Mitchell would have to do it. As Maud later put it, the "ruse of a reconciliation" was the only way one of them could get close to George.[16]

Esther, who the day before had told her brother Fred that she would not go to see George and Perry off, arrived at the crowded train depot shortly after 4 p.m.,[17] and after a few minutes located her brothers. There was an awkward meeting, Fred trying as before to get the principal enemies to talk.[18] Some desultory conversation followed, George and Esther shaking hands at Fred's suggestion, although George was apparently "discouraged" because he could see in Esther's eyes that she hated him still for what he had done. At about 4:25 Perry and George walked side by side towards the exit from the waiting area, and Fred and Esther fell in behind them. Dressed in a white shirtwaist and a light skirt, Esther had her jacket over her arm, the gun concealed beneath it. As they walked Fred offered to carry her coat. The moment she was relieved of the burden she levelled the gun at George, in front of her, and fired; the bullet went through the back of his head below the brain, severing his carotid artery. He died very shortly afterwards from loss of blood.

Pandemonium erupted as the noise brought bystanders rushing to the area. Fred grabbed Esther, but only in time to stop her firing a second shot. She clung to him as he took the gun from her. Perry fell on his knees beside George and demanded, "Esther! Esther! How could you? How could you?" Esther did not answer but sat down to await her arrest, which occurred just minutes later. She "submitted quietly and without remonstrance." Although according to one report she said that she was "commanded" to kill George, implying that the command came from God,[19] Esther later maintained that her action was impelled by human emotion, not divine instruction. The statement was probably put in her mouth by a reporter wishing to make her crime an exact replica of George's.

George's body lay on the floor of the waiting room until Deputy Coroner Shirley Wiltsie arrived to supervise its removal to the Bonney-Watson Funeral Home, where Creffield's had gone just over two months before. John Miller, who had heard of the tragedy while in his office, made a dramatic entrance. "Pale and excited," he kept repeating, "I don't believe it," and asked to see the body. He then rushed off to police headquarters, where Esther had been taken. Seattle had yet another sensational murder case on its hands, and many must have felt the same way as Miller, who asked, "My God, what is this country coming to?"[20]

REVENGE OR RELIGION?

Seattle's interest in George Mitchell's killing of Creffield paled in comparison to the sensation caused by Esther Mitchell's murder of her brother. The *Times* rushed out nine extra editions that evening, the last at about 8 p.m., and "newsboys carried [it] to all parts of the city and the suburban towns and many thousands were sold to the people who were clamoring for the facts." The next day all the city newspapers carried the story at great length; the *Times* had no less than twelve articles on the murder, the reaction to it, and Creffield's cult, as well as a pictorial reproduction of the murder and a photograph of George Mitchell. The *Post-Intelligencer* had sixteen articles in its July 13 edition, with the murder the principal front-page story, while the *Star* went one better that day. Hundreds of people flocked to the jail to try to get a glimpse of the girl who murdered her brother, and as many visited the mortuary to view George's body. The authorities had not planned on visits, but so many thronged the doors that they were let in to file past the body. At 9 p.m. the doors were finally closed, despite the line of people still waiting to get in. Many people sent flowers, including the mystery girl who had regularly attended the trial and brought Mitchell flowers.[21]

All the newspapers provided extensive coverage of a variety of events that followed the murder: Mrs Kelly being officially reprimanded for not reporting that Maud Creffield had asked for the return of her guns;[22] a cursory investigation into whether others, particularly Frank Hurt, had been involved;[23] and George Mitchell's final journey. His body was taken back to Newberg by his grieving brothers on July 16 and laid to rest by his mother's side the following day. Most of the expenses were paid for by donations: the *Star* set up a fund in Seattle, and people from Newberg contributed locally. Enough was contributed for a rather handsome gravestone, and somebody thought enough of George's actions that it is inscribed with the well-known verse from John 15:13: "Greater love hath no man than this, that a man lays down his life for his friends."[24]

No aspect of the sorry tale was as interesting, however, as the character and motivations of George Mitchell's killer. Why she did it, and why Maud Creffield aided and abetted her, were questions to which people desperately wanted answers. Both Esther Mitchell and Maud Creffield, who surrendered herself to the police on the evening of July 12,[25] were happy to provide them, although they were not the answers the city wanted to hear. People wished Esther Mitchell in particular to be a demented girl driven to an insane act by some combination of Creffield's teaching, Maud

Creffield's evil influence, and, most of all, religious fanaticism. A number of people, Fred and Perry Mitchell chief among them, immediately assigned the lion's share of the blame to Maud.[26]

What the city got was quite different – a calm, rational person who insisted that she had the same right as her brother to take the law into her own hands, and that she had killed not because God told her to or because Maud made her, but, for the most part, because she was entitled to do what the law had failed to do – exact justice for the death of Creffield. The first discussion of Esther Mitchell's motives came via a reporter's account of what she told Chief Wappenstein on the evening of July 12. Esther had resolved to kill her brother the moment he had been acquitted because he had killed Creffield and "must die for his crime."[27] Similar assertions appeared in other newspapers as journalists interviewed both the police-men who had talked to her and, in time, Esther Mitchell herself after she had been moved to the county jail. In one statement she noted that she knew full well that her reason "would not be considered by the court." In another she combined her contempt for those who did not share her beliefs with an assertion that she had simply acted where the law had failed. Creffield was "a holy man," she said, whereas George "was of the world and was defiled," and "it was right that he should be punished for what he did, and the law set him free."[28] The irony of such assertions, of course, was that they dovetailed precisely with claims by others – the Corvallis white caps and George Mitchell – that a person had the right to take the law into their own hands in appropriate circumstances. But Esther did not have to rely on natural law for an argument that George had committed an offence. As we have seen, one of the principal defences offered by contemporary Americans of vigilante justice, including lynch-ing, was the failure of legal systems overburdened with technicalities and process concerns to exact swift and certain justice. As Esther pointed out, George had murdered Creffield and the law had signally failed to do anything about it. She had the right to punish him to fill the gap in law enforcement revealed by his acquittal.

Soon the justice rationale was joined by another: that "her brother had blighted her life by spreading broadcast the statement that Creffield had ruined her, which was a lie." It was George, not Creffield, who had despoiled her reputation. Esther Mitchell repeated this on other occa-sions: "The reason I killed George," she told a *Times* reporter, "was that he had killed an innocent man, and ruined my reputation, by stating that Creffield had seduced me." The *Times* thought this was her principal rea-son: "Mainly she justifies her act upon the ground that he had ruined her reputation." The reporter evinced a rare show of sympathy for this motive; it was "a distinctly human, rather than supernatural element" of the affair.[29]

Esther Mitchell also made it clear that had she not been able to kill her brother at the station, she would have used the little money she had to travel on to Portland and seek another opportunity, perhaps on the train itself. What she did not say, and what she consistently denied throughout the summer of 1906, was that she had committed the murder for religious reasons – that she had been commanded by God.[30] Mitchell also denied that she was in any way insane and insisted that she would never plead insanity to escape the law, as her brother had done. Later in the year she would change her line on this, claim that God had commanded her to kill George, and cooperate in efforts to have her declared insane. This change of attitude may have been expedient; her statements in the immediate aftermath of the killing have an air of conviction to them and, as we shall see, citing a religious basis for the murder helped her avoid a trial. Yet whether or not she believed specifically that God had ordered the killing, that she killed her brother is a remarkable testament to the general influence that Creffield's teachings had had on her and Maud Creffield. Murder was as "un-Christian" an act as could be imagined, and one Bible literalists should have shunned. By mid-1906, however, Bible literalism had long given way to personal allegiance to Creffield's revelations, such that murder could be carried out without emotion by these most Christian of women. Here we see the ultimate expression of the emotional dependence on Creffield that his followers developed, a dependence that survived his death months earlier.

As if the views she expressed were not troubling enough, all the reports of interviews with Mitchell marvelled at her demeanour. Esther was as calm as though she were discussing "some event of most ordinary character." She and Maud were a "revelation" to jailers and police, remarkable among criminals for their "indifference" to their acts. They showed no signs of "regret" nor any "fear of the consequences" of their actions.[31] As the *Post-Intelligencer* noted, Esther Mitchell was unique: her "absolute lack of any feeling, save that of elation at the accomplishment of her purpose and her cold-blooded way of relating the details of the murder," were "marks of character never seen in the ordinary criminal."[32] The *Star* professed to know that, on the night of the murder, Mitchell "slept the sleep of a school girl," with "no blood-stained phantoms of a murdered brother to trouble her."[33] What this behaviour amounted to, of course, was that Esther was unnatural, less an unusual example of womanhood than hardly a woman at all. She was like her sister Donna, who simply gave an "odd smile" when told of George's death. But this, the *Post-Intelligencer* reminded its readers, was the woman who had "deserted her babies in the dead of night."[34]

The two women were incarcerated separately, Esther Mitchell in her own cell and Maud Creffield with the habitual inhabitants of the jail in the "women's tank."[35] When Maud Creffield was interviewed, her story was little different.[36] She said that she wanted George Mitchell dead as revenge for her husband. According to the *Post-Intelligencer,* it was "not religious fanaticism" but "the desire of a wife whose husband has been killed . . . to see that payment of a life for a life has been made" that led her to do what she did. She believes, said the *Times,* "in the doctrine of an eye for an eye and a tooth for a tooth."[37] Maud Creffield also claimed that she had made up her mind about this as soon as Creffield had been shot, not after the acquittal. Whether that was true or not, there is some evidence, from Donna Starr, that the decision to take revenge had been made before the acquittal.[38] Like Esther Mitchell, Maud Creffield refuted any suggestion that she was insane and insisted that she would not offer that plea if tried. Indeed, she told one reporter that she was "just as happy here as I have been at any time since my husband was killed, and I don't care what comes now." And she also denied that any religious motives or instructions lay behind the killing. The *Times* man tried to draw her into ascribing the killing to religion, but she would have none of it, insisting rather that, "George Mitchell killed my husband and I had just as good a right to kill him." The reporter thought it "strange" that she did not refer to religion, that "she justifies the killing of George Mitchell upon the simple ground of personal revenge . . . [just as] if her husband had been some hard-working laborer instead of a professional prophet."[39]

Whatever the two women said, many in Seattle and Oregon were convinced that religion was the root cause of the murder, even if the women had not acted on some kind of message from God.[40] The killing was simply the "work of fanatics." So sure was the *Times* that Esther and Maud had killed because God had commanded them to do so that it sarcastically called for the "conviction" of "the being or thing that is 'commanding' that all these murders be committed . . . for he is certainly a bloody commander."[41] Morris, Shipley, and Wappenstein, among others, insisted that the women were insane. The women had to be depicted as insane and perverted by religion, we would argue, because it made their actions understandable. Men like George Mitchell might kill for revenge or honour, whether or not their actions were approved of. But women were not permitted that privilege; they had to be insane to do such a thing, with religion as the obvious cause of that insanity. As the *Telegram* put it: "When women, normally intelligent and gentle in their dispositions, are transformed to moral perverts, when they can be brought to commit murder with a smile and to glorify their act as one of virtue, and not of malignity, society is facing a terrible menace." That menace was the "fundamental evil" of Creffield and his influence, not vigilantism, which simply did not accord with a woman's appropriate role.[42] A man could defend his sisters, but in the particular variant of vigilantism that involved defence of family and female honour, the woman's role was as passive recipient of chivalry. It was rare, although not unknown, for women who were the victims of seducers to successfully invoke the unwritten law. Their male protectors should do this for them.[43]

AN EPIDEMIC OF MURDER AND THE INSANITY DODGE

The other focus of press and public interest after July 12 was the broader issue of law and order in Seattle, first touched on when George Emory was killed. John Miller, in a classic "I told you so," immediately drew links between George Mitchell's acquittal, the insanity defence generally, and what was seen as an epidemic of murder in the city:[44]

> No man's life is safe and law and order is a farce. When a man can deliberately shoot another in the back and be acquitted, simply because a woman is mixed up in the case, it is time to stop this rot about honor. What is going to become of us? What are the courts for? This is no mining camp. We claim it is a civilized community. Yet, what can we do with public sentiment of this sort. The police can arrest murderers and we can prosecute them, but we can't get a jury to punish them.

Mackintosh was just as forthright, reminding people that he had "told the jury that if Mitchell were freed . . . it would mean other killings in the case."[45]

Others joined in with their doubts about the Mitchell verdict, doubts which increased when it was announced that a post-mortem revealed no physical evidence of insanity in George Mitchell's brain; mental illness was generally thought to leave its mark, even if it had been temporary.[46] We have seen that the *Times* performed an about-face over George Mitchell the moment Emory was killed. Now it not only insisted that the killing of Creffield was simple murder – "not justified by either the moral or statutory law" – but that it had also been carried out in a cowardly manner.[47] The *Argus* had long taken this view and insisted again that Mitchell should have been convicted. It later made a little joke out of the news that Milo Rex, one of Mitchell's jurors, had been found insane and taken to the asylum; the fact was not surprising, it noted, "to one who has read the testimony and the verdict."[48] No opinion on the case was more striking than that of Chief of Police Wappenstein. While he deprecated what he saw as a general tendency to acquit the guilty, which was all the fault of foolish juries, he also, inconsistently and incoherently, insisted that "I'm not saying . . . I wouldn't have voted to free Mitchell" as "I think Creffield ought to have been killed." Perhaps realizing that he was making little sense, he ended with the irritable comment, "At any rate, I wish these Oregon people would kill each other on their own side of the river."[49]

The doubts about one case quickly turned into concerns about the insanity defence in general and its relationship to murder. There were two lines of argument. A less important one was that even if a person was insane, too little was done to restrain the successful defendant in the future. Wappenstein was among those who argued that the insane should always be locked up after being acquitted, as did the State Bar Association.[50] The *Post-Intelligencer* made the case forcefully in an editorial: if this were done, "emotions would be restrained and the homicidal impulse would be considerably modified, if not held completely in check."[51]

More importantly, concerns were expressed that the insanity defence was simply too easily exploited, used to acquit unjustifiably, and the result was a perception that people had a licence to kill when they wished. This was an increasingly prevalent view generally in the United States from the 1880s, the insanity defence often being referred to as the "insanity dodge,"[52] but such concerns had not been a feature of the Seattle debate over Mitchell before his trial, perhaps because people knew the insanity defence was simply a mask for justifiable homicide. That now changed dramatically. As it had after Creffield's death, the *Times* set the tone. Blethen's July 13 editorial worried that Seattle was "in the grip of a mania of murder," with homicide "epidemic." On July 14 he ran a long editorial entitled "The Insanity Farce," which makes a wonderful contrast with that of May 8. Seattle had witnessed three killings – of Creffield, Emory, and George Mitchell – which were all cases of "deliberate" murder "remarkable" for "the atrocity of the crime." In each a plea of insanity had been offered by those wanting to defend the murderer; Esther Mitchell had not made this claim, but her brothers among others had done so. This was "absolute folly," each of the murderers being "as sane as the average man or woman who walks the streets." They were not insane but had "permitted themselves to be controlled by their passions and have ignored the law." They "determined to avenge their own wrongs" and "simply held themselves above the law." More followed on the inability of "experts" to tell insanity and on the fact that the line between sanity and insanity "has become in law a farce . . . a joke."

The following day the *Times* went further, arguing not just that the insanity defence was misused but that such misuse encouraged more killings. By the time Chester Thompson stormed into Emory's house with his gun, it was clear that Mitchell was going to be acquitted: "Did the killing of Creffield by Mitchell, and the proclaimed expectation of freedom under the plea of 'insanity' impel Chester Thompson to commit murder under the expectation that he could escape under a like plea?" And the same problem now arose with Esther Mitchell and Maud Creffield. Why, the newspaper asked, "couldn't these women kill Mitchell immediately after a miscarriage of justice from their standpoint, and escape under a like plea?" If the law could not deal properly with murderers, there would be a descent into "the rule of mob law," because sooner or later the public would despair of the ability of the legal system to deal with murderers, and "execute [one] . . . on a telephone pole."[53]

The *Times* had indeed executed a remarkable turnabout, although perhaps a predictable one given that Blethen had already signalled his new views at the time Emory was killed, and his instinct that sensational arguments sold newspapers. He continued to hammer away at the same themes as July wore on.[54] To some extent the rest of the press followed his lead.[55] The *Republican* complained of an "epidemic of insane murderers."[56] All papers agreed that, as one put it, the city had been "shamefully disgraced" by the spate of three murders committed within a few weeks.[57] It was "reaping the whirlwind" of support given for Mitchell.[58] The death of Mitchell himself was a clear example, said the *Post-Intelligencer*, of the fact that "the evil that men do lives after them."[59] Editorials and opinion pieces called for tougher law enforcement and reform of the insanity laws. As it was, insanity acquittals for "perfectly sane people" had led to "appalling miscarriages of justice" and "a general weakening of the regard for the sanctity of human life."[60] Esther Mitchell could expect to live a long time, said the *Argus*, "judging from the way murderers are treated in King County." It put the case against vigilante killing simply and powerfully:[61]

The killing of George Mitchell by his sister Esther emphasizes the fact that constituting one's self judge, jury and executioner doesn't pay. In Mitchell's

eyes his sister had been disgraced . . . Mitchell thought he was ridding the
world of a great scoundrel, and nearly everybody agreed with him. The
holy rollers didn't and Mitchell's murder followed his acquittal. From the
standpoint of Esther Mitchell and Mrs Creffield they had a perfect right
to kill Mitchell. From the standpoint of Mitchell he had a perfect right to
kill Creffield. And that is why our laws must be obeyed, even if a villain does
occasionally escape punishment. If every person who has a private grievance
is allowed to go gunning for his enemy the inevitable result will be that we
will become a nation of barbarians.

The press continued to raise these issues through the rest of the year and
into 1907. The debate over the defence of insanity, initiated by the George
Mitchell and Chester Thompson cases, greatly sharpened by the Esther
Mitchell and Maud Creffield case, and given further impetus by the Sloane
and Constantine trials of 1907, culminated in 1909, when Washington
became the first common-law jurisdiction to abolish the defence. Insanity
became, in effect, a factor that mitigated sentence, but it no longer went
to culpability.[62]

It is much more difficult to know what the general public, rather then
the press, thought of the events. The Sunday after the murder saw the
city's pulpits widely used to talk about the case, the consistent theme being
the need to obey the second commandment.[63] Even before this, Rev.
Myron Haynes, who had contributed to the debate before the trial, was
more forthright, condemning Mitchell and the *Times* for their "disregard
of law," and, as he and others had done earlier, he linked the murders to
broader themes, a "deterioration" in the social, political, and religious life
of the city, from which only reform sentiments could rescue it.[64]

In this atmosphere few were prepared to encourage restraint, but Morris
and Shipley did so. On July 16 they issued a statement to the press that
"deprecate[d] the tendency manifested by many to be borne off from
their equilibrium by these unfortunate and distressing occurrences," and
called for respect for everybody's right to a fair trial.[65] The *Star* also coun-
selled caution, arguing that determinations of guilt should be left to juries
and that Esther Mitchell and Maud Creffield, and anybody else accused
of murder, should be tried for the crime he or she may have committed,
"and not for all the murders that have been committed in King County
during the last year."[66] But in the heated atmosphere of July 1906 these
were not popular sentiments, and Frater for one was happy to accede
to demands for tougher law enforcement. In sentencing one Robert H.
Jones for second-degree murder a few days after the Mitchell acquittal he

referred to the Mitchell case and made it clear that he disapproved of the verdict. Although he told Jones that "he was not being held responsible for any crime other than that for which he had been found guilty," he also said that "it was necessary to inflict punishment as an example to others," and gave him twenty years.[67] Months later Frater was still angry enough to complain that "it seemed impossible to find murderers guilty in this state."[68]

While we can hardly expect outright approval of Esther Mitchell and Maud Creffield's action, some sympathy for their resort to private justice might be anticipated when the law had failed them. Had they been men, such sentiments would surely have been expressed. The eccentric *Patriarch* suggested that Esther Mitchell was no worse than her brother, and a retired superior court judge, William H. Upton of Walla Walla, sent her a telegram stating: "Accept thanks, congratulations and assistance if needed. Talk to your lawyer only." Upton had no sympathy for the Creffield sect, but he was disgusted by the verdict in George Mitchell's trial.[69] He is the only person we have found who sympathized with Esther Mitchell, and he did nothing further to help her. Not even Charles Mitchell could do so. "She will have to abide by the consequences of her crime," he said, adding, "I glory in her determination not to plead insanity," because he did not think she was insane. Esther "had better die upon the scaffold with truth upon her lips" than testify to a falsehood.[70] As matters turned out, neither woman got close to a scaffold. But their treatment by the press suggests, as we have already noted, that honour killings were reserved for men.

12

The Law, Maud Creffield, and Esther Mitchell

Prosecution for Murder

KING COUNTY'S PROSECUTORS had no hesitation in proceed-ing against both Esther Mitchell and Maud Creffield for first-degree murder.[1] Under Washington law an accessory before the fact was just as guilty as if she had fired the shot herself,[2] and the information for what became Case No. 3695 in the superior court, filed on July 18, charged Mitchell with killing her brother and alleged that Maud Creffield "did in-cite, aid, counsel and abet" her in that. The day after the murder a rumour swirled around Seattle that Esther Mitchell would never stand trial because she had committed suicide in her jail cell, but it proved to be untrue. The prosecutors were also adamant that neither of the women was insane. With no trial able to take place before the fall because of the summer recess, they busied themselves with ensuring there would be ample expert evidence to resist any defence claim of insanity – in marked contrast to the earlier approach to George Mitchell's case. Loughary was engaged to examine the women, as was Dr Alexander McLeish, former superintend-ent of the asylum at Steilacoom. By the 14th Loughary had already had "several" talks with the women in the county jail, and his visits continued on a daily basis.[3] The women were held separately and thus had to be seen separately. The doctors were not engaged to make decisions for the prose-cuting attorney's office, however. Miller was determined to prosecute what-ever the physicians came up with. It took weeks for the doctors to report;

when they did it was to the effect that while the women were "possessed of certain peculiarities," they were "not insane."[4]

Although Esther Mitchell told the press that neither she nor Maud had any money and would make do with the court-appointed attorney that had to be provided, if the defendant wished, in a felony case,[5] O.V. Hurt came to Seattle and set about the task of organizing a defence for his daughter and her friend, as he had done for George Mitchell.[6] He tried to engage Morris and Shipley, who resisted despite their affection for Hurt. As one of them put it, it would be "indelicate" to "defend a person charged with the murder of one who was their client."[7] But it must also have been difficult for them to resist the entreaties of Hurt, who a few days after the murder had written plaintively to "Little Maud" asking, "what can your papa do for you, dear" and assuring her that while his heart was broken, "after all I love you more than I ever did." As he told the *Oregonian*, he deplored what Maud had done but believed that "no act of hers can wipe out the tie of paternity." He believed that she and Esther were insane and should be sent to the asylum, and all he wanted to secure, he said, was "a fair trial and no favors."[8] To help get it he was prepared to mortgage his home.[9]

Hurt had trouble finding counsel, especially for Esther Mitchell. Former superior court judge Upton refused. A.J. Speckert of Seattle, who specialized in criminal law, was approached and considered taking on Maud Creffield, but ultimately did not.[10] When the two women were arraigned on July 23, Mitchell was represented by Chauncey Baxter of the Seattle firm of Baxter and Wilson.[11] Baxter had plenty of experience after almost twenty years of practice, but he was little known in Seattle, having moved there from the Midwest only in 1904.[12] In 1906 he was practising in partnership with a young lawyer named John R. Wilson. Although Baxter stayed with Mitchell throughout 1906, he was soon joined by a Portland lawyer, Alfred E. Clark. Clark was a young man who had only just moved to Portland from Minnesota, and was something of a scholar.[13] He was apparently retained by "Portland friends" of Esther but would not say who they were. Maud Creffield was represented at the arraignment by Silas Shipley, although Morris insisted that the involvement of his firm was both temporary, until permanent counsel was secured, and agreed to "entirely out of our regard for Mr Hurt."[14]

The women were arraigned on Tuesday, July 23.[15] Perhaps Frater asked for the case but, if a coincidence, it was an ironic one that saw it added to his docket. Maud Creffield pleaded not guilty in a forthright manner, but

Esther Mitchell was given a week in which to plead. She was in court again on July 31 to plead not guilty. This time she was represented by Clark, who successfully requested a separate trial for her.[16] No trial dates were set at this stage because Chester Thompson's case was due to begin on September 17 and it was unclear how long it might take.[17] Not until September 7 was a date of September 24 set for Esther Mitchell. Her trial would be first, with Maud Creffield's case set down in mid-September for a month later, October 22.[18]

The various pre-trial proceedings provided little to satisfy the curiosity of either press or public in the characters and motivations of the two strange and remarkable women. People attended the relatively brief and dull proceedings in large numbers, with a good percentage of them women, as had been the case for George Mitchell's trial. They "craned" or "edged forward" to catch a glimpse of the accused. When the two women were arraigned, Maud Creffield, still in widow's weeds, "exhibited [not] the least emotion," and both were entirely "self-possessed." They did, however, exchange smiles, it being the first time they had seen each other since their arrests. When Esther Mitchell came to court alone for her plea at the end of July she was said to have sat through the entire proceeding "with her eyes fixed vacantly," although she also, apparently, when her name was called, stood up "calm and smiling to face the bar of justice." When she gave her plea she spoke in "a clear, firm voice."[19]

The women remained objects of considerable attention through the summer, with Esther Mitchell garnering the lion's share. There was a good deal of speculation that she would plead insanity at her trial, fuelled by Clark, who after her not guilty plea started telling the press that the defence would be insanity "induced by religious fanaticism."[20] Stories circulated, again started by Clark, that her brothers were now reconciled to her because they thought her insane, and would assist the defence in establishing this. In the only comment she made on the issue, Esther Mitchell said that she did not know whether her defence would be insanity, but that it might be; she did not rule it out.[21]

Of much more interest than the defence case was Esther Mitchell herself. How could this young girl be so unnatural as to kill a brother in such a cold-blooded and premeditated fashion? People wrote to her, although she evinced little interest in the letters.[22] The press interviewed her, but she would not talk about either her religion or the case. She was, she said, content to live "from day to day" and to "let the future take care of itself." A reporter found it remarkable that Esther "appears absolutely indifferent" to her fate. When "religious workers" visited her they were politely but coldly received, and she insisted that "she had never wronged anyone."[23] The portrait was one of an entirely unnatural stoicism and self-possession, which only increased press fascination with her. When Esther became ill in August there were wild and wholly erroneous rumours of her impending death.[24] Most press commentary was content to assume that she was mentally unbalanced, but the *Times,* one-time champion of George Mitchell, nonetheless complained that "not for one instant so far . . . has this girl suffered the slightest compunction for her crime." How could she be so indifferent to the fact that her brother had killed to "protect the virtue of the sister who repaid his kindness by murdering him?" The *Oregonian* offered an equally harsh assessment, arguing that "no punishment which the law could inflict on this phlegmatic and seemingly heartless creature is adequate for the crime," but nonetheless suggesting that the very enormity of her offence "has raised a question as to the mental responsibility of the murderess."[25]

THE INSANITY COMMISSION

The preparations made for the trial of the two women turned out to be all for naught. In September they were pronounced insane and unfit to stand trial, according to what was called an "insanity commission," appointed pursuant to Washington's procedures for civil commitment for insanity. The origins of this method of dealing with them are murky. Lawyers had begun to talk about an insanity hearing as an alternative to a criminal trial in mid-July,[26] although Mackintosh and Miller were firmly opposed to the idea. Mackintosh insisted that he did not wish to "waste any time with a medical commission," and argued that any proceeding other than a trial "would be equivalent to announcing to the world at large that King County had rather save a little money than prosecute the people who commit murder within its boundaries." He also insisted, wrongly as it turned out, that the law allowed him to try the prisoners, whatever an insanity commission might conclude.[27]

Frater, Morris, and Shipley, among others, were early supporters of the idea. Frater raised the possibility with the prosecutors within days of the murder, but they would not agree to take the initiative and ask for a hearing.[28] Frater was open about his attitude, stating when the two were arraigned on July 23 that "he supposed . . . the defense would be insanity," and that it would be a "good thing for the county and the state" if "the prisoners could be declared insane at once."[29] He continued to attempt to get the prosecutors to agree to hold a hearing into sanity but met with consistent refusals coupled with statements that the prosecution was having its own experts examine the two women and that the verdict would be that they were sane.[30]

Before and after the insanity hearings two reasons were given for why the civil insanity laws should be employed. First, it was cheaper. The Mitchell trial had cost the county over $2,500, and two further trials would allegedly cost twice that.[31] Second, a recent statute required anybody found insane by a Washington court who was not a legal resident of the state to be deported to his or her home state.[32] This too would save King County money, for the costs of the women's incarceration could be foisted onto some other community. Sending the women back to Oregon would also provide the Seattle citizenry with the satisfaction of at last making Oregon deal with Oregon's problems. As the *Post-Intelligencer* succinctly put it in arguing for deportation, "Oregon washes too much dirty linen in Washington."[33]

Saving money and dumping Oregon's problems in their rightful place were good arguments for avoiding a trial, but not, we think, sufficient in themselves. For one thing, the savings would probably not have been as great as some suggested.[34] More importantly, any savings would surely not override the moral value that would attach to bringing to book the perpetrators of yet another murder in a catalogue of killings that had so besmirched the city's reputation. What better opportunity was there for asserting the power and the majesty of the law than the prosecution of these two women, who, like George Mitchell, had no conventional defence and who also, unlike George Mitchell, were widely reviled and condemned in the court of public opinion? That was certainly the opinion of Blethen, now a staunch proponent of law and order.[35] However, a trial of the two women, while it may have vindicated law and order, also posed two very real dangers.

First, many people genuinely believed Creffield and Mitchell were insane, and it was generally thought that despite their assertions to the contrary they would ultimately make that plea.[36] If they were acquitted on the ground of insanity, the trial would reinforce Seattle's reputation as the place where the insanity dodge worked well, where people got away with murder. The second danger a trial posed would arise if the women did not plead insanity but simply asserted that they had killed George in revenge because he had killed Creffield and been allowed to get away with it. This was no legal defence but, as we have seen, Seattle had quickly lost its taste for lionizing George Mitchell, and nobody wanted dramatic public statements of what was true – that the community had let him get away with murder.

Related to these two reasons for preferring a civil insanity commission to a criminal trial was an increasing distrust of juries among the elite. An insanity hearing with doctors as the effective decision makers was preferred precisely because those experts, not lay jurors, would decide the issue. As the *Post-Intelligencer* put it: "Insanity is a matter for alienists to determine by a direct examination of the subject. It should not be settled by a jury on 'expert' testimony given on hypothetical questions, as is the case when the plea is interposed as a defence to a crime. It should be settled definitely in advance of trial and the decision should be final."[37] In arguing for the commission to be able to give a "final" decision on insanity, the paper was asking for the impossible, because a commission could legally determine only sanity as of the time it sat, not whether its subjects had been insane at the time the crime had been committed. But that does not matter; the city's elite was searching for a solution to the "insanity dodge," and for a way to make insanity determinations more "scientifically."[38] Finally, capacity to stand trial was generally a matter raised once the trial began, and it was then ruled on by a jury.[39] Had this been done, and the women found not fit to stand trial, they would have been incarcerated somewhere in Washington against the day when they had recovered and could stand trial. They could not be deported other than under the civil insanity process. If the Seattle elite did not want a trial, deportation was valuable in achieving this end as well – it got the women out of the jurisdiction, ensuring that there would never be a trial unless they were extradited.

The reasons we have offered for the decision to invoke an insanity hearing are somewhat speculative, and the evidence for them circumstantial. But given that the publicly stated reasons are unconvincing, given that Esther Mitchell was later quietly released from the asylum and never tried, and given the intensity of the debate over murder and insanity in Seattle in the summer of 1906, we are confident that a consensus emerged in the city that it was simply not a good idea to put on more high-profile trials. The *Post-Intelligencer,* the paper most closely tied to the city's establishment, was pushing for a commission by mid-July, continuing to argue in its favour throughout the summer.[40]

For all his confidence that an insanity hearing was unnecessary and unwise, Mackintosh also knew that it was easy to invoke the insanity commitment statute, the Washington equivalent of the Oregon law that had been used against the Creffield sect in 1904.[41] And when on September 7

Esther Mitchell's trial was set down to begin on the 24th of that month, that is what happened. Washington provided that if one person submitted an affidavit attesting his or her belief that somebody was insane and thereby "unsafe to be at large," the court was obliged to hold a hearing. In Washington the jurisdiction was given to the superior court, a higher body than in Oregon where the county court had it, but otherwise the process was very similar. The judge was obliged to call in "two reputable physicians" to hear the evidence with him. If the physicians and the judge thought the insanity claim made out, and the person a danger to self, or to others, commitment to the asylum would follow.[42]

Frank Hurt invoked this procedure, swearing two affidavits on Saturday, September 8, that he believed his sister and Esther Mitchell were insane.[43] The affidavits and applications for a hearing were presented in Frater's court by Clark (for Esther Mitchell) and W.A. Holzheimer (for Maud Creffield) on Monday, September 10. Holzheimer was a member of the Baxter and Wilson firm, Esther Mitchell's lawyers, and the man chosen by O.V. Hurt when Morris and Shipley kept their resolution not to represent her in the long term.[44] Frater immediately granted the applications. He did so over prosecution objections, Mackintosh and Miller arguing that while the civil commitment procedure was appropriate in the ordinary case, where there was a serious criminal charge pending against the person alleged to be insane, the issue should be decided by a jury.[45] That was certainly the usual procedure, derived from common law, with the jury being either one specially called for the purpose or, if the trial had actually started before an issue about the capacity was raised, the trial jury itself. However, the state statutes were silent on whether this method of proceeding was required in the case of a criminal defendant.[46] This issue of which procedure should be used to determine fitness to stand trial became the central one in the case that Mackintosh later took to the state supreme court.

Frater named three doctors to hear the case, none expert alienists. Appointed "chairman" of the commission was Dr Kenneth Turner, Frater's family physician.[47] The other members were Dr J. Howard Snively and Dr R.M. Eames (sometimes called Ames). Frater appointed "men whose names are almost unknown in this community," and who were undistinguished, complained the *Times*.[48] This was true of Snively, who not only had no experience in mental illness but had graduated from medical school in Portland just over a year previously.[49] Turner was also a young man, "long on theories if not on experience."[50] Eames was a more substantial figure, a sometime state legislative representative who had served

as Seattle health officer and county physician; he was credited with establishing the city health department. But he specialized in diseases of the
lung and heart, and in smallpox.[51] Frater's selections were unusual ones
and contributed to later intimations that the commission was fixed to get
the result he and others desired.

The commission's task was not to determine whether the women had
been insane when George Mitchell was killed, nor to find whether they
were then insane such that they should be committed to an asylum. It was
to assess their capacity to stand trial, which meant asking whether they
understood the proceedings and could make a rational defence.[52] As we
shall see, this was the one thing the doctors did not actually determine.
The commission got under way more or less immediately, on Wednesday,
September 12, and met on all or part of eight days, some days adding an
evening session to the morning and afternoon.[53] The first six, up to and
including Tuesday, September 18, were taken up with witnesses; the reports
were released on Thursday, September 20, and formally delivered to Frater
the next day. In addition to Esther Mitchell and Maud Creffield, the commission heard from a wide variety of witnesses – twenty-four in total.
They included family members O.V. Hurt, Frank Hurt, Perry Mitchell,
and Fred Mitchell. A number of law enforcement officials gave evidence –
Dr Snyder, the jail physician; Mrs Kelly; John Miller; Chief of Police
Wappenstein and some police officers, including Officer Mason who had
arrested Esther Mitchell; Sheriff Lou Smith; and county jailer Emil Larsen.
And a number of people who had had some experience with one or both
of the women testified – Will Morris, James Berry, William Gardner,
Mary Graham, *Times* reporter E.O. Kelsey, and Dr Bories. Two insanity
experts, Drs. Loughary and Nicholson, rounded out the witness list. The
prosecuting attorney wanted Dr McLeish to testify as well, but the commission declined to hear him on the ground that he would add nothing
to Loughary's testimony. About half the witnesses were brought in by
defendants' counsel, the other half by the state.[54]

The proceedings were relatively informal, although the women were
represented by counsel and Miller attended as well. The rules of evidence
did not apply, and most of the sessions were held in Frater's chambers
rather than in the courtroom. Frater gave control of the whole process to
the doctors: they were "to pursue the inquiry in your own way and as you
think best."[55] The lawyers asked few if any questions, interrogations being
done by the doctors. Frater was often not there at all, spending most of his
time conducting trials in the courtroom while the commission met in his
chambers. He heard the testimony of only two witnesses in full, and parts

of the testimony of two others.[56] As we shall see, many aspects of these arrangements were later criticized by the prosecutors.

Most of the witnesses examined extensively were there to provide evidence that the two women were insane. Moreover, if the press reports are any guide, most of that evidence pointed to the strange beliefs and practices of the Creffield sect as illustrative of insanity. O.V. Hurt, for example, after depicting Maud as always having been a difficult person when it came to religion, talked about her food taboos, her "melancholy weeping spells" after her release from the asylum, her destruction of clothing, and her persistent claim that "God will protect me." He and Frank were also asked about unspecified "vile" practices of the sect. O.V. ended his evidence by asserting that in his view Maud had been "partially insane" for years.[57] Berry's evidence was also principally about Maud's beliefs, including her conviction that she received messages from God, while Gardner and Graham described Esther Mitchell's behaviour in the Portland home – not dressing properly, refusing to associate with others, constant Bible reading and praying. Perry Mitchell, some of whose evidence may have been given in secret, discussed his sister's involvement in the sect and her and other members' distrust of outsiders because they believed they were persecuted. Of course, nobody suggested that a belief in persecution was entirely rational in the circumstances. Some non-family witnesses also talked about religious belief, especially Dr Bories, who recounted Maud Creffield's insistence immediately after the murder that her husband would rise again. We can read between the lines the same kinds of things that helped the Oregon courts earlier to commit sect members. These religious beliefs and practices were so irrational, and so unnatural in women in particular, that people who adhered to them must be insane.

Evidence about religious practices was not the only testimony the doctors heard. We have already seen that there was a belief in heredity as a partial cause of insanity, and Sarah Hurt's mental stability was therefore an issue for the panel. O.V. Hurt was asked about this, and the doctors wanted her to testify, as did Holzheimer. Telegrams flew back and forth to Corvallis, and at various times Sarah was expected to come north, but she never did. On Esther Mitchell's side, the doctors had the testimony of Perry Mitchell that his father "had been a religious and political crank for years and had a quick temper."[58] They also questioned Fred Mitchell about his attempted suicide. He was not pleased about this, and at the end of his examination demanded to know why the questions had been asked; Turner responded that "in dealing with such cases it is necessary to know the temperament and general mental and physical conditions of those nearest to the one alleged to be afflicted."[59] Fred's attempted suicide duly made its way onto the official form committing Esther Mitchell. The search for signs of hereditary insanity also resulted in Frank and O.V. Hurt, and Perry and Fred Mitchell, being given "physical examinations."[60] Will Morris also testified, insisting that Esther Mitchell was insane when he first met her and had remained so ever since, because of what he saw as her entirely unnatural attitude about helping her brother. Her "indifference" to George's fate was a clear sign of insanity. Thus, as with religious beliefs, what could not be comprehended because it was so far outside the realm of natural feminine behaviour was condemned as mental illness.

Of the non-medical witnesses for the state the most important was John Miller. He recounted conversations he had had with the women, which revealed, he said, the love they had for each other and Esther's resentment for her brothers. He testified that Esther had told him she had shot George partly because he had killed Creffield and partly because of the statements he had made about her after his arrest. Miller insisted that in his view the women had not killed out of religious conviction or inspiration. The doctors let Miller have his say without interrupting him with questions even once, suggesting that they had little interest in his testimony. Also there to advance the proposition that the women were sane were officials such as Wappenstein, Smith, Mason, and Larsen, who talked about the women's cool demeanour and the fact that they acted normally in jail.

Some testimony concerned physiological and sexual matters, but since it was taken in private and kept confidential we know very little of it. Mrs Kelly gave some evidence in public about the women's deportment and "personal habits," but this apparently contained little of interest to the press. In private she was examined on more delicate matters – "the menses and personal habits" of the two women. It must have been her evidence that allowed the doctors to certify that Esther Mitchell went in for "suppression of menses at times."[61] The doctors must have believed they had discovered more evidence of mental disease, since female insanity was often associated with dysfunction of the reproductive organs.[62] Maud Creffield did not receive the same notation, but in the section of the physician's certificate made out for her at the conclusion of the commission asking about "filthy habits" she got a "yes."[63] We assume this meant masturbation, and that the evidence of it came from Kelly. How Kelly knew is not clear, and the practice seems incongruous for one of Maud Creffield's religious beliefs. But the important point is that such behaviour was also seen as a sign of mental imbalance in women.

The doctors also conducted a "physical examination" of the two women, although we do not know when and where this took place, or what its scope was.[64] The sessions at which the physical examinations took place and at which Kelly testified were not the only closed ones. Drs. Loughary and Nicholson gave their testimony on Friday, September 14, in camera, because it was a recounting of information derived from doctor-patient confidences.[65] And some of the testimony of Esther Mitchell, Maud Creffield, James Berry, O.V. Hurt, Perry Mitchell, and Fred Mitchell may have been given in secret. These closed sessions later drew bitter complaints from the prosecution.

The most important witnesses, of course, were Esther Mitchell and Maud Creffield. The commission had two kinds of sessions with them. On Saturday, September 15, the doctors visited them at the county jail in order to find out about "the general habits and condition of the women and the manner in which they cared for themselves." They found the cell "as neat as it can be kept, with white linen on the cot, clean towels and handkerchiefs and other necessary articles hung about the place."[66] The doctors talked to the women about a variety of topics, including what the press referred to as personal matters.

The principal examinations took place in the courthouse, Maud Creffield being questioned for many hours on Monday and Tuesday, September 17 and 18, and Esther Mitchell for a long time on the latter day. They were asked about their backgrounds and their time in the sect generally, with much of the questioning focusing on their religious beliefs and knowledge.[67] Attention in both cases, however, centred on the murder of George Mitchell. Maud Creffield was asked if she was willing to be punished for the murder; she replied that she was indeed anxious for that to happen, because she had "fulfilled the purpose for which God placed me in the world" and did not now care what happened to her. There was a good deal more along the same lines about God and Creffield's spirit telling her what to do. She was indifferent to the possibility of hanging because "I never consider the laws of man when the will of God has been known to me." When asked why she had allowed Esther to do the killing if it was God's will that she do it, she said that "Esther came to me and said that God had made known to her that it was his will that she should kill her brother." At first Maud did not believe it, but they both prayed, with the result that "it was witnesseth that Esther was correct and that it was God's will that she should do the killing." Esther Mitchell's examination was very similar. Like Maud Creffield, she had been led by God to commit the murder. Indeed, God had given her the strength to do it and if God commanded her to kill another person, or herself, she would obey that command. She vehemently denied being insane, repeating thereby what she had said earlier in the proceedings when she talked to Fred and Perry. She had also said on that occasion that "I did a good deed, and want the world to know it."[68]

The statements from both women that they believed they were divinely ordained to kill George Mitchell were the most important part of the evidence given before the commission. The women provided exactly the same explanation that George Mitchell had, and if such beliefs had shown insanity in George, presumably they would show it in his sister and Maud Creffield. During the examination of Maud Creffield, Turner noted that her statements were inconsistent with her confession to the police. But she explained that she and Esther had agreed beforehand to say the same things to the police and not to mention the religious motive because "the public would laugh" at a claim that God had ordered the killing, and "mock and scoff." Since she had been incarcerated, God had told her that she should "make public the true nature of her act regardless of consequences." Asked if she was happy to have taken part in the killing, she replied: "I am satisfied. I am certain that I have fulfilled God's will. I was not happy. I am never happy. I care nothing for happiness on earth. I simply wish to do God's will." Esther's explanation of her earlier statements to the police was different. She had put it down to simple revenge "in hopes that it would so arouse the public that she would be lynched." She was "tired of living" and "would have welcomed death."[69]

Esther Mitchell and Maud Creffield provided the commission with all the evidence it could possibly need to find them insane. We suspect that the women's evidence was concocted as some of the evidence at George Mitchell's trial had been. While Esther Mitchell in particular insisted she was not insane, her and Maud's testimony was designed to show the opposite. This conclusion accords with the role played by their counsel, who supported the initial application for a sanity hearing and took a full part in the proceedings, attending at all times and suggesting witnesses who would give evidence that their clients were insane. They could not have done this had their clients instructed them otherwise; indeed, it is hard to see how they could have acted the way they did unless they had positive instructions to do so. George Mitchell had likewise consistently maintained that he was not insane while allowing his lawyers to say the opposite.

After deliberating for a day or so, the doctors presented their reports on Thursday, September 20, and formally delivered them to Frater the next day, at which time they were also published in the newspapers.[70] The reports were identical apart from the names. They were short, and the crucial parts can be reproduced in full:

> the commission is unanimously of the opinion that the subject of this investigation was at the time of the commission of the crime charged against her, and is now, suffering from a form of insanity commonly classified as paranoia, which has its origins in structural defects of the nervous system. Further, that because of this disease she was at the time of the commission of the crime as charged, possessed of such a deranged mentality as to make her unable to distinguish between right and wrong, and therefore irresponsible criminally. Further, that this individual belongs to a class of lunatics dangerous to be at large, who persistently follow their morbid inclinations regardless of law or ethics, and should be placed under restraint in an institution for the proper treatment of such cases.

Paranoia was a term of relatively recent origin among alienists, defined as a form of insanity "characterized by systematized delusions, or by the tendency to form such delusions." It was considered a primary form of insanity, not a symptom or consequence of some other kind. By a "systematized" delusion doctors meant one that was logically constructed throughout, except for the erroneous false premise, and that conclusions and actions therefore followed logically. It might lead to a belief in persecution or to delusions of grandeur, exaltation of the self. Delusions of grandeur were varied, and while none of the textbook examples included a belief that God had ordered a killing, that idea could clearly be included within the general instances given. Indeed, it was believed that "religious paranoiacs" were a particular subgroup of paranoiacs with delusions of grandeur.[71]

The report of the insanity commission simply referred to a conclusion that the women suffered from paranoia, but their analysis is apparent in the "Physician's Certificates," which had to be signed in each case. These noted as the evidence of insanity, "logical and systemilical [sic] delusions of persecution and self exaltation." Both were also said to have "homicidal," "suicidal," and "incendiary" dispositions, the last being a reference to the destruction of personal property, and neither had "rational intervals." For both the insanity was said to be "increasing" and the delusions "permanent."[72] This was the usual view when delusions had progressed from the persecution to the grandeur stage, for delusions of grandeur represented "a transformation which is profound and complete."[73]

Perhaps not surprisingly, given their lack of prior experience, the doctors arrived at their conclusions by relying heavily on textbooks. One of the physicians told the press that they had found *Berkley on Mental Disease* very useful, a text that seemed to describe "the exact cases in question." It stated that women were more prone to paranoia than men, and also that women with the condition were likely to "attend revival meetings, become excitable and uncontrollable," and generally be fanatical about religion. Other texts also gave descriptions of paranoia that seemed "to tally with the cases in question so closely as to make it appear that the subjects in question might have been those under discussion in the work."[74]

Whatever their quality as contemporary examples of diagnosis of mental illness, there were two aspects of the physicians' reports that made them both inappropriate and incomplete, given the specific legal context for which they were produced. First, they stated that the women had not only been insane when George Mitchell was killed, they had been at that time "unable to distinguish between right and wrong" and "irresponsible criminally." An inquiry into fitness to stand trial was not for the purpose of making any finding about the past. Evidence of past insanity might well be relevant to the present, but the statements about right and wrong and criminal responsibility were wholly inappropriate. The doctors had pronounced on something that was clearly a matter only for a criminal trial jury, and a matter that should have been decided only after a hearing of all the evidence, a hearing that would include cross-examination of witnesses – including medical experts – by the prosecution. The commission purported, quite improperly, to acquit the women on the ground of insanity.

The second, and more serious, problem with the reports was that they were incomplete – they did not state whether the women were unfit to stand trial. They said only that Esther and Maud were suffering from paranoia. But it was not sufficient simply to show some measure of insanity, it also had to be demonstrated that a person was not "mentally competent to make a rational defense." The leading medico-legal textbook put it this way: "A person arraigned for crime ... who is capable of understanding the nature and object of the proceeding against him, and who comprehends his own condition in reference to it, and can conduct his defense in a rational manner, is to be deemed sane for the purpose of being tried, although on some other subject his mind may be unsound."[75] The doctors' reports actually said nothing at all about whether the insanity resulted in incapacity. Moreover, it cannot be said that the conclusion was an obvious one from the finding of paranoia. It could perhaps be argued that the women's belief that they had killed George Mitchell because they had been ordered by God to do so rendered them unfit to stand trial because it made them incapable of offering a defence. But the evidence before the commission showed clearly that they understood the charges against them, understood the nature of the trial proceedings, and understood the legal consequences they faced. Could they, in the words of the test quoted above, have conducted their defence in a rational manner? They were rational enough to understand that their explanation that God had ordered them to kill George was not an excuse in law and if stated in court would incriminate them. That a defendant admit an offence rather than put forward an affirmative defence was not, and is not, an indication of incapacity – only, perhaps, of poor judgment.

Frater, however, accepted the reports without hesitation. John Miller objected heatedly to that acceptance, and he made it clear that he would seek review by a higher court. He "denounced the commission in the strongest terms,"[76] but as far as we can tell he did not, at the time or later, question either the finding that the women had not been criminally responsible when George Mitchell was killed, or whether the doctors' conclusions actually meant they were unfit to stand trial. The Mitchell case was stricken from the trial calendar, again in the face of objections from the prosecutors, who argued that the criminal trial should go ahead pending the result of their application to the state supreme court.[77] Frater also ordered both women deported to Oregon, although this order was stayed until the supreme court had ruled. The order stated that the women were to be placed in the Salem Asylum, something a judge of the Washington Superior Court had no authority to do;[78] Frater could order the women transported to the Oregon border, but only an Oregon court could commit them in that state.

Reactions to the commission's finding varied. When her father told Maud Creffield the result, she apparently said, "I am glad for your sake." Esther Mitchell made no comment.[79] There was generally disapproval in Oregon and a mixed reaction in the Seattle press. Most of the adverse comment in Corvallis and Portland concentrated on the deportation order, rightly pointing out that the women would be free the moment they crossed into the state, and that it would take an Oregon court to commit them to an asylum there.[80] Even Oregon Governor George Chamberlain weighed in, calling the deportation order "illogical" and noting that all states held non-residents in their asylums.[81] Frater was unfairly criticized in this respect, for the statute made deportation mandatory, but the concern about exceeding his jurisdiction was a valid one. John Manning, as might be expected, also weighed in with an opinion, suggesting that the women were indeed insane and should simply be brought before an Oregon court for commitment. He could not resist his personal hobby horse, the rectitude of George Mitchell's act: "he did a very laudable act in eliminating that miserable animal Creffield from the face of the earth."[82] Unlike some others, Manning's views had not been altered by subsequent events.

In Seattle, the *Times,* which as we have seen had turned from supporter of vigilante justice to advocate of law and order the moment George Mitchell was killed, led its story on the commission's conclusions with the headline, "Legal Way is Opened for Epidemic of Murder." A front-page cartoon in the same issue, reproduced below, was pure Blethen, suggesting that Frater was as "crazy" as any insane murderer.[83] An editorial the same day attacked the whole process, using many of Mackintosh's legal arguments. "What a farce," it concluded, adding that Seattle "was sick and tired of this insanity plea being made every time cold-blooded murder is committed."[84] Other newspapers, however, were more restrained. The *Post-Intelligencer* simply made no comment on the matter at all, suggesting that it silently approved of this way of dealing with the problem and wanted the whole matter forgotten as quickly and quietly as possible. The *Argus* disapproved, suggesting that the "wiseacres" on the commission ought to have realized that all murderers were "a little off" and worrying that "it will be another stigma on the name of Seattle if these women are permitted to escape trial." The *Republican* took a pragmatic approach: Esther Mitchell was "as crazy as a March hare" and Maud Creffield even worse, and everybody thought that. Thus they would be acquitted if tried, and "if there be any loop hole whereby they can be incarcerated in an insane asylum for life, we see no impropriety in doing so."[85]

Not surprisingly, Mackintosh condemned the proceeding. The law should prosecute the people responsible for "the most brutal assassination ever perpetrated in King County," he said, and the precedent now set meant that "anyone may allege insanity after having been charged with a crime and escape the consequences of the law."[86] Mackintosh doubted not just the expediency of the process but also its legality, and he immediately took the case to the Washington Supreme Court. When he did so, the deportation order was stayed and there was no place else for the two women to go but back to the county jail. Now incarcerated together in their own cell, they whiled away the time waiting for the outcome of the supreme court case. They read and played cards with other women prisoners – perhaps not something Creffield would have approved of – but they took no part in religious exercises and did not proselytize. They would not discuss their case with reporters and had few visitors beyond their lawyers, although any visitors who came were given a welcome "neither cold nor cordial," and "sympathy or kindnesses are not well received." "Gifts are welcome," with "deeds more than words . . . appreciated." One consistent visitor by the fall of 1906 was Attie (Bray) Levins, who had married Sampson Levins on October 18, 1906, in Seattle, and was now living in the city.[87]

The Insanity Commission: Was the Fix In?

From the moment the commission reported, the prosecutors and others complained that the entire proceeding was essentially predetermined, a "fix." Miller put this as forcefully as perhaps he could in Frater's courtroom, stating that "the commission knew what its findings would be after the first day's hearing." But in truth he and Mackintosh had come to believe by then that the commission was designed to produce the result it did from long before it began to hear evidence. Mackintosh told the press that the commission was "simply a subterfuge, conceived and engineered for the purpose of saving the women from a trial for a brutal homicide." He later claimed that in the discussions about whether there should be a commission, Frater had told him "he would find a commission to declare them insane," and the entire proceeding – the timing of Frank Hurt's affidavits, the secret sessions, the limited role the prosecutors were allowed to play, the lack of interest shown in Miller's testimony – only served to convince the prosecutors that the result had been manipulated. Especially damning in their eyes was the refusal to hear their most important witness, Dr Alexander McLeish. For Miller this in particular was proof the commission "had been framed up to find the women insane."[88]

There was no real evidence of this, however, until December, after the case had been argued in the supreme court. At a December 3 meeting of the King County Medical Society, ostensibly on the subject of crime and insanity but in fact organized to provide a forum for the allegations, Dr Caspar Sharples made some startling accusations.[89] Sharples had been in practice in the city since 1890, was an eminent surgeon, variously chief of staff at the Children's Orthopedic Hospital, head of the Seattle General Hospital, and president of the Washington State Medical Association, and he was described by the *Times* as "one of the leading practitioners of the state."[90] He read one of three papers presented that evening, on "The Relation of the State to Criminal Cases." Part of his paper concerned the insanity commission: he alleged that the commission members were chosen only after they had been sounded out for their opinions by someone acting for Frater and it was clear that they would find the women guilty; that the commission was Frater's idea; and that the women's attorneys had also sounded out the commissioners, and others, about their views before appointment.

Sharples' principal evidence for these allegations consisted of two letters he had received from other doctors, which he read at the meeting and which were published in the newspapers. The first was from a Dr Ivan A. Perry, or Parry, and read:

> Mr. A.E. Clark of Portland, attorney for the Mitchells, came to my office and asked if I could sit on an insanity commission, consisting of three. Then asked if I could suggest two other doctors. My suggestion was Dr. Nickelson and Dr. Sharples. Then he said would we all be willing to report her insane? I told him it was an insult to ask for such an opinion before examination. He then said Judge Frater wanted the case tried out of this state and wanted, of course, to be sure that the report of the commission be insanity. I told him my opinion of the action of himself and Judge Frater and he afterwards secured three doctors who brought in the report he wanted.

The second letter was from a Dr H.M. Reid, or Read. It stated that another doctor had telephoned Reid:

> [He] first asked me if I had any objections to finding in favour of their insanity, stating that it was desirable that such a finding could be made so that these women could be sent out of the state. I very promptly told him I would do nothing of the kind; that if I ever accepted a position as an expert or in any other way, that I must be allowed to do exactly as I pleased according to the facts as I saw them, or I would not serve. At this point another voice than this doctor's, who had evidently heard the conversation (my part of it), said to him, "tell him we do not want him." And then the physician said, "Well, I guess you will not be satisfactory under those conditions." I am not certain who the physician was, and of course it would not be just to guess. It was my opinion at that time, however, and still is, that it was a part of a deliberate effort on the part of somebody interested in securing the removal of these women from Seattle, to manufacture a case looking to such an end. I am reliably informed that other physicians were approached more or less openly before the commission was finally secured. I am very glad to learn that most of these attempts were not successful.

After reading the letters Sharples denounced the whole enterprise as "unlawful," a breach of medical ethics, and "a travesty on the dignity of the legal profession." In short: "To free these two women, two shrewd lawyers were willing to pervert an innocent and useful law, . . . a judge was willing to aid the perversion, and three doctors were found who brought it to a successful consummation and debauched the sane sense of the community."[91]

Turner denied the allegations and asked the Medical Society to strike a committee to look into them. Snively, Eames, and Frater all also issued denials.[92] As they did so a story made the rounds that a total of five doctors had been approached to serve on the commission before the three were appointed.[93] Frater pitched in, saying that he and he alone had chosen the commission members, and that he had "full confidence in their integrity."[94] He did not believe Perry's statement about speaking to Clark and also denied that Clark had acted on his authority. As well, Frater stated that when he had originally decided on a commission he told the attorneys that the issue should be given to Judge Griffin; it was attorneys for both sides who had asked him to preside, as the case was on his docket. Otto Case, Frater's clerk, was quoted as corroborating the statement that Frater wanted the issue handled by Griffin. Frater quickly received the support of his colleagues; the superior court judges held a meeting the day the allegations were published and "expressed their confidence in the integrity of Judge Frater." He also received an endorsement from the *Argus,* which did not believe that the accusations "can possibly be true."[95]

There is no way to uncover the truth of all this. Both the King County Medical Society and the Seattle Bar Association announced that they would investigate, but we have been unable to find any record of any inquiries, if they took place.[96] They would probably not have found against their members on the basis of Sharples' evidence, for it was very thin. Perry's evidence was not from his own knowledge but from what he said Clark had said, and Reid's was from a telephone conversation with an unknown person. In the face of denials by those accused, this evidence would never have been sufficient for an adverse finding.

The meeting of the Medical Society was something of a staged event, postponed once and held after consultations with Mackintosh.[97] Sharples was a vehement critic of the way the insanity defence operated, and thus to that extent biased.[98] Yet we think the allegations were probably essentially true. Otherwise three doctors would have to have been prepared to forge letters and risk defamation actions. The evidence given at the meeting explains why the commission had been so oddly constituted, with no experts, a rookie, and Frater's family doctor. And we know that Frater and probably others had worked behind the scenes for weeks to get a commission appointed; it is reasonable to think they would have made sure of the result as well. The *Times* believed the allegations, insisting also that they came as no surprise, as for some time there had been rumours that the commission was fixed.[99] The *Times* had been a critic of the commission for months; more importantly, the *Post-Intelligencer* conceded that the charges had to be looked into, although it cast doubt on the reliability of "telephonic messages from indeterminate sources."[100] The *Argus* was also sure an attempt had been made to fix the membership of the commission, although it insisted that Frater would not have been a party to that.[101] The evidence put forward by Frater of his apparent unwillingness to take the case is not very persuasive. Naturally the attorneys would want the trial judge to preside over a hearing into the fitness to plead of the defendants; indeed, as we shall shortly see, many of Mackintosh's complaints about the process related to Frater's lack of participation in it. If anything, Frater's offer to have Griffin preside seems contrived, an offer he knew would be refused but that would stand him in good stead later if stories about the fix got out. And Frater did not sue anybody for defamation; somebody in his position, if innocent, would ordinarily feel compelled to do so in the face of such an allegation of impropriety.

THE WASHINGTON SUPREME COURT

The conclusion of the commission brought a flurry of complaints from the prosecutors, both in the press and in Frater's courtroom. Mackintosh and Miller complained they had not been allowed to ask questions, only suggest the names of witnesses; they condemned the in-camera hearings, dramatically called "star chamber" sessions; and they denounced the refusal to allow Dr McLeish to testify because he would have said the women were sane.[102] It was true that the doctors had declined to call McLeish, although they had an explanation for that: his evidence would only have corroborated Loughary's, who had in any event worked from McLeish's notes as well as his own.[103] The complaint about the right to ask questions had little merit. A civil insanity hearing was not a criminal trial, and the procedure was always different, especially as regards the right of the public prosecutor and other lawyers to cross-examine witnesses. Miller had been allowed to suggest names of people to be examined and questions to be put to witnesses, and indeed had testified himself.

As for "star chamber" sessions, Miller probably had a point about some of the proceedings. The doctors claimed that there were only a few of them and they were used for physical examinations, Mrs Kelly's evidence about personal matters, and revelations from Loughary and Nicholson of privileged information derived from the doctor-patient relationship.[104] Esther Mitchell's and Maud Creffield's lawyers said the same thing,[105] and secret sessions for these purposes were later held by the Washington Supreme Court to be probably reasonable and necessary.[106] However, the court reporter swore in an affidavit presented to the supreme court that witnesses other than Kelly and the doctors gave secret testimony in whole or in part, and his evidence is supported by the reports on the women, which state that secret sessions were used not just for physical examinations and privileged information but also when the commission believed it would not otherwise get all the facts – when people were reluctant to speak in public.[107] James Berry may have given some of his evidence in secret,[108] and things could have been said when people such as O.V. and Frank Hurt went behind closed doors for their "physical examinations." For obvious reasons we cannot be sure how much the doctors did hear in camera, but it was probably more than they later admitted. The secret sessions lent a suspicious air to the entire proceeding, compounding concerns that it was fixed.

The prosecutors got nowhere with these complaints to Frater, and so wasted no time taking their case to the state supreme court. Although all these issues were discussed in the various briefs and affidavits presented to the court, none of them proved important in the subsequent litigation. A majority of the supreme court judges concluded that Frater had a broad discretion to employ almost any procedure he wanted in an inquiry about fitness to stand trial. Miller presented an application for a hearing on a writ of prohibition to the supreme court, at the state capital of Olympia, on Monday, September 24. Chief Justice Wallace Mount heard the application and granted it immediately, setting October 26 as the date for a hearing before the full court and in the meantime staying the deportation order.[109]

The prosecutors' application was not an appeal, because Frater's decision to certify the women could not be appealed, could not simply be said to have been wrong in law. The writ of prohibition was for cases where it was alleged that a decision maker did not have the jurisdiction to decide the issue given to him. Jurisdiction can be by subject matter or territorial, and thus, for example, a court established to hear disputes arising within one county would have no jurisdiction to hear a dispute from another county. Similarly, a court given power to hear small debts cannot rule on a divorce petition. Thus a writ of prohibition literally prohibits the wrong body from deciding a matter. Using a writ of prohibition to challenge a superior court of common law was an unusual proceeding, because superior courts generally have "inherent jurisdiction" over all subject matters. But the arguments about jurisdiction did not turn on a suggestion that Frater could not hear insanity cases in King County. They relied principally on the idea that he could not use the civil commitment for insanity process to decide whether a criminal defendant was insane at the time of trial. In using the wrong process he had acted "in excess of his jurisdiction," had dealt with the case in a sufficiently improper way as to deprive himself of jurisdiction.

The full court of seven judges heard oral argument in the case on Friday, October 26. Presiding was Chief Justice Wallace Mount; he was joined by Justices Herman Crow, Ralph Oregon Dunbar, Mark Fullerton, Hiram Elwood Hadley, Milo Adelbert Root, and Frank Rudkin.[110] Five of the judges were elected, two – Crow and Root – had been appointed in 1905 when the court was expanded to seven judges. Four (Dunbar, Fullerton, Mount, and Root) were former prosecutors, and three (Dunbar, Fullerton, Mount) were Oregonians. Only Hadley and Rudkin had served as superior court judges, neither in King County. Of these judges Root perhaps had the most difficult time avoiding being influenced by preconceived ideas about the case. As a former prosecuting attorney for Thurston County he might well have sympathized with Mackintosh, and we know that he was concerned enough about the George Mitchell case to have written disparagingly of the *Times'* support of Mitchell.[111] Yet he was also a former law partner of Frater.

There was an impressive array of lawyers present for argument, which probably took some hours.[112] Mackintosh, Miller, and George Vanderveer, another deputy prosecuting attorney,[113] argued Mackintosh's case – Miller did most of the talking. Formally, the "respondents," the term we will use here, were the King County Superior Court and Frater as a judge of the court. Anthony M. Arston represented the superior court of King County; Frater had felt it necessary to also engage one George H. Walker as his personal counsel, and Walker presented oral arguments to the judges.[114] Also listed as attorneys for the respondents on the respondents' brief were Baxter, Holzheimer, and Clark, and the latter two appeared for oral argument at Olympia. State Attorney-General Atkinson participated as *amicus curiae,* suggesting that the court considered the case an important and potentially difficult one. That they heard the case on a Friday also suggests they saw it as urgent, for that was one of two days usually employed in internal meetings and discussions of the cases argued earlier in the week.[115]

We do not know on exactly what basis the lawyers for Esther Mitchell and Maud Creffield participated in this litigation. The women obviously had an interest in the outcome of the case, and on the one hand the presence in court of their lawyers, and the fact that they argued for the respondents' side, suggests that all the women's protestations that they were not insane, and that they were indifferent to what happened to them, were untrue. When the King County prosecuting attorney sought to overturn a finding that they were insane, their lawyers were front and centre in the battle to keep them so classified. As we suggested above, by the fall of 1906 they were happy to acquiesce in a procedure that would avoid a criminal trial and a possible death sentence. On the other hand, their counsel may have had no choice in whether to participate, and the women no capacity to instruct them one way or the other, for they had been found insane. It may be that in those circumstances court rules would have obliged their lawyers to continue to represent their best interests, and defined their best interests as upholding the doctors' verdict.

There is no transcript of the arguments, although they likely concentrated on the issue that dominated the judgment – whether Frater had been within his jurisdiction to appoint the commission and allow it to run the proceedings the way it did. As was normal practice, the court reserved its decision following the argument, although it was not initially expected that a decision and written reasons would take long – both were anticipated on November 3.[116] But once it began to think about the case the court decided there was a serious issue with the validity of the deportation statute and asked for further briefs on that point.[117] It ultimately took until January 5 before written judgments were issued.

We will not detail here all the arguments made by the prosecutors, for some turned out not to be relevant. The principal one was the same point that had been rejected by Frater – that when an accused person's fitness to stand trial was in question, the issue should be resolved by having a jury rule on it.[118] This argument was jurisdictional, and therefore within the scope of the writ of prohibition asked for, because an essential element to the claim that a jury should decide was the corollary proposition that an insanity commission should not, and thus in appointing the commission Frater had assumed a jurisdiction he did not have. This argument relied on an implication from the statutes, and that turned out to be its downfall. Only three parts of the state code dealt with insanity. One was the section requiring a jury that acquitted a person by reason of insanity to state that fact, which we have discussed in connection with George Mitchell's trial; it had no relevance here. Another was the section laying out the civil insanity commitment procedure. The third, and the one relied on by the prosecutors, stated: "Superior Courts of the State of Washington shall have power to commit to the hospital for the insane any person who, having been arraigned for an indictable offense, shall be found by the jury to be insane at the time of such arraignment."[119] The problem with this section for the prosecutors' case was that it did not explicitly require a person's sanity to be decided by a jury; all it did was say what could happen to a person who was found insane and unfit to stand trial. Mackintosh's brief argued that a jury was required, by necessary implication. The civil insanity commitment provision invoked by Frater was for those not charged with a serious crime, the provision mentioning persons "arraigned for an indictable offense" was for such people, and the two "tracks" were not interchangeable. This was a good argument, and it was supported by practice. But it was far from conclusive.

The respondents' answer is not entirely clear from the written brief, but we assume that they argued that Frater could use any process he wished to assess fitness to stand trial. The brief began by asserting that if Mackintosh was correct that Frater had no jurisdiction to do what he did, "then an insane person may be placed on trial for his life, a proposal contrary not only to the dictates of humanity but of reason and authority."[120] This was simply not true, of course – a person's fitness to stand trial could be tested by some other method. But the brief, having made this assertion, concentrated on citing authorities for the obvious proposition that an insane person could not be tried. Mackintosh did not contest this point; he said that the wrong procedure had been used to determine sanity. The respondents' written argument ignored all discussion of why the procedure chosen was acceptable. We suspect that in oral argument they developed the point that the court itself relied on – that there was no statutory requirement to use any particular procedure. The respondents' brief may not have been strong on the law, but it turned out that it was tactically correct to concentrate on putting into the judges' minds the concern about placing an insane person on trial.

On this key point the five-person majority judgment of the court, written by Justice Crow and concurred in by Justices Dunbar, Hadley, Root,[121] and Rudkin, held that the insanity commission was a perfectly valid way of determining fitness to stand trial. Crow made two points, although not in the order we have them here.[122] First, he established why an insane person could not be tried. He thought such a practice was self-evidently "not to be tolerated by the courts of any civilized nation." It was also antithetical to the fifth amendment of the constitution, because it would deprive a person of life or liberty without due process of law, and was a violation of the sixth amendment guarantee that an accused be informed of "the nature and cause of the accusation against him." The principle that a person could not be tried while insane had a long history, and Blackstone was cited in support of it. Washington did not have a statutory rule that an insane person could not be tried, but that did not matter, for it was clearly a common law rule.

Crow's second finding was that a trial judge could go about making sure that an insane person was not tried in any way suitable.[123] As it was part of the court's inherent jurisdiction to ascertain sanity if the issue was raised, Frater had the power to inquire, and did so. In the process he "endeavored to proceed in substantial compliance" with the provisions of the insanity commitment statute, as that was "the most pertinent statute we have upon the subject." But in calling that statute the "most pertinent" Crow was also saying that it was not required that it, or any other statute, be followed. In the absence of a Washington statute specifying the procedure to determine fitness to stand trial, "the common law rule ... must apply here." Crow cited, with approval, a statement in a Georgia case that at common law a trial judge may inquire into fitness to plead "in any right and proper manner – by impaneling another jury if he deem it best to do so, by considering the affidavits of experts, by a personal examination, or otherwise." Thus Frater's action was perfectly acceptable. The supreme court's judgment on this point was largely in accord with contemporary understandings of the law, although there was no Washington authority on the point. At common law, where there was an issue about the sanity of the defendant, the judge could "engraft upon a criminal proceeding ... a proceeding for determination as to present sanity or insanity of the person on trial."[124] Mackintosh's only hope had been to convince the court that in Washington the statutory scheme mandated that a jury be called, and it clearly did not do this. Mackintosh made a series of other arguments critiquing the way in which the investigation into sanity had been carried out. For example, he pointed out that Frater had certified the women as insane without hearing most of the evidence himself, and that he had delegated what was a judicial function to the doctors.[125] These were good grounds on which to criticize Frater in an ordinary case, for it was, and is, a foundational principle that a judge should not decide a case without hearing the evidence. But as good as this and other arguments would have been in the vast majority of cases, they did not at all avail Mackintosh because Crow did not say that the insanity commitment process had to be used. He said that it could be, if the judge so chose, and if it was used, there was no need to use it precisely according to the statute. If Frater wanted to effectively delegate to three doctors, he could. There must have been some limit to this, for the court took pains to suggest that he had "endeavored to proceed in substantial compliance" with the statutory process. The procedure used was within the bounds of an obviously very broad discretion.

The decision was not unanimous. Chief Justice Wallace Mount, with whom Justice Fullerton agreed, dissented on this point, arguing that if Frater had the right to use the insanity commitment statute, then he should have used it properly.[126] Mount and Fullerton, however, concurred with Crow on the second issue dealt with by the court – the validity of the deportation statute. The majority's conclusion was that the statute was nugatory because it was unenforceable. It required the sheriff to take an insane person to his or her home in another state, but the sheriff did not have authority to act outside Washington. In line with the usual practice when a statute was found to be invalid as to its principal purpose, it was declared entirely void. Thus a writ of prohibition was issued to prevent the women being deported.[127] As a result, therefore, the insanity commission and its findings were upheld, but the deportation order was quashed.

Reaction to the supreme court's decision varied. Not surprisingly, the *Seattle Times* disagreed strongly with the majority opinion, arguing that the practice had been that "no person could be adjudged insane without the determination of a jury properly selected" and "after hearing the testimony of medical experts." Frater had decided he had the right to call a commission and let them decide, despite "an entirely plain statute." Of course the statute was not plain, but the real issue for Blethen was his view of insanity experts: now any murderer could "escape justice" provided "his attorneys have a sufficient pull with the trial court to induce the appointment of a commission which can always be relied upon to render the kind of verdict wanted."[128] The *Post-Intelligencer,* which had approved the commission earlier, now expressed concern based on a misunderstanding of the judgment. The court's decision, it said, was "far reaching" because "no person who may be insane can be placed on trial for a capital offense unless his or her sanity is established."[129] The court had not laid down a rule that the prosecution had to establish sanity. The rule was still that the defendant had to show otherwise. The Seattle press seemed not to care about the deportation statute, but the *Oregonian* approved that part of the decision, arguing that Esther Mitchell should not be deported to Oregon because her crime had not taken place in that jurisdiction.[130]

As for the others centrally concerned with the decision, Frater was obviously pleased with approval of his use of the insanity commission.[131] Esther Mitchell was "glad the suspense is ended," but "I do not care," she said. Asked if she preferred the asylum to the penitentiary, she nominated the former: "I am nervous, and that is the place for me." Asked if she would have liked to go back to Oregon, she professed indifference, as "it's all the same." Other kinds of questions got similar answers. Overall she "appears but little different from the day she was taken to the county jail after the murder of her brother ... the nervous fingers twine and intertwine, and there is an appealing sorrowful air about the slender figure."[132]

Epilogue

The Death of Maud Creffield

FRANZ CREFFIELD AND GEORGE MITCHELL died in 1906, and so too did one other of the principals in this story, Maud Creffield. The placid existence she and Esther Mitchell appeared to lead in the county jail while waiting for the Washington Supreme Court to decide their fates must have concealed considerable mental anguish in Maud, for on the night of Thursday, November 16, she took a fatal dose of strychnine.[1] It had been an evening the same as any other, and she and Esther had gone to bed at about 10 p.m. At 11 p.m. the jail was electrified by a scream, and the jailers found Maud standing by the bed with distorted face, clutching at her heart. A doctor was called but she died before he arrived. For a few days there was uncertainty about the cause of death. Poison was initially suspected but a thorough search of the cell failed to turn up any. Deputy Coroner Shirley Wiltsie suggested a heart attack, for Maud was known to have heart trouble. An autopsy was performed the next day, one so extensive that afterwards the undertakers were unable to keep the embalming fluid in the body. All the organs were found to be in good condition, including the heart and the brain; the latter discovery led Dr Eames to insist that insanity did not necessarily leave physical signs. The autopsy itself did not discover the cause of death, but an analysis of the stomach contents revealed enough strychnine to kill several people, and the official verdict was given as suicide.

In death as in life Maud Creffield excited controversy. Esther Mitchell vehemently denied that Maud would have committed suicide, saying that Maud believed it was "cowardly" and that there was no way she could have taken a poison without her, Esther, knowing. Attie Levins also denied that Maud would do something so much against her religion, a point made as well by Will Morris. Frank Hurt and others were still denying the suicide explanation weeks and months later, but it was the official explanation and seems the most likely.[2] The only other one is that the strychnine was given to her by somebody else, and that person would have to have been Esther Mitchell. But the two women were the greatest of friends, and while Esther had shown no compunction to kill she had no reason whatever to kill Maud Creffield. Maud did commit suicide, and in doing so she gives us one more indication, if such were necessary, of Creffield's remarkable influence on his followers. Contemporaries were absolutely correct to point out that suicide was antithetical to her religious beliefs, but Maud's beliefs, like those of many of Creffield's followers, were only partly based on Christian teaching per se. The prophet had taught her that the Bible could be disregarded when it clashed with his, or their, personal revelations.

One person not surprised at the suicide was O.V. Hurt, who now had one more trouble to add to his long list. Maud had seemed "depressed and despondent" when O.V. and Sarah Hurt had visited her the previous weekend, and she had told them that if anything happened to her she should be buried beside Creffield. O.V.'s response when he was informed of the death was that he had been expecting it for a long time.[3] Accompanied by Mae but not Sarah, he rushed back to Seattle to arrange for the funeral. He may have expected the tragedy in a general sense, but was nonetheless "overcome with emotion at the receipt of the news." He told the press that Maud had felt that "all the life had been taken from her" when Creffield was killed, and he was sure she had died "from grief and a broken heart."[4] She had lost a lot of weight in jail, and much strength with it, he thought. Maud was granted her wish about burial, being interred in Seattle on November 19 next to Creffield in the Lakeview Cemetery; O.V. Hurt bought her a plot, and Creffield's body was exhumed from the pauper section and reburied beside hers. Their small, simple tombstones are still there, so modest they are hard to find, especially compared with the large elaborate memorial to George Meade Emory in another section of the cemetery.

At the private funeral a short sermon was pronounced by a Rev. W.J. Wilson. Mourners were few – her father, sister, and brother; Mollie Hurt; lawyers Holzheimer, Shipley, and Morris; and Esther Mitchell and the sheriff's deputy who had to accompany her. Esther "broke down and wept bitterly when she lookt upon the face of the woman who had been her companion thru all the dark days."[5] Indeed, she had been distraught continually since Maud's death, so much so that there were concerns that she too might commit suicide. The press could not help but remark on the fact that she had broken down now, at Maud's loss, while staying so emotionless from the day she had killed her brother.

An issue never resolved was how Maud Creffield had obtained the strychnine. Speculation fingered Attie Levins as a possible supplier, for she had visited Maud the day before she died and had been the last outside visitor to see her. She denied it. Esther Mitchell was also suggested; indeed, she was searched and her clothes completely changed. But if Esther had been the supplier, how would she have got the poison? An investigation was carried out, but it proved inconclusive.[6] Maud's death occasioned an obituary in the *Corvallis Gazette* by "A Friend"; it contained some of the kindest words said publicly about her in nearly three years: she had always had strong religious convictions but was "kindly and generous, with an even temper and a good disposition."[7] But in Seattle she was not generally mourned. The *Republican* said that whether or not there was poison in her stomach, "there were wheels in her head," and the city should forget about "a woman whose life was so little worthy of emulation." The *Times* chalked it up to "the reign of Holy Rollerism" and was pleased that it would save the county money should the supreme court overturn the insanity commission and order a trial. The *Post-Intelligencer* also preferred to see the suicide as further illustration of Creffield's evil: "The Holy Roller harvest of tragedy sown by lack of legal restraint in Oregon, has been reaped in Washington. This sequence of murder and violence should be a lesson to both states."[8]

THE CREFFIELD SECT AND ITS OPPONENTS AFTER 1906

For some people the events described here occupied but a small place in their lives. Kenneth Mackintosh went on to a distinguished career as a judge. He served six years as Frater's colleague on the superior court of King County, and eleven years, including two as chief justice, on the state supreme court, where he likely had opportunities to review some of Frater's judgments. John Miller became mayor of Seattle and served seven terms as a US congressional representative for Washington. Will Morris and Silas Shipley continued their successful and remunerative careers, while Archibald Frater went on with his, serving on the bench until his death in 1925 at the age of sixty-nine.

As for the "ordinary people" caught up in the Creffield story, if aspects of our account have seemed at times hard to believe – truth is stranger than fiction is the phrase that comes to mind – that sense is not diminished by subsequent events. Many of the principals moved to where Creffield had tried to establish his colony in April 1906 – the Waldport-Yachats-Alsea Bay region of Lincoln County.[9] It is easy to see why many of those in the Creffield sect might have wanted to move away from Corvallis and people's memories of what they had believed and done. And they likely stayed together because they all shared the same memories, the same past. Less explicable is that marriages were contracted between people who had had diametrically opposite views of Creffield and the events of 1903-1906. Perhaps Creffield drew people together no matter what side they had been on.

O.V. Hurt was probably the first person to relocate from Corvallis to the coast, he and Sarah returning to where they had first met and married, probably in 1907.[10] He had prepared the way in late 1906 by selling his Corvallis house and purchasing a forty-two-acre farm a mile from Waldport on the shores of Alsea Bay. He farmed, obtained a federal appointment as collector of customs under the Taft administration (presumably through his Republican Party contacts, for he seems to have kept up his political activities through all his travails),[11] and for four years served as county commissioner. He did well in some real estate speculation, selling the land that became the township of Yachats (called Oceanview until 1917) for $25,000, and by April 1909 was referred to as a "wealthy rancher."[12] He returned for some time to Corvallis in 1919, working as Kline's "outside man," and moved to the town of Waldport when he retired. O.V. died there on June 14, 1943 at the age of eighty-five, of a failed heart, after some years as an invalid. His obituary said nothing about his involvement with the Creffield sect, merely noting that he had lived most of his life in Lincoln County "except for a few years spent in Corvallis" and that two of his children had died "some years ago." He and Sarah, who survived him by almost three years, were both buried at Yachats. Sarah also died of heart failure, at the age of eighty-four, although she had suffered from breast cancer for seventeen years. A brief obituary noted that she was known to everyone as "Mother Hurt," the name that Creffield had given her over forty years before.[13] There is no evidence, however, in her case or that of any other former sect members, that she continued to believe in the things that had so vigorously animated her in 1903-1904.

The Hurts enjoyed the companionship of their children in their new surroundings. Mae moved with them to the coast, and in 1909 married Frank Oscar Johnson in Lincoln County, with Frank and Mollie Hurt serving as witnesses, as they had done for Maud's marriages to Creffield.[14] Johnson was a farmer who also drove the stage coach and ran the Yachats Hotel. He and Mae had two sons and three daughters. Mae became a member of the Presbyterian Church and lived to be ninety-four, dying in 1980. She is buried in Yachats like her parents. She was predeceased by her husband, in 1950, and her twenty-year-old daughter Deborah, in 1931, both killed in road accidents.

Frank and Mollie Hurt lived in Seattle, initially both working for a department store, until about 1916, when they also moved to the coast, choosing the village of Tidewater in the Alsea region, where Frank took up farming and ranching.[15] They had five children before Frank, out hunting with his brother-in-law Frank Johnson, was shot in the head by his own gun in 1920 at the age of thirty-eight. A coroner's inquiry deemed it a hunting accident. His funeral was conducted by undertaker Warren B. Hartley of Newport, Louis and Cora's son. Mollie later remarried, choosing, remarkably, that inveterate opponent of Creffield, James Berry, and becoming his sixth and final wife in 1930.[16] Mollie died in 1959, and her and Frank's daughter Ruth was the last person involved in this story to die – at Waldport, on April 16, 1999. Mollie's sister, Olive, also settled in Lincoln County, homesteading with her husband near Cummins Creek.[17]

Other former members of the Creffield sect also went to Lincoln County. Soon after Attie Bray and Sampson Levins married, they moved to the Yachats area, homesteaded 160 acres, and had two children. Sampson also worked as a mail carrier. Attie, who maintained contact with the Hurts, died in June 1967 at the age of eighty-six. Sampson Levins predeceased her by a decade, and both are buried at Yachats.[18] The Hartleys also ended up in Lincoln County. By the late summer of 1906 Louis and Cora had reconciled, and he withdrew his divorce petition.[19] They did, however, divorce in November 1908, as a result of Cora's desertion, at which time Louis was still in Corvallis. Cora went to Washington for a while, and at some point relocated to the Oregon coast. She was living with Donna Starr in Newport in 1910 and with Esther Mitchell at Waldport in 1914. After all this, Louis and Cora were remarried on July 22, 1917, in Lincoln County; the witnesses were Perry Mitchell and Donna Starr. The Hartleys also went to live at Yachats, where Louis died twenty years later. Cora lived on until 1945, when she succumbed to a cerebral hemorrhage at the age of eighty-six.

Both the Hartleys' children moved west as well. Warren set up in business as an undertaker in Newport. He took care of his father's body when he died.[20] Sophia Hartley went to Lincoln County, and in November 1913 married Perry Mitchell.[21] The witnesses were James K. Berry and Esther Mitchell, who both also moved to the coast. The newlyweds ran a general store in Yachats and had one child, Sylvia. Sophia served thirty-three years as the Yachats postmistress. She died on June 18, 1970, at Yachats, and is buried there, in the same cemetery as Perry and her parents. Perry must have seen plenty of his father, for Charles and his eldest son David Perley Mitchell also moved to Yachats.

The Mitchell sisters moved west as well. Donna and Burgess Starr's marriage did not survive the turbulent events of 1906.[22] We do not know when they were divorced, but it was probably before 1910.[23] They may even have contemplated remarriage at one point but did not go through with it,[24] and Burgess married one Evelyn Marks in September 1919, in Lincoln County. He resided at Yachats until his death in 1936 at the age of sixty-four, working mostly as a cook in a logging camp although he also cooked for Frank and Mae Johnson's hotel guests. Donna Starr was living at Yachats in 1914, and in 1916 she married James Berry, becoming his fourth wife and running a store with him. The witnesses at their wedding were Cora Hartley and Perry Mitchell, by then married to Sophia Hartley. Donna's marriage to Berry lasted only until 1919, for he was a drunk and physically abusive when under the influence. Berry was married again in 1920, to an Alice Kent,[25] and after her divorce from Berry Donna moved to Portland. She died there as Donna Victoria Berry on December 23, 1947, of stomach cancer. She was thus the only one of this group who did not end her days in Lincoln County.

Finally, we turn to Esther Mitchell. After the state supreme court had affirmed the finding that she was insane, Esther remained in the King County jail for many weeks. She was, according to Sheriff Lou Smith, a model prisoner, never causing any disturbances, never discussing religion. He insisted that the "religious frenzy to which she was subject" had "entirely disappeared" and she was "as sane as anybody."[26] On February 20 Esther was taken to the asylum at Steilacoom, in the charge of Mrs Kelly, where she joined the other 900 or so patients housed there.[27] The delay was caused by the fact that Frater did not receive a formal notification of the supreme court's decision until that morning, and he could not sign the paper to commit Esther to Steilacoom until he had it. Financial responsibility for her upkeep at the asylum was also something of an issue.[28] Esther took the news of her move "as stoically as she has received everything that has to do with her since she shot her brother."[29] Two months later she was said to be remaining true to her faith in Creffield, to her belief that he would be resurrected, and to her conviction that she had done the right thing in killing her brother. Most of all, she continued to assert that "her relations with Creffield" were "quite proper." Her cheerful disposition and willingness to work made her popular, and she was lightly guarded, as she was not considered an escape risk.[30]

Although she had been found not fit to stand trial rather than acquitted, Esther Mitchell was never tried for the murder of her brother. The usual procedure in a serious case would be to try her if and when she recovered her sanity, but Mackintosh was quoted at the time of her commitment as saying that he would take no further action as he considered the case "a closed incident."[31] We can only assume that he did not want to bother with a trial that would end in a finding of not guilty by reason of insanity. The defence would be able to use the finding of the insanity commission, which had concluded that she had been insane at the time she committed the offence. That finding would not have been conclusive at a trial, but would be very difficult to refute. A trial could only take place once Esther Mitchell was declared sane again, and the result would therefore be the same as in George Mitchell's case – not guilty because insane at the time of the offence, but now sane and free to go. Mackintosh doubtless had better things to do with his time.

There remained the question of what would happen to her. Some speculated that Esther would end her days in the asylum,[32] but she stayed only slightly more than two years, released on parole late on March 28, 1909, to be returned "if she shows any symptoms of a return of her malady."[33] By that time the superintendent considered that she had been cured for about eight months, and according to asylum workers she was by then "thoroughly disgusted with herself" and ashamed of both her involvement in the sect and the murder of George.[34] Although he considered her completely sane, Superintendent Calhoun did not agree to her release without first consulting Frater and George Vanderveer, by then the prosecuting attorney. The latter, taking the same approach as Mackintosh in 1907, had no objection, even though the information charging her with murder had never been withdrawn. Her manner of leaving was odd. She simply walked out of the asylum with Mollie Hurt the day before an official parole was to be issued. Superintendent Calhoun, after consulting with Vanderveer, signed the parole, ignoring what was technically an escape. The Seattle press did not object to her release; the *Times* thought that although she "should have been hanged directly after her crime," in the circumstances of 1909, release was best.[35]

O.V. Hurt re-enters our story here. He had visited the asylum early in 1909 and agreed to take Esther in. Armed with a recommendation from no less a person than Oregon Governor Chamberlain, he was appointed her guardian and gave her a home as one of the family after Mollie had taken her from the asylum to Waldport. She lived out the rest of her life in Lincoln County.[36] The parole was removed on a doctor's recommendation and she was formally discharged on September 23, 1909. She stayed with the Hurts for some years, "a quiet and respected resident of Waldport."[37] We have no evidence about her religious beliefs during these years; she may have continued to yearn for the excitement of radical holiness, or she may indeed have become entirely disillusioned with all forms of belief. We think it more likely that her religious views were as conventional as those of the Hurts.

In April 1914 Esther married, at the age of twenty-six, thirty-six-year-old James Berry, and the couple then made their home at Waldport with Cora Hartley and Berry's eight-year-old son. Berry had relocated to the coast sometime between 1906 and 1910, when he married his second wife in Lincoln County.[38] He continued the trade he had followed in Corvallis, running a farm implement store and general mechanics repair shop. Always the innovator, he learned to fly and was the pilot of the first plane to land at Waldport. Esther Mitchell was his third wife. While Berry had not cared for the sect in 1903 and fought it then and in 1904 and 1906, he seems to have developed a remarkable liking for its female adherents. As already noted, he not only married Esther Mitchell but later her sister Donna Starr, and then Mollie Hurt. To explain both why he should have chosen three of the Creffield sect women, and why they were in turn willing to join with him, requires an appreciation of psychology that is beyond us.

After a little more than three months of marriage, on August 1, 1914, Esther Mitchell committed suicide by taking strychnine, the same method employed by Maud Creffield some eight years previously. Nobody had any premonition of it; she was apparently happy at dinner but later, at about 9:30 p.m., went upstairs and took the poison. She had, however, complained of feeling ill for some time, "and it was noticed by her friends that she was failing in health and losing flesh."[39] Perhaps she had cancer, or had previously poisoned herself and was suffering from the effects of that, or perhaps she had been injured by an abusive husband, for we know that Berry assaulted Donna and one of his later wives.[40] The Portland *Telegram* had a simpler explanation – she had long been depressed at the thought of what she had done to her brother.[41] As with Maud Creffield, whose suicide may have helped Esther justify her own, we do not know how she reconciled the act with any remaining ardent Christian beliefs she may have had.

When the alarm was raised and neighbours and friends rushed over, Sarah Hurt was the first to arrive. Esther's suicide note tells us much more about the Hurts than about her reasons for taking that drastic step. It reveals that Esther Mitchell owned the house she lived in and two other lots, and had a little money in the bank. She could only, we think, have acquired property to that extent from O.V. Hurt, and she asked for the two lots to be given "to mother and father" – surely the Hurts. Her other requests were for her piano and a ring to go to "Martha," which we assume was Martha Hurt, O.V. and Sarah's adopted daughter, who had been an infant when the Creffield sect had operated in Corvallis, and for a silver watch to go to Attie Levins.[42] Esther Mitchell Berry was buried in the Fern Ridge Cemetery near Waldport. Her husband, as we have seen, married three more times: Donna Starr in 1916, Alice Kent in 1920, and Mollie Hurt sometime thereafter. He was still married to Mollie when he died in 1943.[43]

Esther Mitchell's obituary in the Toledo newspaper, the *Lincoln County Leader,* said nothing about her past, but the *Yaquina Bay News* of Newport knew all about it and devoted a column or so to a brief history. Press reports from Corvallis and Portland show that, not surprisingly, people there remembered her. "Esther Mitchell-Berry, of 'Holy Roller' fame," the *Corvallis Gazette-Times* called her. Both that paper and the *Oregonian* recounted the Creffield sect story.[44]

THE MEANINGS OF THE AFFAIR

The death of Esther Mitchell, ultimately the most notorious of Creffield's followers, marks the end of the tale told in this book. As we suggested in the Introduction, our aim has been to use this case study to illustrate the ways in which individual aspirations and actions, and broad social processes, interacted in a particular time and place. As Natalie Davis notes, an unusual story has the power to "uncover motivations and values that are lost in the welter of the everyday."[45] The Creffield story, we believe, demonstrates the enormous power of religious conviction in the period, strong enough not only to induce Creffield's mostly female followers to desert homes and families and social roles, but in the case of two of them to plan and carry out a murder. Holiness was, for a moment, deadly, with an otherwise unimaginable act carried out in the name of its adherents' God. The converse of murdering holiness, of course, was its earlier repression, and the Creffield story exemplifies both the relative ease with which those who stand outside the mainstream of religious belief could be attacked, literally and figuratively, and the fragility of the constitutional protection of religious conscience.

These are not the only lessons that can be taken from this book. We have shown that the rule of law, often referred to as the American religion, was subject to manipulation to serve what contemporaries saw as the greater social good – the very suppression of religious difference in the name of cultural homogeneity referred to above. What John McLaren has called "the deployment of law to produce social or cultural homogenity" has been a feature of the legal histories of both the United States and Canada, with the law's targets often comprising "heretical" sects, from the Shakers to the Mormons, Mennonites, and Doukhobors.[46] In our case insanity laws were easily manipulable to this end, both in 1904 and, rather differently, in September 1906, when Seattle decided that another high-profile murder case was not to its liking. Otherwise "law-abiding" citizens had no compunction in resorting to vigilante acts when they believed that Creffield and his followers were offending against basic mores of their community. The Corvallis white caps and George Mitchell, Louis Hartley, and Ed Baldwin all developed, and acted on, their own ideas of justice, whether or not those accorded with the formal law of the state.

Perhaps the starkest example of the manipulation, and making, of law is the way in which homicide law – often thought of as the least contentious of all criminal law – was applied in the trial of George Mitchell, a trial that declared it acceptable to murder holiness in appropriate circumstances. Most Americans in 1906 would have been certain that they lived under the rule of fixed and determined state law, and that that included the elementary proposition that no man had the right to kill another for some real or imagined offence to his family. But the George Mitchell trial shows us, as other case studies have done, that the law "draws its meaning from contemporary ideologies, not transhistorical categorizations."[47]

It would not be useful to cite all the other examples of ways in which we think this book shows in microcosm large historical processes at work. We would, though, wish to stress a theme that runs throughout our story even if it is not frequently explicitly stated. In addition to being a book about the broader meanings of the history of the Creffield sect, this is also a book about the small group of ordinary people involved, people who strove both to remake or repair, according to their own visions, the world in which they lived. The sources for our story do not, unfortunately, include diaries and letters of these people. But we have uncovered enough about them, and can extrapolate sufficiently from their actions, to say with confidence that in a real sense many of these people were not ordinary, but extraordinary. Immigrant Franz Creffield's version of the American dream was an unusual one, but he pursued it with passion, great fortitude, and some success. He played a highly significant role in the history of the holiness movement in Oregon and Washington, albeit a negative one. George Mitchell's belief in his right to kill another man in defence of his sisters led him to commit an act that could well have cost him his life on the gallows, and resulted in his death in a different way. Esther Mitchell's faith was such that she could not only bring herself to kill, but to kill a brother. Without the extraordinary convictions and actions of these people we would know much less than we do about religion, law, and gender in the Pacific Northwest in these years.

But these are not the only notable "characters" in our story. In some ways, the most remarkable one is O.V. Hurt. Had Creffield not appeared, nobody would have written, then or now, about a department store employee from a small town in Oregon in 1902. He would have lived out his unremarkable life, providing for and raising an unremarkable family. But the events in which he and his family were involved provide insight into the strength and consistency of character of an early twentieth-century Everyman. He never stopped loving and trying to help his family, no matter what anguish they caused him and how painfully they rejected him. He acted throughout the story according to what he thought was right, although that must at times have caused him misgivings. In public matters he must have been greatly conflicted; we see him disapproving vigilante action against Creffield in 1904 and yet countenancing George Mitchell's murder of Creffield. He even likely committed a little perjury to help Mitchell get acquitted. In private matters O.V. was more consistent. He took his wife and youngest daughter back more than once. Most strikingly, he never stopped trying to help his older daughter. Maud caused him immense difficulties time and again, but even when she had conspired to kill George Mitchell he could not neglect paternal duty and asked "What can your papa do for you?" Nor could he fail to take care of his daughter's greatest friend after her release from the asylum. Ending the book by stressing the character of O.V. Hurt is appropriate for a story about human emotions and actions, for of all the characters discussed here, he is, we think, the most admirably human.

The Creffield Sect Membership

SMITH ISLAND PERIOD: SUMMER 1903

Women (16)

Ona Baldwin
Attie Bray
Cora Hartley
Sophia Hartley
Maud Hurt
Mae Hurt
Molly Hurt
Sarah Hurt
Esther Mitchell
Olive Sandell
Edna Seeley
Florence Seeley
Rose Seeley
Donna Starr
Hattie Starr
Coral Worrell

Men (7)

Charles Brooks
Lee Campbell
Franz Creffield
Frank Hurt
Sampson Levins
Wesley Seeley
Clarence Starr

Hurt House Period: September-November 1903

All the above were active members during the late summer and fall of 1903 while the sect used the Hurt house as a headquarters, except for five: Edna Seeley, Clarence and Hattie Starr, Mrs Worrell, and Wesley Seeley. O.V. Hurt joined the group around October 28, 1903, and left around November 20, 1903. Total membership during this period, excluding O.V. Hurt, was therefore thirteen women and five men.

Other Adherents for Brief Periods

James Berry: an early and tepid member, left in the early summer of 1903
Terry Mercer: an early follower, left early in 1903
Ed Sharp: might have briefly been with the group on Smith Island

Notes

NEWSPAPERS

Albany Herald	*Albany Weekly Herald-Disseminator* and *Albany Weekly Herald*
Oregonian	*Morning Oregonian* and *Sunday Oregonian,* Portland
PI	*Seattle Post-Intelligencer*
Republican	*Seattle Republican*
Star	*Seattle Star*
Telegram	*Evening Telegram,* Portland

OTHER SOURCES

BCHM	Benton County Historical Museum, Philomath, Oregon
BGAS	Boys and Girls Aid Society of Oregon
Bellinger and Cotton	*The Codes and Statutes of Oregon ... Compiled and Annotated by Charles B. Bellinger and William W. Cotton,* 2 vols. (San Francisco: Bancroft-Whitney, 1902)
KCA	King County Archives, Seattle
OSA	Oregon State Archives, Salem
OSH	Oregon State Hospital
Remington and Ballinger	*Remington and Ballinger's Annotated Codes and Statutes of Washington,* 2 vols. (Seattle and San Francisco: Bancroft-Whitney, 1910)
SC-KC	Superior Court of King County
UWL	University of Washington Libraries, Special Collections, Seattle

WLR   Washington Law Reports, 1st Series
WSA   Washington State Archives
WSA-PS   Washington State Archives, Puget Sound Regional Branch,
                    Bellevue

CHAPTER 1: INTRODUCTION

1 Quotations from *Seattle Times*, 7 May 1906; *Oregon Statesman*, 6 January 1904; *Corvallis Gazette*, 31 July 1906.
2 *Corvallis Times*, 3 and 6 February 1904.
3 The earliest Holbrook account is a two-part article in *Oregonian*, 22 and 29 November 1936. The most substantial is "Death and Times of a Prophet," in Holbrook, *Murder Out Yonder: An Informal Study of Certain Classic Crimes in Back-Country America*, ed. S. Holbrook (New York: Macmillan, 1941), 1-21. Other Holbrook versions, of varying length but all very similar, are: "Oregon's Secret Love Cult," in *Grand Deception: The World's Most Spectacular and Successful Hoaxes, Impostures, Ruses and Frauds*, ed. A. Klein (Philadelphia: Lippincott, 1955), 16-23; "Death and Times of a Prophet," in *Wildmen, Wobblies and Whistle Punks*, ed. S. Holbrook (Corvallis, OR: Oregon State University Press, 1992), 41-60; "Murder Without Tears," *Oregonian*, 4 parts, 8, 15, and 22 February, and 1 March, 1953. On at least two occasions Holbrook also wrote up the story in "true crime" magazines under pseudonyms: see S. Underwood, "Blonde Esther and the Seducing Prophet," *True Detective Mysteries* 27 (March 1937): 10-15 and 92-94; and C.K. Stanton, "The Enigma of the Sex-Crazed Prophet," *Front Page Detective* (January 1938): 4-9 and 108-10. For the use of these pseudonyms see the Contents List to the Stewart Hall Holbrook Papers, Acc. No. 701, UWL. He may also have been the author of L. Thompson, "Nemesis of the Nudist High Priest," *Startling Detective* 42 (March 1951).
4 See M. Beam, "Crazy After Women," in *Cults of America*, ed. M. Beam (New York: McFadden Books, 1964), 35-58; A. Hynd, "Prophet Joshua and His Holy Rollers," in *Murder, Mayhem and Mystery: An Album of American Crime*, ed. A. Hynd (New York: Barnes, 1950), 265-73; J. Parrott-Holden, "Joshua the Second: The Man Who Put the Hex on San Francisco," *Columbia* 11, 4 (1997-98): 35-37; D. Pintarich, "The Gospel According to Edmond Creffield," in *Great Moments in Oregon History*, ed. Pintarich and W. McCormack (Portland: New Oregon Publishers, 1987), 105-10; E.A. Johnson, "History of the Benton County Courthouse," unpublished ms., c. 1988, BCHM; J.R. Nash, *Encyclopedia of World Crime* (Wilmette, IL: Crime Books, 1989), vol. 1, 815, and vol. 2, 2191, and *Murder America: Homicide in the United States from the Revolution to the Present* (New York: Simon and Schuster, 1980), 182-84; R. Mathison, "Franz Creffield: Naked Reformer," in *Faiths, Cults, and Sects of America*, ed. R. Mathison (Indianapolis: Bobbs-Merrill, 1960), 301-305; and T. Miller, *The Quest for Utopia in Twentieth-Century America*, 2 vols. (Syracuse, NY: Syracuse University Press, 1998), vol. 1, 113-14.
5 We are sure that we have not located all the magazine and newspaper articles, but we have found many, almost all of which are based on Holbrook or other prior magazine articles. See *Benton Bulletin*, 1 June 1989; *Corvallis Gazette-Times*, July 1937 (75th Anniversary Edition), 19 March 1976, and 29 May 1988; *Oregonian*, 28 August 1934,

10 March 1946, 24 February 1980, 7 January 1986, 21 April 1997, and 29 July 2001; *Journal American*, 24 December 1979; *The Weekly* (Seattle), 4 December 1985; *Oregon Magazine*, March 1983; *Oregon Journal*, 14 June 1982; *Seattle Times*, 13 May 1988; *The West*, March 1972; *Argus*, 16 June 1978; *Corvallis Magazine*, Spring 1964; *Seattle Post-Intelligencer*, 19 November 1941; *Newberg Graphic*, 1 February 1995. We thank Derrol Hockett, Sexton, Newberg Friends Cemetery, for some of these references.

6 L. Crew, *Brides of Eden: A True Story Imagined* (New York: HarperCollins, 2001); T. McCracken and R. Blodgett: *Holy Rollers: Murder and Madness in Oregon's Love Cult* (Caldwell, ID: Caxton Press, 2002); M. McDonald, "Roll Ye Sinners Roll: The Story of the Creffield Cult, Corvallis, Oregon, 1903-1909," unpublished ms, 2002, available at BCHM.

7 Cambridge: Harvard University Press, 1983. On "micro-history" see, *inter alia*, G. Levi, "On Microhistory," in *New Perspectives on Historical Writing*, ed. P. Burke (Cambridge: Polity Press, 1991); J. Lepore, "Historians Who Love Too Much: Reflections on Microhistory and Biography," *Journal of American History* 88 (2001): 129-44; D.A. Bell, "Total History and Microhistory: The French and Italian Paradigms," in *A Companion to Western Historical Thought*, ed. L. Kramer and S. Maza (Oxford: Blackwell, 2002); and R.J. Scott, "Small-Scale Dynamics of Large-Scale Processes," *American Historical Review* 105 (2000): 472-79. While initially most case studies dealt with the medieval and early-modern periods (see C. Ginzburg, *The Cheese and the Worms: The Cosmos of a Sixteenth-Century Miller* (Baltimore: Johns Hopkins University Press, 1980) and G. Geis and I. Bunn, *A Trial of Witches: A Seventeenth-Century Witchcraft Prosecution* (London: Routledge, 1997), in more recent years they have been used to illustrate a wide variety of periods and places: monographs we have found most useful include L. Gordon, *The Great Arizona Orphan Abduction* (Cambridge: Harvard University Press, 1999); M. Grossberg, *A Judgement for Solomon: The D'Hauteville Case and Legal Experience in Antebellum America* (Cambridge: Cambridge University Press, 1996); C.B. Herrup, *A House in Gross Disorder: Sex, Law, and the 2nd Earl of Castlehaven* (Oxford: Oxford University Press, 1999); P.C. Cohen, *The Murder of Helen Jewett: The Life and Death of a Prostitute in Nineteenth Century New York* (New York: Knopf, 1998); S. Weisenburger, *Modern Medea: A Family Story of Slavery and Child Murder from the Old South* (New York: Hill and Wang, 1998); R. McGowen and D.T. Andrew, *The Perreaus and Mrs Rudd: Forgery and Betrayal in Eighteenth-Century London* (Berkeley: University of California Press, 2001); R.R. Harris, *Murders and Madness: Medicine, Law and Society in the Fin-de-Siècle* (Oxford: Clarendon Press, 1989); C. and T. Hoffman, *Brotherly Love: Murder and the Politics of Prejudice in Nineteenth-Century Rhode Island* (Amherst, MA: University of Massachusetts Press, 1993); E. Lewis and H. Ardizzone, *Love on Trial: An American Scandal in Black and White* (New York: Norton, 2001).

8 Davis, *The Return of Martin Guerre* (Cambridge: Harvard University Press, 1983), 1.

9 For a useful insistence on continuing to study those large-scale processes, on not assuming that micro-history can replace such work, see B. Gregory, "Is Small Beautiful? Microhistory and the History of Everyday Life," *History and Theory* 39 (1999): 100-10.

10 Grossberg, *A Judgement for Solomon*, xii.

11 R. Finlay, "The Refashioning of Martin Guerre," *American Historical Review* 93 (1983): 553. See also Herrup, *A House in Gross Disorder*, 152, noting that trials are

"moments of social disclosure" that allow us to "hear within legal records the voices of the usually voiceless." For general discussions see R.A. Ferguson, "Untold Stories in the Law," in *Law's Stories: Narrative and Rhetoric in the Law,* ed. P. Brooks and P. Gerwitz (New Haven, CT: Yale University Press, 1996), and C. Ginzburg, "Checking the Evidence: The Judge and the Historian," in *Questions of Evidence: Proof, Practice and Persuasion Across the Disciplines,* ed. J. Chandler et al. (Chicago: University of Chicago Press, 1994).

12 Herrup, *A House in Gross Disorder,* 153.

13 As Davis puts it, "a remarkable dispute can sometimes uncover motivations and values that are lost in the welter of the everyday": *Return of Martin Guerre,* 4.

14 Gordon, *Great Arizona Orphan Abduction,* ix.

15 All official sources except one give this as his year of birth: see *inter alia,* King County Medical Examiner's Records, File 551, KCA; Death Certificate, vol. 1906, No. 16307, WSA-PS; Police Circular, March 1904, in *Corvallis Times,* 30 March 1904; Inmate Records, Oregon State Penitentiary, OSA; Creffield's "Career Sheet," Salvation Army National Archives, Alexandria, VA; Police Arrest Book, Portland City Archives, 240-41. See also *Seattle Times,* 7 May 1906; *Oregonian,* 8 May 1906. However, his age was given as thirty-five in 1906 on the wooden board set up to mark his grave, which would make his birthdate 1871 (*Corvallis Times,* 11 May 1906) and the 1900 federal census lists him as born in May 1864, which we assume is an error: 1900 Federal Census, King County, Washington, Seattle 3rd Precinct, Sheet 9B [hereafter Census–Creffield]. As discussed below, this could also be another person. Most of these sources, including the census, also say that he was from Germany. There are contemporary suggestions that he was from Sweden (see, *inter alia, Seattle Times,* 7 May 1906; *Corvallis Times,* 31 October 1903; *Oregonian,* 8 May 1906; *Oregon Statesman,* 31 October 1903), but we would discount these.

16 The immigration date is from Census–Creffield. For the story about his mother see *Telegram,* 2 August 1904.

17 See Inmate Records, Oregon State Penitentiary, OSA. This is likely more reliable than the description put out by the Corvallis police in 1904 (*Corvallis Times,* 30 March 1904), which gave his height as five feet six inches. A Portland *Evening Telegram* reporter described him as "not over five feet high" and about 130 pounds: *Telegram,* 1 August 1904.

18 The *Seattle Post-Intelligencer* always used "Crefeld," which also appears on his gravestone in Lakeview Cemetery, Seattle, and on Census–Creffield. He was also referred to by that name in the Salvation Army newspaper *War Cry:* see, for example, the issues of 25 November 1899 and 21 September 1901. Most newspapers as well as the Oregon State Penitentiary officials and other official sources preferred "Creffield," which we have adopted. Some early newspaper reports also called him "Krofield" (*Corvallis Gazette,* 3 November 1903) and "Krafel" (*Telegram,* 2 November 1903, and *Oregon Statesman,* 31 October 1903).

19 Even his wife claimed she knew nothing about his early life: *Seattle Times,* 7 May 1906. A few stories did circulate, but we cannot attach any reliability to them. One said that he was a deserter from the German army, another that he was highly educated and had trained in Germany for the priesthood. It was also claimed that he worked as a labourer in Portland: see variously *Corvallis Times,* 21 September 1904; *Oregonian,* 8 May and 13 July 1906; *Oregon Journal,* 8 May 1906. Robert Blodgett of

Corvallis has searched without success for information that might establish where Creffield came from in Germany and when and how he moved to the United States, although he suspects that Creffield's family was from the Aachen area: correspondence with Robert Blodgett, on file with the authors.

20 His "Career Sheet" at the Salvation Army Archives describes him as "Out of the Corps at Seattle, WA" but does not say that he was a soldier there, which the career sheets usually specify.

21 Information on the Salvation Army in Portland in this period is principally from unpublished histories in the Portland files of the Salvation Army National Archives. Especially useful is "The Salvation Army: Its Beginnings in Portland, Compiled by an Old Timer." There are also brief accounts in *Oregonian*, 31 July 1904 and 30 September 1934, and in the Army newspaper the *War Cry*, especially 3 January and 14 March 1903 and 10 December 1904. See also J. Gaston, *Portland, Oregon: Its History and Builders*, 3 vols. (Chicago: S.J. Clarke, 1911), vol. 1, 476. Violent and other opposition to the Army was common in the late nineteenth century, making for a "depressingly long ... catalogue of hostile acts" and including a number of deaths of Army members: see E.H. McKinley, *Marching to Glory: The History of the Salvation Army in the United States, 1880-1992* (Grand Rapids: W.B. Eerdmans, 1995), 81-82.

22 *Telegram*, 3 August 1904; the quotations that follow are from this source.

23 Ibid., 6 August 1904.

24 See the list of promotions in *War Cry*, 25 November 1899.

25 Information on Creffield's postings is from the "Disposition of Forces" books and Creffield's "Career Sheet," Salvation Army National Archives. See also *War Cry*, 25 November 1899, and 16 March 1901.

26 There are two other explanations for Creffield being on the Seattle census at the same time that he was moving from post to post in the Salvation Army in Oregon. One is that the lodging housekeeper with whom he resided in Seattle (see Census–Creffield) added his name because she assumed Creffield would return; if so, that suggests that Creffield had been resident in Seattle for some time and was seen by his acquaintances as at least a semi-permanent resident. The other, alluded to above, is that the Edmund Crefeld of the Seattle census was a different man from the Franz Edmund Crefeld featured in this book.

27 See McKinley, *Marching to Glory*, passim, and D. Winston, *Red-Hot and Righteous: The Urban Religion of the Salvation Army* (Cambridge: Harvard University Press, 1999), 81. See generally the "Disposition of Forces" books noted above, which indicate frequent changes in personnel for many Oregon communities.

28 *Corvallis Times*, 21 September 1904, quoting Creffield's defence speech at his adultery trial.

29 Captain Edmund Crefeld, "Holiness," *War Cry*, 8 September 1901.

30 *Corvallis Times*, 31 October 1903; *Yamhill County Reporter*, 6 and 13 November 1903, 8 January and 23 September 1904; *McMinnville Reporter*, 11 and 18 May and 13 and 20 July 1906; *McMinnville Telephone Register*, 14 and 21 July 1906.

31 *Seattle Times*, 17 September 1906; *Star*, 7 May 1906.

32 *Telegram*, 5 and 13 August 1904. See also *Corvallis Gazette*, 12 August 1904, and *Oregonian*, 8 May and 15 July 1906. For Creffield's interest in Ryan see C.M. Robeck, "The Dog Days of Summer: 1906," unpublished ms; we are grateful to Professor Robeck for the opportunity to read this account. For Ryan in Salem in 1902 see

Oregon Statesman, 13 and 16 July 1902, and for his later leadership of the "Tongues of Fire" Pentecostalists there see *Gazette,* 19 October 1906, and *Oregonian,* 15 July 1906. A search of the *Oregon Statesman* for 1902 turned up no mention of Creffield, but he is listed in the *Salem and Marion County Directory* for 1902, 58, as "Frank E. Crefeld," a student living at the Mission and Training School run by Ryan. (We thank Robert Blodgett of Corvallis for this last piece of information.)

33 *Oregon Statesman,* 25 November 1906. (We thank Robert Blodgett of Corvallis for this reference.)

34 For Creffield's presence in the Dalles see principally *The Dalles Weekly Chronicle,* 4 November 1903 and 3 August and 21 September 1904; *Telegram,* 6 August 1904. See also *Oregon Journal,* 9 May 1906, and *Corvallis Times,* 21 September 1904. There is no mention of Creffield in *The Dalles Weekly Chronicle* for 1902. Van Zandt and Cooper were active in The Dalles in 1902, both described as travelling evangelists and as Salvation Army men: see *The Dalles Weekly Chronicle,* 19 and 23 April and 1 October 1902.

CHAPTER 2: THE CREFFIELD SECT IN CORVALLIS, 1903

1 The literature on Corvallis history is limited. The best source is M.K. Gallagher, *Historic Context Statement: City of Corvallis, Oregon* (Corvallis: Benton County Historical Museum, 1993), a good deal of which is also at <http://www.ci.corvallis.or.us/historic>. Gallagher is the source of the population calculation; according to census records she employs, the population was 1,819 in 1900 and 4,552 in 1910. In addition, M. Phinney, *Historical Sketches of Benton County* (Salem: Oregon State Archives, 1942) and B. Martin, "History of Corvallis, 1846-1900," MA thesis, University of Oregon, 1938, can be mined with profit. For the history of the city's best-known institution see J.W. Goshong, *The Making of a University, 1868-1968* (Corvallis, OR: Oregon State University Press, 1968), and J.B. Horner, "History of Oregon State College, 1865-1907," *Oregon Historical Quarterly* 31 (1930): 42-50. Of rather more limited use are D. Fagan, *History of Benton County* (Portland: A.G. Walling, 1894), and M.K. Reynolds, "Corvallis in 1900," typescript, n.d., a fifty-seven-page set of reminiscences at the Benton County Historical Museum. The Willamette Valley generally has been better served: see especially W.A. Bowen, *The Willamette Valley: Migration and Settlement on the Oregon Frontier* (Seattle: University of Washington Press, 1978); D.L. May, *Three Frontiers: Family, Land, and Society in the American West, 1850-1900* (Cambridge: Cambridge University Press, 1994), passim; and P.G. Boag, *Environment and Experience: Settlement Culture in Nineteenth Century Oregon* (Berkeley: University of California Press, 1992).

2 Ethnic homogeneity was a matter of pride for many. See Corvallis Commercial Club, *Benton: The Blue Ribbon County of Oregon* (1920): "Corvallis has no slums and the foreign element is conspicuous by its absence, most of the residents being native Americans of the better class."

3 We have found no evidence of suffrage campaigns in the town. There are a few references to women's organizations, such as the WCTU and the Coffee Club, a group that served coffee to the volunteer fire department when it was called out. This later became the Corvallis Women's Club: see *Corvallis Gazette,* 17 March 1903; Reynolds

"Corvallis in 1900"; Martin, "History of Corvallis." For the blue laws and voting patterns see Phinney, *Historical Sketches of Benton County,* A-22-A-23 and A-80.

4 *Corvallis Gazette,* 3 October 1902; *Corvallis Times,* 6 September 1902.

5 This paragraph is from *Corvallis Gazette,* 5 and 12 December 1902, and 6 August 1904;
   Corvallis Times, 10 January, 10 June, and 31 October 1903; *Telegram,* 7 November 1903;
   Eugene Register, 3 November 1903.

6 The Corvallis corps' activities were quite frequently reported in the press: see, *inter
   alia, Corvallis Times,* 4, 15, and 22 October 1902, and *Corvallis Gazette,* 1 July and 17
   October 1902.

7 *Corvallis Gazette,* 6 August 1904. The Pacific Northwest commander for the Salvation
   Army, Colonel French, claimed in 1899 that the Corvallis contingent had some fifty
   members: *War Cry,* 28 October 1899. Whether this had been true then, the numbers
   were down by 1902-1903, for as we shall see, the Creffield sect never numbered more
   than about half that number.

8 Information on Sarah Hurt and on the early life of O.V. Hurt is drawn from Death
   Certificate, Sarah M. Hurt, 1946, No. 2682, OSA; "Descendants of Captain John
   Starr," at genealogy.com; *Oregon Journal,* 31 October 1932, 8; Marriage Certificate,
   Sarah Starr and O.V. Hurt, Benton County, vol. 5, 163, OSA; M.H. Hays, *The Land
   That Kept Its Promise: A History of South Lincoln County* (Newport: Lincoln County
   Historical Society, 1976), 118 and 131-33.

9 This account of Hurt in Corvallis is drawn from *Oregon Journal,* 31 October 1932,
   8; *Lincoln County Leader,* 17 June 1943; *Corvallis Gazette,* 30 October 1903 and 19
   January, 2 August, and 15 November 1904; *Corvallis Times,* 7 April, 6 May, and 31
   October 1903, 16 April and 12 November 1904, 23 October and 21 December 1906;
   Oregon Statesman, 31 October 1903; *Telegram,* 23 November 1903 and 5 January 1904.

10 The 1904 tax assessments for Benton County show his personal property to be
   assessed at $90, his real estate at $400: *Corvallis Times,* 17 September 1904. These are
   modest sums compared with most others on the same roll. Although the personal
   property figure could be much lower than the year before because the sect destroyed
   his possessions, an incident discussed below and in Chapter 3, this qualification does
   not apply to the house. Only about 20 percent of residents had real estate worth $400
   or less, with most land holdings valued at between $500 and $1,000; the wealthiest
   men had property worth over $10,000. See also his statement in 1904 that "I am only
   on a small salary": Hurt to William Gardner, 21 June 1904, Case File 2430, BGAS
   Records. For his level of education see this and other letters in Case File 2430, BGAS
   Records, which contain a number of spelling and grammatical errors.

11 *Oregonian,* 8 May 1906; *Albany Herald,* 19 July 1906.

12 See *Corvallis Gazette,* 11 July 1902.

13 For Maud Hurt see OSH Records, Personal and Medical Histories, vol. 4B, 277,
   OSA, describing her as five feet two inches tall and weighing 160 pounds. See also the
   description of her in July 1906 as having a "rather short, rotund figure": *PI,* 14 July
   1906. In addition to the sources cited in this paragraph, for Maud Hurt see Crew,
   Brides of Eden, passim; *Corvallis Times,* 14 September 1906; *Oregonian,* 6 January 1904
   and 13 September 1906; *Seattle Times,* 12 September 1906; *Star,* 7 May 1906.

14 *PI,* 13 September 1906, and *Oregonian,* 13 September 1906.

15 *Corvallis Gazette,* 30 November 1906. See also her one-time fiancé James Berry's statement that she "was always very devout": *PI,* 13 September 1906.

16 Quotation from *Oregonian,* 8 May 1906. Maud herself later stated that "while a member of the Salvation Army her relations with the other members were pleasant" but that she had some trouble with the "higher officers" because "they took offense at her criticisms of the methods by which the army collected subscriptions." In addition, she also "had trouble in the army by expressing her opinion that the army was teaching the Bible in a narrow manner": *Seattle Times,* 17 September 1906.

17 *Oregonian,* 1 May 1904. For other information on Frank Hurt see *Telegram,* 7 and 11 November 1903; Death Certificate, Frank C. Hurt, 1920, No. 1, OSA; *Corvallis Gazette,* 3 May 1904; OSH Records, Personal and Medical Histories, Frank Hurt, vol. 6A, 445, OSA.

18 For Mae Hurt see Crew, *Brides of Eden,* esp. at 3 and 5; Benton County Court Case File No. 778, 1904, Benton County Courthouse; Register Book, Girls C, Case 2430, BGAS Records. See her photograph, with Attie Bray, this book.

19 For the arrival and activities of Brooks and Lieutenant C.E. Maness see *War Cry,* 24 January and 21 and 28 February 1903; *Corvallis Times,* 7 and 10 January, and 14 and 28 March, 1903; *Corvallis Gazette,* 3 February 1903; *Telegram,* 3 August 1904. For Brooks' defection see *Corvallis Times,* 10 June 1903; see also *Oregon Statesman,* 31 October 1903 and *Eugene Register,* 3 November 1903. There are references to the Army parading in Corvallis in early May, although Brooks is not mentioned: *Corvallis Times,* 13 May 1903, and *Corvallis Gazette,* 12 May 1903. A Canadian, Brooks had been a solider in the Army for eleven years before becoming an officer in 1902 while living in Baker City, Oregon. He had one posting to Astoria before being sent to Corvallis: see the "Disposition of Forces" book, entry for Corvallis, and Brooks' "Career Sheet," both at Salvation Army National Archives.

20 A year later the Salvation Army hall was being used by the Corvallis Steam Laundry: *Corvallis Gazette,* 19 April 1904. The Corvallis Corps has no "Disposition of Forces" listing in the Salvation Army Archives from 1903 until August 1923, and it disappears again after October 1924. The corps did not return to Corvallis until the 1990s (information from Judy Juntunen, archivist at the Benton County Historical Museum).

21 They rented the hall from member and local entrepreneur James Berry, who is likewise discussed below: see *Seattle Times,* 7 July 1906. This account of the early period is drawn from a variety of newspaper reports, including some from 1906. Especially useful are *Corvallis Times,* 10 June, 31 October, and 7 November 1903, and 27 February 1904; *Oregonian,* 8 May and 13 and 14 July 1906; *PI,* 8 May 1906; *Seattle Times,* 13 July and 17 September 1906; *Oregon Statesman,* 31 October 1903; *Telegram,* 30 October 1903. Also a good source for the chronology of the sect is Louis Hartley's Divorce Petition, Benton County Divorces, No. 4377, OSA. See also Reynolds, "Corvallis in 1900," 50-51.

22 Just south of Corvallis the Willamette River forks into the main channel and what is known as the Booneville Channel. Between the two forks lies Kiger's Island, a large area used then and now for orchards. Between the island and the west bank of the river sits a much smaller piece of land, Smith Island, and it was here that the sect established its camp. In the summer, with the Willamette running low, both Smith and Kiger's Islands were reachable by shallow fords. This description is from Reynolds, "Corvallis in 1900," 52, and Creffield File, BCHM. See also Crew, *Brides of Eden,* 35-36.

23 The *Oregonian,* 8 May and 14 July 1906, states that the camp lasted for six weeks;

Crew, *Brides of Eden*, 59-60, says it began in June and went to the end of August. Other sources simply refer to "the summer."

24 Reynolds, "Corvallis in 1900," 53.

25 *Corvallis Times*, 10 June 1903.

26 Versions of the picture reproduced here appeared in various newspapers, first in the Portland *Evening Telegram* of 2 November 1903. We have ones published in *Telegram*, 2 November 1903 and *Oregon Journal*, 16 May 1906; the photograph also appears in *Telegram*, 13 August 1904, *Oregonian*, 13 July 1906, *Oregon Journal*, 13 July 1906, and *Seattle Times*, 13 July 1906. Although they are all undoubtedly the same picture, the versions are a little different, with two of them having only twenty-one people because Wesley Seeley, standing in the back row, was obscured. The *Telegram* picture used here has only twenty because Hattie Starr's image was covered with biblical verses after she left the group, and the verses also hid another woman seated close by, we assume by accident. We assume the portrait was taken by a professional, although we do not know whom. The various versions agree on the identification of just fourteen of the twenty-two but are not consistent for the other eight; we have used other photographs and descriptions of members to identify them.

27 For "Army of Holiness" see *Corvallis Gazette*, 5 December 1902. For "holiness mission" see *Albany Herald*, 5 May 1904. For both "come-outers" and "Holy Rollers" see *Corvallis Times*, 10 June 1903.

28 *Corvallis Gazette*, 5 December 1902; *Corvallis Times*, 10 June 1903.

29 *Corvallis Times*, 31 October 1903.

30 Ibid., 31 October 1903; *Oregon Statesman*, 31 October 1903; *Telegram*, 30 October 1903.

31 *Corvallis Times*, 10 June 1903; *Corvallis Gazette*, 5 December 1902.

32 The principal destination was Newport. In the summer the local news pages of both newspapers were replete with stories about comings and goings from the coast: see, for example, *Corvallis Gazette*, 11 July 1902. For the rise of Newport as a summer resort see R.M. Price, *Newport, Oregon, 1866-1936: Portrait of a Coast Resort* (Dallas, OR: Lincoln County Historical Society, 1975).

33 See *Corvallis Times*, 10 June 1903, noting that "many" wished to visit the island "through curiosity." See also the account of Minerva Kiger Reynolds, who claimed to have witnessed both the group's activities and community reaction as a small girl. The group "became the talk of the town," with reactions ranging from curiosity to annoyance to alarm. But the account does not suggest there was any serious opposition: Reynolds, "Corvallis in 1900," 51. See also the report of the marriage of two members, Frank Hurt and Mollie Sandell, in July 1903. It was a standard, bland account, and the paper saw no need to make any mention of their involvement in the sect: *Corvallis Gazette*, 24 July 1903.

34 In this survey we will have more to say about the central, and steadfast, members than about the others, but we will at least note everybody who is mentioned in any source as being an adherent; the members are also listed in the Appendix.

35 For Mollie Sandell Hurt and her sister Olive see variously *Albany Herald*, 5 May and 30 June 1904; *Corvallis Gazette*, 24 July 1903; "Disposition of Forces" books and "Career Sheet," Salvation Army National Archives; *Oregonian*, 1 May 1904; OSH Records, Admissions Registers – Female, vol. E, 83, OSA; *PI*, 13 July 1906; *Seattle City Directory*, 1907; *Corvallis Gazette-Times*, 20 May 1959.

36 See Marriage Certificate, Frank Hurt and Mollie Sandell, Benton County, vol. 7, 257, OSA; *Corvallis Times,* 22 July 1903; *Corvallis Gazette,* 24 July 1903.

37 See *War Cry,* 18 August 1900 and 6 July 1901; *PI,* 13 July 1906.

38 For Attie Bray and her family see J. Gaston, *The Centennial History of Oregon, 1811-1912,* 3 vols. (Chicago: S.J. Clarke, 1912), vol. 3, 680-81; B. Bogue, B. and S.B. Yunker, "Proved Up on Ten Mile Creek: The Story of the Early Settlers of Lane County, Oregon," bound typescript, n.p., n.d., 4-8; "Descendants of Captain John Starr"; *Corvallis Times,* 7 May and 11 June 1904; OSH Records, Admissions Register – Female, vol. E, 83, and Personal and Medical Histories, vol. 4B, 278, OSA; Lane County Census, 1900, Heceta Precinct, vol. 7; E. Parry, *At Rest in Lincoln County* (Newport, OR: Lincoln County Historical Society, 1979), 231.

39 For Hattie and Clarence Starr see *Albany Herald,* 5 May 1904; Death Certificate, Clarence M. Starr, 1939, No. 69, OSA; "Descendants of Captain John Starr"; Hattie A. Starr, in Index to Oregon Death Records, ancestry.com; Marriage Licence for Clarence Starr and Harriet Baldwin, Benton County, vol. 6, 241, OSA; *Oregon Journal,* 29 July and 19 August 1936.

40 For Burgess and Donna Starr see *Newberg Graphic,* 3 May 1906; *Telegram,* 17 March 1904; "Descendants of Captain John Starr"; Marriage Certificate, Burgess Starr and Donna Mitchell, Multnomah County, 1899-1901, 340, OSA; *Portland City Directories,* 1901-1904. The Salvation Army connection is evidenced by the fact that they were married by a Salvation Army officer. Donna Starr's family background is discussed in more detail below, where we deal with Esther Mitchell.

41 He brought it from Portland and sold it to one August Fischer: see *Corvallis Times,* 4 July and 8 August 1903. For Berry see Death Certificate, James Berry, 1943, No. 9, OSA; Marriage Certificate, James Berry and Clara King, Benton County, vol. 7, 273; *Corvallis Gazette,* 3 March, 27 June, 31 July, and 7 and 30 August 1903; 8 April and 7 and 12 October 1904; *Corvallis Times,* 4 July 1903 and 9 January 1904; *PI,* 13 September 1906.

42 For the Baldwins see *Corvallis Gazette,* 17 March 1903; *Seattle Times,* 5 July 1906; *Oregon Journal,* 29 July 1936; *Corvallis Gazette-Times,* 12 December 1947; Mark Phinney Interviews – David Ruble, WPA Historical Records, Benton County, OSA; Hays, *The Land That Kept Its Promise,* 108.

43 In addition to the specific references cited below, this account of the Mitchell family is based on *Seattle Times,* 2 July 1906; *Corvallis Gazette,* 20 July 1906; *Oregonian,* 18 July 1906; Ruth Mitchell Pritchard, "The Genealogical Record of the Ancestors and Descendants of Perley and Phebe Mitchell," at ancestry.com; *Newberg Graphic,* 1889-1895, passim, and 11 August 1904; Register Book, Girls C, Case 2251, BGAS Records; H.S. Nedry, "The Friends Come to Oregon: 1, Newberg Meeting," *Oregon Historical Quarterly* 45 (1944): 195-217; Marriage Certificate of Phoebe Mitchell and Peter Vanderkellen, Multnomah County Marriages, vol. 16, 387, OSA.

44 *Corvallis Gazette,* 12 December 1902.

45 See principally *Star,* 7 May 1906.

46 See *Catalogue of the O.S.A.C. for 1902-1903,* in Oregon State University Archives. The program in household science required courses in math, English, botany, history, chemistry, American literature, economics, geology, German, and physiology in addition to household science courses.

47 *Corvallis Times,* 4 May 1904. For the Hartleys see Death Certificates, Lewis Hartley and Cora Hartley, 1937, No. 2, and 1945, No. 5853, OSA; Divorce Petition, Louis

Hartley, Benton County Divorces, No. 4377, OSA; *Corvallis Gazette*, 17 and 31 March 1903; *Corvallis Times*, 14 March 1903. For the Bohemia Mines see *Corvallis Gazette*, 2 June and 14 July 1903, and for Louis' economic status see the list of incorporators in the Great Eastern Mining Company (*Corvallis Times*, 12 July 1902), and note that early in 1903 he started building a ten-room, two-storey house in Corvallis: *Corvallis Times*, 14 March 1903. For his many business trips see also *Corvallis Gazette*, 13 January, 31 March, and 8 and 29 December 1903.

48 *Telegram*, 30 October 1903.

49 See *Catalogue of the O.S.A.C. for 1902-1903*, in Oregon State University Archives.

50 For the Seeleys see Linn County Court Judicial Journals, 1904, 574, OSA; OSH Records, Personal and Medical Histories, vol. 4B, 278, OSA; 1900 US census, cited in McDonald, "Roll Ye Sinners Roll," 10; McCracken and Blodgett, *Holy Rollers*, 17; Register Book, Girls C, Case 2397, BGAS Records; Benton County Insane Record, vol. 2, 3-4, BCHM; *Corvallis Times*, 7 May 1904; *Oregonian*, 7 May 1904; *Corvallis Gazette*, 3 and 10 May 1904; *Albany Herald*, 5 May 1904; *Telegram*, 3 May 1904 (quotations); Crew, *Brides of Eden*, 50-51.

51 Another Seeley sister, Daisy, also lived in Corvallis, as did a younger brother, Ben: Register Book, Girls C, Case 2397, BGAS Records.

52 *Telegram*, 16 September 1904 and *Oregonian*, 17 September 1904. Other newspapers' versions of the group portrait identify this woman as a Julia Lamberson of Portland and as a Mrs Waldron of Portland. We think she was Mrs Worrell because she does reappear, as a follower, when Creffield was in Portland, whereas there are no further mentions of the other two.

53 *Telegram*, 7 November 1903.

54 *Corvallis Times*, 10 July 1906; Death Certificate, Milton Lee Campbell, 1912, No. 458, OSA; Crew, *Brides of Eden*, 19.

55 *Telegram*, 6 November 1903. For Levins generally see also *Corvallis Times*, 10 July 1906; *Telegram*, 7 November 1903; *Corvallis Gazette-Times*, 4 November 1957; Parry, *At Rest in Lincoln County*, 231; Bogue and Yunker, "Proved Up on Ten Mile Creek," 9.

56 A letter about his conversion from a Sampson Lewis of Oregon, almost certainly Levins, appeared in *God's Revivalist and Bible Advocate* in October 1902 (information from Robert Blodgett of Corvallis).

57 He is mentioned in, *inter alia, Seattle Times*, 13 July 1906, *Telegram*, 13 August 1904, and *Oregonian*, 8 May 1906. Some of our information on him is courtesy of Robert Blodgett of Corvallis.

58 *Corvallis Times*, 7 November 1903.

59 Our calculation of the total number of members is at odds with all prior accounts, which typically suggest much larger numbers, as do the wildly exaggerated accounts in some 1906 newspapers. Even Crew, *Brides of Eden*, generally very accurate, suggests as many as thirty-five in 1903 (p. 27). We believe, however, that our figures are correct, unless there were many more members who were never mentioned in any of the numerous accounts of the sect. It is supported by the first extended discussion of the group in the Corvallis press, which estimated a membership of "about 20": *Corvallis Times*, 31 October 1903. See also the figure of twenty or so given in *Corvallis Times*, 18 November 1903, and *Oregon Statesman*, 31 October 1903, and twenty-one in *Telegram*, 19 November 1903. Florence Seeley gave the number as seventeen in May 1904, but that was after a few people had left: *Telegram*, 3 May 1904.

60 M.E. Dieter, *The Holiness Revival of the Nineteenth Century* (Metuchen, NJ: Scarecrow Press, 1980), 72. The literature on the holiness movement and the related issues discussed here is extensive. In addition to Dieter, we have found most useful, and largely based this section on: R.M. Anderson, *Vision of the Disinherited: The Making of American Pentecostalism* (New York: Oxford University Press, 1979); C.E. Jones, *Perfectionist Persuasion: The Holiness Movement and American Methodism, 1867-1936* (Metuchen, NJ: Scarecrow Press, 1974); S.S. Frankiel, *California's Spiritual Frontiers: Religious Alternatives to Anglo-Protestantism, 1850-1910* (Berkeley: University of California Press, 1988); J.L. Brasher, *The Sanctified South: John Lakin Brasher and the Holiness Movement* (Urbana, IL: University of Illinois Press, 1994). Also useful are E.L. Queen, S.R. Porthero, and G.H. Shattuck Jr., *The Encyclopedia of American Religious History,* 2 vols. (New York: Facts on File, 1996), vol. 1, 295-98; J.G. Melton, *Encyclopedia of American Religions* (Detroit: Gale Research, 1996), ch. 7 ("Holiness Family"); J.M. Schmidt, "Holiness and Perfectionism," in *Encyclopedia of the American Religious Experience: Studies of Traditions and Movements,* ed. C.H. Lippy and P.W. Williams (New York: Scribner, 1988); M.E. Marty, *Modern American Religion,* vol. 1, *The Irony of It All: 1893-1919* (Chicago: University of Chicago Press, 1986).
61 Melton, *Encyclopedia of American Religions,* ch. 7 ("Holiness Family"), 75.
62 Queen et al., *Encyclopedia of American Religious History,* vol. 1, 295.
63 Frankiel, *California's Spiritual Frontiers,* 103.
64 2 Corinthians 6:17.
65 Melton, *Encyclopedia of American Religions,* ch. 7 ("Holiness Family"), 76.
66 Quotations from Queen et al., *Encyclopedia of American Religious History,* vol. 1, 298, and C.E. Jones, "Symbol and Sign in Methodist Holiness and Pentecostal Spirituality," in *America's Alternative Religions,* ed. T. Miller (Albany, NY: State University of New York Press, 1995), 24. Jones analogizes the relationship between holiness and Pentecostalism to that of "mother and daughter." For the day of the Pentecost see Acts of the Apostles, chapter 2.
67 *God's Revivalist and Bible Advocate,* 21 August 1902. We are indebted to Professor Mel Robeck of the Fuller Theological Seminary in Pasadena for alerting us to this article.
68 Crefeld, "Holiness."
69 *Oregon Statesman* (Salem), 25 November 1906; we thank Robert Blodgett for this reference.
70 Crefeld, "Holiness."
71 This paragraph is largely based on interviews with Creffield by a reporter for the Portland *Evening Telegram,* published in early August 1904. Quotations are from the issues of 5 and 6 August 1904.
72 Ibid., 7 November 1903.
73 Brasher, *The Sanctified South,* 64.
74 There are many references to the prophet Joshua, although the first does not appear until March 1904: see *Corvallis Times,* 30 March 1904. Before that the Corvallis press referred to him as "Parson Creffield" or "Apostle Creffield."
75 Quotation from Deuteronomy 34:9. See also Joshua 1:5 and 6:27: "He enjoyed the presence of God" and "He was indwelt by the word of God." For Joshua see generally H. Lockyer, *All the Men of the Bible* (Grand Rapids, MI: Zondervan Publishing House, 1958), 205-207, and P.J. Achtemeier, ed., *Harper's Dictionary of the Bible* (San Francisco: Harper, 1985), 509-10.

76 See *Telegram,* 6 November 1903, quoting Sampson Levins. See also Frank Hurt's statement that Creffield was "an apostle the same as those mentioned in the Bible": *Telegram,* 7 November 1903. See also *Eugene Register,* 3 November 1903.

77 Crefeld, "Holiness."

78 Quotations from *Telegram,* 5 and 6 August 1904.

79 See J.G. Melton, *Religious Leaders of America: A Biographical Guide to Founders and Leaders of Religious Bodies, Churches, and Spiritual Groups in North America* (Detroit: Gale Research, 1991), 255; Queen et al., *Encyclopedia of American Religious History,* vol. 1, 297; "The Formation and Development of the Pilgrim Holiness Church," at <http://campus.arbot.edu:8880/~markw/howe/pilgrimh>; L. Haines, "A Pilgrim's Progress," at <http://www.wesleyan.org/doc/history/heritage/histknapp>. Knapp's holiness writings included *Holiness Triumphant; Or, Pearls from Patmos, Being the Secret of Revelation Revealed* (Cincinnati: God's Bible School, 1900). For others see Melton, *Religious Leaders of America,* 255, and <http://www.watchword.org/knapp>.

80 *Telegram,* 7 November 1903 and 6 August 1904; *The Dalles Weekly Chronicle,* 3 August 1904. They presumably used *Bible Songs of Salvation and Victory Compiled by M.W. Knapp and E. McNeill* (Cincinnati: God's Bible School, 1902).

81 *Oregonian,* 1 May 1904, and *Telegram,* 7 November 1903. The following account of the sect's beliefs and practices is drawn mostly from press reports, emanating both from Oregon papers in 1903-1904 and from Seattle and Oregon papers in 1906, after Creffield had been killed in Seattle.

82 *Corvallis Times,* 18 November 1903.

83 *Telegram,* 6 November 1903.

84 Ibid., 7 November 1903.

85 *Corvallis Times,* 31 October 1903; *The Dalles Weekly Chronicle,* 4 November 1903; *Telegram,* 6 and 7 November 1903.

86 *Telegram,* 2 and 6 November 1903, 6 August 1904, and 12 May 1906; *Oregon Journal,* 8 May 1906. Indeed, Creffield's occupation is given as "Holy Roller" in the coroner's file on his death in 1906 and on his death certificate: See Medical Examiner Files, No. 551, KCA, and State of Washington Death Certificate, vol. 1906, No. 16307, WSA – PS.

87 See Robeck, "The Dog Days of Summer: 1906."

88 Brasher, *The Sanctified South,* 88.

89 *Telegram,* 6, 7, and 11 November 1903.

90 *Seattle Times,* 3 July 1906; *Corvallis Times,* 31 October 1903. See also *Telegram,* 7 November 1903: "At all times of the day and night . . . the air . . . is rent with groans, screams, wailings and shouts."

91 *PI,* 3 July 1906.

92 *Corvallis Times,* 23 December 1903; *Oregonian,* 1 May 1904.

93 *Telegram,* 7 November 1903, quoting Frank Hurt.

94 See the report of his trial testimony in *Oregonian,* 4 July 1906. For other accounts of the rolling see O.V. Hurt's trial testimony, *Seattle Times,* 3 July 1906; and *PI,* 3 July 1906.

95 *Seattle Times,* 7 May 1906.

96 See especially L. Taiz, "Applying the Devil's Work in a Holy Cause: Working-Class Popular Culture and the Salvation Army in the United States, 1879-1900," *Religion and American Culture* 7 (1997): 195-223.

97 A. Taves, *Fits, Trances and Visions: Experiencing Religion and Explaining Experience from Wesley to James* (Princeton, NJ: Princeton University Press, 1999), 3.

98 See here Frankiel's description of Bresee's teaching, that the coming of the Holy Ghost meant that a person "would not seem to be in his ordinary personality." Frankiel also quotes Bresee to similar effect: A holy person "is personally enlarged and strengthened . . . filled with and clothed upon with power so much greater than himself that he is comparatively lost sight of": *Holiness in California*, 113. Ann Taves has termed this a "dissociative state," one in which "something that is 'not me' can be present in place of or along side what I experience or believe to be 'me'": A. Taves, "Knowing Through the Body: Dissociative Religious Experience in African and British-American Methodist Traditions," *Journal of Religion* 73 (1993): 201-202.

99 For the links between holiness and Pentecostalism see especially Anderson, *Vision of the Disinherited*. Creffield himself referred to the need to "see people through on Pentecostal lines" in "He'll Not Compromise," but that was likely a general reference to it being on the day of the Pentecost that the Apostles received the Holy Spirit.

100 *Corvallis Times*, 31 October 1903.

101 *Telegram*, 7 November 1903.

102 *Seattle Times*, 3 July 1906.

103 *Oregonian*, 1 May 1904. See also Florence Seeley's statement that, "We received messages direct from [God] . . . Sometimes we would all receive them together": *Telegram*, 3 May 1904.

104 Berry's evidence before the September 1906 insanity commission, in *PI*, 13 September 1906.

105 *Corvallis Times*, 4 November 1903.

106 See James Berry's testimony before the 1906 insanity commission that Maud Hurt "had often been known to fast for three days at a time": *PI*, 13 September 1906. On fasting generally see also *Oregon Journal*, 8 May 1906.

107 *Telegram*, 5 August 1904.

108 Ibid., 7 November 1903.

109 *Seattle Times*, 15 May 1906.

110 *PI*, 6 July 1906, citing Louis Hartley's trial testimony, and Louis Hartley's Divorce Petition, Benton County Divorces, 1906, No. 4337, OSA.

111 *PI*, 3 July 1906; *Oregon Journal*, 3 July 1906; *Star*, 7 May 1906.

112 See *Telegram*, 5 August 1904. See also James Berry's trial testimony to the effect that he had stopped going to meetings in the spring of 1903 when Creffield ordered him to "sell all his personal belongings, including an automobile," and give the proceeds to the sect: *Seattle Times*, 7 July 1906.

113 See *Albany Herald*, 5 May 1904, and the discussion in Chapter 5.

114 *Telegram*, 4 August 1904.

115 Ibid., 7 November 1903.

116 S. Rushing, *The Magdalene Legacy: Exploring the Wounded Icon of Sexuality* (Westport, CT: Bergin and Garvey, 1994), 118. See also R.R. Ruether, *Women and Redemption: A Theological History* (Minneapolis: Fortress Press, 1998).

117 *Albany Herald*, 5 May 1904.

118 *Corvallis Times*, 6 July 1906, citing O.V. Hurt's evidence at George Mitchell's trial. For a similar account see *Seattle Times*, 3 July 1906. For other trial witnesses' testimonies about these "wrappers" see *PI*, 3 July 1906 and *Corvallis Times*, 10 July 1906.

119 Reynolds, "Corvallis in 1900," 51.

120 Dieter, *The Holiness Revival*, 214. See also Anderson, *Vision of the Disinherited*, 36,

discussing "prohibitions against eating meat, sweets, and 'medicinal foods,' against wearing neckties and other 'worldly ornamentations,' and against using hair curlers and cosmetics." See also Frankiel, *California's Spiritual Frontiers*, 104-106.

121 Melton, *Encyclopedia of American Religions*, ch. 7 ("Holiness Family"), 76.

122 *Oregonian*, 7 May 1904. For a complaint about Creffield "subsisting wholly on their [his adherents] labour," see *Corvallis Times*, 4 November 1903. See also for similar comments *Corvallis Times*, 7 May 1904; *Telegram*, 5 August 1904; and *Oregonian*, 1 May 1904.

123 See Frank Hurt's interview with a Portland *Evening Telegram* reporter in November 1903, in which he stressed that "we will ask the public for no contributions. I have been cutting wood this summer and have a little money put away": *Telegram*, 7 November 1903.

124 See ibid., 25 November 1903, and Berry's later trial testimony, reported in *Seattle Times*, 7 July 1906, and *PI*, 7 July 1906.

125 *The Dalles Weekly Chronicle*, 3 August 1904. In addition to the quotations, this paragraph is based on reports in *Corvallis Times*, 10 June and 7 November 1903, and *Corvallis Gazette*, 14 June 1904.

126 *Corvallis Times*, 4 November 1903, and Personal and Medical History, Sophia Hartley, OSH Records, vol. 4B, 277, OSA.

127 From his trial testimony, in *Seattle Times*, 7 July 1906.

128 Ibid., 1 June 1906.

129 *Telegram*, 17 March 1904.

130 Personal and Medical History, Sarah Hurt, OSH Records, vol. 4B, 287, OSA.

131 *Eugene Register*, 3 November 1903.

132 Melton, *Encyclopedia of American Religions*, ch. 7 ("Holiness Family"), 76.

133 Louis Hartley's Divorce Petition, Benton County Divorces, 1906, No. 4337, OSA. See also Hartley's later statement that his wife and daughter "observed all the rites of the Holy Rollers ... so that [he] ... had to cook his own meals, even after he came in from work": *PI*, 6 July 1906.

134 *Corvallis Times*, 4 November 1903.

135 See *Star*, 3 July 1906.

136 *Oregonian*, 13 September 1906.

137 *Oregon Journal*, 3 July 1906.

138 In addition to the groups in The Dalles and Salem, we have evidence of holiness activity in Portland, Woodburn, Baker City, and New Era in the 1902-1904 period: see *The Dalles Weekly Chronicle*, 25 June 1902; *Oregon Journal*, 9, 16, 23, and 30 January, and 13 February 1904; *Oregon Statesman*, 28 January 1904; *Oregonian*, 1 December 1903. One newspaper reported in late 1903 that there were "a few of them [holy rollers] all over the state," suggesting small, isolated groups scattered throughout the area: *The Dalles Weekly Chronicle*, 4 November 1903. There is evidence that the Pentecostal movement had a rather more substantial impact from mid-1906 onwards: see *Corvallis Gazette*, 19 October 1906 and 4, 8, 25, and 29 January, and 12 February 1907; *Oregonian*, 15 July 1906; *Herald*, 3 January 1907. The *Corvallis Times*, 24 July 1906, called the rise of Pentecostalism "a wave of Holy Rollerism."

139 For "occult influence" or similar comments see *Corvallis Times*, 6 August 1904, and *PI*, 8 May 1906. For the hypnotism theory see O.V. Hurt's statements, in *Oregonian*, 8 May 1906; others made the same claim in *Corvallis Times*, 3 and 21 September and

10 December 1904; *Eugene Register,* 3 November 1903; *Star,* 11 May 1906; *Telegram,* 7 November 1903 and 3, 4, and 6 August 1904; and *Oregonian,* 14 July 1906. The *Oregon Observer* of Grant's Pass, 24 September 1904, also accepted the hypnotism idea and ran a long editorial calling for regulation of the practice. For "mental telepathy" see *Oregon Journal,* 8 May 1906, stating that "during his schooling he made a particular study of mental telepathy and . . . became something of an expert in the science of thought transference." The *Oregonian* suggested in an editorial that Creffield was a master of "the well-known power of suggestion": *Oregonian,* 9 May 1906.

140 For references to the weak-mindedness of Creffield's followers see, *inter alia, Corvallis Times,* 4 November 1903 and 6 August 1904; *Eugene Register,* 3 November 1903; *Albany Herald,* 10 May 1906. *The Dalles Weekly Chronicle,* 11 May 1906, did not call his female followers weak-minded, but it did argue that women were particularly susceptible to religious extremism. For the association between religious enthusiasm and women's "weak-mindedness" see Taves, *Fits, Trances and Visions,* and for psychiatric opinion, discussed in more detail in Chapter 5, see L. Marks, "Hysterical Frenzies and Religious Legitimacy: Women, Sexuality, Madness, and Religion in North American and British Psychiatry, 1850-1890," unpublished paper, 1995. We thank Professor Marks for allowing us to read and cite this work.

141 *Corvallis Times,* 3 September 1904.

142 Quotations from *Seattle Times,* 1 July 1906; *Corvallis Times,* 21 September 1904; *Oregon Journal,* 8 May 1906. See also to similar effect Reynolds, "Corvallis in 1900," 50, and *Telegram,* 2 August 1904.

143 *Oregonian,* 8 May 1906, and *PI,* 3 July 1906. See also for his being intelligent and well educated, *Oregon Journal,* 8 May 1906.

144 *Corvallis Times,* 3 September 1904.

145 *Corvallis Gazette,* 11 July 1902. For revival meetings in the Corvallis area see *Corvallis Gazette,* 14 and 22 July 1903 and 28 April 1905, and, generally, H.M. Corning, ed., *Dictionary of Oregon History* (Portland: Binford and Mort, 1956), 41, and the sources cited therein. The *Corvallis Gazette* carried notices for the Catholic Church and eight Protestant denominations in this period, plus the Salvation Army. The Protestant churches were the Baptist Church, the First Spiritual Union of Corvallis, the Methodist Episcopal Church, the Episcopal Church, the Christian Church, the United Evangelical Church, the Presbyterian Church, and the Congregational Church. See *Corvallis Gazette,* passim. The history of many of these churches is traced in Phinney, *Historical Sketches,* 71-76.

146 *Corvallis Times,* 10 and 27 February, and 5 and 30 March, 1904.

147 The exception, of course, is the well-known Aurora Colony, a religious commune that operated in the Willamette Valley for nearly thirty years until its dissolution in 1881: see L.K. Jacobs et al., "The Stauffer-Will Farmstead: Historical Archeology of an Aurora Colony Farm," University of Oregon Anthropological papers, 1981, and E.E. Snyder, *Aurora, their Last Utopia: Oregon's Christian Commune, 1856-1883* (Portland: Binford and Mort, 1993). But Oregon saw nothing like the number of communal experiments that have marked the history of neighbouring Washington state: see C.P. LeWarne, *Utopias on Puget Sound, 1885-1915,* 2nd ed. (Seattle: University of Washington Press, 1995). There is no general history of religion in Oregon, although there are some good accounts of particular movements and churches: see especially E.S. Oliver, *Saints and Sinners: The Planting of New England Congregationalists in Portland, Oregon,*

1851-1876 (Portland: Hapi Press, 1987), and E.S. Oliver, ed., *Obed Dickinson's War Against Sin in Salem, 1853-1867* (Portland: Hapi Press, 1987). The lack of interest in the subject in itself suggests the relative unimportance of religion in the state's history.

148 The 1900 federal census showed just 29 percent of Oregonians having a denominational affiliation compared with a national average of 43 percent: G. Dodds, *Oregon: A Bicentennial History* (New York: Norton, 1977), 149. Indeed, an "indifference" to religion, notes Dodds, which was "planted in the first decades," continues to be a "distinguishing feature of the state's cultural life": ibid., 107.

149 *Corvallis Gazette*, 14 July 1903.

150 Ibid., 14 June 1904.

151 See generally S.H. Armitage, "Tied to Others' Lives: Women in Pacific Northwest History," in *Women in Pacific Northwest History: An Anthology*, ed. K.J. Blair, rev. 2nd ed. (Seattle: University of Washington Press, 2001), lamenting the lack of research.

152 R. Chused, "Late Nineteenth-Century Married Women's Property Law," *American Journal of Legal History* 29 (1985): 3-35; D. Peterson Del March, *What Trouble I Have Seen: A History of Violence Against Wives* (Cambridge: Harvard University Press, 1996).

153 Women's clubs were active in Washington and other parts of the Pacific Northwest and over time grew into "domestic feminist" organizations through which women engaged in civic activism. However, the only reference to them in Corvallis that we have found is to the Coffee Club, noted above in the section on Corvallis. The only work on the club movement in Oregon is a brief study of The Dalles in S. Haarsager, *Organized Womanhood: Cultural Politics in the Pacific Northwest* (Norman, OK: University of Oklahoma Press, 1997).

154 There is a large literature on women and religion in this period. What follows is based on L.D. Scanzoni and S. Setta, "Women in Evangelical, Holiness and Pentecostal Traditions," and M.T. Blauvelt, "Women and Revivalism," both in *Women and Religion in America*, ed. R.R. Ruether and R.S. Keller, 3 vols. (San Francisco: Harper and Row, 1981), vol. 1, 1-45 and 223-65; M.T. Blauvelt and R.S. Keller, "Women and Revivalism: The Puritan and Wesleyan Traditions," in ibid., vol. 2, 316-67; R.M. Griffith, "American Religious History and Women's History: Old Divides and Recent Developments," *Reviews in American History* 25 (1997): 220-26; C.A. Haynes, *Divine Destiny: Gender and Race in Nineteenth-Century Protestantism* (Jackson, MS: University Press of Mississippi, 1998); L. Marks, *Revivals and Roller Rinks: Religion, Leisure, and Identity in Nineteenth-Century Small Town Ontario* (Toronto: University of Toronto Press, 1996); M.J. Westerkamp, *Women and Religion in Early America, 1660-1850* (New York: Routledge, 1999); N.A. Hardesty, *Your Daughters Shall Prophesy: Revivalism and Feminism in the Age of Finney* (Brooklyn: Carlson Publishing, 1991); B.A. DeBerg, *Ungodly Women: Gender and the First Wave of American Fundamentalism* (Minneapolis: Fortress Press, 1990); B.L. Epstein, *The Politics of Domesticity: Women, Evangelicalism, and Temperance in Nineteenth-Century America* (Middletown, CT: Wesleyan University Press, 1981); L. Taiz, "Hallelujah Lasses in the Battle for Souls: Working and Middle-Class Women in the Salvation Army, 1872-1896," *Journal of Women's History* 9 (1997): 84-107; C. Smith-Rosenberg, "The Cross and the Pedestal: Women, Anti-Ritualism, and the Emergence of the American Bourgeoisie," in Smith-Rosenberg, *Disorderly Conduct: Visions of Gender in Victorian America* (New York: Oxford University Press, 1985); A. Douglas, *The Feminization of American Culture* (New York: Knopf, 1977).

155 See Marks, *Revivals and Roller Rinks.*
156 Haynes, *Divine Destiny,* 100.
157 Winston, *Red-Hot and Righteous,* 22; Blauvelt, "Women and Revivalism," 5. See also Haynes, *Divine Destiny,* 101, arguing that "while women may not have been given a legitimate public role in society, they could authoritatively devote themselves to revivals and other evangelical endeavors and thus gain a measure of public agency and power."
158 Rose to Florence Seeley, 19 June 1904, Case File 2397, BGAS Records.
159 For the social origins of American Salvation Army women in the period, and for the freedom membership bestowed, see Winston, *Red-Hot and Righteous,* 65-67. For similar arguments about that freedom see L. Marks, "The Knights of Labour and the Salvation Army: Religion and Working Class Culture in Ontario, 1882-1890," *Labour/Le Travail* 28 (1991): 113-14, and "The 'Hallelujah Lasses': Working-Class Women in the Salvation Army in English Canada, 1882-1892," in *Gender Conflicts: New Essays in Women's History,* ed. F. Iacovetta and M. Valverde (Toronto: University of Toronto Press, 1990), and Taiz, "Hallelujah Lasses."

CHAPTER 3: DRIVING OUT THE SECT

1 *Telegram,* 7 November 1903. For the group living at the Hurt house see also *Corvallis Times,* 31 October, 4 November, and 23 December 1903.
2 See Louis Hartley's Divorce Petition, Benton County Divorces, No. 4377, OSA.
3 *Telegram,* 2 November 1903.
4 *Corvallis Times,* 31 October 1903. The account that follows of the events of late October is drawn largely from this source, including the quotations unless otherwise stated, and from *Telegram,* 2 November 1903, and *Corvallis Times,* 4 November 1903. The resignation of O.V. Hurt was also reported in *Corvallis Gazette,* 30 October 1903, and *Oregon Statesman,* 31 October 1903.
5 *Corvallis Times,* 7 November 1903.
6 Savonarola ordered cosmetics, fine clothes, and items of adornment to be burned, as well as furniture and musical instruments: see R. Erlanger, *The Unarmed Prophet: Savonarola in Florence* (New York: McGraw-Hill, 1988), 172-75.
7 *Eugene Register,* 3 November 1903.
8 *Oregonian,* 1 May 1904.
9 Bryson, just twenty-seven in 1903, was a Corvallis native who had earned his law degree from Columbia Law School before returning home to practise in 1898: see C.W. Taylor, *Eminent Judges and Lawyers of the Northwest, 1843-1955* (Palo Alto, CA: privately printed, 1954), 89. He combined private practice with the deputy district attorney's job for Corvallis. Burnett was the nephew of Peter Burnett, the first governor of California. Born in California in 1861, he went to Oregon with his father in 1867, and to Corvallis in the 1880s. Variously a farmer, clerk, and businessman, he held several public offices, including that of Benton County sheriff from 1900 to 1907. See *Portrait and Biographical Record of the Willamette Valley, Oregon* (Chicago: Chapman Publishing, 1903), 976-77; File – Benton County Public Officials, BCHM.
10 *Corvallis Times,* 31 October 1903.
11 This account of the insanity hearing is drawn from *Corvallis Times,* 31 October and 4

and 7 November 1903, and 3 July 1906; *Telegram,* 2 November 1903; and *The Dalles Weekly Chronicle,* 4 November 1903. No official records have survived; indeed, given the absence of any reference to the hearing in the county court journal, it may be that a record was not kept when the subject was not found insane. Watters was a Kansas native brought to Oregon by his father in 1877. He worked as a journalist and a jeweller, and was best known in Corvallis for his real estate business in partnership with one Ambler. He served as Benton County recorder 1894-96 and 1898-1902. A Democrat, he had been elected county judge in 1902 for a four-year term: See *Portrait and Biographical Record of the Willamette Valley,* 1131-32; *Corvallis Times,* 17 August 1904; File – Benton County Public Officials, BCHM. The county court judge was a powerful man, for although the court dealt only with suits for less than $500 and various specialized jurisdictions like probate and estate administration, it doubled as the county's administrative agency, the judge sitting with two other county commissioners when it met in that capacity. For the court structure see *Bellinger and Cotton,* vol. 1, 422 et seq; the county court statute is at 430-36.

12 Pernot and Cathey were two of just five doctors whose services were advertised in the local press. The Pernot family had located in Corvallis in 1889, and both sons became prominent community members. Emile Pernot was professor of bacteriology at the Oregon Agricultural College, and Henry practised medicine in the town for thirty-four years. He was an 1882 graduate of the Cincinnati College of Medicine and Surgery. Cathey was the most eminent of the town's doctors, although also the most recent arrival among them. A Multnomah County native who had taught school while learning medicine from a practitioner in Albany, he had then practised medicine without any formal training in Woodburn in the days before certification was necessary. He then attended medical school at Willamette University, graduating in 1890. He later returned to the University as Professor of Physiology before moving to Corvallis in 1903 and building the largest surgical practice in the county. See *Portrait and Biographical Record of the Willamette Valley,* 1011-13 and 1258; O. Larsell, *The Doctor in Oregon: A Medical History* (Portland: Oregon Historical Society, 1947), 241; H.K. Hines, *An Illustrated History of the State of Oregon* (Chicago: Lewis Publishing, 1893), 319-20.

13 *The Dalles Weekly Chronicle,* 4 November 1903.

14 Louis Hartley's Divorce Petition, Benton County Divorces, No. 4337, OSA.

15 *Telegram,* 2 November 1903.

16 *Corvallis Times,* 4 November 1903. The rest of this paragraph, and the next, is from this source, unless otherwise stated. See also *Telegram,* 3, 5, and 7 November 1903, and *Oregonian,* 3 November 1903.

17 *Telegram,* 3 November 1903. See also *Corvallis Gazette,* 6 November 1903, reporting that there had been "threatened mobbing of these fanatics" in the air. See also *Albany Democrat,* 6 November 1903.

18 *Telegram,* 7 November 1903.

19 *Corvallis Times,* 4 November 1903. The rest of this paragraph, and the next, are from this source, unless otherwise stated. See also *Eugene Register,* 3 November 1903: "The community . . . was incensed at the men, and it was thought they had worked on the weak-minded."

20 *Corvallis Gazette,* 10 November 1903.

21 *Oregonian,* 3 November 1903.

22 *Telegram,* 7 November 1903.
23 Ibid., 5 January 1904.
24 *Corvallis Gazette,* 6 November 1903.
25 Ibid., 6 and 10 November 1903; *Corvallis Times,* 7 November 1903; *Telegram,* 5 November 1903.
26 *Corvallis Times,* 18 November 1903. See also *Oregon Statesman,* 20 November 1903, and *Telegram,* 6 and 7 November 1903.
27 *Telegram,* 6 November 1903.
28 *Corvallis Times,* 2 December 1903.
29 Ibid., 7 November 1903; *Telegram,* 7 November 1903.
30 *Telegram,* 7 November 1903.
31 The following account is drawn from ibid., 7 November 1903. The *Telegram* also interviewed Levins and O.V. Hurt, but most of its space was devoted to Frank.
32 Ibid., 11 November 1903. The rest of this paragraph is drawn from this source.
33 *Corvallis Times,* 18 November 1903. The rest of this paragraph is drawn from this source, unless otherwise stated. The interview was reproduced in its entirety in *Eugene Register,* 22 November 1903. A similar set of statements was given to a *Telegram* reporter a little later: *Telegram,* 24 November 1903.
34 For Frank Hurt's acknowledgment that "cats and dogs" had been destroyed see *Oregonian,* 1 May 1904. For O.V. Hurt's testimony at George Mitchell's trial see *PI,* 3 July 1906, and Chapter 9.
35 This account of Creffield's and Brooks' departures is from *Corvallis Gazette,* 24 November 1903; *Telegram,* 23, 24, and 25 November 1903; *Corvallis Times,* 18 and 25 November 1903; *Eugene Register,* 25 November 1903.
36 *Telegram,* 17 March 1904.
37 Ibid., 24 November 1903.
38 *Corvallis Times,* 25 November 1903; *Corvallis Gazette,* 24 November 1903. See also the approving editorial in *Telegram,* 24 November 1903.
39 Our knowledge of this incident is derived from Register Book, Girls C, Case 2251, and Case File 2251, BGAS Records, and from later trial testimony, especially that of Perry Mitchell, William Gardner, and Burgess Starr: see *Seattle Times,* 6 July 1906; *PI,* 4, 6, and 7 July 1906. See also *Telegram,* 1 June 1906; *Corvallis Times,* 22 May and 13 July 1906; *Corvallis Gazette,* 11 December 1903.
40 See Register Book, Girls C, Case 2251, BGAS Records. There are many reports from 1906 of his having lived in Portland for five or six years: see *Seattle Times,* 7 May and 28 June 1906; *Corvallis Times,* 10 July 1906. For his work see *Seattle Times,* 2 July 1906; *Corvallis Times,* 13 July 1906.
41 There is no substantial history of the Society, although a few details can be gleaned from P. Collmeyer, "From 'Operation Brown Baby' to 'Opportunity': The Placement of Children of Color at the Boys and Girls Aid Society of Oregon," *Child Welfare* 74 (1995): 242-63. The social reform efforts of the Portland middle classes, and the origins of the Society, are discussed briefly in Dodds, *Oregon,* 150; Gaston, *Portland,* vol. 1, 460-62; and E.K. McColl, *Merchants, Money and Power: The Portland Establishment, 1843-1913* (Portland: Georgian Press, 1988), 188-89 and 241-42. For the nationwide child-saving movement of the period see, *inter alia,* J.R. Sutton, "The Juvenile Court and Social Welfare: Dynamics of Progressive Reform," *Law and Society Review* 19 (1985): 197-245; A.M. Platt, *The Child Savers: The Invention of Delinquency,* 2nd ed.

(Chicago: University of Chicago Press, 1977); S.L. Schlossman, *Love and the American Delinquent: The Theory and Practice of "Progressive" Juvenile Justice, 1825-1920* (Chicago: University of Chicago Press, 1977); and the introduction to E.J. Clapp, *Mothers of All Children: Women Reformers and the Rise of Juvenile Courts in Progressive Era America* (University Park, PA: Pennsylvania State University Press, 1998). The work of the Society can be traced through these brief accounts and the numerous stories that appeared on it in Oregon newspapers; for examples see *Corvallis Times,* 24 September 1902; *Oregonian,* 12 December 1903, 20 and 21 May 1904; *Oregon Journal,* 22 January 1904; *The Dalles Weekly Chronicle,* 23 April 1902.

42 For state grants see the appropriations statute for 1905, in *Oregon Statutes,* 1905, 286-87, and Gaston, *Portland,* vol. 1, 460-62. Counties were required to pay for each child sent to the Society: see *Oregonian,* 11 May 1904.

43 A juvenile court system was established in 1905: see *Oregon Statutes,* 1905, c. 80, and Gaston, *Portland,* vol. 1, 471-73.

44 For this statute see *Bellinger and Cotton,* vol. 2, 1221-22.

45 For Gardner see variously *Seattle Times,* 6 and 8 July 1906; *PI,* 6 July 1906; Gaston, *Portland,* vol. 1, 460-62; Oregon Historical Society, Scrapbook SB 59, 166.

46 Register Book, Girls C, Case 2251, BGAS Records. See also Perry Mitchell's later statement that Esther "was taken to the Boys and Girls Home ... because her relatives feared that if she was not removed from the influence of her former associates she would have to be sent to the state asylum": *PI,* 13 September 1906. For suggestions of a court order see the reference to her having been "pronounced insane and sent to the Society for proper care" and being "committed" to the Society's care: *Oregonian,* 25 November 1903. See also to similar effect *Telegram,* 7 December 1903 and 1 June 1906. Many of the press reports about her refer to Esther or Annie Taylor, but the context makes it clear that it was Esther Mitchell being referred to: see *Gazette,* 11 December 1903, and 1 January 1904; *Eugene Register,* 9 December 1903; *Telegram,* 21 December 1903; *The Dalles Weekly Chronicle,* 28 November 1903; *Oregonian,* 25 November 1903; Anne was Esther's middle name, and she worked as a tailor, which likely accounts for the choice of alias.

47 We checked the Benton County Court Journals and Case Files, BCHM, and Multnomah County Court Journals and Multnomah County Insane Commitments, Multnomah County Court House, Portland. Although insanity hearings were within the jurisdiction of the county court (see the more detailed discussion in Chapter 5, and *Oregonian,* 30 June 1904), we also checked the records of the circuit court, to no avail.

48 Register Book, Girls C, Case 2251, BGAS Records, and *Telegram,* 1 June 1906. For other references to Esther Mitchell's "insanity" and "mental derangement" see *Corvallis Gazette,* 11 December 1903, and *Telegram,* 21 December 1903. The process for asylum commitments, and the concept of religious mania, are discussed in Chapter 5.

49 See *Oregonian,* 16 November 1903: "No boy or girl in distress is refused admission to the ... Home." See also the fact that of twenty-four girls placed in the home in 1903, only thirteen were put there by court order: Register Book, Girls C, BGAS Records. A typical example was Case 2245, "sent by her mother for discipline" on November 3, 1903, and "returned to her mother" on December 12 of the same year. For Gardner's preference see Gardner to O.V. Hurt, 8 June 1904, Letter Books, BGAS Records.

50 *Corvallis Times,* 6 January 1904.

51 See the discussion of this and other allegations of sexual relations in Chapter 4.

52 Quotations from *The Dalles Weekly Chronicle*, 28 November 1903; *Oregonian*, 13 September 1906; *Corvallis Times*, 10 July 1906; *Telegram*, 21 December 1903. For similar
reports of her behaviour see also *Corvallis Times*, 23 December 1903, and 9 January
1904; *Telegram*, 21 December 1903; *PI*, 13 September 1906.

53 For her release and the move to Illinois see also the statements of William Gardner
and the trial testimony of Gardner and Perry Mitchell: *Telegram*, 1 June 1906, and *PI*,
6 and 7 July 1906. See also *PI*, 23 June 1906; *Albany Herald*, 28 June 1906; *Corvallis
Times*, 10 July 1906.

54 In Newberg Mitchell tried his hand at many things – grain farming, well digging,
wood cutting, horticulture, even a little subscription bookselling – but without being
able to make much of a go of any of them: see *Newberg Graphic*, 11 January, 22 February, and 29 March, 12 September, 24 October, 28 November, and 5 December 1890;
20 February and 14 August 1891; 1 and 8 September, 13 October, 24 November, and 15
December 1893; 12 January and 15 February 1894; 19 July 1906. For the family being
"in poor circumstances" when they lived in Oregon see *Albany Herald*, 19 July 1906,
and for his being "a man of very small means" in Illinois see *Oregonian*, 29 June 1906.
For his remarriage see Pritchard, "The Genealogical Record of . . . Perley and Phebe
Mitchell."

55 For Charles' personality and religious beliefs see *Seattle Times*, 2 July 1906; *Corvallis
Gazette*, 20 July 1906; *Oregonian*, 18 July 1906. His son Perry called him "a religious
and political crank" with "a quick temper": *PI*, 13 September 1906.

56 *Corvallis Times*, 10 July 1906.

57 This paragraph is from ibid., 28 November and 16 December 1903; *Telegram*, 23
November 1903; *Eugene Register*, 11 December 1903; *Oregon Statesman*, 13 December
1903.

58 *Corvallis Gazette*, 11 December 1903. For other accounts of this incident see *Oregonian*, 6 July 1906; *Oregon Statesman*, 13 December 1903; *Telegram*, 7 and 21 December
1903; *Eugene Register*, 9 December 1903.

59 *PI*, 6 July 1906.

60 *Oregonian*, 4 July 1906, and *Star*, 3 July 1906.

61 This paragraph is based on reports in *Telegram*, 22 and 30 December 1903, and 12 May
1906; *Corvallis Gazette*, 22 December 1903, and 8 and 12 January and 3 May 1904; *Corvallis Times*, 23 December 1903, and 6 January 1904; *Albany Democrat*, 25 December
1903. The Linn County colony was roughly where the Harrison Street Bridge crosses
the Willamette: see D. Shaw, "When Creffield's Cult Went to Corvallis," *Oregonian*,
24 February 1980.

62 *Corvallis Gazette*, 22 December 1903.

63 Ibid., 1 January 1904. See also *Corvallis Times*, 9 January 1904, and *Albany Herald*, 30
December 1903. A little later the *Oregonian*, 7 January 1904, noted that "warnings
have repeatedly been given him that violent demonstration was sure to follow if he
persisted in his fanatic zeal and methods." It seems likely that pressure was put on Mrs
Beach to get rid of them as well, and one report states that she intended to: see
Telegram, 30 December 1903. But she did not, presumably because there was a valid
lease.

64 Gallagher, *Historic Context*, 127.

65 The following account of the actions on the night of January 4 is principally based on
Corvallis Gazette, 8 and 12 January 1904, and *Corvallis Times*, 6 January 1904. Detailed

accounts also appeared in *Oregonian,* 6 and 7 January 1904; *Albany Herald,* 7 January 1904; *Albany Democrat,* 8 January 1904; *Oregon Journal,* 5 and 6 January 1904; *Oregon Statesman,* 6 January 1904; *Telegram,* 5 January 1904. Quotations are from *Corvallis Gazette,* 8 January 1904, and *Corvallis Times,* 6 January 1904.

66 The contemporary reports in the *Corvallis Gazette* state both that only Creffield and Brooks were taken out, and that all four men were. The *Corvallis Times* reported only the first two as involved, as did the Portland newspapers, although the *Evening Telegram,* issue of 12 January 1904, carries a report that Campbell and Levins were taken along as well and made to witness what was done to Creffield and Brooks. The only detailed account of Levins and Campbell being disciplined comes from a much later source, which states that they were not ordered to strip but had a "gob of tar" put on their heads into which feathers were stuck and were then "let off": *Corvallis Times,* 10 July 1906.

67 *Corvallis Times,* 6 January 1904.

68 For the threatened November assault see *Telegram,* 25 November 1903. James Berry, Maud Hurt's one-time fiancé, and Clara King were married on January 4 in Corvallis: Benton County Marriage Records, vol. 7, 273, OSA.

69 *Corvallis Gazette,* 12 January 1904.

70 Ibid., 29 December 1903.

71 *Albany Democrat,* 25 December 1903.

72 *Corvallis Times,* 9 January 1904.

73 *Telegram,* 12 January 1904.

74 In addition to the sources already cited for this section see *Corvallis Times,* 9 and 13 January 1904; *Corvallis Gazette,* 8 and 19 January 1904; Linn County Marriage Records, Marriage Certificate, 5 January 1904, No. 203, OSA.

75 *Oregonian,* 6 January 1904, and *Corvallis Times,* 6 January 1904.

76 Two sources say that Creffield was disguised as a woman for fear of further reprisals: *Telegram,* 6 January 1904, and *Eugene Register,* 8 January 1904.

77 *Eugene Register,* 8 January 1904.

78 *Oregon Statesman,* 6 January 1904.

79 *Lebanon Express Advance,* 8 January 1904.

80 Hurt had a brief meeting with Maud after the newlyweds returned from Albany, meeting her in a Corvallis back street: *Eugene Register,* 8 January 1904. O.V. was said to be livid: *Corvallis Gazette,* 8 January 1904; see also *Telegram,* 5 January 1904. The *Albany Herald,* 7 January 1904, quotes him as saying that he knew nothing about it and did not consent, "but as both parties are of age I could not have stopped it." Others were also annoyed, and one man who had taken part in the tarring and feathering apparently said that had he known of the planned marriage the white caps "would have taken steps to render such a contract null and void": *Telegram,* 5 January 1904.

81 *Telegram,* 5 January 1904. This account is drawn from *Corvallis Times,* 9 January 1904 (quotations); *Corvallis Gazette,* 8 January 1904; and *Telegram,* 12 January 1904.

82 For use of the term "white caps" see especially *Corvallis Times,* 6 January 1904. There is no general history of white capping, although there are a number of local studies. We have found most useful B. Palmer, "Discordant Music: Charivaris and Whitecapping in British North America," *Labour/Le Travail* 3 (1978): 5-62. The phenomenon is also discussed briefly in R. Brown, "Historical Patterns of Violence in America," in *Violence in America: Historical and Comparative Perspectives,* ed. H.D. Graham and

T. Gurr (Beverley Hills: Sage, 1979). For case studies see E.W. Crozier, *The White-Caps: A History of the Organization in Sevier County* (Knoxville, TN: Bean, Warters and Gaut, 1899); H. Goss, *The California White-Cap Murders: An Episode in Vigilantism* (Santa Barbara, CA: privately printed, 1969); and M. Hartman and E. Ingenthron, *Bald Knobbers: Vigilantes on the Ozarks Frontier* (Gretna, LA: Pelican Publishing, 1988). For the history of informal violent sanctions in the United States such as tarring and feathering see, *inter alia*, Palmer, "Discordant Music," and P. Gilje, *Rioting in America* (Bloomington, IN: Indiana University Press, 1996).

83 There have been three distinct Klans. The first originated in the reconstruction period and employed violence or its threat against both radical Republicans and blacks. It largely died out in the late 1870s, but the Klan was reborn in Atlanta in 1915. See generally E.V. Toy, "Right-Wing Extremism from the Ku Klux Klan to the Order, 1915-1988," in *Violence in America*, vol. 2, *Protest, Rebellion, and Reform*, ed. H.D. Graham and T. Gurr (Newbury Park, CA: Sage, 1989).

84 For these regional differences see, *inter alia*, the use of white capping to drive out black share croppers and tenant farmers in the south: W.F. Holmes, "Whitecapping: Agrarian Violence in Mississippi, 1902-1906," *Journal of Southern History* 35 (1969): 165-85, and "Whitecapping in Georgia: Carroll and Houston Counties, 1893," *Georgia Historical Quarterly* 64 (1980): 388-404. "Whitecapping" is still an offence under the *Mississippi Code*, sec. 97-3-87, defined as threats to a person or property designed to intimidate that person "into an abandonment or change of home or employment." In some places white capping extended to actions against radical labour leaders and political dissidents, and elsewhere was employed to the opposite effect, against strikebreakers: see Palmer, "Discordant Music," 41, 43, 45, and 48-49. In some areas of the Southwest it was used by peasants with grievances over land: see, *inter alia*, R.W. Larson, "The White Caps of New Mexico: A Study of Ethnic Militancy in the South West," *Pacific Historical Review* 44 (1975): 171-85.

85 See also M. Matthews, *A Dictionary of Americanisms on Historical Principles* (Chicago: University of Chicago Press, 1951), 1865, which defines white caps as a "voluntary group formed ostensibly for punishing offenders not adequately dealt with by law." J.S. Farmer, *Americanisms – Old and New* (London: privately printed, 1889), cited in Palmer, "Discordant Music," 39, defines white capping as a "mysterious organization in Indiana, who take it upon themselves to administer justice to offenders independent of the law . . . They are particularly severe against wife beaters." As Palmer notes, to some extent white capping drew on the White Cross Movement, "a religious crusade of the 1880s raging against prostitution, drink, and lewdness." It also, of course, drew on the older folk tradition of the charivari: see "Discordant Music," 41 and 44.

86 Booth Tarkington, *The Gentleman from Indiana* (New York: Doubleday and McClure, 1900), 43.

87 *Oregonian,* 17 and 19 March 1904.

88 Palmer, "Discordant Music," 46-47.

89 It did not use the term white cap, but it did say that the tarring and feathering was done "in the style adopted years ago": *Albany Herald,* 7 January 1904.

90 Gordon, *The Great Arizona Orphan Abduction,* 261.

91 This was the Crook County Vigilance Committee, which operated in Princeville in the early to mid-1880s: see C. Elton, "Reign of the Vigilantes," *Frontier Times* 44 (1970): 34-35 and 48-50. R.M. Brown, *Strain of Violence: Historical Studies of American*

Violence and Vigilantism (New York: Oxford University Press, 1975), purports to list all such vigilante committees in the United States, and found none for Oregon.

92 These examples can be found in *Corvallis Times,* 16 December 1903; *The Dalles Weekly Chronicle,* 20 September 1902; *Corvallis Gazette,* 25 January 1907; E. McLagan, *A Peculiar Paradise: A History of Blacks in Oregon, 1788-1940* (Portland: Georgian Press, 1980), 135-37. There was also an attempted lynching in Baker City in 1903, a confession forcibly extracted from a man the community believed to be an arsonist in Lebanon, and other instances of the use of force, on one occasion deadly force, against blacks: see *Corvallis Times,* 7 March 1903; *Albany Democrat,* 25 December 1903; and McLagan, *A Peculiar Paradise,* 137-38. According to one person's recollections, the charivari, a similar folk practice to white capping, was still practised in Oregon in the early twentieth century: see L. Stone, *The Family, Sex and Marriage in England, 1500-1800* (New York: Harper and Row, 1977), 504.

93 For the Klu Klux Klan in Oregon see D.A. Horowitz, ed., *Inside the Klavern: The Secret History of a Ku Klux Klan of the 1920s* (Carbondale, IL: Southern Illinois University Press, 1999), and "Oregon's Ku Klux Klan in the 1920s," *Oregon Historical Quarterly* 90 (1989): 364-84; McLagan, *A Peculiar Paradise,* 138 et seq.

94 *Albany Herald,* 7 January 1904; *Corvallis Times,* 9 January 1904. For similar statements see also *Corvallis Gazette,* 8 and 12 January 1904; *Oregonian,* 6 January 1904; *Oregon Statesman,* 6 January 1904.

95 See *Corvallis Gazette,* 21 August 1903.

96 *Corvallis Times,* 9 January 1904.

97 *Corvallis Gazette,* 12 January 1904. See also a later editorial regretting state law's inability to deal with someone like Creffield: *Corvallis Gazette,* 22 March 1904.

98 See Gilje, *Rioting in America,* 77.

99 R.M. Brown, "The American Vigilante Tradition," in Graham and Gurr, eds., *Violence in America,* vol. 1, 141. See also Gordon, *Arizona Orphan Abduction,* 258, noting that the "imperative of justice" was often thought to override the law. C. Waldrep, "Word and Deed: The Language of Lynching, 1820-1953," in *Lethal Imagination: Violence and Brutality in American History,* ed. M. Bellesiles (New York: New York University Press, 1999), 230-32, also has a useful summary of justifications for vigilantism. C.G. Fritz locates this argument in ideas of popular sovereignty in "Popular Sovereignty, Vigilantism, and the Constitutional Right of Revolution," *Pacific Historical Review* 66 (1994): 39-66. For specific examples see, *inter alia,* R. McGrath, *Gunfighters, Highwaymen, and Vigilantes: Violence on the Frontier* (Berkeley: University of California Press, 1984), 100-101, quoting an 1864 source to the effect that the community had a right to "assert the right of self-preservation and the supremacy of natural law." See also an 1867 vigilante group statement that "the right of the people to take care of themselves, if the law does not, is an indisputable right," cited in Brown, "The American Vigilante Tradition," 142.

100 Gordon, *Great Arizona Orphan Abduction,* 257.

101 *Corvallis Times,* 6 January 1904; *Albany Herald,* 7 January 1904.

102 *Corvallis Times,* 6 January 1904.

103 For a review of the class background of rural lynch mobs, for example, see R. Slotkin, "Apotheosis of the Lynching: The Political Uses of Symbolic Violence," *Western Legal History* 6 (1993): 1-15.

104 *Albany Herald,* 7 January 1904.

105 *Corvallis Gazette*, 8 January 1904.

106 See, *inter alia*, Waldrep, "Words and Deeds," 231-32, for a discussion of the frequent references to regularity and good order.

107 For these arguments see *The Dalles Weekly Chronicle*, 9 January 1904; *Salem Journal* and *Lebanon Criterion*, January 1904 (both cited in *Corvallis Gazette*, 19 January 1904); and *Albany Democrat*, 8 January 1904. Approval of the tarring and feathering can be found in *Telegram*, 12 January 1904; *Albany Herald*, 7 January 1904; *Oregon Statesman*, 9 January 1904.

108 This paragraph is drawn largely from *Corvallis Gazette*, 8 and 12 January 1904, and *Corvallis Times*, 9 January 1904.

109 *Corvallis Times*, 29 July 1903; see also the issue of 25 July 1903.

110 The *Corvallis Gazette*'s willingness to go this far was confirmed a little later when it was reported that Creffield was hiding near Lebanon, Oregon; it proclaimed: "Johnny get your gun!": *Corvallis Gazette*, 26 January 1904.

111 *Corvallis Times*, 23 March 1904; *Corvallis Gazette*, 3 and 10 May 1904; *Albany Herald*, 5 May 1904. By June 1904 Wesley Seeley was likely living with his older married sister in British Columbia, although we do not know when he left: see Gardner to Mrs J.A. Wilson, 21 June 1904, Letter Books, and Rose to Florence Seeley, 19 June 1904, Case File 2397, BGAS Records.

112 *Corvallis Times*, 7 May 1904; *Albany Herald*, 5 May 1904.

113 *Oregonian*, 6 January 1904.

114 Reports of their camp and their movements in January 1904 appear in various newspapers. This account is based on *Corvallis Times*, 16 and 20 January, and 3 February 1904; *Corvallis Gazette*, 26 January and 2 February 1904; *Oregonian*, 1 February 1904; *Oregon Journal*, 1 February 1904; *Albany Democrat*, 15 and 22 January 1904; *Oregon Statesman*, 28 January 1904; *Lebanon Advance*, 2 February 1904.

115 *Oregon Journal*, 1 February 1904.

116 *Corvallis Times*, 3 February 1904.

117 *Oregon Journal*, 1 February 1904. See also *Corvallis Gazette*, 2 February 1904.

118 See Chapter 11.

119 See Chapter 10. One remarkable story is that Louis Hartley may have pursued and killed one or more of the men. In March 1904 it was reported that a man, unnamed but whose description makes it Hartley, had followed the men and found them near Rainier. They "were made to line up at the muzzle of a revolver and marched seven miles and then—." Showing his revolver, the man then apparently assured the reporter that "the Holy Rollers will not trouble any one any more." All this is from *Albany Democrat*, 25 March 1904, but there is no further evidence for it. Hartley, as we shall see, was prepared to shoot Creffield in 1906.

CHAPTER 4: "SENSUALIST PRACTICES PRESCRIBED AND ORDAINED AS COMING FROM HEAVEN"

1 Suggested in *Oregon Journal*, 9 January 1904.

2 For Maud's return to Corvallis see *Corvallis Times*, 3 February 1904; *Corvallis Gazette*, 22 March 1904. The following account of Creffield's time in Portland is based on

Oregonian, 17 and 20 March 1904, and 8 May 1906; *Telegram,* 16 and 17 March 1904; *Corvallis Gazette,* 22 and 25 March 1904; *Corvallis Times,* 19 and 23 March, 27 April, and 21 September 1904; *Oregon Journal,* 16 and 17 March 1904; Benton County Divorces, File 4334, 1905, OSA; Arrest Warrant, Case File A8559, Circuit Court Records, Multnomah County Courthouse.

3 *Telegram,* 17 March 1904.

4 For the statute law see *Bellinger and Cotton,* vol. 1, 679-80, and *Oregon Laws, Showing All the Laws of a General Nature in Force in the State of Oregon, Compiled and Annotated by Charles P. Olson,* 2 vols. (San Francisco: Bancroft-Whitney, 1920), vol. 1, 1229-30. A 1917 amendment also made it possible for a parent to be the complainant in a case where a married man had sex with an unmarried female under the age of twenty: *Olson's Oregon Laws,* vol. 1, 1230.

5 For a prosecution of both parties for adultery see *Corvallis Gazette,* 17 February 1903.

6 Ibid., 22 and 25 March 1904.

7 He was reported to have walked to Corvallis from Albany on the evening of Thursday, March 17, in the company of a man named Breon, although Breon could not positively identify him. There was also a rumour in Corvallis that a sect member had admitted seeing Creffield at this time: see *Corvallis Gazette,* 22 March 1904; *Corvallis Times,* 23 March 1904; *Oregon Journal,* 18 and 22 March 1904.

8 This paragraph and the next are based on *Telegram,* 21, 24, and 31 March 1904; *Corvallis Gazette,* 22, 25, and 29 March, and 14 June 1904; *Corvallis Times,* 23 March, 13 April, 11 and 22 June, and 30 July 1904; *Oregonian,* 22 March, 24 April, 1 May, and 11 June 1904; *Albany Herald,* 21 April 1904.

9 *Telegram,* 21 March 1904. Also questioned was Florence Seeley, by then in the BGAS Home in Portland (see Chapter 5), but she refused to help if she did know where Creffield was: see Sheriff M.P. Burnett to Gardner, 14 June 1904, Case File 2397, BGAS Records.

10 *Oregonian,* 17 May 1906. This was a little after Attie Bray had been sent to the asylum, an event discussed in Chapter 5.

11 See the *Corvallis Gazette's* lament that his followers were "completely secretive" about his whereabouts: *Corvallis Gazette,* 14 June 1904.

12 Gardner to M.P. Burnett, June 1904, Letter Books, BGAS Records.

13 *Corvallis Times,* 30 March 1904.

14 Ibid., 22 June 1904.

15 This account of Creffield's apprehension is from *Corvallis Gazette,* 2 August 1904; *Corvallis Times,* 30 July 1904; *Albany Herald,* 4 August 1904; *Oregonian,* 30 and 31 July 1904; *Telegram,* 29 July 1904.

16 The claim was made by O.V. Hurt: see *Oregonian,* 4 July 1906.

17 *Corvallis Times,* 30 July 1904.

18 *Telegram,* 17 March 1904.

19 For accounts of what happened on the night of July 29 see *Corvallis Times,* 3 August 1904; *Albany Herald,* 4 August 1904; *Telegram,* 30 July and 3 August 1904; *Oregonian,* 30 and 31 July, and 2 August 1904. O.V. Hurt later said that he had worried about mob violence when Creffield was first captured and had taken him to jail as quietly as possible as a result: *Oregonian,* 4 July 1906. The suggestion that Hartley's presence

might have made a difference was made, albeit implicitly, at the time: see *Oregonian*, 31 July 1904.

20 For the again inconsistent accounts see *Albany Herald*, 4 August 1904; *Oregonian*, 31 July and 2 August 1904; *Corvallis Times*, 3 August 1904.

21 *Corvallis Times*, 3 August 1904.

22 Ibid., 3 and 20 August 1904.

23 *Corvallis Gazette*, 2 August 1904.

24 See principally *Corvallis Times*, 3 August 1904.

25 This section on Creffield in the jail is from *Oregonian*, 31 July, and 1 and 3 August 1904; *Corvallis Times*, 3 August 1904; *Telegram*, 1 and 2 August 1904; Portland Police Arrest Book, City of Portland Archives, 1904, 240-41.

26 *Oregonian*, 31 July 1904.

27 *Telegram*, 1 August 1904.

28 For Elijah see especially D.N. Freedman, ed., *Eerdman's Dictionary of the Bible* (Grand Rapids, MI: W.B. Eerdmans, 2000), 325-27. See also Achtemeier, ed., *Harper's Dictionary*, 256-58.

29 *Telegram*, 13 August 1904.

30 *Oregonian*, 3 August 1904.

31 *Telegram*, 11 August 1904.

32 He appeared before Judge Hogue in municipal court for this, although the trial would be in the superior criminal court, the circuit court. For the arraignment and other pre-trial proceedings see *Telegram*, 1 and 4 August 1904; *Oregonian*, 2 and 6 August 1904; *Corvallis Times*, 6 and 7 August 1904; *Corvallis Gazette*, 9 and 26 August 1904.

33 *Telegram*, 4 August 1904.

34 There is a copy of the information in Benton County Divorces, Franz and Maud Creffield, File 4334, OSA. Manning was a Wisconsin native who practised law in Nebraska before moving to Oregon in 1893. In 1900 he was appointed chief deputy district attorney under George Chamberlain, and in 1902 became district attorney when the latter won the governorship. He was re-elected in 1904 with a large majority, and served until 1907. See especially Gaston, *Portland*, vol. 3, 476-77, and M. Colmer, comp., *History of the Bench and Bar of Oregon* (Portland: Historical Publishing Company, 1910), 183. See also *Times*, 4 July 1906; *Oregonian*, 2 and 3 December 1903; McColl, *Merchants, Money and Power*, 244; F. Leeson, *Rose City Justice: A Legal History of Portland, Oregon* (Portland: Oregon Historical Society, 1998), 243.

35 For the trial see *Telegram*, 16 September 1904; *Corvallis Gazette*, 20 September 1904; *Corvallis Times*, 17 and 21 September 1904; *Oregonian*, 17 September 1904; *The Dalles Weekly Chronicle*, 21 September 1904; *Oregon Observer*, 21 September 1904; *Oregon Journal*, 16 September 1904; Case File A8559, Circuit Court Records, Multnomah County Courthouse. A former assistant district attorney, Sears was one of four judges of the circuit court for Multnomah County, serving from 1896 to 1907: see Leeson, *Rose City Justice*, 244.

36 *Oregonian*, 17 September 1904.

37 This is our best interpretation of the reports. The *Telegram*, 16 September 1904, says that Judge Sears "ordered the doors of the courtroom closed" because some of the testimony was "indecent," and the *Oregon Journal*, 16 September 1904, also states that the trial "was behind closed doors." These statements suggest that the public were excluded, in whole or in part. But it is unlikely that a criminal trial would have been

held in camera, even in part, and perhaps Sears satisfied the requirement of a public trial by letting the press stay – we know reporters were there.

38 *Corvallis Times,* 21 September 1904.

39 *Corvallis Gazette,* 20 September 1904.

40 Quotations in this paragraph are from *Oregon Journal,* 16 September 1904.

41 *Telegram,* 16 September 1904.

42 *Corvallis Gazette,* 20 September 1904.

43 *Corvallis Times,* 21 September 1904.

44 *Seattle Times,* 15 May 1906. For similar references, among many, see *Seattle Times,* 27 June and 1 July 1906.

45 See again, for example, the letter from "An Oregon Girl," which the *Times* apparently censored, inserting in parentheses: "Here are related some of Creffield's practices which cannot be printed": *Seattle Times,* 15 May 1906. See also the report of the trial testimony of Louis Sandell, brother of Molly Hurt (Sandell) and Olive Sandell, which stated that he "told unprintable things of what he had learned concerning Creffield's holy roller orgies": *Corvallis Times,* 10 July 1906. And see also the report of Burgess Starr's trial testimony about Donna in Corvallis in 1903, which included "details of her practices that would not bear mention": *Oregonian,* 4 July 1906.

46 *PI,* 9 May 1906.

47 *Corvallis Times,* 4 November 1903.

48 *Corvallis Gazette,* 12 January 1904.

49 *Corvallis Times,* 13 July 1906.

50 *Telegram,* 21 March 1904.

51 *Albany Herald,* 5 May 1904; *Corvallis Gazette,* 3 May 1904.

52 *Corvallis Gazette,* 3 May 1904.

53 *Corvallis Times,* 6 August 1904.

54 Ibid., 4 November 1903; *Albany Herald,* 5 May 1904; *Oregonian,* 20 March 1904.

55 *Telegram,* 13 August 1904; *Oregonian,* 31 July 1904; *Corvallis Times,* 21 September 1904.

56 *Telegram,* 9 May 1906.

57 Ibid., 17 September 1904.

58 *Corvallis Gazette,* 27 April 1906; *Oregonian,* 3 May 1906.

59 *Seattle Times,* 5 July 1906.

60 See, for example, *Oregon Journal,* 8 May 1906, and *Telegram,* 4 July 1906.

61 See Louis Hartley's Divorce Petition, Benton County Divorces, 1906, No. 4337, OSA: the "sensualist practices" were "prescribed and ordained as coming from Heaven by and through the mediation of the aforesaid Joshua." On "justifications" there is also a reference to the fact that Creffield preached about the story of David and Bathsheba: see the letter from "An Oregon Girl" in *Seattle Times,* 15 May 1906. Bathsheba was the wife of Uriah the Hittite. King David impregnated her and then got rid of Uriah by sending him into battle with instructions to the general to set Uriah "in the forefront of the hardest fighting, and then draw back from him, that he may be struck down and die." For the story see the Second Book of Samuel, ch. 11. It is difficult, however, to see how this could function as some kind of rationale or justification for sex.

62 *Oregonian,* 17 September 1904. See also *Corvallis Times,* 21 September 1904.

63 For the Salvation Army see Marks, *Revivals and Roller Rinks,* 174-76; for a Texas example of a group with sex as part of its regular practices see Dieter, *Holiness Revival,* 215.

64 See, *inter alia,* L. Foster, *Religion and Sexuality: Three American Communal Experiments*

of the Nineteenth Century (New York: Oxford University Press, 1981); R.L. Muncy, *Sex and Marriage in Utopian Communities: Nineteenth Century America* (Bloomington, IN: Indiana University Press, 1973); L. Foster, ed., *Free Love in Utopia: John Humphrey Noyes and the Origin of the Oneida Community* (Urbana, IL: University of Illinois Press, 2001); R. Strachey, ed., *Religious Fanaticism: Extracts from the Papers of Hannah Whitall Smith* (London: Faber and Gwyer, 1928); L. Bromfield, ed., *The Strange Case of Miss Anne Spragg* (New York: Stokes, 1920); Queen et al., *Encyclopedia of American Religious History*, 613-14.

65 For a rare Oregon example of such radicalism see the account of a late nineteenth-century anarchist newspaper in Portland, which also advocated the abandonment of marriage laws, in C. Schwantes, "Free Love and Free Speech on the Pacific Northwest Frontier," *Oregon Historical Quarterly* 82 (1981): 271-93.

66 *Telegram*, 15 May 1906, and *Seattle Times*, 6 July 1906; see also to the same effect *Seattle Times*, 12 May 1906; *Star*, 12 May 1906; *PI*, 13 May 1906.

67 See Register Books, Girls C, Cases 2251, 2397, and 2430, and Letter Books, and Case Files 2251, 2397, and 2430, BGAS Records.

68 Statutory rape was defined as carnal knowledge of any female under the age of sixteen and carried a minimum sentence of three years and a maximum of twenty: *Bellinger and Cotton*, vol. 1, 635. Florence Seeley turned sixteen on August 19, 1903, and thus might just have been of age when Creffield had sex with her, if he did. Esther Mitchell was definitely under age; she did not turn sixteen until January 1904. Mae Hurt was sixteen and seventeen in 1903, her birthday being on August 23. Just after our period, in 1905, the offence of fornication was introduced in Oregon, making it a crime to have sex with a female under eighteen if other than a wife: see *Olson's Oregon Laws*, vol. 1, 1231-32.

69 *PI*, 10 May 1906; *Seattle Times*, 4 July 1906.

70 *PI*, 13 May 1906.

71 *Albany Herald*, 4 August 1904.

72 *Telegram*, 15 May 1906.

73 For an extended discussion of the defence of Mitchell see below, esp. Chapters 8 and 10.

74 *Corvallis Times*, 6 July 1906.

75 Louis Hartley's Divorce Petition, Benton County Divorces, No. 4377, OSA.

76 See her statements following the death of Creffield, Chapter 8.

77 *Albany Democrat*, 6 May 1904.

78 *Telegram*, 11 July 1906.

79 See *PI*, 15 September 1906. Miller is discussed extensively in Chapter 7.

80 *Telegram*, 19 July 1906; *PI*, 19 July 1906.

81 *PI*, 13 September 1906.

82 See Ruether, *Women and Redemption*, 140-41, and D. Soden, *The Reverend Mark Matthews: An Activist in the Progressive Era* (Seattle: University of Washington Press, 2001), 48.

83 *Telegram*, 4 July 1906.

84 Compare, for example, Crew's version of the sex, which suggests private liaisons between Creffield and others in his tent on Smith Island, with that of McCracken and Blodgett's, which has both individual couplings and mass orgies with all the men

involved. The point is that none of the authors knows what, if anything, happened, because the evidence is not sufficient to tell us. See Crew, *Brides of Eden*, 55-57, and McCracken and Blodgett, *Holy Rollers*, 28-29 and 101-102. The earliest writer on Creffield, Stewart Holbrook, perhaps responded to the problem of uncertain sources by claiming that sometime in the fall of 1903 a photograph was circulated in Corvallis showing a naked Creffield surrounded by naked women and girls on Smith Island, some of them standing, some rolling in the lush, wild grass. He professed to have been told of this photograph in an interview, but there is no hint of it in any of the sources, and it is impossible to believe that not one of the voluminous newspaper reports in the Seattle and Oregon press would have picked it up. It also seems inconceivable that had such a photograph been circulated the community would have waited weeks before taking the action against Creffield that occurred in early January. For the supposed photograph see Holbrook, *Murder Out Yonder*, 7.

85 *Corvallis Times,* 4 November 1903. See also the comment by a Linn County newspaper early in 1904 that the sect members "are accused of nothing worse than praying long and loud": *Lebanon Criterion,* January 1904, cited in *Corvallis Gazette,* 19 January 1904. And see the *Corvallis Gazette*'s comment the same month that the sect was a "nuisance": issue of 8 January 1904. Note also that in February 1904, in a story about a holiness revival among the Quinault Indians reproduced in the *Corvallis Gazette,* the *Oregonian* noted that "there is no record ... that they [the Quinaults] have broken up their furniture, roasted dogs and cats alive, or performed other sacrificial rites which lately made the Corvallis contingent conspicuous": *Corvallis Gazette,* 19 February 1904. Again, there is no hint here of sex.

86 *Telegram,* 7 November 1903.

87 *Corvallis Times,* 6 July 1906, citing O.V. Hurt's trial evidence. See also the version of his testimony reported in the *Seattle Times*: "his own women folk and Esther Mitchell ... would spend hours tumbling about the floor ... almost nude because of having burned all their clothing, with the exception of light wrappers": *Seattle Times,* 3 July 1906.

88 Interestingly, the *Seattle Times,* which printed many of the sex allegations, later defined the "free love" issue in exactly the way we have. The sect, it said, believed in "free love," and this meant "men, women, and children lived in camps ... and all slept in the same room, without beds or cots": *Seattle Times,* 7 May 1906.

89 Louis Hartley's Divorce Petition, Benton County Divorces, 1906, No. 4337, OSA.

90 *Albany Herald,* 5 May 1904.

91 This was one of five grounds for divorce, the others being impotency at the time of the marriage, adultery, conviction for felony, and habitual gross drunkenness: see *Bellinger and Cotton,* vol. 1, 275.

92 Marks, "Hysterical Frenzies and Religious Legitimacy," 18. This brief summary is taken from, in addition to Marks, E. Showalter, *The Female Malady: Women, Madness, and English Culture, 1830-1980* (New York: Pantheon Books, 1985); B. Welter, "Female Complaints: Medical Views of American Women," in *Dimity Convictions: The American Woman in the Nineteenth Century,* ed. B. Welter (Athens, OH: Ohio University Press, 1976); S.E.D. Shortt, *Victorian Lunacy: Richard M. Bucke and the Practice of Late Nineteenth-Century Psychiatry* (Cambridge: Cambridge University Press, 1986), 142-43; and W. Mitchinson, *The Nature of Their Bodies: Women and Their Doctors in Victorian Canada* (Toronto: University of Toronto Press, 1991).

CHAPTER 5: DISCIPLINING THE SECT

1 Parts of this chapter have been previously published in J. Phillips, K. De Luca, and R. Gartner, "Incarcerating Holiness: Religious Enthusiasm and the Law in Oregon, 1904," in *People and Place: Historical Influences on Legal Culture,* ed. C. Backhouse and J. Swainger (Vancouver: UBC Press, 2003).

2 Quotations from *Corvallis Gazette,* 3 May 1904, and *Albany Herald,* 30 June 1904. See also for similar descriptions *Oregonian,* 1 May and 30 July 1904, and *Albany Herald,* 5 May 1904.

3 Quotations from *Albany Herald,* 5 May 1904. The following account of Florence Seeley's commitment is from this source and *Telegram,* 3 May 1904; *Corvallis Gazette,* 3 May 1904; *Oregonian,* 29 April 1904; *Albany Democrat,* 6 May 1904; Linn County Court Journal, vol. 2, 1904, 574-75, OSA; Case File 2397, BGAS Records.

4 Quoted in *Albany Herald,* 5 May 1904.

5 Linn County Court Journal, vol. 2, 1904, 575, OSA.

6 *Albany Herald,* 5 May 1904.

7 Ibid., 5 May 1904. See also to similar effect *Corvallis Gazette,* 3 May 1904.

8 For commitment procedures in late nineteenth-century America see G.N. Grob, *Mental Illness and American Society, 1875-1940* (Princeton, NJ: Princeton University Press, 1983), and R.D. Miller, *Involuntary Civil Commitment of the Mentally Ill in the Post-Reform Era* (Springfield, IL: Thomas, 1987).

9 For the statutory scheme for insanity see *Bellinger and Cotton,* vol. 2, 1223-28. With one or two minor exceptions that do not concern us, the scheme laid out in this 1902 code was still in force in 1904: see *Lord's Oregon Laws, Showing All the Laws of a General Nature in Force in the State of Oregon,* 2 vols. (Salem: State Printer, 1910), vol. 2, 1705-1706. The essence of this statutory scheme was established in 1862 (*Oregon Statutes,* 1862, 54), although there had been some changes in detail between then and 1904.

10 Insanity Records, Linn County, Case 1036 (Mollie Hurt) and 1067 (Frank Hurt), OSA. The following account of the Hurts' commitment is from this source, which includes the official complaints, the certificates of the examining physicians, and the commitment orders, and from *Albany Herald,* 5 May 1904; *Corvallis Gazette,* 3 May 1904; *Oregonian,* 1 May 1904; *Lebanon Advance,* 3 May 1904; *Albany Democrat,* 6 May 1904. The hearing was held in Albany because the arrest warrant had been obtained from the Linn County district attorney. It would not have been returnable in a Benton County court.

11 They were J.P. Wallace and W.A. Trimble. We know nothing more about them than what is stated in their certificates of insanity, which is that Wallace had practised for twenty-four years and Trimble for nine: Physicians' Certificates, Insanity Records, Linn County, Cases 1036 and 1067, OSA.

12 *Oregonian,* 1 May 1904.

13 Quotations from *Corvallis Gazette,* 3 May 1904, and *Oregonian,* 1 May 1904.

14 *Albany Herald,* 5 May 1904.

15 *Oregonian,* 1 May 1904.

16 Physicians Certificates, Insanity Records, Linn County, Case 1036 (Mollie Hurt) and 1067 (Frank Hurt), OSA.

17 OSH Records, Personal and Medical Histories, vol. 4B, 276, and vol. 6A, 445, OSH Records, OSA.

18 For the proceedings against the first two see *Corvallis Gazette,* 6 May 1904; *Albany Herald,* 5 May 1904; *Corvallis Times,* 4 May 1904; *Oregonian,* 4 May 1904; Extract from Insane Record, Creffield File, BCHM; OSH Records, Admissions Register – Female, vol. E, 83, OSA. For the proceedings against Bray and Seeley see the OSH Records already cited; Benton County Insane Record, vol. 2, 1-4, BCHM; *Corvallis Times,* 7 and 10 May 1904; *Corvallis Gazette,* 10 May 1904; *Albany Herald,* 12 May 1904; *Albany Democrat,* 13 May 1904.

19 For Mae Hurt see *Corvallis Gazette,* 14 June 1904; *Corvallis Times,* 11 June 1904; Benton County Court Journals, vol. 2, 636, and Case File No. 778, Benton County Courthouse; Gardner to O.V. Hurt, 8 June 1904, Letter Books, and Case File 2430, BGAS Records. For Sarah Hurt see Benton County Insane Record, vol. 2, 8-9, BCHM; *Corvallis Gazette,* 28 June 1904; *Corvallis Times,* 29 June 1904.

20 *Star,* 3 July 1906.

21 Physicians' Certificate, Insanity Records, Linn County, Case 1067, OSA.

22 See the reference above to Frank and Mollie Hurt. For more on the fact that Sophia Hartley and Maud Creffield "conversed quietly and rationally" at the train station when being taken to Salem, that they uttered "not a murmur" of complaint, see *Albany Herald,* 5 May 1904. Sophia Hartley was also said to be "deluded on religious subjects but entirely intelligent and amiable otherwise": *Oregonian,* 4 May 1904. Attie Bray and Rose Seeley were "perfectly rational on all ordinary subjects": *Corvallis Times,* 7 May 1904. See also, re Sarah Hurt, *Albany Herald,* 30 June 1904.

23 See Benton County Court Journals, vol. 2, 636, and Case File No. 778, Benton County Courthouse.

24 *Corvallis Times,* 11 June 1904.

25 *Albany Herald,* 30 June 1904.

26 Personal and Medical Histories, Frank Hurt and Mollie Hurt, OSH Records, OSA. Sophia Hartley's asylum record states that she was a "religious fanatic" who "does not believe there is a Christian in any of the other churches." That for Rose Seeley talks of her belief that "her church is the only church": Sarah Hurt's record said that she "claims husband is not related to her and that Christ is her husband": OSH Records, Personal and Medical Histories, vol. 4B, 277, 278, and 287, OSA.

27 Register Book, Girls C, Case 2430 (Mae Hurt), BGAS Records.

28 See on this point Marks, "Hysterical Frenzies and Religious Legitimacy"; G. Grob, *The Mad Among Us: A History of the Care of America's Mentally Ill* (Toronto: Maxwell Macmillan, 1994), 60 et seq; D.J. Rothman, *The Discovery of the Asylum: Social Order and Disorder in the New Republic,* rev. ed. (Toronto: University of Toronto Press, 1990), 111 et seq; J. Melling and B. Forsythe, eds., *Insanity, Institutions and Society, 1800-1914: A Social History of Madness in Comparative Perspective* (London: Routledge, 1999), passim; F. Wharton and M. Stille, *Wharton and Stille's Medical Jurisprudence,* 5th ed., 3 vols. (Rochester, NY: Lawyers' Cooperative Publishing, 1905), vol. 1, 591-93. In 1860 some 8 percent of asylum incarcerations in the United States were attributed to "religious excitement" or the like: see W.S. Bainbridge, "Religious Insanity in America: The Official Nineteenth Century Theory," *Sociological Analysis* 45 (1984): 226. See also Rothman's suggestion that popular religious movements which produced "excitement in the community" were in an earlier period seen as contributing to higher rates of insanity: Rothman, *Discovery of the Asylum,* 119. Some modern commentators continue to identify a link between religion and insanity: see Bainbridge,

"Religious Insanity in America," 224. For an argument that by 1900 religion was no longer seen as a cause of insanity, but had been "relegated to the status of a delusion associated with an underlying mental disease," see J.H. Rubin, *Religious Melancholy and Protestant Experience in America* (New York: Oxford University Press, 1994), vii, and 197 et seq. While contemporary psychiatric literature may give that impression, the evidence presented here shows that this was not true "on the ground" in Oregon.

29 Wharton and Stille, *Wharton and Stille's Medical Jurisprudence,* vol. 1, 591. On this point, and for a contrary belief that more "rational" religions, which taught that salvation was the personal responsibility of the individual, would lead to greater anxiety and despair, see O. Walsh, "'The Designs of Providence': Race, Religion, and Irish Insanity," in *Insanity, Institutions, and Society,* ed. Melling and Forsythe, 230-31, and Bainbridge, "Religious Insanity," 227-28 and 232-34.

30 *Corvallis Times,* 4 November 1903.

31 For the 1904 figures, and those for 1903 and 1905 given below, see OSH Records, Admissions Registers, vols. D148, D149, D150, D152, D154, D155, D156, E84, and E85, OSA. There may have been another case, one Thomas Mimmick, who is reported in *Oregonian,* 14 July 1904, as being committed, but he does not appear in the asylum registers. Those committed in 1904 came from all over Oregon, from eight different counties, and all were incarcerated as individuals, not as members of a group. Two were ministers, including one Henry Ellis, a Portland evangelist: see *Oregonian,* 30 June, and 1, 6, and 8 July, and 13 and 14 September 1904. 1904 was a roughly typical year: in 1903 there were seventeen people committed with religion given as the cause, and in 1905 there were fifteen.

32 Quotations from Marks, "Hysterical Frenzies and Religious Legitimacy," 11 and 14.

33 Seeley and Bray left their situations as domestics in late April, drawing the comment that "it is supposed they intended to spend their time idly, on Creffield's plan that 'God will provide'": *Corvallis Times,* 7 May 1904. A similar sneering comment was offered in *Oregonian,* 1 May 1904, the paper noting that a "further teaching of Creffield, which is claimed to be a direct message from God, is that the Holy Rollers must not work, that God will care for his children." For Mae Hurt see Gardner to O.V. Hurt, 18 June 1904, Letter Books, BGAS Records.

34 *Albany Herald,* 5 May 1904; OSH Records, Personal and Medical Histories, vol. 4B, 277, OSA.

35 *Corvallis Times,* 7 May 1904.

36 *Oregonian,* 3 May 1904, and *Albany Herald,* 5 May 1904. For similar approving comments on these and other commitments see *Corvallis Times,* 4 and 7 May 1906; *Oregonian,* 4 May 1904; *Corvallis Gazette,* 6 and 10 May 1904.

37 Extract from Insane Record, Creffield File, BCHM. For similar comments about "good" habits in the cases of Rose Seeley and Attie Bray see Benton County Insane Record, vol. 2, 2 and 4, BCHM.

38 *Corvallis Gazette,* 10 May 1904.

39 See variously *Albany Herald,* 5 May and 30 June 1904; Extract from Insane Record, Creffield File, BCHM; Benton County Insane Record, vol. 1, 2 and 4, BCHM.

40 Gardner to O.V. Hurt, 18 June 1904, Letter Books, BGAS Records.

41 In addition to those discussed in this paragraph, Wesley Seeley was also not incarcerated. As noted in Chapter 3, he may have left the Beach house after the tarring and

feathering, or he may have decamped when the colony was broken up at the end of April.

42 For all this see *Corvallis Times,* 30 July, 20 August (quotation), and 3 September 1904; *Telegram,* 1 June 1906; OSH Records, Personal and Medical Histories, vol. 4B, 277, OSA.

43 For all this see *Corvallis Gazette,* 6 and 10 May 1904; *Albany Herald,* 12 May 1904; *Oregonian,* 11 June 1904; *Corvallis Times,* 29 June 1904; Benton County Insane Record, vol. 2, 1-4 and 8, BCHM; Extract from Insane Record, Creffield File, BCHM. The Farmers' Hotel proudly advertised itself as a whites-only employer: see *Corvallis Gazette,* 22 April 1904.

44 See variously Benton County Insane Record, vol. 2, 8, BCHM; *Corvallis Gazette,* 6 May 1904; Extract from Insane Record, Creffield File, BCHM. Bayne, also referred to as Bain and Bane, was well known in the county, and indeed throughout the Willamette valley, as a producer of china pheasants: see *Corvallis Gazette,* 11 July and 19 August 1902, and *Oregon Journal,* 21 January 1904.

45 For the presence of these doctors in the various proceedings see Extract from Insane Record, Creffield File, BCHM, and Insane Record, Benton County Court, vol. 2, 1-4 and 8, BCHM. Altman, born 1852, was a graduate of Hahnemann Medical College in Chicago and had practised in Indiana and Kansas before migrating to Oregon. Farra graduated from the University of Louisville in 1877 and immediately relocated to Corvallis. He was president and chief stockholder of the Corvallis Water Company from 1885, when it was first incorporated, a director of the railroad that served Corvallis, and "a large stockholder in many of the important enterprises of Corvallis and vicinity." He practised in Corvallis for almost fifty years before retiring in 1924. See *Portrait and Biographical Record of the Willamette Valley,* 743; Larsell, *The Doctor in Oregon,* 240-41; Hines, *Illustrated History of Oregon,* 449 and 517-18; *Corvallis Gazette,* 22 April 1904.

46 See Hines, *Illustrated History of Oregon,* 319-20, and *Corvallis Gazette,* 14 July 1903. For Cathey generally see Chapter 3.

47 *Portrait and Biographical Record of the Willamette Valley Oregon,* 1258.

48 Ibid., 1131-32.

49 See Benton County Court Journals, vol. 2, 636, and Case File No. 778, Benton County Courthouse. For the legislation see Chapter 3.

50 Gardner to O.V. Hurt, 8 June 1904, Letter Books, BGAS Records.

51 This is a necessarily greatly truncated account. For classic statements of the social control argument see especially A. Scull, *Social Order/Mental Disorder: Anglo-American Psychiatry in Historical Perspective* (Berkeley: University of California Press, 1989); and Rothman, *The Discovery of the Asylum.* See also Lasch's argument that society increasingly "insisted that all citizens live by the same rules of character and conduct": C. Lasch, *The World of Nations: Reflections on American History, Politics and Culture* (New York: Knopf, 1973), 17. For a very useful review of the historiography of the asylum see the Introduction to J. Moran, *Committed to the State Asylum: Insanity and Society in Nineteenth-Century Quebec and Ontario* (Montreal and Kingston: McGill-Queen's University Press, 2000).

52 Not surprisingly, the result was relatively high rates of asylum incarceration in most states; Oregon's was among the highest, although by no means out of proportion to many others. Incarceration rates for 1890 are provided in H.M. Hurd, ed., *The*

Institutional Care of the Insane in the United States and Canada, 3 vols. (Baltimore: Johns Hopkins Press, 1916-17), vol. 1, 418. Oregon's was 204 per 100,000 population, putting it well into the upper third of states but below some others – California with 309, for example. By 1910 the Oregon rate had risen to 233 per 100,000. In August 1904 the Oregon Asylum at Salem held 1,375 patients: *Corvallis Gazette*, 16 September 1904.

53 For this recent work see J. Melling, "Accommodating Madness: New Research in the Social History of Insanity and Institutions," in *Insanity, Institutions and Society*, ed. Melling and Forsythe. For examples see Moran, *Committed to the State Asylum*; Grob, *The Mad Among Us*, and *Mental Illness and American Society*; and N. Tomes, *A Generous Confidence: Thomas Story Kirkbride and the Art of Asylum-Keeping, 1840-1883* (Cambridge: Cambridge University Press, 1984). For similar arguments about England see D.N. Wright, "The Discharge of Pauper Lunatics from County Asylums in mid-Victorian England: The Case of Buckinghamshire, 1853-1872," and B. Forsythe, "Politics of Lunacy: Central Sate Regulation and the Devon Pauper Lunatic Asylum, 1845-1914," both in Melling and Forsythe, eds., *Insanity, Institutions and Society*; J. Melling, B. Forsythe, and R. Adair, "Families, Communities and the Legal Regulation of Lunacy in Victorian England: Assessments of Crime, Violence and Welfare in Admissions to the Devon Asylum, 1815-1914," in *Outside the Walls of the Asylum: The History of Care in the Community, 1750-2000*, ed. P. Bartlett and D. Wright (London: Athlone, 1999).

54 C. McGovern, "The Community, the Hospital, and the Working-Class Patient: The Multiple Uses of Asylum in Nineteenth-Century America," *Pennsylvania History* 54 (1987): 17.

55 Grob, *Mental Illness and American Society*, 10-11.

56 The first such institution in Oregon was the private Hawthorne Asylum in Portland, established in 1861. For some years it took state patients also, until the establishment of the state asylum at Salem, properly called the Oregon State Hospital, in 1883. This development occurred rather later in Oregon than elsewhere, most states having built state facilities before or during the third quarter of the century. For all this see the limited literature on the history of the Oregon Asylum: Hurd, *Institutional Care of the Insane*, vol. 3, 368-80; O. Larsell, "History of the Care of the Insane in the State of Oregon," *Oregon Historical Quarterly* 46 (1945): 295-326, and *The Doctor in Oregon*, ch. 15; R. Higgins-Evenson, "The Political Asylum: State Making and the Medical Profession in Oregon, 1862-1900," *Pacific Northwest Quarterly* 89 (1998): 136-48.

57 Benton County Insane Record, vol. 2, BCHM.

58 *Oregon Statesman*, 11 October 1902.

59 See E. Lunbeck, *The Psychiatric Persuasion: Knowledge, Gender and Power in Modern America* (Princeton, NJ: Princeton University Press, 1994), ch. 10. For a similar suggestion that women who refused to conform to gender roles were especially vulnerable to being labelled insane see Y. Ripa, *Women and Madness: The Incarceration of Women in Nineteenth-Century France* (Cambridge: Polity Press, 1990). One author has also argued that contemporary medical opinion held that women and the aged were especially susceptible to mental illness, and that women were thus more readily diagnosed as insane than men. For the same reason it was easier for relatives to commit a woman for opportunistic reasons, as less compelling evidence was required. See on this point R.W. Fox, *So Far Disordered in Mind: Insanity in California, 1870-1930*

(Berkeley: University of California Press, 1978), 94-95. Most recent research, however, suggests that women were not more likely to be committed than men: see, *inter alia,* Tomes, *A Generous Confidence* and P. McCandless, *Moonlight, Magnolias, Madness: Insanity in South Carolina from the Colonial Period to the Progressive Era* (Chapel Hill, NC: University of North Carolina Press, 1996).

60 For a similar case at this time of using asylum commitment when other measures of social and legal coercion failed see G. Andrews, *Insane Sisters, Or, The Price Paid for Challenging a Company Town* (Columbia, MO: University of Missouri Press, 1999).

61 See the monthly asylum reports reproduced in *Oregonian,* 12 June and 2 August 1904.

62 For the asylum regime see the sources cited above for the history of the institution.

63 *Albany Herald,* 5 May 1904. For orders that Sophia Hartley and Maud Creffield be kept apart, and that Maud Creffield be kept away from Frank and Mollie Hurt, see *Corvallis Gazette,* 6 May 1904, and Extract from Insane Record, Creffield File, BCHM.

64 *Oregonian,* 31 July 1904.

65 *Telegram,* 20 August 1904.

66 This is according to the evidence of O.V. Hurt at Maud's second insanity hearing, in Seattle in 1906: see *Corvallis Times,* 14 September 1906, and *PI,* 13 September 1906.

67 Rose to Florence Seeley, 19 June 1904, Case File 2397, and O.V. Hurt to Gardner, 29 June 1904, Case File 2430, BGAS Records.

68 *Corvallis Times,* 11 June 1904; Benton County Insane Record, vol. 2, 7, BCHM.

69 *Corvallis Times,* 20 August 1904.

70 *Albany Herald,* 6 October 1904. For these events see also *Corvallis Gazette,* 23 September and 4 October 1904; *Corvallis Times,* 21 September and 1 October 1904; Discharge Register, OSH Records, vol. F, 113, OSA; Admissions Register, OSH Records, vol. E, 85, OSA; Benton County Insane Record, vol. 2, 10 and 12, BCHM.

71 *Corvallis Times,* 20 August 1904. See the same source for similar comments about Maud Creffield, and Frank and Mollie Hurt.

72 Mary Graham to O.V. Hurt, 6 July 1904, Letter Books, and O.V. Hurt to Gardner, 29 June 1904, Case File 2430, BGAS Records; Discharge Register, OSH Records, vol. F, 112, OSA; *Corvallis Times,* 13 July 1904; *Corvallis Gazette,* 15 July 1904.

73 See Discharge Register, OSH Records, vol. F, 113 and 115, OSA; Benton County Insane Record, vol. 2, 11 and 15, BCHM; Discharge Certificates, Insanity Records, Linn County, Cases 1036 and 1067, OSA.

74 *Telegram,* 22 March 1905.

75 Register Book, Girls C, Case 2397; Gardner to Mrs Wilson, 7 June 1904, and Graham to Same, 8 July 1904, Letter Books; and J.A. and Lilly Wilson to Gardner, 11 and 25 June 1904, and Florence Seeley to Graham, 2 July and 12 August 1904, Case File 2397 – all BGAS Records. The Wilsons' home was variously given as Mud Bay, Allavia, and Alluvia, BC, which according to one of these letters was nine miles from Blaine, Washington, in southern British Columbia.

76 Quotations from Gardner to Mrs J.A. Wilson, 7 June 1904, and Graham to Rose Seeley, 21 June 1904, Letter Books, BGAS Records, and *Corvallis Times,* 13 July 1904. For her assertions of faith in Creffield on incarceration see *Telegram,* 3 May 1904. For the correspondence with her sister see Graham to Rose Seeley, 21 June 1904, Letter Books, BGAS Records, and Rose to Florence Seeley, 19 June 1904, Case File 2397, BGAS Records.

77 Florence Seeley to Graham, 12 August 1904, Case File 2397, BGAS Records.
78 See Gardner to O.V. Hurt, 18 and 23 June 1904, and Mary Graham to Same, 6 July 1904, Letter Books, and O.V. Hurt to Gardner, 15 and 21 June 1904, Case File 2430, BGAS Records.
79 For Hurt's expressions of affection see Hurt to Gardner, 15 and 29 June 1904, and to Mae Hurt, 16 July 1904, Case File 2430, BGAS Records. For other parts of this account see also Gardner to O.V. Hurt, 29 July 1904, Letter Books, ibid. For earlier indications of her "improvement" see Graham to O.V. Hurt, 18 and 22 July 1904, ibid. See also Graham to Florence Seeley, 29 September 1904, ibid.
80 Hurt to Graham, 21 July 1904, and to Gardner, 28 July 1904, Case File 2430, BGAS Records.
81 Register Book, Girls C, Case 2430, BGAS Records and *Albany Herald,* 4 August 1904.
82 Graham to Florence Seeley, 29 September 1904, Letter Books, BGAS Records.
83 See generally Miller, *Involuntary Commitment,* 31. For Oregon see Hurd, *Institutional Care of the Insane,* vol. 1, 338-43: "Recovered patients must be discharged, also other patients whenever the superintendent may think the best interests of the state institution require it."
84 For an example see O. Walsh, "Lunatic and Criminal Alliances in Nineteenth-Century Ireland," in *Outside the Walls of the Asylum,* ed. Bartlett and Wrights.
85 Bainbridge, "Religious Insanity," 235.
86 *Corvallis Gazette,* 2 December 1904.
87 This is from O.V. Hurt's testimony at Maud Creffield's 1906 insanity hearing in Seattle: see *Oregonian,* 13 September 1906.

CHAPTER 6: REVIVAL AND REVENGE, JANUARY TO MAY 1906

1 *Telegram,* 12 May 1906. Information on Creffield's time in the penitentiary is from a press report in ibid., 22 March 1905, reproduced in *Corvallis Gazette,* 24 March 1905, and from Oregon State Penitentiary Records, Convict Record Book, OSA. For the law on remission see *Oregon Statutes,* 1903, 113-14, and *Bellinger and Cotton,* vol. 2, 1567-68. The law allowed prisoners 2 days' remission for every day worked. Penitentiary records suggest that Creffield worked 160 days up to the end of November 1905; we do not know why he did not get out earlier.
2 See Benton County Divorces, No. 4334, OSA, and brief reports in *Corvallis Times,* 8 and 12 July 1905, and *Corvallis Gazette,* 11 July 1905.
3 *PI,* 19 September 1906.
4 *Corvallis Gazette,* 16 May 1905.
5 For the $5 see *Bellinger and Cotton,* vol. 2, 1239. In addition to sources cited for specific points below, this section on Creffield's activities following his release is based on reports in *Telegram,* 2 May and 4 July 1906; *Oregonian,* 24 April, 8 May, and 4 July 1906; *PI,* 9 May and 13 July 1906; *Seattle Times,* 7 and 8 May, 1 June, and 3, 4, 5, and 6 July 1906; *Corvallis Times,* 24 April and 11 May 1906; *Corvallis Gazette,* 11 May 1906; *Star,* 11 May 1906. Note that all these sources are from a later period than the one discussed; contemporaries other than the sect members knew little or nothing about his movements.
6 This seems most probable, although the only direct evidence for it is a letter he

supposedly wrote to O.V. Hurt from Los Angeles, in reply to one from Hurt warning him to stay out of Oregon. Creffield's response was bellicose: "Hurt, . . . God has resurrected me. I have got my foot on your neck. God has given me back my own. I will return to Oregon, and again gather up all my people. Place no obstacles in my way or God will smite you." This is from Hurt's testimony at George Mitchell's trial: *PI*, 4 July 1906. See also similar statements in May in *Telegram*, 9 May 1906.

7   For the Hurts' move to Seattle in 1905, which presumably included Olive Sandell, see the statement of Louis Sandell in *Star*, 11 May 1906. See also *Corvallis Gazette*, 9 January 1906, and *PI*, 8 May 1906.

8   *Corvallis Gazette*, 9 and 20 February 1906.

9   For Esther's continued adherence to radical holiness see *Corvallis Times*, 10 July 1906, stating that she "refused to call her own father by that name, saying that her only father was God and that she had no father on earth." For her return to Oregon and work in the mills see ibid.; *Oregonian*, 7 and 14 July 1906; *Star*, 7 May 1906; *Seattle Times*, 13 July 1906.

10 For this claim see *Star*, 11 May 1906.

11 *Corvallis Times*, 24 April 1906. The fate of Rose Seeley after her release from the asylum is unclear. As noted in Chapter 5, Florence went to British Columbia in 1904, and one report says that Rose did also: see *The Dalles Weekly Chronicle*, 3 August 1904.

12 After his death, a number of envelopes were found among Creffield's effects with this address on them, post-marked from various places in Oregon, although the letters had been removed and were not found: *Seattle Times*, 8 May 1906.

13 See King County Marriage Licence Register No. 19, 212, Licence No. 14343, and King County Record of Marriages, 1906, Certificate 18756, both at WSA-PS.

14 *Corvallis Times*, 24 April 1906.

15 *PI*, 19 July 1906. For the adultery see her statement that Donna Starr "did not know what she was signing" when she put her name to statements: *PI*, 16 July 1906.

16 *Oregonian*, 24 April 1906.

17 See also Maud Creffield's later comment that the trip to Waldport was to "places where I had spent many childhood days": *PI*, 16 July 1906.

18 See *Telegram*, 7 May 1906, for Frank's actions, and *PI*, 8 May 1906, for the homesteading. The latter's reference was to "taking up government land" at Ocean View; Ocean View is now Yachats.

19 *Corvallis Times*, 13 March 1906.

20 The following account of the journey to the coast is from a variety of sources: see *Yaquina Bay News* (Newport), 26 April 1906; *Oregonian*, 24 April and 2 and 8 May 1906; *Corvallis Gazette*, 27 April 1906; *Corvallis Times*, 24 April and 1 May 1906; *PI*, 16 July 1906; Louis Hartley's Divorce Petition, 1906, Benton County Divorces, No. 4377, OSA.

21 We are not entirely certain about the Seeleys, for the only source that mentions their presence on the coast is Crew, *Brides of Eden*, 144. Although Crew's book is usually very reliable, we would prefer some contemporary evidence. Florence Seeley had gone to British Columbia after her release from the BGAS home in 1904, and at least for some time maintained both her apostasy and a correspondence with matron Mary Graham: see Graham to Florence Seeley, 29 September 1904, Letter Books, BGAS Records.

22 See O.V. Hurt's testimony at George Mitchell's trial, cited in *Oregonian*, 4 July 1906.

23 Ibid., 8 May 1906.

24 *Seattle Times,* 5 July 1906, citing Baldwin's testimony at George Mitchell's trial. See also *Oregon Journal,* 5 July 1906.

25 For this part of the story see the sources noted above, and reports of Hartley's testimony at George Mitchell's trial in *Corvallis Times,* 10 and 11 July 1906; *Seattle Times,* 6 July 1906; and *Oregonian,* 6 July 1906.

26 Louis Hartley's Divorce Petition, 1906, Benton County Divorces, No. 4377, OSA.

27 None of the sources describes fully the journey to the Waldport area, although a report in the Newport *Yaquina Bay News* of April 26 says that the party went across to South Beach on the evening of Saturday, April 21, the day the Creffields arrived on the coast. See also *Corvallis Times,* 24 April 1906, for the crossing to South Beach, and see generally Louis Hartley's Divorce Petition, 1906, Benton County Divorces, No. 4377, OSA. The suggestion about the wagon comes from Crew, *Brides of Eden,* 167-68, a reasonable assumption given that that was the usual mode of travel. Only two sources give the location of the camp as Hosford's land: *Star,* 17 May 1906, and *Telegram,* 16 May 1906. Others simply locate it on the north shore of Alsea Bay, near Waldport: see *Oregonian,* 24 April and 2 May 1906; *Lincoln County Leader* (Toledo), 4 May 1906. Crew, *Brides of Eden,* 168-69, has the camp on the beach.

28 See the suggestion in the Newport *Yaquina Bay News,* 26 April 1906, that the intended destination was Ten-Mile Creek in Lane County, some fifteen miles farther south and near the Bray family homestead.

29 *Oregonian,* 2 May 1906.

30 All except the Seeleys are mentioned in the various contemporary accounts. Crew says that the Seeleys were there also, having come from Oregon City (see *Brides of Eden,* 173), but it must be remembered that they were supposed to have gone to Levins' British Columbia colony in 1904-1905. They may, of course, have done so, and then returned to Oregon.

31 On this see Louis Hartley's Divorce Petition, 1906, Benton County Divorces, No. 4377, OSA. He states that they were there, but that he did not know how they got to the camp. If they had been with the main party Hartley would have seen them when he tried to shoot Creffield, unless perhaps they had hidden themselves on the ferry when they saw him running from the other ferry.

32 There are many accounts of this. See Burgess Starr's trial testimony in *Times,* 4 July 1906. See also *Corvallis Times,* 1 May 1906, and *Oregonian,* 2 and 8 May 1906. There is a good description in McDonald, "Roll Ye Sinners Roll," 89. The report in the *Telegram,* 16 May 1906, has Donna walking to Corvallis from Portland, not taking the train.

33 *Corvallis Gazette,* 27 April 1906.

34 According to the *Oregonian,* "he alleges now that he is Christ risen from the dead, his death being the two years incarcerated at the Oregon State Penitentiary": *Oregonian,* 24 April 1906. The *Corvallis Times* asserted similarly that, "this time he is palming himself off on his foolish followers as Jesus Christ," with "his resurrection having been his emergence from the state penitentiary": *Corvallis Times,* 24 April 1906.

35 *Corvallis Times,* 22 May 1906, and *Seattle Times,* 13 July 1906. For similar statements attributed to her see *Times,* 7 May and 6 and 7 July 1906, and *Corvallis Gazette,* 11 May 1906. For other evidence of Creffield asserting his own divinity and for his followers believing it see *Seattle Times,* 7 and 16 May, 1 June, and 16 July 1906; *PI,* 8

and 9 May 1906; *Corvallis Times,* 6 July 1906; *Oregon Journal,* 9 and 13 May 1906. See also the account of the women discovered on the beach in mid-May 1906, below, and that of his followers' belief in his resurrection in Chapter 7.

36 There are many accounts of this: see in particular *Oregonian,* 2 May 1906, and *Corvallis Times,* 1 May 1906.

37 *Corvallis Times,* 1 May 1906, and *PI,* 8 May 1906. For other contemporary indications of his early departure see *Oregonian,* 2 and 8 May 1906.

38 See *Telegram,* 2 and 8 May 1906. Some people were back in Corvallis by the end of April, although we do not know who: see *Corvallis Times,* 1 May 1906; *Oregonian,* 2 May 1906. The latter source states that two people took the April 30 train from Yaquina Bay to Corvallis. Those departing likely included Frank Hurt and Esther Mitchell, who were not among those not taken out until mid-May. In addition, Maud Creffield stated on May 7 that Esther Mitchell was staying with Frank Hurt in Corvallis: *Star,* 7 May 1906. See also *Seattle Times,* 13 July 1906, and *Oregonian,* 14 July 1906.

39 The *Oregonian,* 17 May 1906, has only five women and a baby left after Creffield and other followers quickly departed, but the *Oregon Journal,* 17 May 1906, states that Frank Hurt was with these women until Friday, May 11.

40 *Lincoln County Leader* (Toledo), 11 May 1906.

41 See his evidence at George Mitchell's trial, reported in *Corvallis Times,* 10 July 1906, *Seattle Times,* 6 July 1906, and *PI,* 6 July 1906. See also generally *Herald,* 10 May 1906, and *Seattle Times,* 1 June 1906.

42 Louis Hartley's Divorce Petition, 1906, Benton County Divorces, No. 4377, OSA. She left his house shortly afterwards, and he finally gave up, suing in early May for divorce.

43 For Baldwin see his evidence at George Mitchell's trial, reported in *Corvallis Times,* 10 July 1906, and *Seattle Times,* 5 July 1906; see also *Oregonian,* 14 July 1906. For Mitchell see *Star,* 7 May 1906.

44 *Telegram,* 9 May 1906.

45 See O.V. Hurt's statement about this in *PI,* 9 May 1906. See also *Oregon Journal,* 9 May 1906.

46 *Corvallis Times,* 1 May 1906. See also, to the same effect, *Oregonian,* 2 May 1906, and *PI,* 8 May 1906. The *Star,* 7 May 1906, refers to a "threatened raid" on the camp. And see also a later reference to men who "drove Creffield from the beach at Wallport": *Seattle Times,* 19 June 1906.

47 *Oregonian,* 2 May 1906.

48 *Seattle Times,* 16 May 1906; *Telegram,* 16 May 1906; *Oregonian,* 17 May 1906. The rest of this paragraph, including the quotations, is from the last source. Crew, *Brides of Eden,* 181-84, graphically recreates the journey, and there is a good description in McDonald, "Roll Ye Sinners Roll," 99-100.

49 *Oregon Journal,* 19 August 1936.

50 Bogue and Yunker, "Proved Up on Ten Mile Creek," 6.

51 *Oregonian,* 17 May 1906.

52 *Star,* 11 May 1906; *Oregon Journal,* 16 May 1906.

53 *Oregonian,* 16 May 1906. The essence of this story was also published in *Seattle Times,* 16 May 1906; *Star,* 17 May 1906; *Oregon Journal,* 16 May 1906; *Corvallis Times,* 18 May 1906; and *Eugene Register,* 17 May 1906. This paragraph is based largely on these sources.

54 *Star,* 17 May 1906; they "seemed to fear that the slightest act of kindness toward the women would encourage the men of the party to return."

55 *Oregonian,* 17 May 1906. The rest of the paragraph is from this source, and *Oregon Journal,* 17 May 1906.

56 *Corvallis Times,* 13 July 1906. See also *Oregonian,* 8 May 1906, and *Telegram,* 2 May 1906. The *Telegram,* 2 and 8 May 1906, and the *Star,* 7 May 1906, give a different story: that Creffield took the Corvallis train but got off at Blodgett, walked the roughly thirty-five miles south to Junction City, and from there took the Portland train. We think these newspapers got it wrong, however, for most sources agree on the walk to Eugene.

57 *Telegram,* 17 March 1904 and 7 May 1906.

58 *Oregonian,* 8 May 1906; *Seattle Times,* 6 July 1906; *PI,* 8 May 1906; *Telegram,* 2 May 1906. The date is from an interview with Maud herself.

59 *Seattle Times,* 7 May 1906. See also *PI,* 8 May 1906.

60 See the report in the *Star* of her going back to the room to pick up her belongings after Creffield had been murdered: "There was a small Bible, some writing paper, a few pens and pencils, combs, a couple of hair ribbons, and a package of tobacco." The last is an interesting item for the ascetic Creffield sect. The police also found her revolver and took it away. See *Star,* 7 May 1906.

61 *PI,* 19 July 1906.

62 Only one source gives the precise timing; according to the *Star,* 6 July 1906, he was in the hospital from April 10 to April 20. For Mitchell generally see ibid., 7 May 1906.

63 See Hurt's testimony reported in *Oregonian,* 4 July 1906. For other accounts of his stay in the hospital see, *inter alia, Corvallis Times,* 10 July 1906; *Seattle Times,* 2 and 6 July 1906.

64 Cited *PI,* 7 July 1906.

65 Mitchell's movements described in this paragraph are well documented, principally in *Telegram,* 2 May 1906. See also numerous reports immediately after the murder and in later trial testimony in, *inter alia, Seattle Times,* 7 May, 29 June, and 5, 6, and 7 July 1906; *Star,* 7 and 11 May 1906; *PI,* 8 May and 7 July 1906; *Oregonian,* 10 May 1906; *Corvallis Times,* 11 May 1906.

66 The murder of Creffield was extensively reported in all the Seattle, Portland, and Corvallis newspapers, and the following account is taken from those reports, variously appearing between the May 7 and May 10. It is supplemented by the prosecution evidence at George Mitchell's trial, also extensively reported; we have relied principally on the reports in *Times,* 29 June 1906; *Star,* 29 June 1906; and *PI,* 30 June 1906. The only non-newspaper source used here is the Creffield file, No. 551, in the King County Medical Examiner Records, KCA.

67 *PI,* 9 May 1906.

68 *Seattle Times,* 7 May 1906. The same words were reported in *PI,* 8 May 1906.

69 *Seattle Times,* 29 June 1906; *PI,* 8 May 1906.

70 Bories emigrated from Austria to the United States as a young man. His medical degree was from the University of Vermont (1885) and he practised in Seattle thereafter. A faculty member at the University of Washington and an author of many medical papers, he was one of the city's best-known doctors as well as a successful businessman, and he was known for his fine tastes, well-appointed house, and voluminous library. See J. Hawthorne, *History of Washington: The Evergreen State,* 2 vols. (New

York: American Historical Publishing, 1893), vol. 2, 584; *Argus*, 18 December 1897; *PI*, 13 July 1901; Washington State Biography Files, UWL.

CHAPTER 7: SEATTLE PREPARES FOR TRIAL, MAY AND JUNE 1906

1 This necessarily brief overview is derived from a number of sources. The standard general histories are R. Berner, *Seattle 1900-1920: From Boomtown, Urban Turbulence, to Restoration* (Seattle: Charles Press, 1991), and R. Sale, *Seattle: Past to Present* (Seattle: University of Washington Press, 1976). An excellent study of the economy and social structure is N. MacDonald, *Distant Neighbors: A Comparative History of Seattle and Vancouver* (Lincoln, NE: University of Nebraska Press, 1987), and much useful data can be gleaned from C. Schmid, *Social Trends in Seattle* (Seattle: University of Washington Press, 1944). See also G.A. Frykman, *Seattle's Historian and Promoter: The Life of Edward Stephen Meany* (Pullman, WA: Washington State University Press, 1998). Other sources are referred to below in relation to specific topics. For the history of Washington in this period see C.O. Schwantes, *The Pacific Northwest: An Interpretive History* (Lincoln, NE: University of Nebraska Press, 1989); R. Ficken and C.P. LeWarne, *Washington: A Centennial History* (Seattle: University of Washington Press, 1988); and the introduction to LeWarne, *Utopias on Puget Sound.*

2 The best description of this aspect Seattle's social life is M. Morgan, *Skid Road: Seattle, Her First 125 Years* (Sausalito, CA: Comstock Press, 1978), esp. ch. 3. For violence in the city, see D. Peterson Del Mar, *Beaton Down: A History of Interpersonal Violence in the West* (Seattle: University of Washington Press, 2002), 94-96.

3 Seattle's annual homicide rate in the first decade of the twentieth century ranged between 6 and 12 per 100,000 population, and averaged 8.2. This figure is from data collected for a project on homicide in twentieth-century Seattle by Rosemary Gartner and Professor Bill McCarthy. Among other major cities in this period, Buffalo's homicide rate ranged between 2 and 5 per 100,000 population, Los Angeles' between 6 and 8, and New York's between 3 and 6: E. Monkkonen, "Estimating the Accuracy of Historic Homicide Rates: New York City and Los Angeles," *The Varieties of Homicide and Its Research: Proceedings of the 1999 Meeting of the Homicide Research Working Group* (Washington: US Department of Justice, 1999), 13-21, and *Murder in New York City* (Berkeley: University of California Press, 2001); D. Eckberg, "Using Econometric Forecasting to Correct for Missing Data: Homicide and the Early Registration Area," *Trends, Risks and Interventions in Lethal Violence: Proceedings of the Third Annual Symposium of the Homicide Research Working Group* (Washington: US Department of Justice, 1995), 51-64. Note, however, that by no means all Seattle homicides led to prosecutions. Only eleven people were prosecuted in 1906, from nine cases, including the three people this book is about – George Mitchell, Esther Mitchell, and Maud Creffield: see Prosecuting Attorney's Criminal Docket, vol. 8, passim, KCA.

4 The background to the shooting of William Meredith by John Considine is too complicated to reproduce here, but the immediate cause was that Considine had testified before an investigating committee to bribing Meredith, who was a former business associate of his before Meredith briefly became police chief. Meredith was fired, and went after Considine with a shotgun. Considine and his brother Tom got the better

of the altercation and both were later tried for murder but acquitted. For the affair see Morgan, *Skid Road*, ch. 3; *PI*, 25 June-13 July and 5-21 November 1901.

5 See R.H. Engeman, "The 'Seattle Spirit' Meets The Alaskan: A Study of Business, Boosterism and the Arts," *Pacific Northwest Quarterly* 81 (1990): 54-66. For the reform movement generally see M.G. Blackford, "Reform Politics in Seattle During the Progressive Era, 1902-1906," *Pacific Northwest Quarterly* 59 (1968): 177-85.

6 The largest exception was the 1896-1901 period, during which populist governor John Rogers was twice elected. His administration was able to do little, however, given the dominance of the legislature by railroad interests, and he died shortly after the start of his second term.

7 The most comprehensive study of progressivism in Washington remains R. Saltvig, "The Progressive Movement in Washington," PhD dissertation, University of Washington, 1966.

8 Strictly speaking, Washington women got the vote back in 1910, having had it during the Territorial period, from 1883 to 1887, when a court decision removed it.

9 Matthews is ably discussed in Soden, *The Reverend Mark Matthews*.

10 For Blethen see especially S. Boswell and L. McConaghy, *Raise Hell and Sell Newspapers: Alden J. Blethen and the Seattle Times* (Pullman, WA: Washington State University Press, 1996).

11 Accounts of Creffield's funeral are in *PI*, 9 and 10 May 1906; *Oregonian*, 10 May 1906; *Corvallis Times*, 11 May 1906; *Star*, 9 May 1906.

12 *PI*, 14 May 1906. The police matron took charge of female witnesses being held for trial but dealt mostly with young girls held for truancy, delinquency, running away, and so on. See Police Department Reports, 1905 and 1908, Seattle Municipal Archives.

13 The *Post-Intelligencer* reported on May 9 that "several followers" of Creffield had gone to the morgue to view his remains but did not say who they were, and we cannot guess who they might have been. We suspect that the paper was wrong about this, for there were no other adherents that we know of in the city so soon after the killing. Other papers, however, carried the same report: see *Star*, 9 May 1906, and *Oregon Journal*, 9 May 1906.

14 For Maud's death see Chapter 12. The two simple headstones still stand in Lakeview Cemetery, Seattle.

15 Quotations from *PI*, 10 May 1906, and *Corvallis Times*, 11 May 1906. See also *Seattle Times*, 13 May 1906; *Corvallis Times*, 15 May 1906; *Oregon Journal*, 13 May 1906.

16 *Seattle Times*, 13 May 1906. See also *PI*, 14 May 1906.

17 Quotation from *Albany Herald*, 17 May 1906. See also for Maud's beliefs and visits to Creffield's grave *Corvallis Times*, 15 May 1906; *Oregon Journal*, 13 May 1906; *Seattle Times*, 13 July 1906; *Star*, 14 and 28 May 1906; *Oregonian*, 9 July 1906.

18 *Seattle Times*, 15 May, 30 June, and 13 July 1906; *Star*, 15 May 1906; *Corvallis Times*, 13 July 1906.

19 For Frank and Mollie's arrivals see *Star*, 24 and 28 May 1906, and *Oregon Journal*, 17 and 22 May 1906. For Frank's later views see *Oregonian*, 9 July 1906; *Corvallis Times*, 10 July 1906; *Seattle Times*, 13 July 1906.

20 *Remington and Ballinger*, vol. 1, 1229. Second-degree murder was also a purposeful killing, but without premeditation: see ibid., 1230.

21 A proceeding by information permits the state to bypass the grand jury. The prosecutor simply "informed" the court on oath of his belief that a crime had been committed: see the information in the Mitchell case, in SC-KC Case File No. 3652, WSA-PS.

Washington law provided that either method could be employed in any case. Some state constitutions required a preliminary examination when the prosecution was by information, but not Washington's. See *Remington and Ballinger*, vol. 1, 1012-13, and the cases cited therein on the constitutionality of the legislative provisions.

22 Washington named its county-based public prosecutor the "prosecuting attorney" rather than the more common "district attorney." For the statutory basis of the term see *Remington and Ballinger*, vol. 1, 189. Deputies were appointed by the prosecuting attorney, not elected: see ibid., vol. 1, 190.

23 For Mackintosh see C.H. Sheldon, *The Washington High Bench: A Biographical History of the State Supreme Court, 1889-1991* (Pullman, WA: Washington State University Press, 1992), 234-37; H.J. Boswell, *The American Blue Book: Western Washington* (Seattle: Lowman and Hanford, 1922), 20; Taylor, *Eminent Judges and Lawyers*, 177; *Mail and Herald*, 30 December 1905, 1; C. Bagley, *History of Seattle From the Earliest Settlement to the Present Time*, 3 vols. (Chicago: Chicago: S.J. Clarke, 1916), vol. 3, 841; *PI*, 8 November 1904 and 23 August 1906; *Seattle Times*, 11 July 1906; *Republican*, 25 December 1903.

24 He served two terms as prosecuting attorney (1905-1907 and 1907-1909) and was elected as a judge of the King County Superior Court (1912-18) and a judge of the Washington Supreme Court (1918-29). He was chief justice of Washington from 1927 to 1929.

25 For his philosophy of office see Mackintosh to Erastus Brainerd, 14 March 1908, Erastus Brainerd Papers, Acc. No. 4624-1, folder 3-36, UWL. See also *Seattle Times*, 1 March 1905, on his campaign for stiffer sentences for major felonies.

26 See C.H. Sheldon, *A Century of Judging: A Political History of the Washington Supreme Court* (Seattle: University of Washington Press, 1988), 276; County Commissioners' Proceedings, vol. 15, 6 November 1906. KCA. As well as professionalizing the office, Mackintosh hired its first woman deputy prosecuting attorney: Sheldon, *The Washington High Bench*, 235.

27 For Miller see the biographical notes in John Franklin Miller Papers, Acc. No. 1267, Box 3, UWL; Bagley, *History of Seattle*, vol. 2, 373; *Seattle Times*, 6 July 1906; Berner, *Seattle 1900-1920*, 112-14.

28 For their friendship see J. Sundwall to E. Brainerd, 4 March 1908, Erastus Brainerd Papers, Acc. No. 4624-1, folder 5-13, UWL.

29 "Garbed in an immaculate suit of blue, with tan vest, shoes polished and void of dust and in his hand a straw hat of the very latest style, Mr Miller looked his right to the title of the Chesterfield of the local bar": *Star*, 6 July 1906.

30 *Seattle Times*, 8 May 1906. Morris was reported as Mitchell's lawyer in the morning edition of the *PI*, 8 May 1906. For Hurt's travels see *Oregonian*, 8 and 9 May 1906.

31 For Morris see Bagley, *History of Seattle*, vol. 3, 786-87; Boswell, *American Blue Book*, 43; *Argus*, 21 December 1895; *Star*, 11 July 1906.

32 *Oregonian*, 11 July 1906. The newspaper seems to have known of what it spake, for it provided a list of the cases. It included the Considine case, discussed earlier in this chapter, in which Morris was junior defence counsel to James F. McElroy: see *PI*, 20 November 1901. According to an account written in 1916, when Miller was still practising, by that time the list had expanded to twenty-six cases, from which came twenty-four outright acquittals and one conviction for the reduced charge of manslaughter: Bagley, *History of Seattle*, vol. 3, 787. Morris did take on a variety of defences, not just murder and other high-profile ones. Between April 1905 and October 1907 he acted in thirteen cases, including two each of murder, attempted murder, and rape, but also

cases of grand larceny, burglary, and assault with a deadly weapon. He succeeded in either having the case dismissed, securing an acquittal, getting a conviction on a lesser included offence than the one charged, or having a conviction reversed in the supreme court, in all but one of them: see Prosecuting Attorney's Criminal Docket, vol. 8, passim, KCA.

33 *Corvallis Times,* 22 June 1906. See also *Republican,* 25 December 1903, describing him as a man who "has won more murder cases than any lawyer in the state."

34 *Corvallis Times,* 22 June 1906. Material on Shipley is also drawn from Hawthorne, *History of Washington,* vol. 2, 620; Boswell, *American Blue Book,* 198; Family Records of Washington Pioneers, vol. 8, 1938, UWL.

35 *Seattle Times,* 11 July 1906.

36 See *Remington and Ballinger,* vol. 1, 1037-38 and 1122.

37 *PI,* 11 May 1906; Prosecuting Attorney's Criminal Docket, vol. 8, 211, Case No. 3652, KCA. The information is in Case File 3652, SC-KC, WSA-PS.

38 See *Remington and Ballinger,* vol. 1, 165. For the court system see D. Hastings, "Introduction," in *Guide to the Judicial Records of King County* (Seattle: Washington State Archives, 1977).

39 There had been three in 1895, with occasional increases from time to time as population grew. The sixth judge was added only in 1905: see *Pierce's Code: A Compilation of all the Laws in Force in the State of Washington Including the Session of 1905* (Seattle: Tribune Printing, 1905), 715-15A.

40 *PI,* 13 May 1906.

41 For Frater see Memorial Pamphlet, 2 January 1926, in Stephen James Chadwick Papers, Acc. No. 7, Box 2, folder 2-1, UWL. This was produced for a Masons' meeting, Frater having been grand master of the Washington Lodge in 1897-98. See also *Argus,* 29 August 1908; *Mail and Herald,* 14 October 1905; *Patriarch,* 24 November 1906, 7 and 28 January 1911, and 26 April 1913.

42 *Mail and Herald,* 3 June 1905. For his temperament see the discussion of the Beede-MacDonald case, below, and a story that came up during jury selection for the Mitchell trial. When Dr George Thompson, a dentist, asked to be excused on the grounds that he was not a citizen, Frater asked him how long he had lived in the United States. The reply was sixteen years, which led Frater to give him a stinging lecture before excusing him: "You have lived here for sixteen years enjoying the privileges and emoluments of a citizen without taking any part in the duties of a citizen which make these privileges possible, or performing your proper share of the duties involved in the well-being of the community. The least thing you can do is to go directly to the clerk's office and take the necessary steps to become a citizen of the United States": *Seattle Times,* 26 June 1906.

43 This discussion of the Beede-MacDonald case, including the quotations, is principally from *Oregonian,* 11 May 1906. See also *Star,* 9 May 1906, and Prosecuting Attorney's Criminal Docket, vol. 8, 121, Case No. 3572, KCA. See also *Argus,* 28 April 1906, for acerbic criticism of Frater for comments "in mighty poor taste," which showed that "he is not fit to be on the bench."

44 For the unwritten law see principally two articles: R.M. Ireland, "The Libertine Must Die: Sexual Dishonor and the Unwritten Law in the Nineteenth-Century United States," *Journal of Social History* 23 (1989): 27-44; and H. Hartog, "Lawyering, Husbands' Rights, and the 'Unwritten Law' in Nineteenth-Century America," *Journal of*

American History 84 (1997): 67-96. See also R.M. Ireland, "The Thompson-Davis Case and the Unwritten Law," *Filson Club History Quarterly* 62 (1988): 417-41; "Death to the Libertine: The McFarland-Richardson Case Revisited," *New York History* 68 (1987): 191-217; "Frenzied and Fallen Females: Women and Sexual Dishonor in the Nineteenth-Century United States," *Journal of Women's History* 3 (1992): 95-117; and "Insanity and the Unwritten Law," *American Journal of Legal History* 32 (1988): 157-72; M.M. Umphrey, "The Dialogics of Legal Meaning: Spectacular Trials, the Unwritten Law, and Narratives of Criminal Responsibility," *Law and Society Review* 33 (1999): 393-422.

45 A defence lawyer in an 1868 case claimed he could cite twenty-eight previous trials invoking the unwritten law: Ireland, "The Libertine Must Die," 31.

46 Hartog, "Lawyering, Husbands' Rights, and the 'Unwritten Law,'" argues that the term should properly be understood as applying only to a husband who killed his wife's lover, having caught them in the act, and that acquittal was always the result in such cases. He sees it as effectively a part of the law. The killing of adulterers in other circumstances, and the killing of seducers, also often led to acquittals if juries were sympathetic, but those cases were not true instances of the operation of the unwritten law. Ireland, "The Libertine Must Die," includes all adultery and seduction cases under the rubric, and argues that most, though not all, appeals to the unwritten law were successful. The differences between the two are not important to us, largely because Mitchell's was a case of killing the alleged seducer and thus not covered by Hartog's apparently stricter rule. In addition, Hartog's study revolves principally around three cases where the adulterer was not caught in the act but where juries acquitted; he argues that they represented an extension of the unwritten law, but it seems to us better to see them as part of it.

47 Three states did make the killing of an adulterer if the murderer caught him in the act a justifiable homicide: Hartog, "Lawyering, Husbands' Rights, and the 'Unwritten Law,'" 67-68. The best-known was Texas, for which see P. Kens, "Don't Mess Around in Texas: Adultery and Justifiable Homicide in the Lone Star State," in *Law in the Western United States,* ed. G.M. Bakken (Norman, OK: University of Oklahoma Press, 2000).

48 *Telegram,* 28 June 1906.

49 *Star,* 12 May 1906.

50 For the arraignment see SC-KC Journals, vol. 218, 575, WSA- PS.

51 *Remington and Ballinger,* vol. 1, 1034. The statutory bail provision was actually a close paraphrase of Article 1, s. 20, of the state constitution, which also guaranteed bail except in capital cases "when the proof is evident or the presumption great."

52 See *PI,* 13 July 1901. Other cases cited by the defence, according to press reports, were those of Nellie Underwood, jointly charged with her husband, of William E. Langdon, and of McCann. We know nothing about the first two, but the third involved a circumstantial case against James and John McCann for killing one Joseph Cicero, in which much of the state's evidence concerned prior bad feelings and altercations between the deceased and the defendants: see *State* v. *McCann,* 16 *WLR* 249 (1896).

53 The following account of the bail hearing is from *Seattle Times,* 12 May 1906.

54 Ireland, "The Libertine Must Die," 31.

55 The *Telegram,* 15 May 1906, quotes Morris to similar effect: "I appeal to you as a Judge

and as a man. I ask you if the slaying of a human leper . . . is a deed to make this man a criminal, to make him a desperate murderer, a man too dangerous to be set at liberty in this community on bail. Can you call this boy . . . a criminal when he, a green country youth, has arisen in his manhood and taken the vengeance of nature upon the viper who has stolen the honor of his sisters."

56 *Star,* 12 May 1906.

57 *Seattle Times,* 13 May 1906; *Corvallis Times,* 15 May 1906.

58 *Seattle Times,* 19 May 1906; *PI,* 20 May 1906; Prosecuting Attorney's Criminal Docket, vol. 8, 211, Case No. 3652, KCA; SC-KC Journals, vol. 218, 575, WSA-PS. The set date notice is in SC-KC Case File 3652, WSA-PS.

59 See the short list of prosecution witness subpoenaed, in SC-KC Case File 3652, WSA-PS.

60 *Seattle Times,* 8 and 15 May 1906; *Corvallis Times,* 11 May 1906; *Star,* 10 and 14 May 1906.

61 See his comments that temporary insanity was the only plea that would give Mitchell "the slightest chance" of an acquittal, for it was the only way that "testimony [about Creffield] will be entered . . . that otherwise will be excluded": *PI,* 11 and 18 May 1906.

62 The subpoenas are in SC-KC Case File 3652, WSA-PS.

63 For Miller's trip see *Seattle Times,* 19 and 20 June, and 6 July 1906; *Telegram,* 1 and 23 June 1906; *Corvallis Gazette,* 22 June 1906; *Corvallis Times,* 13 and 17 July 1906; *PI,* 23 June 1906; *Herald,* 28 June 1906; *Star,* 19 June 1906.

64 *Star,* 22 June 1906.

65 *Seattle Times,* 15 May 1906.

66 For Morris' trip see *Corvallis Times,* 22 June 1906; *Telegram,* 1 June 1906; *Seattle Times,* 1 June 1906; *Albany Herald,* 28 June 1906. Hurt quickly returned to Corvallis and did not go back to Seattle until just before the trial began (*Corvallis Gazette,* 11 May and 26 June 1906), but he corresponded with the defence team regularly: see *Star,* 21 May 1906. Moser was in Seattle in the week ending Friday, May 18, supposedly for a convention, but he was also said to be "taking a deep interest in the case" and to have "spent some time" with Mitchell's lawyers on the 17th: *PI,* 18 May 1906.

67 The subpoenas were issued on June 19: see SC-KC Journals, vol. 233, 115-16, WSA-PS. Some newspapers carried the list: see *Seattle Times,* 19 June 1906, *Corvallis Times,* 22 June 1906, and *Corvallis Gazette,* 26 June 1906. The defence had the right to subpoena any witnesses it liked, the county was required to pay for the summonses, witness fees per day at a set rate, and travel expenses; the last, though, were only allowed from the point at which the Oregon witnesses entered Washington: see ibid., and *Remington and Ballinger,* vol. 1, 1037, and Witnesses Time Sheets and Witness Cost Bill, both in SC-KC Case File 3652, WSA-PS. Not all individuals' costs were met by the state, and money had also to be raised by Mitchell's supporters to cover them: see *Oregonian,* 26 June 1906.

68 For Fred Mitchell see *Telegram,* 19 May 1906; *Corvallis Times,* 22 May 1906; *Seattle Times,* 2 and 3 July 1906; *Newberg Graphic,* 23 January 1903; Pritchard, "Genealogical Record of the Mitchells."

69 *Seattle Times,* 25 June and 1 July 1906. The *Corvallis Times* was confident that she would "testify in favor of her brother": *Corvallis Times,* 26 June 1906.

70 This discussion of Charles Mitchell is from *Seattle Times,* 28 June and 15 July 1906; *Oregonian,* 29 June 1906; *Newberg Graphic,* 28 June 1906.

71 *Corvallis Times,* 22 May 1906. For Esther's attitudes and actions see also *Star,* 14 and
    15 May 1906; *Oregonian,* 20 May and 27 June 1906, and *Seattle Times,* 30 June 1906.
    Morris later told an insanity hearing for her that her only sympathetic comment
    about her brother to him was a hope that "he would not be killed until he had had
    time to get right with his creator": *PI,* 18 September 1906.

CHAPTER 8: JUSTIFIABLE HOMICIDE AND THE UNWRITTEN LAW

1 *Seattle Times,* 7 May 1906. The same story appeared in the *Oregonian,* 8 May 1906,
   and an essentially similar version was printed in the *PI,* 8 May 1906. The *Star,* which
   like the *Times* published on the evening of May 7, has a similar statement, suggesting
   that a *Star* reporter was there also.
2 *Seattle Times,* 24 June 1906.
3 Quotations from ibid., 8 May 1906, and *Telegram,* 9 May 1906. See also for similar
   statements and for Hurt's actions *Oregon Journal,* 8 May 1906; *PI,* 8 and 9 May 1906;
   Star, 9 May 1906; *Telegram,* 8 May 1906.
4 *Telegram,* 9 May 1906.
5 *PI,* 8 May 1906. In addition to being mayor in 1906 Johnson was one of the city's most
   substantial residents, a former state senator and sometime farmer, merchant, stock
   raiser, and founder of Corvallis' first national bank. From 1900 to 1906 he was national
   bank inspector for the northwest district, which included Oregon, Washington,
   Montana, and Idaho, and it was in connection with this job that he was in Seattle.
   For Johnson see Gaston, *Centennial History of Oregon,* vol. 4, 845-47. For other comments on the popularity of the killing in Corvallis see *Oregon Journal,* 8 May 1906.
6 *Telegram,* 7 May 1906.
7 *PI,* 10 May 1906; *Seattle Times,* 10 May 1906. The letter was also published in the
   Oregonian, 10 May 1906, and *Telegram,* 9 May 1906.
8 *Oregonian,* 3 December 1903. Manning was responsible for closing the Multnomah
   County saloons on Sundays and had the distinction of being the only Oregon district
   attorney to have successfully prosecuted a bank president when he did so following the failure of the Title Guarantee & Trust Company. This apparently cost him re-
   election in 1906: see Gaston, *Portland,* vol. 3, 476-77.
9 For expressions of approval see *Corvallis Gazette,* 8 May and 26 June 1906; *Oregonian,*
   8 and 9 May 1906; *Times,* 8 May 1906; *Albany Herald,* 10 and 17 May 1906; *Telegram,*
   8 and 9 May 1906; *Oregon Journal,* 11 May 1906; *Albany Democrat,* 11 and 18 May
   1906; and *Eugene Register,* 8 May 1906. The *Corvallis Times* was circumspect, though
   not about Creffield, and finally came out in full support of Mitchell once the trial
   began: see *Corvallis Times,* 8, 15, 18, and 22 May, 22 June, and 3 and 10 July 1906. For
   two letters disapproving of Mitchell see *Oregon Journal,* 17 and 21 May 1906.
10 The defence fund was organized by the *Corvallis Gazette,* and calls for subscriptions
   were printed in other newspapers: *Corvallis Gazette,* 11, 15, 18, 22, and 29 May, and 5
   and 15 June 1906; *Oregonian,* 8 May 1906; *PI,* 8 May 1906; *Corvallis Times,* 11 May and
   26 June 1906; *Albany Herald,* 17 and 24 May 1906; *The Dalles Weekly Chronicle,* 18
   May 1906. Louis Hartley played a large role here, travelling to other towns to solicit
   funds for the defence. He had some success: "Quite a number of Eugene people have
   subscribed to the fund, Councilman W.G. Calkins heading the list with $5," reported

the *Oregon Journal,* 15 May 1906. William Gardner was among the Portlanders who contributed: *Telegram,* 24 May 1906, O.V. Hurt to Gardner, 16 May 1906, Case File 2430, and Gardner to O.V. Hurt, 18 May 1906, Letter Books, BGAS Records. For the medal, which was probably newspaper invention and was later denied by O.V. Hurt, see *Seattle Times,* 8 May 1906, and *Telegram,* 8 and 9 May 1906.

11 *Telegram,* 9 May 1906.

12 *Seattle Times,* 11 May 1906, and *Corvallis Times,* 11 May 1906.

13 *Telegram,* 11 May 1906.

14 *PI,* 10 May 1906. Another newspaper quoted him as calling the letter "ridiculous." Mackintosh may also have believed at this time that Mitchell was a hired assassin: *Oregon Journal,* 10 May 1906.

15 *PI,* 11 May 1906. See also *Star,* 10 May 1906.

16 *Seattle Times,* 8 May 1906.

17 See the sources cited in Chapter 3, especially Brown, *Strain of Violence,* ch. 6. See also D. Johnson, "Vigilance and the Law: The Moral Authority of Popular Justice in the Far West," *American Quarterly* 33 (1981): 558-86. We use the term vigilantism here to mean an action of coercion using violence or its threat, in which the perpetrator or perpetrators justify the use of force by reference to law, be it state law or some higher law. Brown, *Strain of Violence,* would limit the term to the phenomenon of organized extra-legal groups on the "frontier," but most other writers on the subject do not, explicitly or implicitly, adopt such a narrow definition. For effective critiques of Brown and a sense of the varieties of vigilantism see Gordon, *Great Arizona Orphan Abduction,* ch. 7; H.J. Rosenbaum and P.C. Sederberg, "Vigilantism: An Analysis of Establishment Violence," in *Vigilante Politics,* ed. Rosenbaum and Sederberg (Philadelphia: University of Pennsylvania Press, 1976); and D. Grimstead, "Making Violence Relevant," *Reviews in American History* 4 (1976): 331-38.

18 Editorial in *Olympia Courier,* 1882, cited in J.R. Warren, "An Explosion of Savagery," *Portage* 9 (1988): 29.

19 For such justifications for Washington lynchings see especially M. Pfeifer, "Midnight Justice: Lynching and Law in the Pacific Northwest," *Pacific Northwest Quarterly* forthcoming, 2003, and "'Midnight Justice' in the Pacific Northwest: Lynching and Law in Washington, Oregon and Idaho, 1882-1919," unpublished paper available at <http://academic.evergreen.edu/users5/pfeifer/PacficiNorthwestLynching>.

20 For the biblical basis of the doctrine see Hartog, "Lawyering, Husbands' Rights, and the 'Unwritten Law,'" 87-88.

21 See T.J. Kernan, "The Jurisprudence of Lawlessness," *American Bar Association, Report of the Annual Meeting* (Philadelphia: American Bar Association, 1906), 451-52. For the apparent decline of the defence see Ireland, "The Libertine Must Die," 37-38. The defence was employed, and the phrase "unwritten law" used to describe it, in the Thaw trial in New York, also in 1906: see Umphrey, "The Dialogics of Legal Meaning."

22 For extended discussions of women as unwritten law defendants, and of feminists' reactions to those cases, see Ireland, "Frenzied and Fallen Females," and G.M. Bakken, "The Limits of Patriarchy: Women's Rights and 'Unwritten Law' in the West," *Historian* 60 (1998): 703-16. For two Canadian cases in which women were acquitted by juries who believed they were defending their sexual honour see C. Strange, "Wounded Womanhood and Dead Men: Chivalry and the Trials of Clara Ford and Carrie

Davis," in *Gender Conflicts: New Essays in Women's History,* ed. F. Iacovetta and M. Valverde (Toronto: University of Toronto Press, 1992).

23 There is now an extensive literature on ideas about masculinity in the nineteenth and early twentieth centuries, which we cannot deal with extensively here. The following brief summary relies principally on G. Bederman, "Civilization, the Decline of Middle-Class Manliness, and Ida B. Wells' Antilynching Campaign, 1892-1894," *Radical History Review* 52 (1992): 5-30, and *Manliness and Civilization: A Cultural History of Gender and Race in the United States, 1880-1917* (Chicago: University of Chicago Press, 1995); E.A. Rotundo, "Learning About Manhood: Gender Ideals and the Middle-Class Family in Nineteenth-Century America," in *Manliness and Morality: Middle-Class Masculinity in Britain and America, 1800-1940,* ed. J.A. Mangam and J. Walvin (New York: St. Martin's Press, 1987), and *American Manhood: Transformations in Masculinity from the Revolution to the Modern Era* (New York: Basic Books, 1993); M. Kimmel, *Manhood in America: A Cultural History* (New York: Free Press, 1966).

24 The phrase is from Bederman, *Manliness and Civilization,* 225.

25 The reasons often ascribed for the "crisis" in ideas of manhood in the period include the rise of large corporate bureaucracies, which undermined the Victorian valorization of self-employment and economic independence; the development of a culture of leisure and consumption, which undermined the ethic of self-restraint and thrift; and the rise of the women's movement. Concerns about the decline of the white race and "civilization" also played a role, although they were both a cause of the resort to a new emphasis on physicality and aggression and a defensive strategy to remake the white masculine ideal. For all this see especially Bederman, *Manliness and Civilization.*

26 See the examples in *Seattle Times,* 12, 13, and 15 May 1906.

27 Ibid., 8, 12, 15, 16, and 19 May 1906.

28 Ibid., 11 and 12 May 1906.

29 Ibid., 12 and 15 May 1906.

30 Ibid., 13 May 1906.

31 Ibid., 12 May 1906.

32 Ibid., 15 May 1906. We suggest it was a plant because it was described as written by "A young married woman whose parents' home was broken up by the teachings of . . . Creffield." The only married couples who fit such a description were O.V. and Sarah Hurt, Cora and Louis Hartley, and Donna and Burgess Starr, and the only married daughter among those families was Maud Hurt Creffield. The circumstances described in the letter best fit the Hartley family, but to the best of our knowledge they did not have a married daughter.

33 Ireland, "The Libertine Must Die," 32.

34 Ibid., 29.

35 For an excellent study of the ways in which this occurred in a number of societies see A. McLaren, *The Trials of Masculinity: Policing Sexual Boundaries, 1870-1930* (Chicago: University of Chicago Press, 1997).

36 *Seattle Times,* 13 May 1906.

37 Ibid., 14 May 1906.

38 Ibid., 1 June 1906; the rest of this paragraph is from this source.

39 This discussion of Blethen is based largely on Boswell and McConaghy, *Raise Hell and Sell Newspapers,* quotations at 91 and 121.

40 For Brainerd see R.C. Berner, "The Brainerd Papers, 1880-1919," in Brainerd Papers, Acc. No. 4624-1, UWL.

41 Blethen claimed in 1905 that his circulation exceeded that of the *Post-Intelligencer* by one-third: Boswell and McConaghy, *Raise Hell and Sell Newspapers,* ch. 5.

42 In addition to the quotations below see also the description of him in the *Seattle Times* issue of 7 May 1906.

43 Ibid., 12, 13, and 15 May 1906.

44 Ibid., 12 May 1906.

45 For the links between the unwritten law and class see Ireland, "The Libertine Must Die," 36-37.

46 *Republican,* 11 May 1906. For Cayton see Q. Taylor, *The Forging of a Black Community: Seattle's Central District from 1870 Through the Civil Rights Era* (Seattle: University of Washington Press, 1994), 19-20 and passim; R.S. Hobbs, *The Cayton Legacy: An African American Family* (Pullman, WA: Washington State University Press, 2002); and E. Diaz, "Horace Roscoe Cayton and the Meredith Scandal," paper presented to the Pacific Northwest History Conference, Seattle, 2002.

47 *Republican,* 18 May 1906.

48 *Star,* 11 May 1906. Other quotations are from the issues of 7 and 19 May. See also the headline of its account of the Creffield sect, "Revolting Creed of Holy Rollers": ibid., 7 May 1906.

49 Ibid., 9 May 1906. The same column noted the irony of Frater, "the judge who applauded Beede," possibly having "to pronounce the death sentence" for Mitchell. A week later the *Star* repeated the theme, through a story about a man called Marshall who was charged with assault and battery for beating up another who was interfering with his wife. He had been discharged by Judge Gordon: "In line with previous decisions already given in this city touching the rights of a man to defend the honor of his home and the prospective attitude that will be taken in connection with the case against George Mitchell, the decision in the Marshall case is interesting": ibid., 16 May 1906.

50 The *Star* was a Scripps paper. E.W. Scripps started the first national newspaper chain in the late nineteenth and early twentieth centuries, his papers being like regular dailies rather than specialized "labour" outlets, but nonetheless concerned with working-class issues. The *Star,* started by Scripps in 1899, sold for one cent and had sister northwest papers in the Spokane *Press,* the Portland *Daily News,* and the Tacoma *Times.* See G.J. Baldasty, "Newspapers for the 'Wage-Earning Class': E.W. Scripps and the Pacific Northwest," *Pacific Northwest Quarterly* 90 (1999): 171-81; and Boswell and McConaghy, *Raise Hell and Sell Newspapers,* 7.

51 *PI,* 20 May 1906. For Paulhamus see W.T. Kerr, "The Progressives of Washington, 1910-1912," *Pacific Northwest Quarterly* 55 (1964): 16-27.

52 *Oregonian,* 11 May 1906.

53 *Seattle Times,* 13 July 1906.

54 *Corvallis Times,* 15 May 1906. The most prominent prior case was the David Van Houten trial in Portland in 1903-1904: see *Oregonian,* 29, 30, and 31 January 1904.

55 For example, when Creffield did not rise from the dead after four days, it commented: "The dupes of the late Mr. Creffield will have to wait more than the four days allotted before they see their Joshua rise from the dead": *PI,* 12 May 1906.

56 Ibid., 9 May 1906.

57 Chadwick was a reform Republican, and his paper regularly attacked ex-senator John L. Wilson, the owner of the *Post-Intelligencer,* for being tied to railroad interests. Chadwick supported municipal ownership, the anti-saloon lobby, and "responsible" trade unionism, although he was a fierce opponent of one plank in the reform movement, female suffrage. See Berner, *Seattle 1900-1920,* 6-7.

58 Quotations from *Argus,* 12 May 1906. See also the issue of 19 May 1906.

59 Quotations from *Mail and Herald,* 12 and 19 May, and 30 June 1906.

60 Quoted in *Oregonian,* 14 July 1906.

61 See generally Brown, *Strain of Violence,* 318. For the 1882 committee see Warren, "An Explosion of Savagery." For an eastern Washington organization see H. Stevens, *Vigilantes Ride in 1882* (Fairfield, WA: Ye Galleon Press, 1975).

62 See Pfeiffer, "Midnight Justice." See also J.F. Hankins, "Whitman County Grit: Palouse Vigilantes and the Press," *Columbia* 6, 1 (Spring 1992): 20-26 – lynchings in Whitman County in 1882, 1884, and 1894; H.D. Baumgart, "Ellensburg's Tree of Justice," *Columbia* 15, 4 (Winter 2001-2002): 7-15 – lynching in Ellensburg, 1895; K.D. Richards, "Regulars and Militia: Washington's Post-Frontier Military," *Columbia* 9, 1 (Spring 1995): 8 – 1891 shooting in Walla Walla; and *Corvallis Times,* 8 August 1903 – a Spokane lynching of a man who had sexually assaulted and killed a young girl.

63 See LeWarne, *Utopias on Puget Sound,* 177-78.

64 *Seattle Times,* 14 November 1906; see also the issues of 11 and 12 November 1906.

65 See variously *Argus,* 19 May 1906; *Mail and Herald,* 30 June 1906; *Patriarch,* 19 and 26 May 1906.

66 *Oregon Journal,* 11 May 1906. See also ibid., 13 May 1906, and *Seattle Times,* 11 May 1906.

67 *Mail and Herald,* 19 May 1906.

68 *Oregon Journal,* 13 May 1906.

69 Mark Matthews Papers, Acc. No. 97-3, Sermon, 9 December 1906, Box 8, UWL; Soden, *The Reverend Mark Matthews,* esp. 57-58, and ch. 6-7.

70 For both the debates over race and civilization, and their link to emerging notions of masculinity, see Bederman, *Manliness and Civilization.*

71 *PI,* 20 May 1906; *Seattle Times,* 19 May 1906.

72 For the former see Clarence Bagley to Edward Huggins, 16 May 1906, Bagley Papers, Acc. No. 36-1, Box 4, folder 4-8, UWL. For the latter see the discussion below.

73 *Seattle Times,* 16 May 1906.

74 Ibid., 11 May 1906.

75 Ross Parker to Erastus Brainerd, 14 July 1906, and Milo Root to Same, 9 July 1906, Brainerd Papers, Acc. No. 4624-1, Box 4, folders 4-20 and 4-26, UWL.

76 *Oregonian,* 27 June 1906.

77 *Seattle Times,* 16 May 1906. For Shorrock see the *Seattle City Directory,* 1906, and *Star,* 16 May 1906.

78 Of the firm of McGraw, Kittinger and Case, which dealt in real estate and fire insurance, McGraw was president of the chamber of commerce for several years: see C. Hanford, *Seattle and Environs, 1852-1924,* 3 vols. (Chicago: Pioneer Historical Publishing, 1924), vol. 2, 271. For his role in the anti-Asian riots of the mid-1880s see C. Schwantes, "Protest in a Promised Land: Unemployment, Disinheritance, and the Origins of Labor Militancy in the Pacific Northwest, 1885-1886," *Western Historical Quarterly* 13 (1982): 384-85.

79 *Patriarch,* 19 May 1906.
80 *Seattle Times,* 13 May 1906.
81 For the supposed views of police and jailers see ibid., 7 May 1906; *Corvallis Gazette,* 11 May 1906; *PI,* 13 July 1906. For statements of widespread support see *Seattle Times,* 15 May 1906; *Oregon Journal,* 10 and 13 May 1906; *Corvallis Times,* 15 May 1906.
82 *Argus,* 14 July 1906. See also to the same effect *Patriarch,* 19 May 1906.
83 *Corvallis Times,* 10 July 1906.
84 *Seattle Times,* 15 May 1906.
85 The historiography of women in Seattle is not as well developed as it might be, but a sense of women's public involvement can be garnered from, *inter alia,* K.J. Blair, "The Limits of Sisterhood: The Woman's Building in Seattle, 1908-1921," and S.H. Armitage, "The Challenge of Women's History," both in Blair, ed., *Women in Pacific Northwest History,* and S.H. Armitage, "Women in Pacific Northwest History," in the second, 2001, revised edition of the same book. For clubs see especially K.J. Blair, *The Club Woman as Feminist: True Womanhood Redefined, 1868-1914* (New York: Holmes and Meier, 1980) and "The Seattle Ladies' Musical Club, 1890-1930," in *Experiences in the Promised Land: Essays in Pacific Northwest History,* ed. C. Schwantes and T.G. Edwards (Seattle: University of Washington Press, 1986); and Haarsager, *Organized Womanhood.* For other aspects of the history of women in the state see N. Clark, *The Dry Years: Prohibition and Social Change in Washington* (Seattle: University of Washington Press, 1988); M.T. Andrews, *Washington Women as Path Breakers* (Dubuque: Kendall/ Hunt, 1989); K. Oberdeck, "Not Pink Teas: The Seattle Working-Class Women's Movement, 1905-1918," *Labor History* 32 (1991): 193-230; T.A. Larson, "The Woman Suffrage Movement in Washington," *Pacific Northwest Quarterly* 67 (1976): 49-62.
86 We searched the women's pages of the *Union Record,* the newspaper of the Washington State Federation of Labor, and the minutes of the Washington State Federation of Women's Clubs, Acc. No. 3463, Box 4, UWL, without success.
87 For brief discussions of women's attitude to the unwritten law, see Ireland, "The Libertine Must Die," 37, and Hartog, "Lawyering, Husbands' Rights, and the 'Unwritten Law,'" 79.
88 For the relatively "unchurched" nature of Washington's population see D.M. Buerge and J. Rochester, *Roots and Branches: The Religious Heritage of Washington State* (Seattle: Church Council of Greater Seattle, 1988), 158-59, and Soden, *The Reverend Mark Matthews,* 43. For the few radical religious movements and communes that did exist see LeWarne, *Utopias on Puget Sound,* 11-12. The holiness movement seems to have had little impact on Seattle before 1906, although the Holiness Pentecostal group of Robert Gourley became notorious in late 1906: see *Seattle Times,* 17 October 1906, and *Oregonian,* 16 November 1906.

CHAPTER 9: THE TRIAL OF GEORGE MITCHELL, PART 1

1 Cases of Thomas Taylor, K. Nakayama, and Robert Jones, Prosecuting Attorney's Criminal Docket, vol. 8, 189, 194, and 199, KCA.
2 Compare Mitchell's case with two others in Seattle in 1906. Robert Jones' trial for first-degree murder and Julius Marfaudille's for second-degree murder each lasted a total of four days: Prosecuting Attorney's Criminal Docket, vol. 8, 149 and 266, KCA.

3 *Remington and Ballinger,* vol. 1, 1229.

4 C. Rosenberg, *The Trial of the Assassin Guiteau: Psychiatry and Law in the Gilded Age* (Chicago: University of Chicago Press, 1968), 253.

5 The observations made in this paragraph have been made in many other case studies. See, *inter alia,* Herrup, *A House in Gross Disorder,* esp. at xiv; Grossberg, *A Judgement for Solomon,* esp. at 228-29; P. Gerwitz, "Narrative and Rhetoric in Law," in *Law's Stories,* ed. Brooks and Gerwitz; and Umphrey, "The Dialogics of Legal Meaning."

6 C. Strange, "Murder and Meanings in US Historiography," *Feminist Studies* 25 (1999): 683.

7 The courthouse was opened in 1891 after its predecessor was destroyed in the great fire of 1889. It was situated between Seventh and Eight Avenues, at the top of one of Seattle's steepest hills. The nickname came from the oaths attorneys were supposed to have uttered as they slogged up the hill to get to work: see M. Lampson, *From Profanity Hill: King County Bar Association's Story* (Kirkland, WA: Documentary Book Publishers, 1993), 34.

8 *Star,* 25 June 1906. The jury selection stage of the trial was extensively reported in the *Seattle Times, Seattle Post-Intelligencer, Seattle Star,* and the Portland newspapers – the *Oregonian, Telegram,* and *Oregon Journal.* There were also reports, often reproductions of other newspapers' stories, in the *Corvallis Gazette,* the *Corvallis Times,* and the *Albany Weekly Herald.* The account that follows is a composite one based on all these reports. We provide notes only for quotations and where specific information about a juror is given. Jury selection is also briefly noted in SC-KC Journals, vol. 233, 131, 133, and 135-36, WSA-PS.

9 Most of the Oregon residents subpoenaed were not yet in Seattle, however. They would not travel until it became clear "just what testimony would be admitted" and when, for the defence did not want the expense of having almost thirty witnesses waiting around for days or weeks: *Oregonian,* 26 June 1906. They would "come whenever summoned by telegraph": *PI,* 23 June 1906.

10 *Seattle Times,* 25 June 1906.

11 *Seattle Times,* 26 June 1906. The incident was also reported in *Oregonian,* 27 June 1906, and *Oregon Journal,* 26 June 1906.

12 *Seattle Times,* 25 June 1906. The rest of this paragraph is from this source.

13 For example, with jury selection over, the *Seattle Times* stated that the trial was about whether Mitchell was a murderer or a follower of the "unwritten code of human law" that states that "a wrong committed against the women folk of a household is punishable by death at the hands of the ablest male relative." Mitchell had been "thrust into the position of the male protector of his sisters," and, in that role, had "done his duty as he saw it": ibid., 28 June 1906.

14 *Republican,* 29 June 1906.

15 *Seattle Times,* 26 June 1906.

16 For Washington law on the choosing of the array see *Pierce's Code,* 1026-31.

17 Note that women were excluded twice, first by the suffrage requirement and then again by the "male inhabitant" criterion.

18 Daniel Myers or Meyer, "a negro," was examined on June 25 and excused because he thought Mitchell was justified: *PI,* 26 June 1906; *Seattle Times,* 26 June 1906. Myers had been allowed to serve on three juries the previous week: see SC-KC Journals, vol. 233, 105, 120, and 124, WSA-PS. George Bill, a miner from Cedar Mountain, was a

"quarterbreed Indian": *Seattle Times,* 26 June 1906. As discussed below, he was passed initially and then removed by agreement of both sides.

19 See SC-KC Jury Journals, vol. 235, 14-17 and 18-20, and Journals, vol. 233, 105 et seq, WSA-PS. Another 100 men had been drawn to serve in three other departments in May; as we shall see, some of these men ended up on Mitchell's jury.

20 For these exemptions see *Pierce's Code,* 1026-27.

21 *Remington and Ballinger,* vol. 1, 1049.

22 Newspaper reports contain mentions of fifty-nine, but there may have been more.

23 According to the *Seattle Times,* thirty-three of the sixty in the special panel made excuses or were found to be unqualified: *Seattle Times,* 28 June 1906. A few had excuses such as illness in the family; one George Chute was excused because his brother was about to die: *Times,* 25 June 1906. Of those found to be unqualified, one was not a citizen and another one not a freeholder or householder: see *Seattle Times,* 26 June 1906, and *PI,* 27 June 1906.

24 For this see SC-KC Jury Journals, vol. 235, 22-23, WSA-PS.

25 *Seattle Times,* 28 June 1906.

26 *Remington and Ballinger,* vol. 1, 1050. This summary of the statutory law is drawn from this source, 1049-50, and from *Pierce's Code,* 115-16.

27 See the fact that all the reported Washington cases on actual bias, some of which are discussed below, concerned pre-trial opinions about guilt or innocence.

28 For these points see *State* v. *Rutten,* 13 *WLR* 203 (1896), and *State* v. *Blanton,* 1 *WLR* 265 (1890).

29 *State* v. *Riley,* 36 *WLR* 441 at 448 (1904). The first case to lay down this rule after statehood was *State* v. *Rose,* 2 *WLR* 310 (1891), and it was followed also in, *inter alia, State* v. *Coella,* 3 *WLR* 99 (1891), *State* v. *Murphy,* 9 *WLR* 204 (1894), *State* v. *Wilcox,* 11 *WLR* 215 (1895), and *State* v. *Lattin,* 19 *WLR* 57 (1898). There was a further statutory provision directly on the issue of pre-formed opinion. The civil procedure rule defining actual bias cited above went on to provide that, even if a juror "has formed or expressed an opinion upon what he may have heard or read," that opinion in itself did not disqualify; "the court must be satisfied from all the circumstances, that the juror cannot disregard such opinion and try the issue impartially": *Pierce's Code,* 116. This seems to set up a laxer standard than that laid down by the supreme court, but we conclude that it was not considered applicable to criminal cases. None of the seventeen supreme court cases from 1891 on mentions this provision, and although we have no direct evidence for this belief, it seems likely that the qualifying phrase in the rule for criminal challenges, that the "causes of challenge prescribed for civil cases" be used "as far as they may be applicable," was seen as sufficient to ignore the lower standard statutorily prescribed for civil cases.

30 For cases in which the court held that the juror had only an "impression" that would not affect his ability to accord the defendant the presumption of innocence and decide the case entirely on the evidence see *State* v. *Croney,* 31 *WLR* 122 (1902), *State* v. *Gile,* 8 *WLR* 12 (1894), and *State* v. *Carey,* 15 *WLR* 549 (1896).

31 *Seattle Times,* 25 June 1906.

32 *Star,* 25 June 1906.

33 *Seattle Times,* 27 June 1906. See also a similar comment in *Telegram,* 27 June 1906.

34 Quotations in this paragraph from *Oregonian,* 26 June 1906; *Star,* 25 and 26 June 1906; *PI,* 26 June 1906.

35 *Seattle Times,* 26 June 1906; *PI,* 27 June 1906.

36 *Star,* 26 June 1906.

37 *Seattle Times,* 26 and 27 June 1906; *Oregonian,* 26 June 1906; *Telegram,* 27 June 1906.

38 *Oregonian,* 27 June 1906.

39 Ibid., 28 June 1906.

40 *PI,* 28 June 1906; *Corvallis Times,* 29 June 1906. This was perhaps a typical example of such questioning by the defence: "If it is shown in the course of this trial that the deceased Creffield exercised such an influence upon certain women . . . that they submitted themselves to the gratification of his beastly lust": *Star,* 27 June 1906.

41 The *Oregonian,* 28 June 1906, stated that Frater's lecture did have the effect of shortening the examinations, but the *Seattle Times,* 27 June 1906, insisted that the questioning continued in the same vein. Our conclusion is based on the fact that only ten men were examined on the 27th, and that in the afternoon of June 27, after this lecture from Frater, Mackintosh took an hour with one man: *PI,* 28 June 1906.

42 See, *inter alia,* the cases of L.M. Bechtel of Houghton and James Cass, a farmer from Maple Valley: *PI,* 26 and 27 June 1906.

43 This was George Bill, a "quarterbreed Siwash," who was passed on June 26. The first order of business on the 27th was his removal by agreement of both sides. The joint stipulation to this effect is in SC-KC, Case File 3652, WSA-PS. The *Times* said that it was "feared that his understanding of the English language was scarcely broad enough to comprehend the ponderous diction of legal practices" (*Seattle Times,* 27 June 1906), but the *Oregonian* noted, more correctly, that while neither side "had a specific objection to him," he was "not regarded as a satisfactory juror," being "of Indian descent": *Oregonian,* 28 June 1906. For his service on two trials for larceny and burglary see SC-KC Journals, vol. 233, 107 and 124, WSA-PS.

44 *Star,* 26 June 1906.

45 *PI,* 26 June 1906.

46 Ibid., 27 June 1906.

47 But see the somewhat inconsistent summaries in *Corvallis Times,* 29 June 1906, and *Oregonian,* 27 June 1906.

48 *Oregon Journal,* 26 June 1906.

49 *Oregonian,* 27 June 1906. For Swanson's examination see *Seattle Times,* 25 June 1906, and *Oregonian,* 26 June 1906.

50 *Oregonian,* 28 June 1906.

51 *PI,* 27 June 1906.

52 *Seattle Times,* 27 June 1906; *PI,* 27 June 1906.

53 Quotations from *Seattle Times,* 27 June 1906; see also *PI,* 28 June 1906. Re Evans, note the *Star*'s suggestion that the defence was keen to retain "men who have families of their own, preferably grown and married daughters": *Star,* 26 June 1906.

54 *Oregonian,* 29 June 1906.

55 These references to the jurors are variously from *Seattle Times,* 26-29 June 1906, and 11 July 1906; *PI,* 26, 27, and 29 June 1906; *Oregonian,* 28 June 1906. Information derived from the newspapers has been supplemented by the references to eight of them in the *Seattle City Directory,* 1906, and by tax assessment information for 1904, 1905, and 1909 in WSA-PS.

56 Many professionals were in any event exempted, including lawyers, clergymen, and doctors: see *Pierce's Code,* 1026.

57 Personal Property Assessment Rolls, 1909, Country, vol. 4, 162, and Seattle, vol. 2, 201, WSA-PS.
58 In 1904 he was assessed as having personal property worth $1,020. Of the fifty-one people listed on the same page in the tax rolls, only four were assessed for more than him, and over forty were assessed at $500 or less: Personal Property Assessment Rolls, 1904, Seattle, vol. 1-A, 45, WSA-PS.
59 See the jury lists in SC-KC Jury Journals, vol. 235, 13-20, WSA-PS.
60 For comments by all the lawyers to this effect see *PI*, 29 June 1906, and *Oregonian*, 29 June 1906. These two papers, in their issues of 30 June 1906, as well as the *Seattle Times*, on 29 and 30 June, the *Star*, 30 June 1906, and *Telegram*, 29 June 1906, carried reports on the proceedings, and what follows is drawn variously from these sources. Only quotations and some particular points are footnoted specifically. See also *Oregon Journal*, 30 June 1906, and the brief minutes of proceedings in SC-KC Journals, vol. 233, 137, WSA-PS.
61 The *Post-Intelligencer*, 30 June 1906, reported "hundreds of men and women" in the hall, and while this was surely an exaggeration, there were obviously a large number of disappointed people unable to get a seat.
62 *Seattle Times*, 29 June 1906.
63 For Bories see Chapter 6. Carroll was from Louisiana and earned his medical degree in San Francisco. A republican, he was city physician and health officer from 1899 to 1903, King County coroner from 1904 to 1908, and in January 1906 elected treasurer of the King County Medical Society: see L. Spencer and L. Pollard, *A History of the State of Washington*, 4 vols. (New York: American Historical Society, 1937), vol. 4, 488-89; C.B. Bagley, *History of King County, Washington*, 3 vols. (Chicago: S.J. Clarke, 1929), vol. 2, 282-84; *Seattle Mail and Herald*, 20 February and 5 November 1904; *Republican*, 11 August 1905; *PI*, 9 January 1906.
64 Quotations from *Seattle Times*, 29 June 1906.
65 Quotations from ibid., 30 June 1906, and *PI*, 30 June 1906.
66 Quotations from *PI*, 30 June 1906.
67 *Seattle Times*, 30 June 1906.
68 Ibid., 13 July 1906.
69 Ibid., 29 June 1906.
70 Ibid., 2 July 1906.
71 *PI*, 29 June 1906.
72 *Seattle Mail and Herald*, 30 June 1906.

CHAPTER 10: THE TRIAL OF GEORGE MITCHELL, PART 2

1 The chronology of the defence case can be followed in SC-KC Journals, vol. 233, 142, 143, 145-47, and 149, WSA-PS. The account that follows is taken from the various Seattle and Oregon newspapers already cited; again, only quotations have been specifically footnoted.
2 Obviously those thirty included most of those to whom subpoenas had been issued. It did not include six of them, however – Phoebe Vanderkellen, Milt Beer, William MacMillan, Mae Hurt, A.J. Johnson, and Fred Mitchell. And six witnesses testified

who were not on the list of those subpoenaed: Esther Mitchell, Perry Mitchell, and Doctors Crookall, Witherspoon, Miles, and Wright.

3 *Seattle Times,* 1 July 1906.

4 *Star,* 30 June 1906.

5 Ibid., 14 July 1906.

6 Ireland, "The Libertine Must Die," 31 and 32.

7 *Telegram,* 1 June 1906.

8 *McNaughtan's Case,* [1843] 8 *English Reports* 718; R. Moran, *Knowing Right from Wrong: The Insanity Defence of Daniel M'Naghten* (New York: Free Press, 1981). For the use of the *McNaughtan* standard in Washington see *State* v. *Strasburg,* 60 *WLR* 106 (1910); *State* v. *Hawkins,* 23 *WLR* 289 (1900); and *State* v. *Craig,* 52 *WLR* 66 (1909). See also generally D.F. Ross, "The Spirit of M'Naghten," *Gonzaga Law Review* 9 (1974): 806-15. Judge Frater's instructions to the jury in the Mitchell case, discussed below, also make it clear that Washington law was essentially *McNaughtan.* The only statutory provision in force dealing with insanity did not alter the test and is discussed in the final section of this chapter. The literature on the insanity defence is extensive, although there is no history of it for Washington state. The following summary is drawn principally from Rosenberg, *Trial of the Assassin Guiteau;* D.A. Robinson, *Wild Beasts and Evil Humors: The Insanity Defence from Antiquity to the Present* (Cambridge: Harvard University Press, 1996); T. Maeder, *Crime and Madness: The Origins and Evolution of the Insanity Defence* (New York: Harper and Row, 1985); R. Smith, *Trial By Medicine: Insanity and Responsibility in Victorian Trials* (Edinburgh: Edinburgh University Press, 1981); N. Walker, *Crime and Insanity in England: The Historical Perspective* (Edinburgh: Edinburgh University Press, 1968); J. Mohr, *Doctors and the Law: Medical Jurisprudence in Nineteenth-Century America* (New York: Oxford University Press, 1993); H. Weihofen, *Insanity as a Defence in Criminal Law* (New York: Oxford University Press, 1933); Ireland, "Insanity and the Unwritten Law"; and H. Hovenkamp, "Insanity and Criminal Responsibility in Progressive America," *North Dakota Law Review* 57 (1981): 541-75. Also very useful for the law as of c. 1906 is J.H. Lloyd, "Insanity: Forms and Medico-Legal Relations," in *Wharton and Stille's Medical Jurisprudence.* For analyses of the adoption of the *McNaughtan* rules in the United States see A. Platt and B. Diamond, "The Origins of the 'Right and Wrong' Test of Criminal Responsibility and Its Subsequent Development in the United States: An Historical Survey," *California Law Review* 54 (1966): 1227-60; Weihofen, *Insanity as a Defence,* passim; A. Morris, "Criminal Insanity," *Washington Law Review* 43 (1968): esp. at 594-95.

9 See generally Lloyd, "Insanity," 183-85. For a Washington case on this see *State* v. *Craig,* 52 *WLR* 66 (1909), at 69: "A person may be partially insane on all subjects, and yet be criminally responsible if he have sufficient capacity to distinguish right from wrong with reference to the crime committed. On the other hand, he may be mentally sound upon almost all subjects, with power of rational thought and capacity to meet the ordinary affairs of life; and yet upon some one or a particular group of subjects manifest a mental excitement, either of desire or aversion, that makes him wholly irresponsible within the limit of his aberration."

10 For Washington cases on the points discussed in this paragraph see *McAllister* v. *Washington Territory,* 1 *Washington Territory Reports* 360 (1881); *State* v. *Craig,* 52 *WLR* 66

(1909); and *State* v. *Clark,* 34 *WLR* 485 (1904). See also the discussion of Frater's instructions to the jury, below.

11 For these points see generally F. Wharton, *A Treatise of the Law of Evidence in Criminal Cases,* 9th ed. (Philadelphia: Kay and Brother, 1884), 348-49, and *Wharton and Stille's Medical Jurisprudence,* 392-93. For Washington law see *State* v. *Brooks,* 4 *WLR* 328 (1892); *State* v. *Bridgham,* 51 *WLR* 18 (1908); *State* v. *Craig,* 52 *WLR* 66 (1909); *State* v. *Constantine,* 48 *WLR* 219 (1908).

12 These controversies are well canvassed in the sources already cited. For an overview, and for attempts at medico-legal cooperation to reduce controversy, see J. Tighe, "Reforming the Insanity Defence in the Progressive Era," *Bulletin of the History of Medicine* 57 (1983): 397-411.

13 Lloyd, "Insanity," 192, and J.P. Bishop, *Commentaries on the Criminal Law,* 7th ed., 2 vols. (Boston: Little, Brown, 1882), 254-55. For acceptance of this principle in Washington see one of Frater's instructions to the jury, which included the statement that a person was not criminally responsible if his mind was "dominated by an insane delusion impelling his act": Defence Request for Jury Instructions, SC-KC, Case File 3652, WSA-PS.

14 See the excellent discussion of this, from which this paragraph is drawn, in Rosenberg, *Trial of the Assassin Guiteau,* 64-65. See also Lloyd, "Insanity," 228-29.

15 Rosenberg, *Trial of the Assassin Guiteau,* 53.

16 On the Thaw case see, *inter alia,* Umphrey, "The Dialogics of Legal Meaning," and G. Langford, *The Murder of Stanford White* (Indianapolis: Bobbs-Merrill, 1962).

17 *McAllister* v. *Washington Territory,* 1 *Washington Territory Reports* 360 at 367-68 (1881).

18 Unless otherwise stated, quotations from Shipley's opening address are all from *Seattle Times,* 2 July 1906.

19 Rosenberg, *Trial of the Assassin Guiteau.*

20 *PI,* 3 July 1906.

21 See *Telegram,* 1 June 1906.

22 *PI,* 3 July 1906.

23 See Shipley's comment to the press before the trial began that he expected a "great fight" in "securing the admission of testimony of our witnesses regarding the doings of Creffield in Oregon": ibid., 23 June 1906.

24 *Albany Herald,* 5 July 1906. The *Corvallis Times* also knew what was going on: "For fear that the court will not admit much of the evidence touching upon Creffield's religious fanaticism the attorney for the defense crowded it all into his opening statement so as to get it before the jury": *Corvallis Times,* 3 July 1906.

25 In "Insanity and the Unwritten Law," Ireland argues that some insanity defences were less of a sham than is generally thought, but his evidence is unconvincing and his argument somewhat inconsistent with his other articles on the subject, especially "The Libertine Must Die."

26 Ireland, "Insanity and the Unwritten Law," 158-59.

27 See the arrest warrant for contempt of court in SC-KC Case File 3652, WSA-PS.

28 *Oregonian,* 27 June 1906.

29 *Seattle Times,* 30 June 1906.

30 Quotations from ibid., 2 July 1906.

31 Ibid., 2 July 1906. The story also appeared in *PI,* 3 July 1906.

32 *Seattle Times,* 1 July 1906.
33 Ibid., 4 July 1906. See also *Star,* 3 July 1906: Hurt was "doing all within his power to free Mitchell."
34 On this issue see Wharton, *A Treatise of the Law of Evidence,* 362, 368, and 419-22, esp. at 368: "A defendant when a witness, . . . may be contradicted by proof of prior incon- sistent statements."
35 *PI,* 6 July 1906.
36 A little later Miller complained that "the effort seems to be to get in everything that is immaterial to this issue, and some things that are material": ibid., 6 July 1906.
37 *Oregonian,* 4 July 1906.
38 *Seattle Times,* 16 July 1906. This was the case of Robert Jones, convicted of second- degree murder. Frater used the Mitchell case to illustrate the need for deterrence in sentencing and gave Jones twenty years. It was a not untypical example, as we have seen, of his tendency to say more than he should on the bench.
39 Ibid., 30 June 1906. This assessment was based on Morris' attempts the previous week to question Maud Creffield about the Creffield sect.
40 Ibid., 4 July 1906.
41 Quotations from *Gazette,* 6 July 1906; *Star,* 14 July 1906; *Oregonian,* 4 July 1906.
42 This was Charles Shires of North Yamhill, who testified for only a few minutes to the effect that he had known Mitchell for six or seven years and that he had always borne a good reputation. Mitchell had worked for him in his shingle mill a few years before.
43 *PI,* 4 July 1906.
44 Quotations from *Star,* 3 July 1906; *Oregonian,* 4 July 1906; *Seattle Times,* 4 July 1906.
45 Quotations from *PI,* 4 July 1906.
46 Quotations from *Seattle Times,* 3, 4, 6, and 9 July 1906, and *Oregonian,* 7 July 1906.
47 *Corvallis Times,* 10 July 1906. See also the fact that Miller was often "ridiculed" when he got up to make his objections: *Republican,* 13 July 1906. See also *Oregonian,* 6 July 1906, reporting that the spectators greeted some of his objections with "laughter and hisses," to the point that three times Frater was required to "quell demonstrations."
48 *Seattle Times,* 13 July 1906.
49 Crookall was a Californian who migrated to Seattle in 1893, obtained a BA from the University of Washington, and then tried his luck in the Klondike in 1897. After a year or so he returned and went to medical school in San Francisco. After graduating he went back to Seattle to practise. He was successful and well known, and in 1906 he was president of the University of Washington Alumni Association and ran, unsuc- cessfully, for coroner later that year: see *Mail and Herald,* 27 October 1906; County Commissioners' Proceedings, vol. 15, 6 November 1906, KCA.
50 *Seattle Times,* 5 July 1906.
51 They are not discussed here in the order in which they appeared.
52 This was Armstrong Glover, a mill foreman from Portland, for whom Mitchell had worked in 1905.
53 *Seattle Times,* 6 July 1906.
54 Quotations from *Corvallis Times,* 10 July 1906.
55 Quotations from *Seattle Times,* 6 July 1906.
56 Gardner to O.V. Hurt, 18 May 1906, Letter Books, BGAS Records.
57 *PI,* 6 July 1906.

58 *Corvallis Times,* 10 July 1906.

59 *Star,* 5 July 1906.

60 *Oregonian,* 7 July 1906; *Seattle Times,* 6 July 1906. A less favourable view of these women was taken by the misogynistic *Patriarch,* which suggested that "the pictures of these 'ladies' should be placed in the rogues' gallery with their peers, as they have shown their sympathy with crime": *Patriarch,* 7 July 1906.

61 *Seattle Times,* 6 July 1906.

62 Quotations from *Corvallis Times,* 10 July 1906; *Seattle Times,* 7 July 1906; and *PI,* 7 July 1906.

63 *PI,* 7 July 1906.

64 *Corvallis Times,* 10 July 1906. Indeed, the same report claimed that "close observation of the jurors during the court sessions reveals plainly that the frequent arguments of the state over minor legal technicalities is irritating to them."

65 Frater greatly disapproved of Manning. He said nothing at the time, of course, but less than a week after the conclusion of the Mitchell case, in a sentencing speech following another murder trial, he castigated Manning and others for the stand they took. "Human life is held too cheaply in this country," he said, and he noted the "anomaly" of "seeing sworn officers of the law using every effort at their disposal to secure the acquittal of a man who committed murder." He was "glad" to see the King County prosecutors doing their duty, but "the officers of another state have even gone on the witness stand in behalf of a man charged with murder in the first degree, and who did not deny that he had taken a human life": *Seattle Times,* 16 July 1906.

66 *Star,* 7 July 1906.

67 This is more or less how the *Star* and *Telegram* reported it, and we have taken their reports as correct because they tally with what happened later: *Star,* 7 July 1906, and *Telegram,* 7 July 1906. The *Seattle Times* report stated that Frater ruled in favour of the defence being now able to introduce expert evidence as well as what testimony it liked about Charles Mitchell and other members of the family, but given later events we think this wrong. The *Post-Intelligencer* did not report the argument or the ruling.

68 For Nicholson see *PI,* 8 July 1906; *Seattle Times,* 7 July 1906; J.W. Haviland and N. Rockafeller, eds., *Saddlebags to Scanners: The First 100 Years of Medicine in Washington State* (Seattle: Washington State Medical Association, 1989), 293; H.A. Dickel, "Early Pioneers and Leaders in Psychiatry in the Pacific Northwest," *Northwest Medicine* 65 (1966): 41.

69 *PI,* 8 July 1906. The quotations that follow are from the same source.

70 See on this point Ireland, "Insanity and the Unwritten Law," 168-69.

71 He said that he had thirteen people lined up "to show facts concerned with the mentality of relatives of George Mitchell": *PI,* 8 July 1906.

72 Ibid., 8 July 1906.

73 This account is taken from *Seattle Times,* 8 and 9 July 1906, and *PI,* 8 and 9 July 1906. A brief summary of the case can be found in W. Hunt, "Spurned Love and a Dead Judge," *Journal American,* 19 May 1908, A5. William S. Thompson was a Georgia-born veteran of the Confederate army, who practised law in Indiana before migrating west in 1889. As well as being a successful attorney, he was also a published poet: see *PI,* 11 August 1918.

74 George Meade Emory, of Maryland, went to Seattle as a young lawyer of twenty-one in 1890. He was a King County assistant prosecuting attorney until his appointment to the superior court bench in 1901, filling a vacancy created by the expansion of the bench from three to four judges. He served a little more than a year, resigning at the end of his term in 1902 to practise law: *PI,* 8 July 1906.

75 In fact he did plead insanity and was acquitted on that ground in January 1907 after being defended by his father and by Will Morris. The trial was postponed more than once, and then moved to Tacoma on the grounds that public antipathy towards Thompson was too great for him to get a fair trial in Seattle. He was finally released from the asylum in 1958. The progress of the case can be followed in both the *Seattle Times* and the *Seattle Post-Intelligencer* from July 1906 through January 1907. For his release see *PI,* 14 February 1958.

76 *Seattle Times,* 9 July 1906; the other quotations in this paragraph are from this source.

77 *Star,* 10 July 1906. See also a similar critique in *Republican,* 13 July 1906, and *Mail and Herald,* 14 July 1906.

78 *PI,* 8 July 1906; the other quotations in this paragraph are from the same source.

79 *Argus,* 14 July 1906. Although this article was published after George Mitchell's acquittal and death, it was written before those events.

80 *Corvallis Times,* 13 July 1906.

81 *Seattle Times,* 9 July 1906.

82 Ibid.; the other quotations in this paragraph are from this source.

83 We know little about Miles. He is listed as a physician in the *Seattle City Directory* for 1906, and a Portland newspaper described him as "one of the foremost medical men in the city": *Oregon Journal,* 10 July 1906.

84 *Oregonian,* 10 July 1906; the other quotations in this paragraph are from this source.

85 Lloyd, "Insanity," 194.

86 Another Midwesterner, the Iowa-born Loughary had moved to Seattle in 1888 when he was in his late twenties and quickly established himself as the best-known author-ity on insanity in the state. In 1908 he founded the first private sanatorium for the mentally ill in the state, the Puget Sound Sanatorium: see Washington State Biogra-phy Files, UWL, and Dickel, "Early Pioneers and Leaders in Psychiatry," 41.

87 *Oregonian,* 10 July 1906.

88 On this see generally Rosenberg, *Trial of the Assassin Guiteau,* 61 et seq. Simplifying a complex debate, conservative alienists resisted an expanded version of the notion of "moral insanity," the idea that people might be unable to conform to society's moral dictates as a result of disease, not innate depravity. The suggestion that such inability to conform could serve as the only sign of mental disease was seen by many as a dan-gerous doctrine, with the potential to excuse all crime as caused by external factors, and many doctors insisted that other symptoms had to be present for a diagnosis of insanity to be made.

89 Ireland labels most prosecutors' efforts in this regard "pathetic": see "Insanity and the Unwritten Law," 170.

90 Quotations from *Oregonian,* 10 July 1906.

91 J.B. Mitchell, "Why Should the Prosecutor Get the Last Word?" *American Journal of Criminal Law* 27 (2000): 139-216.

92 *Seattle Times,* 10 July 1906.

93 See *Oregonian*, 10 July 1906, suggesting there might be a "chance remark" or "slight intimation." This would be "desperate" and get them cited for contempt, but "the attorneys representing the state may attempt to influence the jury by letting the arbiters of Mitchell's fate know that another man has been shot down in Seattle by a youth who will plead insanity."

94 The *Seattle Post-Intelligencer* did not report the substance of the speech, and this account, including all quotations unless otherwise indicated, is from *Seattle Times*, 10 July 1906.

95 *Oregonian*, 11 July 1906. The *Star* agreed with this, noting that "Miller, the brilliant deputy prosecutor, was being saved by the state for its closing address": *Star*, 10 July 1906.

96 *Oregon Journal*, 10 July 1906.

97 *Telegram*, 10 July 1906.

98 *Oregonian*, 11 July 1906.

99 Defence Request for Jury Instructions, SC-KC Case File 3652, WSA-PS.

100 *Seattle Times*, 11 July 1906. Other quotations are from the same source.

101 See, *inter alia*, *Albany Herald*, 12 July 1906 – it was "longer than was expected by the friends of the defendant." The same newspaper insisted that "there was at no time any danger of a different verdict" and explained the time taken by the jury thoroughly canvassing all the testimony they had heard before ballotting.

102 *Corvallis Times*, 13 July 1906; see also *Oregonian*, 11 July 1906.

103 Less than a week later, in sentencing another man, Frater referred to the Mitchell case. He complained about the demonstration of approval that had greeted the verdict and, according to the *Seattle Times*, stated that "a man who was, under the evidence, clearly guilty of murder, was set free": *Seattle Times*, 16 July 1906. See also *PI*, 17 July 1906.

104 See *Washington Statutes*, 1891, c. 29, 61, and *Pierce's Code*, 340-41. For the origins of the special verdict in an 1800 English statute that followed the famous Hadfield trial see Walker, *Crime and Insanity*, 78.

105 See the verdict form in SC-KC Case File 3652, WSA-PS.

106 In this respect Washington was more liberal towards those acquitted by reason of insanity. Britain, for example, mandated that a person found not guilty by reason of insanity be kept in custody "until His Majesty's pleasure be known," which often amounted to a life sentence in an asylum. See Walker, *Crime and Insanity*, 78.

107 The following day the *Seattle Times* asked why, if Mitchell had been insane when he killed Creffield, he was not still insane, and why had he not been taken to the asylum? (*Seattle Times*, 11 July 1906). Similarly the *Argus*, 14 July 1906, asserted that "had Mitchell been insane it was the duty of Judge Frater to commit him to the asylum," and lamented that "nobody entertained a serious thought to that effect."

108 See *PI*, 13 July 1906, asserting that Mitchell had been "declared by a jury of his peers to have been justified in taking the law into his own hands." See also *Star*, 14 July 1906. However, the *Seattle Times* clung to the view that the jury had considered Mitchell insane: *Seattle Times*, 11 July 1906.

109 Quotations from Herrup, *A House in Gross Disorder*, xiv and 7. For similar observations see Grossberg, *A Judgement for Solomon*, xiii.

110 *Corvallis Times*, 13 July 1906.

CHAPTER 11: "AND THE EVIL THAT MEN DO LIVES AFTER THEM"

1 For this paragraph see *Seattle Times,* 11, 12, and 13 July 1906; *Oregonian,* 11 July 1906; *Star,* 11 July 1906; *Corvallis Times,* 13 July 1906.

2 Ireland, "The Libertine Must Die," 37.

3 *Corvallis Times,* 13 July 1906. See also for general comments about the reaction and atmosphere in Corvallis, *PI,* 13 July 1906, and *Oregonian,* 11 July 1906.

4 *Telegram,* 11 July 1906.

5 Quotations from *Republican,* 13 July 1906, and *Star,* 11, 13, and 14 July 1906.

6 *Seattle Times,* 12 July 1906. The subsequent quotations in this paragraph are from this source.

7 Quotations from *Patriarch,* 14 July 1906; *Argus,* 14 July 1906; *Seattle Daily Bulletin,* 11 July 1906. See also the *Mail and Herald,* 14 July 1906, linking the Mitchell and Thompson cases and renewing its prior attacks on the *Seattle Times* for its defence of Mitchell.

8 *PI,* 13 July 1906.

9 *Telegram,* 11 July 1906.

10 These events can be followed in *Seattle Times,* 8, 13, 14, and 15 July 1906; *Oregonian,* 12 and 13 July 1906; *Corvallis Times,* 13 July 1906; *PI,* 13 July 1906; *Star,* 10 July 1906; *Oregon Journal,* 11 July 1906; *Telegram,* 11 and 12 July 1906.

11 Esther in her turn complained to Miller about her father, although it is not clear what she hoped he could do: *Corvallis Times,* 13 July 1906.

12 See, *inter alia, Oregonian,* 9 and 12 July 1906; *Corvallis Times,* 22 June 1904, and 10 and 13 July 1906; *Albany Herald,* 12 July 1906; *Star,* 11 and 12 July 1906; *Times,* 13 July 1906; *Oregon Journal,* 11 July 1906; *Telegram,* 11 July 1906. This colony was supposedly at Allavia, British Columbia. It was established, according to these reports, sometime between Levins' expulsion from Corvallis and the death of Creffield, probably much closer to the latter time, as the Seeley girls were supposed to be there. We are not convinced, however, that any such "colony" ever existed. As discussed above, Florence and Wesley Seeley went to British Columbia in 1904, to live with their older sister.

13 The events described in this paragraph, and in the next, can be followed in *Seattle Times,* 13 July 1906; *PI,* 13 July 1906; *Star,* 10 and 13 July 1906; *Corvallis Times,* 13 July 1906; *Oregonian,* 13 and 14 July 1906; *Oregon Journal,* 13 July 1906; *Albany Herald,* 19 July 1906.

14 The sources are inconsistent on exactly when they left the matron's custody. Esther Mitchell picked up her witness fees on July 9: see Receipt and Witness Cost Bill, both in SC-KC Case File 3652, WSA-PS.

15 Quotations from *Oregonian,* 13 July 1906.

16 *Seattle Times,* 13 July 1906.

17 There were, according to one report, some 500 people in the depot: *Oregonian,* 13 July 1906. There is no suggestion that people were drawn there by the prospect of seeing the Mitchells leave. This was tourist season, and the overnight train to Portland was always crowded.

18 There are extensive, although not always entirely consistent, versions of what happened at the depot in *Seattle Times,* 12, 13, and 14 July 1906; *PI,* 13 and 14 July 1906; *Oregonian,* 13 July 1906; *Oregon Journal,* 13 July 1906; *Telegram,* 13 July 1906. This

account is drawn from them collectively; the differences in detail are not germane to the story.

19 Quotations from *Seattle Times*, 13 July 1906, and *PI*, 13 July 1906.

20 *Seattle Times*, 13 July 1906.

21 For all this see *PI*, 13 and 14 July 1906; *Oregonian*, 13 July 1906; *Star*, 13 July 1906.

22 *Seattle Times*, 13 July 1906. She defended her failure to report Maud Creffield's owner-ship of a gun by saying that she had not taken the possibility of her using it seriously.

23 For stories about suspicions that Frank Hurt was involved see *PI*, 13 and 14 July 1906; *Seattle Times*, 13, 14, and 18 July 1906; *Oregonian*, 13 and 14 July 1906; *Star*, 13 July 1906. Perry Mitchell pushed the idea hard, as did Burgess Starr, but although the police could not find him for a few days, they quickly decided he had had nothing to do with the murder. O.V. Hurt vigorously denied that his son had anything more to do with the killing "than a man in Alaska": *Seattle Times*, 16 July 1906.

24 See, *inter alia*, *Corvallis Times*, 20 July 1906; *Star*, 14 and 16 July 1906. We were un-able to discover who proposed the inscription or whether anybody in particular paid for it.

25 Esther Mitchell more or less immediately told Chief Wappenstein what Maud Creffield's role had been. Detectives were dispatched to find her, but Maud, having briefly visited Creffield's grave, called police headquarters and told them where she was: see *Seattle Times*, 12 and 13 July 1906; *PI*, 13 and 16 July 1906.

26 See *PI*, 13 and 14 July 1906; *Seattle Times*, 13 July 1906; *Star*, 13 July 1906. The *Oregonian* claimed that the police and the prosecuting attorney's office also took this view: *Oregonian*, 13 July 1906. There is some support for this, judging by Chief Wappen-stein's comment that Esther Mitchell was "weak-minded and entirely under the influ-ence of the older woman": *Seattle Times*, 13 July 1906.

27 *Seattle Times*, 12 July 1906. The discussion of Esther Mitchell's statements that follows is from this source and *Seattle Times*, 13 and 14 July 1906; *PI*, 13, 14, and 16 July 1906; *Oregonian*, 13 and 14 July 1906; *Corvallis Times*, 13 July 1906; *Oregon Journal*, 14 July 1906; *Albany Herald*, 19 July 1906. Only quotations are specifically referenced.

28 Quotations from *Albany Herald*, 19 July 1906, and *Seattle Times*, 13 July 1906. The *Seattle Times* interview was also published in *Oregonian*, 14 July 1906.

29 Quotations from *PI*, 14 July 1906, and *Seattle Times*, 13 and 14 July 1906.

30 The *Seattle Post-Intelligencer* ran a story to this effect on July 13 but quickly changed its version of her statements. The initial story was probably based on the reporter's assumption and a desire for a good story congruent with George Mitchell's own defence.

31 *Seattle Times*, 13 July 1906.

32 *PI*, 14 July 1906.

33 *Star*, 13 July 1906.

34 *PI*, 13 July 1906.

35 *Seattle Times*, 13 July 1906; *PI*, 14 July 1906. The latter described Maud Creffield as "quietly reading a magazine in the woman's ward of the jail" with around her, "stretched out on beds, generally smoking" were a "large number of women, drawn chiefly from the lower grades of humanity." The *Oregonian* painted a similar picture: she was "surrounded by the off-scouring of the red light district" and "the oaths that fell from the lips of other women prisoners, and the sight of a burly negress sitting on a table smoking cigarettes, disgusted her": *Oregonian*, 14 July 1906.

36 The discussion of Maud Creffield's statements that follows is from *Seattle Times,* 13-15 July 1906; *PI,* 13, 14, and 16 July 1906; *Oregonian,* 14 July 1906; *Corvallis Times,* 17 July 1906; *Albany Herald,* 19 July 1906. Only quotations are specifically referenced.

37 Quotations from *PI,* 14 July 1906, and *Seattle Times,* 13 July 1906.

38 See the story in *PI,* 13 July 1906, about conversations Starr had with her sister on July 6 and 7.

39 *Seattle Times,* 14 July 1906.

40 This paragraph is from *Oregonian,* 13 and 14 July 1906; *Seattle Times,* 13 and 14 July 1906; *Telegram,* 13 July 1906.

41 *Seattle Times,* 14 July 1906.

42 *Telegram,* 13 July 1906.

43 See especially Ireland, "Frenzied and Fallen Females." See also Ireland, "The Libertine Must Die," 30, and, for cases in which women did win acquittals after killing their seducers, Bakken, "The Limits of Patriarchy," and Strange, "Wounded Womanhood and Dead Men."

44 *Seattle Times,* 13 July 1906.

45 *Oregonian,* 13 July 1906.

46 The post-mortem was performed on July 13. Coroner Dr Francis Carroll supervised, and the principal work was done by Dr Loughary, with a number of other surgeons present. The doctors were principally interested in his brain, which was "subjected to an exceptionally close scrutiny" – "as soon as it was removed from the skull the physicians crowded around it." But it was completely normal. Although the doctors acknowledged that it was "possible" for a person to be temporarily insane and have no trace of it, Mitchell had "brooded and schemed on the murder ... for months," and that would be a chronic condition, and "in chronic insanity there was always a physical trace": *PI,* 14 July 1906. See also *Oregonian,* 14 July 1906; *Star,* 14 July 1906.

47 *Seattle Times,* 15 July 1906. In the same editorial it argued that Mitchell's action would have been excusable had he gone to Creffield, remonstrated with him, and "in the heat of temper" killed him. But Mitchell stalked him and cold-bloodedly shot him from behind. This was "direct and positive cowardice on the part of the murderer."

48 *Argus,* 14 July and 4 August 1906. Soon after the trial Rex had two "paralytic strokes" and his mind failed, and he had hallucinations. One was that he was still involved in the trial. His wife had him committed to the asylum: *Seattle Times,* 29 July 1906.

49 *Seattle Times,* 13 July 1906.

50 Ibid., 13 July 1906; *PI,* 14 July 1906. See also the *Seattle Times* editorial of July 15, 1906.

51 *PI,* 19 July 1906. See also *Seattle Daily Bulletin,* 16 July 1906.

52 See Rosenberg, *Trial of the Assassin Guiteau,* esp. 53 and 253 et seq.

53 *Seattle Times,* 15 July 1906.

54 See, for example, "Some one suggests that the 'murder mania' should be pinched in the bud. Pinched in the neck would be better": *Seattle Times,* 16 July 1906. See also the reaction to the news that another person had been found murdered: "The march of Death through Seattle continues": ibid., 17 July 1906. See also editorial commentary in ibid., 17 and 18 July 1906.

55 In addition to the comments cited here see *Seattle Daily Bulletin,* 13 and 16 July 1906.

56 *Republican,* 20 July 1906.

57 *PI,* 13 July 1906. There was one feature of press coverage generally that the *Seattle Times* did not participate in – blaming Blethen for being the problem. Brainerd in

particular had a great opportunity to skewer his rival, and took it. The *Seattle Times'* attitude to murder and vengeance demonstrated the "utter depravity and degradation of the liberty of the press in the United States": *PI*, 14 July 1906.

58 *Seattle Mail and Herald*, 21 July 1906.

59 *PI*, 13 July 1906.

60 Ibid., 19 July 1906. See also *Seattle Mail and Herald*, 21 July 1906, complaining that the community might as well "do away with our criminal courts" and "put a six shooter in the hands of men and women and tell them to shoot down those who wrong them."

61 *Argus*, 18 August and 14 July 1906. See also its issue of 10 November 1906.

62 For the change in the law see *Washington Statutes*, 1909, 892-97, and *Remington and Ballinger*, vol. 1, 1109 and 1114. It was preceded by a less drastic reform in 1907, which toughened up the procedures for pleading insanity and sought to ensure that those acquitted on that ground were confined to an asylum: *Washington Statutes*, 1907, c. 30. The 1909 abolition was short-lived, ruled unconstitutional by the state supreme court in *State* v. *Strasburg*, 60 *WLR* 106 (1910). For a more detailed account, and for the links between the cases in this book and the abolition, see J. Phillips and R. Gartner, "Abolishing the Insanity Dodge: Murder and Insanity Defence Reform in Washington, 1906-1910," unpublished paper, 2002.

63 *PI*, 16 July 1906.

64 *Star*, 14 July 1906.

65 *Seattle Times*, 16 July 1906.

66 *Star*, 17 July 1906.

67 *Seattle Times*, 16 July 1906. See also a later similar case reported in *Seattle Times*, 29 October 1906.

68 *Star*, 13 October 1906.

69 *Seattle Times*, 13 July 1906; *Oregonian*, 13 July 1906. For the *Patriarch's* attitude see the issue of 14 July 1906.

70 *Seattle Times*, 15 July 1906.

CHAPTER 12: THE LAW, MAUD CREFFIELD, AND ESTHER MITCHELL

1 The pre-trial proceedings against the two women are briefly summarized in SC-KC Journals, vol. 233, 166-67, WSA-PS, and Prosecuting Attorney's Criminal Dockets, vol. 8, 247, KCA. For the information and other documents see SC-KC Case File 3695, WSA-PS. See also for various public announcements of the intention to prosecute *Seattle Times*, 13, 14, and 17 July 1906; *PI*, 14, 18, and 19 July 1906; *Oregonian*, 14 July 1906; *Star*, 13 July 1906.

2 See *Remington and Ballinger*, vol. 1, 1110: "No distinction shall exist between an accessory before the fact and a principal . . . , and all persons concerned in the commission of an offence . . . shall hereafter be indicted, tried and punished as principals."

3 See *Seattle Times*, 14 and 17 July 1906; *PI*, 14 and 15 July 1906. For McLeish see R. Hollander, "Incarcerate or Cure? Governor Albert Mead and Progressive Reform of the Washington Mental Health System," *Columbia* 7, 3 (Fall 1993): 17-23.

4 *Seattle Times*, 5 December 1906.

5 See *Remington and Ballinger*, vol. 1, 1037-38.

6 This paragraph is based on reports in *Seattle Times,* 14-17 and 22 July 1906; *PI,* 14, 15, 17, and 19 July 1906; *Corvallis Gazette,* 20 July 1906; *Oregonian,* 15 and 16 July 1906; *Star,* 16 July 1906; *Telegram,* 19 July 1906.

7 *PI,* 17 July 1906.

8 Quotations from ibid., and *Oregonian,* 16 July 1906.

9 *Corvallis Gazette,* 20 July 1906. He likely effectively did so, the house being sold in October to one A.E. Wilkins for $1,225, although "possession is not to be given until later on": *Corvallis Times,* 23 October 1906.

10 *PI,* 17 July 1906. Speckert took a first-degree murder case to the supreme court in 1903, and represented about half a dozen clients in 1906-1907, none before mid-1906: see *State* v. *Champoux,* 33 *WLR* 339 (1903), at 341; Prosecuting Attorney's Criminal Docket, vol. 8, passim, KCA. The *Seattle Times* predicted early on that Hurt would have to find an Oregon lawyer, as "no reputable firm of this city will take the case." All he would find in Seattle would be "lawyers of little practice and less repute who will probably be glad to take the case for the advertising it will give them": *Seattle Times,* 15 July 1906.

11 For the rest of this paragraph see *PI,* 19, 24, and 29 July, and 1 August 1906; *Corvallis Gazette,* 27 July 1906; *Corvallis Times,* 3 August 1906; *Seattle Times,* 22 and 31 July 1906.

12 Baxter was from Minnesota and after getting a law degree from the University of Iowa in 1885 had practised there before moving west. For Baxter see Washington State Biography Files, UWL; Luther Baxter Papers, Acc. No. 4605, Box 1, folder 14, UWL; *PI,* 19 July 1906.

13 Born in 1873 in Canada, he had moved to Minnesota as a child. He studied law privately and joined the Minnesota Bar in 1897. He moved to Portland in 1906 when admitted to the Oregon bar. He was in private practice doing many kinds of law throughout his career and was the author of articles on constitutional and international law: see Taylor, *Eminent Judges and Lawyers,* 107; Gaston, *Portland,* vol. 3, 137; *Telegram,* 21 September 1906.

14 *PI,* 19 July 1906.

15 This discussion of the arraignments is from the accounts in *Corvallis Gazette,* 27 July 1906; *PI,* 24 July and 1 August 1906; *Seattle Times,* 24 and 31 July 1906; *Oregonian,* 24 July 1906; *Star,* 31 July 1906.

16 Her plea was taken by Judge Arthur Griffin because Frater was unexpectedly absent from Seattle, having missed a train in Everett: *Star,* 31 July 1906.

17 *PI,* 12 August 1906. For speculation about when the trials would be see *Corvallis Times,* 14 August 1906; *Corvallis Gazette,* 14 August 1906; *PI,* 1 August 1906. The Thompson case was actually postponed because of the illness of Thompson's mother, and then later moved to Tacoma, Pierce County, following a defence argument that he could not get a fair trial in Seattle. It took place in December 1906 and January 1907. See Prosecuting Attorney's Criminal Dockets, vol. 8, 247, KCA; *PI,* 7 December 1906 to 23 January 1907, passim.

18 SC-KC Journals, WSA-PS, vol. 233, 284 and 322; Prosecuting Attorney's Criminal Dockets, vol. 8, 247, KCA; *PI,* 16 and 21 September 1906; *Corvallis Times,* 11 September and 26 October 1906; *Corvallis Gazette,* 11 September 1906; *Star,* 7, 8, and 15 September 1906.

19 Quotations in this paragraph from *Seattle Times,* 24 and 31 July 1906; *PI,* 1 August 1906; *Oregonian,* 24 July 1906; *Corvallis Times,* 3 August 1906.

20 *PI*, 1 August 1906; *Star*, 30 July 1906. See also *Seattle Times*, 31 July 1906, quoting Clark as saying that Esther's brothers "realize she is mentally irresponsible."

21 *Seattle Times*, 31 July 1906; *PI*, 21 and 23 July 1906; *Corvallis Times*, 3 August 1906.

22 *PI*, 23 and 29 July 1906.

23 Quotations from *PI*, 23 and 29 July 1906, and *Corvallis Times*, 14 August 1906. See also *PI*, 29 July 1906: "Those who see the girl daily" all stated that "her attitude is always the same, serene and seemingly indifferent as to the possible consequences of her act."

24 For this see *Seattle Times*, 12 and 13 August 1906; *Corvallis Times*, 14 August 1906; *Corvallis Gazette*, 14 and 24 August 1906; *PI*, 13 and 16 August 1906; *Argus*, 18 August 1906; *Republican*, 17 August 1906.

25 Quotations from *Seattle Times*, 12 August 1906, and *Oregonian*, 13 August 1906.

26 *PI*, 18 and 24 July 1906; *Corvallis Times*, 20 July 1906; *Corvallis Gazette*, 20 July 1906; *Seattle Times*, 21 September 1906; *Ballard News*, 27 July 1906.

27 *Oregonian*, 24 July 1906; *Seattle Times*, 24 July 1906. Mackintosh cited *State* v. *Champoux*, 33 *WLR* 339 (1903), which was not directly on point. Champoux had been tried for first-degree murder, and an issue arose once the trial started as to whether he was then insane. A special jury was called and it determined that he was fit to stand trial. The evidence of that finding and the testimony given during the hearing were admitted in the trial proper at which Champoux was found guilty. One of the grounds of appeal was that that evidence should not have been admitted, but the supreme court rejected this argument. All the *Champoux* case showed was that in that instance a special jury determined fitness to stand trial; it did not stand for the proposition that one had to be called whenever the issue of fitness was raised.

28 *Seattle Times*, 18 July 1906.

29 *PI*, 24 July 1906. He asserted that evidence in the Mitchell trial had shown that Maud had been in the asylum and Esther in the home: *Oregonian*, 24 July 1906.

30 See variously *PI*, 19 and 24 July, and 1 August 1906; *Corvallis Gazette*, 27 and 31 July, and 14 August 1906; *Seattle Times*, 24 July and 5 December 1906; *Oregonian*, 24 July 1906.

31 *PI*, 18 July 1906; *Corvallis Times*, 20 July 1906. In fact, the trial cost $1,170 in witness fees and $1,627 in food and lodging for the jury, for a total of $2,797: Witness Cost Bill and Bill for Jury Lodging, SC-KC Case File 3652, WSA-PS.

32 *Washington Statutes*, 1905, c. 138.

33 *PI*, 19 July 1906. See also an earlier comment: "Oregon papers are having much to say about 'Seattle's murders,' but are quiet on the fact that the crimes are committed by murderers from Oregon . . . Oregon furnishes the assassins and Washington bears the burden of infamy and pays the bills": *PI*, 14 July 1906. See also the *Corvallis Times*, 20 July 1906, noting that if the women were to be sent to Oregon, "the Oregon officials who were so outspoken in their opinions of the trial of George Mitchell, claim local court officials [in Seattle], would then have a chance to handle the case themselves." And see also Wappenstein's remark, cited in the previous chapter, that "I wish these Oregon people would kill each other on their own side of the river." The *Republican*, 20 July 1906, also called for Oregon's "rollers" to "conduct their killing scrapes at home."

34 Neither trial would have been as complex and long as George Mitchell's trial, even if the women pleaded insanity, although they would not have been short either, for the

information listed seventeen state witnesses, including the Mitchell brothers: *PI,* 18 July 1906; Information Against Esther Mitchell and Maud Creffield, in SC-KC Case File 3695, WSA – PS. Moreover, a civil insanity hearing would also incur costs, including that of transportation if the women were taken to Oregon afterwards.

35 *Seattle Times,* 1 September 1906.

36 *PI,* 18 July 1906.

37 Ibid., 19 July 1906.

38 See also the *Times* comment that it was wrong to blame "the courts" for miscarriages of justice like in the George Mitchell case; juries were responsible: *Seattle Times,* 18 July 1906.

39 See, for example, *State* v. *Champoux,* 33 *WLR* 339 (1903).

40 *PI,* 19 July 1906.

41 *Seattle Times,* 24 July 1906.

42 For this see *Remington and Ballinger,* vol. 2, 943-44. A person alleged to be insane could request a trial of the issue by a jury.

43 This paragraph is principally based on *PI,* 11 September 1906. See also *Seattle Times,* 10 and 24 September 1906. See also the "Complaints" for each, which became Cases 7273 and 7274 in the superior court, in Respondents' Brief, 4, in the documents submitted to the supreme court of Washington in *State ex Rel Mackintosh* v. *Superior Court of . . . King County, and A.W. Frater* [hereafter *Mackintosh v. Superior Court – Documents*], Washington State Archives, Central Regional Branch, Ellensburg.

44 Holzheimer probably did not practise only criminal law, but he was experienced in the area. He defended about a dozen people between April 1905 and October 1907: Prosecuting Attorney's Criminal Docket, vol. 8, passim, KCA. He was counsel for Martin Strasburg in the 1910 case that overturned the abolition of the insanity defence: see *State* v. *Strasburg,* 60 *WLR* 106 (1910), 107. For his association with Baxter and Wilson see *Seattle Times,* 21 October 1906.

45 *Seattle Times,* 10 September 1906. See also Affidavit of John Miller, 22 October 1906, in *Mackintosh v. Superior Court – Documents.*

46 The only statutory provision on the subject did no more than give the court the power "to commit to the hospital for the insane any person who, having been arraigned for an indictable offense, shall be found by the jury to be insane at the time of such arraignment": *Remington and Ballinger,* vol. 2, 945.

47 See *Seattle Times,* 23 September 1906.

48 Ibid., 21 September 1906. See also *Argus,* 22 September 1906, commenting that two of the three doctors, presumably Turner and Snively, "are hardly known."

49 *Seattle Times,* 23 September 1906. We were unable to find out anything more about Snively.

50 *Argus,* 22 September 1906.

51 Eames was from Ohio and earned his medical degree at what was then Western Reserve University, before moving to Seattle in 1888. See Hawthorne, *History of Washington,* vol. 1, 559, and Bagley, *History of Seattle,* vol. 3, 727. He died soon after the events described here, in 1907.

52 Wharton and Stille, *Medical Jurisprudence,* 210-11.

53 The following account of the commission's proceedings is from newspaper and other sources. Among the former we rely principally on *Seattle Times,* 12 and 16-19 September 1906; *PI,* 13-19 September 1906; *Oregonian,* 13, 18, and 21 September 1906. See

also *Corvallis Times,* 14 and 25 September 1906; *Corvallis Gazette,* 18 and 21 September 1906; *Star,* 12, 14, and 18 September 1906. There is also much information in published judgment in *Mackintosh* v. *Superior Court* [hereafter *Mackintosh v. Superior Court – Judgment*] and in *Mackintosh v. Superior Court – Documents.*

54 Affidavit of Holzheimer and Baxter, 23 October 1906, in *Mackintosh v. Superior Court – Documents.*

55 See Petitioner's Brief, 21, and Reports on Esther Mitchell and Maud Creffield, all in ibid.

56 See Petitioner's Brief, 7, and Affidavit of John Miller, 22 October 1906, both in ibid.

57 Quotations from *Oregonian,* 13 September 1906.

58 *PI,* 13 September 1906.

59 Ibid., 14 September 1906.

60 Physician's Certificate, Esther Mitchell, Case No. 7273, and Affidavit of Respondents, 18 October 1906, in *Mackintosh v. Superior Court – Documents.*

61 Affidavit of Turner, Snively and Eames, 23 October 1906, and Physician's Certificate, Esther Mitchell, Case No. 7273, in ibid.

62 For the relationship between female insanity and sex see the sources discussed in Chapter 4. For how women were thought to be able to suppress the menstrual cycle see J. Delaney, M.J. Lupton, and E. Toth, *The Curse: A Cultural History of Menstruation* (Urbana, IL: University of Illinois Press, 1988), 252-57.

63 Physician's Certificate, Maud Creffield, Case No. 7274, in *Mackintosh v. Superior Court – Documents.*

64 References to this "physical examination" are at *Gazette,* 18 September 1906, and *Mackintosh v. Superior Court – Judgment,* 250.

65 *Mackintosh v. Superior Court – Judgment,* 250.

66 *PI,* 16 September 1906.

67 See the *Seattle Times'* statement that Maud Creffield was "subjected ... to an extended examination as to her religious experience and opinions": *Seattle Times,* 17 September 1906. Her answers were full and liberally laced with biblical quotations: ibid., 18 September 1906. See similarly the *Post-Intelligencer's* comment that her answers "showed a thorough study of the Bible and at no time was she unable to give a reason for her actions by quoting scripture": *PI,* 19 September 1906.

68 Quotations from *Corvallis Gazette,* 21 September 1906; and *Seattle Times,* 18 September 1906; *PI,* 18 September 1906.

69 *Seattle Times,* 18 and 19 September 1906.

70 The following account of the presentation of the reports and associated proceedings is from ibid., 20 and 21 September 1906; *PI,* 20 and 21 September 1906; *Oregonian,* 22 September 1906; *Corvallis Times,* 25 September 1906. Copies of the reports are in *Mackintosh v. Superior Court – Documents.*

71 Wharton and Stille, *Medical Jurisprudence,* vol. 1, 820-45; quotation at 820. The delusions of grandeur noted at 823 were: "he believes that he is a personage of importance; that he is reserved for a great destiny; that he is a reformer, an inventor, a prophet, a king, or even a Messiah."

72 Physician's Certificates for Esther Mitchell and Maud Creffield, Case Nos. 7273 and 7274, in *Mackintosh v. Superior Court – Documents.*

73 *Wharton and Stille's Medical Jurisprudence,* vol. 1, 829.

74 *PI,* 22 September 1906, and *Oregonian,* 22 September 1906.

75 See Wharton and Stille, *Medical Jurisprudence*, vol. 1, 210 and 211.

76 *Corvallis Times*, 25 September 1906.

77 SC-KC Journals, vol. 233, 344, WSA-PS. Presumably because trial was not due to start until October 22 Maud Creffield's case was not removed. If Frater's decision was overturned quickly by the state supreme court she could still go to trial as planned.

78 The order is in *Mackintosh v. Superior Court – Documents*. For a more detailed discussion of this see the section below on the Washington Supreme Court.

79 *Corvallis Gazette*, 25 September 1906, and *PI*, 21 September 1906.

80 See *Corvallis Times*, 25 September 1906; *Oregonian*, 22 September 1906; *Corvallis Gazette*, 25 September 1906; *Telegram*, 25 September 1906.

81 *Seattle Times*, 25 September 1906.

82 Ibid., 25 September 1906.

83 Ibid., 21 September 1906.

84 Ibid., 21 September 1906.

85 *Argus*, 22 September 1906, and *Republican*, 28 September 1906. See also for similar comments *Argus*, 23 and 24 September, and 21 October 1906.

86 *Seattle Times*, 23 September 1906, and *PI*, 23 September 1906.

87 *PI*, 21 October and 21 November 1906; *Corvallis Gazette-Times*, 2 November 1957.

88 Quotations from *PI*, 22 September 1906; *Seattle Times*, 21 September and 5 December 1906; *Corvallis Times*, 25 September 1906.

89 The following account is based on reports in *Star*, 4 December 1906; *Seattle Times*, 3,4, and 5 December 1906; *PI*, 4 December 1906; *Oregonian*, 4 December 1906.

90 Sharples was an Oregonian who had obtained his medical degree from the University of Pennsylvania. For this information see *Seattle Times*, 4 December 1906; Washington State Biography Files, UWL; Haviland and Rockafeller, eds., *Saddlebags to Scanners*, 101-102 and 107.

91 *Oregonian*, 4 December 1906.

92 *Seattle Times*, 7 December 1906, and *PI*, 4 December 1906.

93 *Star*, 5 December 1906.

94 *Seattle Times*, 5 December 1906; the other quotations in this paragraph are from this source.

95 *Argus*, 8 December 1906.

96 Neither the King County Medical Society nor the King County Bar Association has any record of an inquiry.

97 *Star*, 4 December 1906.

98 Sharples' views on the defence were made clear in the rest of his paper. He complained that "members of the medical profession were willing to aid lawyers in concocting and putting into execution sham defenses of insanity to free criminals." This applied to the George Mitchell case; the doctors who testified for Mitchell "must share the moral responsibility for the tragedies and crimes that followed his acquittal": *Seattle Times*, 4 December 1906. He also said with reference to that case that "no intelligent person" in Seattle believed George Mitchell was insane: *Oregonian*, 4 December 1906. He was an advocate of the sterilization of criminals: ibid.

99 *Seattle Times*, 5 December 1906. See also *Star*, 4 December 1906.

100 *PI*, 5 December 1906. Only the *Republican* refused to take the accusations seriously. It thought the whole thing a put up job by the *Seattle Times*, which would "rather publish a sensational lie than an actual truth," aided by Mackintosh, who wanted to

influence the jury that would try Chester Thompson against the insanity defence and insanity experts: *Republican,* 7 December 1906.

101 *Argus,* 8 December 1906.

102 For all this see generally *Seattle Times,* 21 and 23 September 1906 (quotation from 23 September); *Corvallis Times,* 25 September 1906; *PI,* 22 September 1906.

103 Affidavit of Turner, Snively and Eames, 23 October 1906, in *Mackintosh v. Superior Court – Documents.*

104 Ibid.

105 Affidavit of Holzheimer and Baxter, 23 October 1906, in ibid.

106 See the discussion below.

107 See Affidavit of Benjamin Strawbridge, Court Reporter, 25 October 1906, and the reports for both women, both in *Mackintosh v. Superior Court – Documents.*

108 There is some confusion over Berry. He is reported as having refused to give his evidence publicly, wanting a private session because he had once been engaged to Maud Hurt. The report also says that his request was granted, and then goes on to report what he said regarding his knowledge of Maud Creffield's religious beliefs. See *PI,* 13 September 1906. The most likely explanation of all this is that he gave some of his evidence in public, and some behind closed doors.

109 *Seattle Times,* 23 and 24 September 1906; *PI,* 23 and 25 September 1906; *Corvallis Gazette,* 28 September 1906; *Mackintosh v. Superior Court – Judgment,* 248; Mackintosh's Petition, and Order to Show Cause, in *Mackintosh v. Superior Court – Documents.* Mount issued what was referred to as an "alternative writ of prohibition," alternative effectively meaning temporary, and the hearing would be to determine whether it was to be made final.

110 Information on the judges is largely from Sheldon, *The Washington High Bench,* 111-12, 134-37, 156-57, 182-84, 258-59, 287-90, and 297-98.

111 See his letter to Erastus Brainerd, 9 July 1906, Brainerd Papers, Acc. No. 4624-1, folder 4-26, UWL, commending Brainerd on an editorial urging stricter law enforcement and deprecating "other newspapers (or alleged newspapers)" for "filling their columns with sensational stuff calculated to make heros [sic] of these offenders in the minds of 'half-baked' and unthinking people." Root was a native of Illinois who had moved to Washington in 1883 and to Seattle in 1897. He served four years on the supreme court, leaving the bench in 1908 as a result of a corruption scandal arising out of his connections to the Great Northern Railway. For Root see also Washington State Biography Files, UWL; Bagley, *History of Seattle,* vol. 3, 843-44; *Seattle Times,* 6 January 1907.

112 For the little we have on the hearing see *Mackintosh v. Superior Court – Judgment,* 249; *Star,* 26 October 1906.

113 Born in Iowa and, like Mackintosh a graduate of Columbia Law School, Vanderveer moved to Seattle in 1901. He was a deputy prosecuting attorney from 1905 and was elected prosecuting attorney in 1908, when Mackintosh did not run for office again. In 1909 he chaired the committee that prepared a revised Washington State Penal Code. See *Argus,* 19 September 1908; Bagley, *History of King County,* 284-85.

114 Walker was originally from Wisconsin and a Columbia Law School graduate, and set up practice in Washington in 1892. He served a stint as the prosecuting attorney for Pierce County, 1899-1900, and must have been a successful and prominent attorney, for he served as president of the Seattle Bar Association in 1912-13: see Washington

Lawyers' Collection, University of Washington Law Library, and Lampson, *From Profanity Hill*, 102. Arston was from Michigan and had qualified there before setting up practice in Seattle in 1902: Washington Lawyers' Collection, University of Washington Law Library.

115 Sheldon, *The Washington High Bench*, 47.
116 *Corvallis Times*, 6 November 1906; *PI*, 17 November 1906.
117 *Mackintosh v. Superior Court – Judgment*, 258.
118 For the prosecution's arguments see Petitioner's Brief, 9-30, in *Mackintosh v. Superior Court – Documents*. The principal argument about the choice of insanity commission or jury is at 10-15.
119 *Remington and Ballinger*, vol. 2, 945.
120 Respondents' Brief, 6-10, in *Mackintosh v. Superior Court – Documents*.
121 Root did not sign Crow's opinion but in a short concurrence stated that he agreed "fully" with the majority "as to the trial court's right to appoint the lunacy commission and adjudge the two women insane": *Mackintosh v. Superior Court – Judgment*, 260.
122 This discussion is from ibid., 252-55; quotations at 252 and 253.
123 This discussion is from ibid., 251-52 and 255-57; quotations at 255, 256, and 257.
124 *Wharton and Stille's Medical Jurisprudence*, vol. 1, 208. Wharton and Stille went on to say that the "general and better practice" was to submit the issue to a jury empanelled for that purpose, but conceded that that was not the only permissible way to do it: ibid., 214.
125 Petitioner's Brief, 15-30, in *Mackintosh v. Superior Court – Documents*.
126 *Mackintosh v. Superior Court – Judgment*, 260-61.
127 For this see ibid., 258-60; quotations at 258 and 259. On this issue, Root did not concur with Crow. He expressed no opinion because neither party had argued the point. He did, however, hint that he thought it might be valid given that "many" states "have, and are enforcing, statutes of this character": ibid., 260.
128 *Seattle Times*, 7 January 1907.
129 *PI*, 6 January 1907.
130 *Oregonian*, 11 January 1907.
131 *PI*, 6 January 1907.
132 Ibid., 6 January 1907. See also a slightly later report that she did not care where she went, was "pale and care worn" with "no life or light in her eye." There was "always the attitude of unconcern, of 'I don't care.'" She had "no animation, no life, no spirit about her," was "like a human being in which the soul is dead": ibid., 9 January 1907.

EPILOGUE

1 The following account of Maud Creffield's death and the autopsy is from *PI*, 17 and 18 November 1906; *Seattle Times*, 17, 18, and 20 November 1906; *Star*, 17, 20, and 21 November 1906; *Oregonian*, 17 November 1906; *Corvallis Times*, 20 November 1906; *Corvallis Gazette*, 20 November 1906. Corvallis' new third newspaper, the *Benton County Republican*, which began publishing in mid-October 1906, also reported the death in its issue of 22 November 1906.
2 See Death Certificate of Ida M. Crefield, vol. 1906, Register No. 17252, WSA – PS.

Quotations and other information in this paragraph are from *Corvallis Times*, 23 November 1906; *Seattle Times*, 20 November 1906, and 6 January 1907; *PI*, 17 and 22 November 1906; *Corvallis Gazette*, 30 November 1906.

3 This paragraph and the next are from *Seattle Times*, 18 and 20 November 1906; *PI*, 17, 18, 20, and 22 November 1906; *Corvallis Times*, 20 November 1906; *Oregonian*, 18 November 1906; *Corvallis Gazette*, 20 and 23 November 1906.

4 Quotations from *Seattle Times*, 18 November 1906, and *PI*, 17 November 1906.

5 *PI*, 20 November 1906. See the Release Form for Mitchell to attend the funeral, in SC-KC Case File 3695, WSA – PS.

6 *Seattle Times*, 20 November 1906; *Corvallis Gazette*, 23 November 1906; *Corvallis Times*, 23 November 1906.

7 *Corvallis Gazette*, 30 November 1906.

8 *Republican*, 30 November 1906; *Seattle Times*, 17 November 1906; *PI*, 22 November 1906.

9 In addition to the people discussed here, note also that Clarence and Hattie Starr relocated to Waldport as well. Clarence ran a store and a dairy and was a two-time mayor of Waldport. He died in June 1939. See *Oregon Journal*, 19 August 1936, and Death Certificate, Clarence M. Starr, 1939, No. 69, OSA.

10 This paragraph is based on *Oregon Journal*, 31 October 1932; *Corvallis Times*, 23 October 1906; *Corvallis Gazette*, 11 January 1907; *Corvallis Gazette-Times*, 15 January 1920; *Lincoln County Leader*, 17 June 1943; Death Certificates, Orlando Victor Hurt and Sarah M. Hurt, 1943, No. 67, and 1946, No. 2682, OSA; Parry, *At Rest in Lincoln County*, 251; Hays, *The Land That Kept Its Promise*, 124 and 140.

11 In January 1907 he went to Salem to witness the election of two US senators, and his views on the event merited a paragraph in *Corvallis Gazette*, 25 January 1907.

12 *PI*, 6 April 1909.

13 *Lincoln County Leader*, 17 June 1943, and *Yachats News*, 11 April 1946; we are indebted to Marlene MacDonald of Philomath for the latter reference.

14 This paragraph is from Lincoln County Marriage Book, vol. 2, 23; Death Certificates, Frank Oscar Johnson and Deborah Mae Johnson, 1950, No. 6218, and 1931, No. 81, OSA; Parry, *At Rest in Lincoln County*, 240; Crew, *Brides of Eden*, 209 and 216; Hays, *The Land That Kept Its Promise*, 118.

15 This paragraph is from *Corvallis Times*, 15 January 1907; *Yaquina Bay News*, 15 January 1920; *Lincoln County Leader*, 16 January 1920; *Corvallis Gazette-Times*, 15 January 1920, and 20 May 1959; Crew, *Brides of Eden*, 215-16; Death Certificate, Frank C. Hurt, 1920, No. 1, OSA; E. Parry, *At Rest in Lincoln County*, 224.

16 The marriage was performed at Vancouver, Washington: *Corvallis Gazette-Times*, 20 May 1959. Berry and Mollie were still married when the former died in 1943: see Death Certificate, James Berry, 1943, No. 9, OSA. It will be recalled that Berry had married Clara King in 1904 (see Chapter 3) and he remarried in 1910, to a Tensie Johnson, in Lincoln County: Lincoln County Marriage Book, vol. 2, 56. His other marriages are discussed below, this chapter.

17 McCracken and Blodgett, *Holy Rollers*, 269.

18 For Bray and Levins see Crew, *Brides of Eden*, 215; J.M. Carson and V.M.W. Stevens, *The Valley Called Home: The Yachats River Valley* (Salem: privately printed, n.d.), 58 and 131; Bogue and Yunker, "Proved Up on Ten Mile Creek," 9; Gaston, *Centennial History of Oregon*, vol. 3, 680; Oregon Death Index, at ancestry.com; Parry, *At Rest in*

Lincoln County, 231; Death Certificate, Frank C. Hurt, 1920, No. 1, OSA; *Corvallis Gazette-Times,* 2 and 4 November 1957.

19 For the Hartleys see *Albany Herald,* 2 August 1906; *Lincoln County Leader,* 7 August 1914; *Telegram,* 26 July 1906; Carson and Stevens, *The Valley Called Home,* 59; Benton County Divorces, No. 4466, OSA; *Federal Census 1910,* Oregon, Lincoln County, vol. 7; Lincoln County Marriage Book, vol. 2, 401; Death Certificates, Lewis Hartley and Cora Hartley, 1937, No. 2, and 1945, No. 5853, OSA; Yachats Cemetery Records, BCHM.

20 Death Certificate, Louis Hartley, 1937, No. 2, OSA.

21 For Sophia Hartley and Perry Mitchell see Crew, *Brides of Eden,* 215; Hays, *The Land That Kept Its Promise,* 51, 119, and 144; Carson and Stevens, *The Valley Called Home,* 9-10 and 95; Lincoln County Marriage Book, vol. 2, 251; Oregon Death Records, at ancestry.com; *Lincoln County Leader,* 7 August 1914; Pritchard, "The Genealogical Record of the . . . Mitchells"; McCracken and Blodgett, *Holy Rollers,* 269.

22 For Donna and Burgess Starr see, in addition to the sources cited in this paragraph, *Lincoln County Leader,* 7 August 1914; Crew, *Brides of Eden,* 216; McCracken and Blodgett, *Holy Rollers,* 266-67; Lincoln County Marriage Book, vol. 2, 354, and vol. 3, 51; Death Certificates, Burgess Ebb Starr and Donna Berry, 1936, No. 18, and 1947, No. 4423, OSA; Hays, *The Land That Kept Its Promise,* 118.

23 The 1910 federal census for Oregon shows Donna Starr as the head of family, living in Newport with three children. As noted above, the other person living in the household was Cora Hartley, a boarder: *Federal Census 1910,* Oregon, Lincoln County, vol. 7.

24 A marriage licence was issued to Burgess Ebb Starr and Donna Victoria Starr. It is not dated but is in the Lincoln County Marriage Book between entries for November and December 1914, so presumably it was issued about this time: Lincoln County Marriage Book, vol. 2, 293. The only explanation we can give for this is a contemplated remarriage, which did not take place.

25 Marriage Certificate, Benton County, vol. 8, 516, OSA.

26 *Corvallis Gazette,* 4 January 1907.

27 The rest of this paragraph is from the Patient Register, Western State Hospital, Washington State Archives, Olympia, and from *Albany Herald,* 28 February 1907; *Corvallis Gazette,* 22 February 1907; *PI,* 9 January and 21 February 1907; *Seattle Times,* 20 February 1907.

28 See *PI,* 9 November 1907, a report based on a conversation with Holzheimer, acting now as her lawyer. There was a state fund for keeping prisoners at the asylum, but it was for temporary maintenance only and had a limit. For Washington residents the county was expected to pay. Holzheimer worried about what authority the superintendent would have to keep her once there was no money coming in to provide for her. See also *Seattle Times,* 20 February 1907, and *Argus,* 12 January 1907.

29 *Corvallis Gazette,* 22 February 1907.

30 *Corvallis Times,* 30 April 1907.

31 *Seattle Times,* 20 February 1907.

32 Ibid., 6 January 1907.

33 *Benton County Republican,* 18 April 1909. What follows on Esther's release is based on this source and on Patient Register, Western State Hospital, Washington State Archives, Olympia; *Seattle Times,* 5-8 April 1909; *PI,* 6 and 7 April 1909; *Star,* 6 April 1909; *Oregonian,* 3 August 1914; *Lincoln County Leader,* 7 August 1914.

34 *Seattle Times*, 6 April 1909.

35 Ibid., 6 April 1909.

36 This account of Esther's remaining years is from Patient Register, Western State Hospital, Washington State Archives; Crew, *Brides of Eden*, 215-16; *PI*, 6 April 1909; *Oregonian*, 3 August 1914; *Lincoln County Leader*, 7 August 1914; *Yaquina Bay News*, 6 August 1914; *Telegram*, 3 August 1914; Lincoln County Marriage Book, vol. 2, 251 and 261; *Corvallis Gazette-Times*, 3 August 1914; Pritchard, "The Genealogical Record of the ... Mitchells"; Parry, *At Rest in Lincoln County*, 224; Register Book, Girls C, Case 2251, and Case File 2251, BGAS Records.

37 *Corvallis Gazette-Times*, 3 August 1914.

38 For Berry see Lincoln County Marriage Book, vol. 2, 56; Death Certificate, James Berry, 1943, No. 9, OSA; Hays, *The Land That Kept Its Promise*, 131.

39 *Lincoln County Leader*, 7 August 1914.

40 McCracken and Blodgett, *Holy Rollers*, 266-67; Crew, *Brides of Eden*, 216.

41 *Telegram*, 3 August 1914.

42 For the note see *Yaquina Bay News*, 6 August 1914, and *Lincoln County Leader*, 7 August 1914.

43 Death Certificate, James Berry, 1943, No. 9, OSA.

44 *Corvallis Gazette-Times*, 3 August 1914, and *Oregonian*, 3 August 1914.

45 Davis, *The Return of Martin Guerre*, 4.

46 J. McLaren, "Creating 'Slaves of Satan' or 'New Canadians'? The Law, Education, and the Socialization of Doukhobour Children, 1911-1935," in *Essays in the History of Canadian Law Volume 6: British Columbia and the Yukon*, ed. McLaren and H. Foster (Toronto: Osgoode Society for Canadian Legal History and University of Toronto Press, 1995), 352. See also J. McLaren, "The State, Child Snatching, and the Law: The Seizure and Indoctrination of Sons of Freedom Children in British Columbia, 1950-1960," in *Regulating Lives: Historical Essays on the State, Society, the Individual and the Law*, ed. McLaren, R. Menzies, and D. Chunn (Vancouver: UBC Press, 2002).

47 Herrup, *A House in Gross Disorder*, 7.

Bibliography

PRIMARY SOURCES

NEWSPAPERS

Seattle

Argus
Patriarch
Republican
Seattle Daily Bulletin
Seattle Mail and Herald
Seattle Post-Intelligencer
Seattle Star
Seattle Times

Oregon

Albany Democrat
Albany Weekly Herald
Benton County Republican (Corvallis)
Corvallis Gazette
Corvallis Gazette-Times
Corvallis Times
Eugene Register
Evening Telegram (Portland)
Lebanon Express Advance
Lincoln County Leader (Toledo)
McMinnville Reporter/Yamhill County Reporter
McMinnville Telephone Register
Newberg Graphic

Oregon Journal (Portland)
Oregon Observer (Grant's Pass)
Oregon Statesman (Salem)
Oregonian (Portland)
The Dalles Weekly Chronicle
Yaquina Bay News (Newport)

OREGON STATE ARCHIVES, SALEM

Linn County Court, Judicial Journals
Linn County Court, Insanity Records
Oregon State Hospital [Asylum] Records
Marriage, Death and Divorce Records
Penitentiary Records
Works Progress Administration, Historical Records, Benton County

WASHINGTON STATE ARCHIVES

Central Regional Branch, Ellensburg – Case File, *Mackintosh v. Superior Court,*
    Supreme Court of Washington Records
Main Branch, Olympia – Western State Hospital Patient Register
Puget Sound Regional Branch, Bellevue – Death Certificates; Marriage Records;
    Superior Court Case Files; Superior Court Journals; Personal Property Assessment
    Rolls, County and Seattle.

UNIVERSITY OF WASHINGTON LIBRARIES, SPECIAL COLLECTIONS

Family Records of Washington Pioneers
Washington State Biography Files
Clarence Bagley Papers
Luther Baxter Papers
Erastus Brainerd Papers
Stewart Hall Holbrook Papers
Mark Matthews Papers
John Franklin Miller Papers
Washington State Federation of Women's Clubs Minutes

OTHER ARCHIVES

Benton County Courthouse, Corvallis, Oregon – County Court Case Files; County
    Court Journals
Benton County Historical Museum, Philomath, Oregon – Benton County Insane
    Record, vol. 2; Franz Creffield File; Yachats Cemetery Records
Boys and Girls Aid Society, Portland – Register Books; Letter Books; Patient Case
    Files
King County Archives, Seattle – Medical Examiner's Records; Prosecuting Attorneys
    Criminal Dockets; County Commissioners' Proceedings

Multnomah County Court House, Portland – Multnomah County Insane Commitments; Multnomah County Court Journals; Multnomah County Circuit Court Records
Oregon Historical Society – Scrapbook SB 59
Oregon State University Archives, Catalogue of the O.S.A.C. for 1902-1903
Portland City Archives – Portland Police Records
Salvation Army National Archives, Alexandria, Virginia – Officers' Career Sheets; Disposition of Forces Records; Portland, Oregon files
Seattle Municipal Archives – Police Department Records
University of Washington Law Library – Washington Lawyers' Collection

MISCELLANEOUS

The Codes and Statutes of Oregon . . . Compiled and Annotated by Charles B. Bellinger and William W. Cotton. 2 vols. San Francisco: Bancroft-Whitney, 1902.
Federal Census, 1900 and 1910
God's Revivalist and Bible Advocate. Cincinnati: God's Bible School.
Knapp, M.W. *Holiness Triumphant; Or, Pearls from Patmos, Being the Secret of Revelation Revealed.* Cincinnati: God's Bible School, 1900.
–. *Bible Songs of Salvation and Victory Compiled by M.W. Knapp and E. McNeill.* Cincinnati: God's Bible School, 1902.
Lord's Oregon Laws, Showing All the Laws of a General Nature in Force in the State of Oregon. 2 vols. Salem: State Printer, 1910.
Oregon Laws, Showing All the Laws of a General Nature in Force in the State of Oregon, Compiled and Annotated by Charles P. Olson. 2 vols. San Francisco: Bancroft-Whitney, 1920.
Pierce's Code: A Compilation of All the Laws in Force in the State of Washington Including the Session of 1905. Seattle: Tribune Printing, 1905.
Portland City Directories, 1901-1904.
Remington and Ballinger's Annotated Codes and Statutes of Washington. 2 vols. Seattle and San Francisco: Bancroft-Whitney, 1910.
Seattle City Directories, 1906, 1907.
War Cry (newspaper of the Salvation Army)
Washington Law Reports, 1st Series
Washington Territory Reports

SECONDARY SOURCES

BOOKS

Achtemeier, P.J., ed. *Harper's Dictionary of the Bible.* San Francisco: Harper, 1985.
Anderson, R.M. *Vision of the Disinherited: The Making of American Pentecostalism.* New York: Oxford University Press, 1979.
Andrews, G. *Insane Sisters, Or, The Price Paid for Challenging a Company Town.* Columbia, MO: University of Missouri Press, 1999.
Andrews, M.T. *Washington Women as Path Breakers.* Dubuque, IA: Kendall/Hunt, 1989.
Bagley, C. *History of King County, Washington.* 3 vols. Chicago: S.J. Clarke, 1929.

–. *History of Seattle From the Earliest Settlement to the Present Time.* 3 vols. Chicago: S.J. Clarke, 1916.

Bartlett, P., and D. Wright, eds. *Outside the Walls of the Asylum: The History of Care in the Community, 1750-2000.* London: Athlone, 1999.

Bederman, G. *Manliness and Civilization: A Cultural History of Gender and Race in the United States, 1880-1917.* Chicago: University of Chicago Press, 1995.

Bellesiles, M., ed. *Lethal Imagination: Violence and Brutality in American History.* New York: New York University Press, 1999.

Berner, R. *Seattle 1900-1920: From Boomtown, Urban Turbulence, to Restoration.* Seattle: Charles Press, 1991.

Bishop, J.P. *Commentaries on the Criminal Law.* 7th ed., 2 vols. Boston: Little, Brown, 1882.

Blair, K.J. *The Club Woman as Feminist: True Womanhood Redefined, 1868-1914.* New York: Holmes and Meier, 1980.

–, ed. *Women in Pacific Northwest History: An Anthology.* Seattle: University of Washington Press, 1st ed., 1988; 2nd rev. ed., 2001.

Boag, P.G. *Environment and Experience: Settlement Culture in Nineteenth Century Oregon.* Berkeley: University of California Press, 1992.

Boswell, H.J. *American Blue Book: Western Washington.* Seattle: Lowman and Hanford, 1922.

Boswell, S., and L. McConaghy. *Raise Hell and Sell Newspapers: Alden J. Blethen and the Seattle Times.* Pullman, WA: Washington State University Press, 1996.

Bowen, W.A. *The Willamette Valley: Migration and Settlement on the Oregon Frontier.* Seattle: University of Washington Press, 1978.

Brasher, J.L. *The Sanctified South: John Lakin Brasher and the Holiness Movement.* Urbana, IL: University of Illinois Press, 1994.

Bromfield, L. *The Strange Case of Miss Anne Spragg.* New York: Stokes, 1928.

Brown, R.M. *Strain of Violence: Historical Studies of American Violence and Vigilantism.* New York: Oxford University Press, 1975.

Buerge, D.M., and J. Rochester. *Roots and Branches: The Religious Heritage of Washington State.* Seattle: Church Council of Greater Seattle, 1988.

Carson, J.M., and V.M.W. Stevens. *The Valley Called Home: The Yachats River Valley.* Salem, OR: privately printed, n.d.

Clapp, E.J. *Mothers of All Children: Women Reformers and the Rise of Juvenile Courts in Progressive Era America.* University Park, PA: Pennsylvania State University Press, 1998.

Clark, N. *The Dry Years: Prohibition and Social Change in Washington.* Seattle: University of Washington Press, 1988.

Cohen, P.C. *The Murder of Helen Jewett: The Life and Death of a Prostitute in Nineteenth Century New York.* New York: Knopf, 1998.

Colmer, M., comp. *History of the Bench and Bar of Oregon.* Portland: Historical Publishing Company, 1910.

Corning, H.M., ed. *Dictionary of Oregon History.* Portland: Binford and Mort, 1956.

Crozier, E.W. *The White-Caps: A History of the Organization in Sevier County.* Knoxville, TN: Bean, Warters and Gaut, 1899.

Davis, N. *The Return of Martin Guerre.* Cambridge: Harvard University Press, 1983.

DeBerg, B.A. *Ungodly Women: Gender and the First Wave of American Fundamentalism*. Minneapolis: Fortress Press, 1990.

Delaney, J., M.J. Lupton, and E. Toth. *The Curse: A Cultural History of Menstruation*. Urbana, IL: University of Illinois Press, 1988.

Del Mar, D.P. *What Trouble I Have Seen: A History of Violence Against Wives*. Cambridge: Harvard University Press, 1996.

–. *Beaten Down: A History of Interpersonal Violence in the West*. Seattle: University of Washington Press, 2002.

Dieter, M.E. *The Holiness Revival of the Nineteenth Century*. Metuchen, NJ: Scarecrow Press, 1980.

Dodds, G.B. *Oregon: A Bicentennial History*. New York: Norton, 1977.

–. *The American Northwest: A History of Oregon and Washington*. Arlington Heights, IL: Forum Press, 1986.

Douglas, A. *The Feminization of American Culture*. New York: Knopf, 1977.

Epstein, B.L. *The Politics of Domesticity: Women, Evangelicalism, and Temperance in Nineteenth-Century America*. Middletown, CT: Wesleyan University Press, 1981.

Erlanger, R. *The Unarmed Prophet: Savonarola in Florence*. New York: McGraw-Hill, 1988.

Fagan, D. *History of Benton County*. Portland: A.G. Walling, 1894.

Farmer, J.S. *Americanisms – Old and New*. London: privately printed, 1889.

Ficken, R., and C.P. LeWarne. *Washington: A Centennial History*. Seattle: University of Washington Press, 1988.

Foster, L. *Religion and Sexuality: Three American Communal Experiments of the Nineteenth Century*. New York: Oxford University Press, 1981.

–, ed. *Free Love in Utopia: John Humphrey Noyes and the Origin of the Oneida Community*. Urbana, IL: University of Illinois Press, 2001.

Fox, R.W. *So Far Disordered in Mind: Insanity in California, 1870-1930*. Berkeley: University of California Press, 1978.

Frankiel, S.S. *California's Spiritual Frontiers: Religious Alternatives to Anglo-Protestantism, 1850-1910*. Berkeley: University of California Press, 1988.

Freedman, D.N., ed. *Eerdmans' Dictionary of the Bible*. Grand Rapids, MI: W.B. Eerdmans, 2000.

Frykman, G.A. *Seattle's Historian and Promoter: The Life of Edward Stephen Meany*. Pullman, WA: Washington State University Press, 1998.

Gallagher, M.K. *Historic Context Statement: City of Corvallis, Oregon*. Corvallis: Benton County Historical Museum, 1993.

Gaston, J. *The Centennial History of Oregon, 1811-1912*. 3 vols. Chicago: S.J. Clarke, 1912.

–. *Portland, Oregon: Its History and Builders*. 3 vols. Chicago: S.J. Clarke, 1911.

Geis, G., and I. Bunn. *A Trial of Witches: A Seventeenth-Century Witchcraft Prosecution*. London: Routledge, 1997.

Gilje, P. *Rioting in America*. Bloomington, IN: Indiana University Press, 1996.

Ginzburg, C. *The Cheese and the Worms: The Cosmos of a Sixteenth-Century Miller*. Baltimore: Johns Hopkins University Press, 1980.

Gordon, L. *The Great Arizona Orphan Abduction*. Cambridge: Harvard University Press, 1999.

Gordon, S.B. *The Mormon Question: Polygamy and Constitutional Conflict in Nineteenth-Century America*. Chapel Hill, NC: University of North Carolina Press, 2002.

Goshong, J. *The Making of a University, 1868-1968*. Corvallis, OR: Oregon State University Press, 1968.

Goss, H. *The California White-Cap Murders: An Episode in Vigilantism*. Santa Barbara, CA: privately printed, 1969.

Graham, H.D., and T. Gurr, eds. *Violence in America: Historical and Comparative Perspectives*. Beverley Hills: Sage, 1979.

Grob, G.N. *The Mad Among Us: A History of the Care of America's Mentally Ill*. Toronto: Maxwell Macmillan, 1994.

–. *Mental Illness and American Society, 1875-1940*. Princeton, NJ: Princeton University Press, 1983.

Grossberg, M. *A Judgement for Solomon: The D'Hauteville Case and Legal Experience in Antebellum America*. Cambridge: Cambridge University Press, 1996.

Gurr, T., ed. *Violence in America*. Vol. 2, *Protest, Rebellion, and Reform*. Newbury Park, CA: Sage, 1989.

Haarsager, S. *Organized Womanhood: Cultural Politics in the Pacific Northwest*. Norman, OK: University of Oklahoma Press, 1997.

Hanford, C. *Seattle and Environs, 1852-1924*. 3 vols. Chicago: Pioneer Historical Publishing, 1924.

Hardesty, N.A. *Your Daughters Shall Prophesy: Revivalism and Feminism in the Age of Finney*. Brooklyn: Carlson Publishing, 1991.

Harris, R.R. *Murders and Madness: Medicine, Law and Society in the Fin-de-Siècle*. Oxford: Clarendon Press, 1989.

Hartman, M., and E. Ingenthron. *Bald Knobbers: Vigilantes on the Ozarks Frontier*. Gretna, LA: Pelican Publishing, 1988.

Haviland, J.W., and N. Rockafeller, eds. *Saddlebags to Scanners: The First 100 Years of Medicine in Washington State*. Seattle: Washington State Medical Association, 1989.

Hawthorne, J. *History of Washington: The Evergreen State*. 2 vols. New York: American Historical Publishing, 1893.

Haynes, C.A. *Divine Destiny: Gender and Race in Nineteenth-Century Protestantism*. Jackson, MS: University Press of Mississippi, 1998.

Hays, M.H. *The Land That Kept Its Promise: A History of South Lincoln County*. Newport, OR: Lincoln County Historical Society, 1976.

Herrup, C.B. *A House in Gross Disorder: Sex, Law, and the 2nd Earl of Castlehaven*. Oxford: Oxford University Press, 1999.

Hines, H.K. *An Illustrated History of the State of Oregon*. Chicago: Lewis Publishing, 1893.

Hobbs, R.S. *The Cayton Legacy: An African American Family*. Pullman, WA: Washington State University Press, 2002.

Hoffman, C., and T. *Brotherly Love: Murder and the Politics of Prejudice in Nineteenth-Century Rhode Island*. Amherst, MA: University of Massachusetts Press, 1993.

Horowitz, D.A., ed. *Inside the Klavern: The Secret History of a Ku Klux Klan of the 1920s*. Carbondale, IL: Southern Illinois University Press, 1999.

Hurd, H.M., ed. *The Institutional Care of the Insane in the United States and Canada*. 3 vols. Baltimore: Johns Hopkins Press, 1916-1917.

Jones, C.E. *Perfectionist Persuasion: The Holiness Movement and American Methodism, 1867-1936*. Metuchen, NJ: Scarecrow Press, 1974.

Kimmel, M. *Manhood in America: A Cultural History.* New York: Free Press, 1996.

Lampson, M. *From Profanity Hill: King County Bar Association's Story.* Kirkland, WA: Documentary Book Publishers, 1993.

Langford, G. *The Murder of Stanford White.* Indianapolis: Bobbs-Merrill, 1962.

Larsell, O. *The Doctor in Oregon: A Medical History.* Portland: Oregon Historical Society, 1947.

Lasch, C. *The World of Nations: Reflections on American History, Politics and Culture.* New York: Knopf, 1973.

Leeson, F. *Rose City Justice: A Legal History of Portland, Oregon.* Portland: Oregon Historical Society, 1998.

LeWarne, C.P. *Utopias on Puget Sound, 1885-1915.* 2nd ed. Seattle: University of Washington Press, 1995.

Lewis, E., and H. Ardizzone. *Love on Trial: An American Scandal in Black and White.* New York: Norton, 2001.

Lippy, C.H., and P.W. Williams, eds. *Encyclopedia of the American Religious Experience: Studies of Traditions and Movements.* New York: Scribner, 1988.

Lockyer, H. *All the Men of the Bible.* Grand Rapids, MI: Zondervan Publishing House, 1958.

Lunbeck, E. *The Psychiatric Persuasion: Knowledge, Gender and Power in Modern America.* Princeton, NJ: Princeton University Press, 1994.

McCandless, P. *Moonlight, Magnolias, Madness: Insanity in South Carolina from the Colonial Period to the Progressive Era.* Chapel Hill, NC: University of North Carolina Press, 1996.

McColl, E.K. *Merchants, Money and Power: The Portland Establishment, 1843-1913.* Portland: Georgian Press, 1988.

MacDonald, N. *Distant Neighbors: A Comparative History of Seattle and Vancouver.* Lincoln, NE: University of Nebraska Press, 1987.

McGowen, R., and D.T. Andrew. *The Perreaus and Mrs Rudd: Forgery and Betrayal in Eighteenth-Century London.* Berkeley: University of California Press, 2001.

McGrath, R. *Gunfighters, Highwaymen, and Vigilantes: Violence on the Frontier.* Berkeley: University of California Press, 1984.

McKinley, E.H. *Marching to Glory: The History of the Salvation Army in the United States, 1880-1992.* Grand Rapids, MI: W.B. Eerdmans, 1995.

McLagan, E. *A Peculiar Paradise: A History of Blacks in Oregon, 1788-1940.* Portland: Georgian Press, 1980.

McLaren, A. *The Trials of Masculinity: Policing Sexual Boundaries, 1870-1930.* Chicago: University of Chicago Press, 1997.

Maeder, T. *Crime and Madness: The Origins and Evolution of the Insanity Defence.* New York: Harper and Row, 1985.

Marks, L. *Revivals and Roller Rinks: Religion, Leisure, and Identity in Nineteenth-Century Small Town Ontario.* Toronto: University of Toronto Press, 1996.

Marty, M.E. *Modern American Religion.* Vol. 1, *The Irony of It All: 1893-1919.* Chicago: University of Chicago Press, 1986.

Matthews, M. *A Dictionary of Americanisms on Historical Principles.* Chicago: University of Chicago Press, 1951.

May, D.L. *Three Frontiers: Family, Land, and Society in the American West, 1850-1900.* Cambridge: Cambridge University Press, 1994.

Melling, J., and B. Forsythe, eds. *Insanity, Institutions and Society, 1800-1914: A Social History of Madness in Comparative Perspective.* London: Routledge, 1999.

Melton, J.G. *Encyclopedia of American Religions.* Detroit: Gale Research, 1996.

–. *Religious Leaders of America: A Biographical Guide to Founders and Leaders of Religious Bodies, Churches, and Spiritual Groups in North America.* Detroit: Gale Research, 1991.

Miller, R.D. *Involuntary Civil Commitment of the Mentally Ill in the Post-Reform Era.* Springfield, IL: Thomas, 1987.

Miller, T., ed. *America's Alternative Religions.* Albany, NY: State University of New York Press, 1995.

Mitchinson, W. *The Nature of their Bodies: Women and Their Doctors in Victorian Canada.* Toronto: University of Toronto Press, 1991.

Mohr, J. *Doctors and the Law: Medical Jurisprudence in Nineteenth-Century America.* New York: Oxford University Press, 1993.

Monkkonen, E. *Murder in New York City.* Berkeley: University of California Press, 2001.

Moran, J. *Committed to the State Asylum: Insanity and Society in Nineteenth-Century Quebec and Ontario.* Montreal and Kingston: McGill-Queen's University Press, 2000.

Moran, R. *Knowing Right from Wrong: The Insanity Defence of Daniel M'Naghten.* New York: Free Press, 1981.

Morgan, M. *Skid Road: Seattle, Her First 125 Years.* 2nd ed. Sausalito, CA: Comstock Press, 1978.

Muncy, R.L. *Sex and Marriage in Utopian Communities: Nineteenth Century America.* Bloomington, IN: Indiana University Press, 1973.

Oliver, E.S. *Saints and Sinners: The Planting of New England Congregationalists in Portland, Oregon, 1851-1876.* Portland: Hapi Press, 1987.

–, ed. *Obed Dickinson's War Against Sin in Salem, 1853-1867.* Portland: Hapi Press, 1987.

Parry, E. *At Rest in Lincoln County.* Newport, OR: Lincoln County Historical Society, 1979.

Phinney, M. *Historical Sketches of Benton County.* Salem: Oregon State Archives, 1942.

Platt, A.M. *The Child Savers: The Invention of Delinquency.* 2nd ed. Chicago: University of Chicago Press, 1977.

Portrait and Biographical Record of the Willamette Valley, Oregon. Chicago: Chapman Publishing, 1903.

Price, R.M. *Newport, Oregon, 1866-1936: Portrait of a Coast Resort.* Dallas, OR: Lincoln County Historical Society, 1975.

Queen, E.L., S.R. Porthero, and G.H. Shattuck Jr. *The Encyclopedia of American Religious History.* 2 vols. New York: Facts on File, 1996.

Ripa, Y. *Women and Madness: The Incarceration of Women in Nineteenth-Century France.* Cambridge: Polity Press, 1990.

Robbins, W.G. *Landscapes of Promise: The Oregon Story, 1800-1940.* Seattle: University of Washington Press, 1997.

Robinson, D.A. *Wild Beasts and Evil Humors: The Insanity Defence from Antiquity to the Present.* Cambridge: Harvard University Press, 1996.

Rosenbaum, H.J., and P.C. Sederberg, eds. *Vigilante Politics.* Philadelphia: University of Pennsylvania Press, 1976.

Rosenberg, C. *The Trial of the Assassin Guiteau: Psychiatry and Law in the Gilded Age.* Chicago: University of Chicago Press, 1968.

Rothman, D.J. *The Discovery of the Asylum: Social Order and Disorder in the New Republic.* Toronto: University of Toronto Press, rev. ed., 1990.

Rotundo, E.A. *American Manhood: Transformations in Masculinity from the Revolution to the Modern Era.* New York: Basic Books, 1993.

Rubin, J.H. *Religious Melancholy and Protestant Experience in America.* New York: Oxford University Press, 1994.

Ruether, R.R. *Women and Redemption: A Theological History.* Minneapolis: Fortress Press, 1998.

Ruether, R.R., and R.S. Keller, eds. *Women and Religion in America.* 3 vols. San Francisco: Harper and Row, 1981.

Rushing, S. *The Magdalene Legacy: Exploring the Wounded Icon of Sexuality.* Westport, CT: Bergin and Garvey, 1994.

Sale, R. *Seattle: Past to Present.* Seattle: University of Washington Press, 1976.

Schlossman, S.L. *Love and the American Delinquent: The Theory and Practice of "Progressive" Juvenile Justice, 1825-1920.* Chicago: University of Chicago Press, 1977.

Schmid, C.F. *Social Trends in Seattle.* Seattle: University of Washington Press, 1944.

Schwantes, C.O. *The Pacific Northwest: An Interpretive History.* Lincoln, NE: University of Nebraska Press, 1989.

Scull, A. *Social Order/Mental Disorder: Anglo-American Psychiatry in Historical Perspective.* Berkeley: University of California Press, 1989.

Sheldon, C.H. *A Century of Judging: A Political History of the Washington Supreme Court.* Seattle: University of Washington Press, 1988.

–. *The Washington High Bench: A Biographical History of the State Supreme Court, 1889-1991.* Pullman, WA: Washington State University Press, 1992.

Shortt, S.E.D. *Victorian Lunacy: Richard M. Bucke and the Practice of Late Nineteenth-Century Psychiatry.* Cambridge: Cambridge University Press 1986.

Showalter, E. *The Female Malady: Women, Madness, and English Culture, 1830-1980.* New York: Pantheon Books, 1985.

Smith, R. *Trial By Medicine: Insanity and Responsibility in Victorian Trials.* Edinburgh: Edinburgh University Press, 1981.

Smith-Rosenberg, C. *Disorderly Conduct: Visions of Gender in Victorian America.* New York: Oxford University Press, 1985.

Snyder, E.E. *Aurora, Their Last Utopia: Oregon's Christian Commune, 1856-1883.* Portland: Binford and Mort, 1993.

Soden, D. *The Reverend Mark Matthews: An Activist in the Progressive Era.* Seattle: University of Washington Press, 2001.

Spencer, L., and L. Pollard, *A History of the State of Washington.* 4 vols. New York: American Historical Society, 1937.

Stevens, H. *Vigilantes Ride in 1882.* Fairfield, WA: Ye Galleon Press, 1975.

Stone, L. *The Family, Sex and Marriage in England, 1500-1800.* New York: Harper and Row, 1977.

Strachey, R., ed. *Religious Fanaticism: Extracts from the Papers of Hannah Whitall Smith.* London: Faber and Gwyer, 1928.

Tarkington, B. *The Gentleman from Indiana.* New York: Doubleday and McClure, 1900.

Taves, A. *Fits, Trances and Visions: Experiencing Religion and Explaining Experience from Wesley to James*. Princeton, NJ: Princeton University Press, 1999.

Taylor, C.W. *Eminent Judges and Lawyers of the Northwest, 1843-1955*. Palo Alto, CA: privately printed, 1954.

Taylor, Q. *The Forging of a Black Community: Seattle's Central District from 1870 Through the Civil Rights Era*. Seattle: University of Washington Press, 1994.

Tomes, N. *A Generous Confidence: Thomas Story Kirkbride and the Art of Asylum-Keeping, 1840-1883*. Cambridge: Cambridge University Press, 1984.

Walker, N. *Crime and Insanity in England: The Historical Perspective*. Edinburgh: Edinburgh University Press, 1968.

Weihofen, H. *Insanity as a Defence in Criminal Law*. New York: Oxford University Press, 1933.

Weisenburger, S. *Modern Medea: A Family Story of Slavery and Child Murder from the Old South*. New York: Hill and Wang, 1998.

Westerkamp, M.J. *Women and Religion in Early America, 1660-1850*. New York: Routledge, 1999.

Wharton, F. *A Treatise of the Law of Evidence in Criminal Cases*. 9th ed. Philadelphia: Kay and Brother, 1884.

Wharton, F., and M. Stille. *Wharton and Stille's Medical Jurisprudence*. 5th ed., 3 vols. Rochester, NY: Lawyers' Cooperative Publishing Company, 1905.

Winston, D. *Red-Hot and Righteous: The Urban Religion of the Salvation Army*. Cambridge: Harvard University Press, 1999.

JOURNAL ARTICLES AND BOOK CHAPTERS

Bainbridge, W.S. "Religious Insanity in America: The Official Nineteenth Century Theory." *Sociological Analysis* 45 (1984): 223-40.

Bakken, G.M. "The Limits of Patriarchy: Women's Rights and 'Unwritten Law' in the West." *Historian* 60 (1998): 703-16.

Baldasty, G.J. "Newspapers for the 'Wage-Earning Class': E.W. Scripps and the Pacific Northwest." *Pacific Northwest Quarterly* 90 (1999): 171-81.

Baumgart, H.D. "Ellensburg's Tree of Justice." *Columbia* 15, 4 (Winter 2001-2002): 7-15.

Bederman, G. "Civilization, the Decline of Middle-Class Manliness, and Ida B. Wells' Antilynching Campaign, 1892-1894." *Radical History Review* 52 (1992): 5-30.

Bell, D.A. "Total History and Microhistory: The French and Italian Paradigms." In *A Companion to Western Historical Thought*, ed. L. Kramer and S. Maza, 262-76. Oxford: Blackwell, 2002.

Blackford, M.G. "Reform Politics in Seattle During the Progressive Era, 1902-1906." *Pacific Northwest Quarterly* 59 (1968): 177-85.

Blair, K.J. "The Seattle Ladies' Musical Club, 1890-1930." In *Experiences in the Promised Land: Essays in Pacific Northwest History*, ed. C. Schwantes and T.G. Edwards, 304-22. Seattle: University of Washington Press, 1986.

Chused, R. "Late Nineteenth-Century Married Women's Property Law." *American Journal of Legal History* 29 (1985): 3-35.

Collmeyer, P. "From 'Operation Brown Baby' to 'Opportunity': The Placement of

Children of Color at the Boys and Girls Aid Society of Oregon." *Child Welfare* 74 (1995): 242-63.

Dickel, H.A. "Early Pioneers and Leaders in Psychiatry in the Pacific Northwest." *Northwest Medicine* 65 (1966): 39-44.

Eckberg, D. "Using Econometric Forecasting to Correct for Missing Data: Homicide and the Early Registration Area." In *Trends, Risks and Interventions in Lethal Violence: Proceedings of the Third Annual Symposium of the Homicide Research Working Group,* 51-64. Washington: US Department of Justice, 1995.

Elton, C. "Reign of the Vigilantes." *Frontier Times* 44 (1970): 34-35 and 48-50.

Engeman, R.H. "The 'Seattle Spirit' Meets the Alaskan: A Study of Business, Boosterism and the Arts." *Pacific Northwest Quarterly* 81 (1990): 54-66.

Ferguson, R.A. "Untold Stories in the Law." In *Law's Stories: Narrative and Rhetoric in the Law,* ed. P. Brooks and P. Gerwitz, 84-98. New Haven, CT: Yale University Press, 1996.

Finlay, R. "The Refashioning of Martin Guerre." *American Historical Review* 93 (1983): 553-71.

Fritz, C.G. "Popular Sovereignty, Vigilantism, and the Constitutional Right of Revolution." *Pacific Historical Review* 66 (1994): 39-66.

Gartner, R., and J. Phillips. "The Creffield-Mitchell Case, Seattle 1906: The Unwritten Law in the Pacific Northwest." *Pacific Northwest Quarterly* forthcoming, 2003.

Gewirtz, P. "Narrative and Rhetoric in Law." In *Law's Stories: Narrative and Rhetoric in the Law,* ed. P. Brooks and P. Gerwitz, 2-13. New Haven, CT: Yale University Press, 1996.

Ginzburg, C. "Checking the Evidence: The Judge and the Historian." In *Questions of Evidence: Proof, Practice and Persuasion Across the Disciplines,* ed. J. Chandler et al., 290-303. Chicago: University of Chicago Press, 1994.

Gregory, B. "Is Small Beautiful? Microhistory and the History of Everyday Life." *History and Theory* 39 (1999): 100-10.

Griffith, R.M. "American Religious History and Women's History: Old Divides and Recent Developments." *Reviews in American History* 25 (1997): 220-26.

Grimstead, D. "Making Violence Relevant." *Reviews in American History* 4 (1976): 331-38.

Hankins, J.F. "Whitman County Grit: Palouse Vigilantes and the Press." *Columbia* 6, 1 (Spring 1992): 20-26.

Hartog, H. "Lawyering, Husbands' Rights, and the 'Unwritten Law' in Nineteenth-Century America." *Journal of American History* 84 (1997): 67-96.

Hastings, D. "Introduction." In *Guide to the Judicial Records of King County,* 1-15. Seattle: Washington State Archives, 1977.

Higgins-Evenson, R. "The Political Asylum: State Making and the Medical Profession in Oregon, 1862-1900." *Pacific Northwest Quarterly* 89 (1998): 136-48.

Hollander, R. "Incarcerate or Cure? Governor Albert Mead and Progressive Reform of the Washington Mental Health System." *Columbia* 7, 3 (Fall 1993): 17-23.

Holmes, W.F. "Whitecapping: Agrarian Violence in Mississippi, 1902-1906." *Journal of Southern History* 35 (1969): 165-85.

–. "Whitecapping in Georgia: Carroll and Houston Counties, 1893." *Georgia Historical Quarterly* 64 (1980): 388-404.

Horner, J.B. "History of Oregon State College, 1865-1907." *Oregon Historical Quarterly* 31 (1930): 42-50.

Horowitz, D.A. "Oregon's Ku Klux Klan in the 1920s." *Oregon Historical Quarterly* 90 (1989): 364-84.

Hovenkamp, H. "Insanity and Criminal Responsibility in Progressive America." *North Dakota Law Review* 57 (1981): 541-75.

Ireland, R.M. "Death to the Libertine: The McFarland-Richardson Case Revisited." *New York History* 68 (1987): 191-217.

–. "Frenzied and Fallen Females: Women and Sexual Dishonor in the Nineteenth-Century United States." *Journal of Women's History* 3 (1992): 95-117.

–. "Insanity and the Unwritten Law." *American Journal of Legal History* 32 (1988): 157-72.

–. "The Libertine Must Die: Sexual Dishonor and the Unwritten Law in the Nineteenth-Century United States." *Journal of Social History* 23 (1989): 27-44.

–. "The Thompson-Davis Case and the Unwritten Law." *Filson Club History Quarterly* 62 (1988): 417-41.

Johnson, D. "Vigilance and the Law: The Moral Authority of Popular Justice in the Far West." *American Quarterly* 33 (1981): 558-86.

Kens, P. "Don't Mess Around in Texas: Adultery and Justifiable Homicide in the Lone Star State." In *Law in the Western United States,* ed. G.M. Bakken, 114-17. Norman, OK: University of Oklahoma Press, 2000.

Kernan, T.J. "The Jurisprudence of Lawlessness." *American Bar Association, Report of the Annual Meeting,* 451-52. Philadelphia: American Bar Association, 1906.

Kerr, W.T. "The Progressives of Washington, 1910-1912." *Pacific Northwest Quarterly* 55 (1964): 16-27.

Larsell, O. "History of the Care of the Insane in the State of Oregon." *Oregon Historical Quarterly* 46 (1945): 295-326.

Larson, R.W. "The White Caps of New Mexico: A Study of Ethnic Militancy in the South West." *Pacific Historical Review* 44 (1975): 171-85.

Larson, T.A. "The Woman Suffrage Movement in Washington." *Pacific Northwest Quarterly* 67 (1976): 49-62.

Lepore, J. "Historians Who Love Too Much: Reflections on Microhistory and Biography." *Journal of American History* 88 (2001): 129-44.

Levi, G. "On Microhistory." In *New Perspectives on Historical Writing,* ed. P. Burke, 93-113. Cambridge: Polity Press, 1991.

McGovern, C. "The Community, the Hospital, and the Working-Class Patient: The Multiple Uses of Asylum in Nineteenth-Century America." *Pennsylvania History* 54 (1987): 17-33.

McLaren, J. "Creating 'Slaves of Satan' or 'New Canadians'? The Law, Education, and the Socialization of Doukhobour Children, 1911-1935." In *Essays in the History of Canadian Law Volume 6: British Columbia and the Yukon,* ed. McLaren and H. Foster, 352-85. Toronto: Osgoode Society for Canadian Legal History and University of Toronto Press, 1995.

–. "The State, Child Snatching, and the Law: The Seizure and Indoctrination of Sons of Freedom Children in British Columbia, 1950-1960." In *Regulating Lives: Historical Essays on the State, Society, the Individual, and the Law,* ed. McLaren, R. Menzies, and D. Chunn, 259-93. Vancouver: UBC Press, 2002.

Marks, L. "The 'Hallelujah Lasses': Working-Class Women in the Salvation Army in English Canada, 1882-1892." In *Gender Conflicts: New Essays in Women's History,* ed. F. Iacovetta and M. Valverde, 67-117. Toronto: University of Toronto Press, 1990.

–. "The Knights of Labour and the Salvation Army: Religion and Working Class Culture in Ontario, 1882-1890." *Labour/Le Travail* 28 (1991): 89-127.

Mitchell, J.B. "Why Should the Prosecutor Get the Last Word?" *American Journal of Criminal Law* 27 (2000): 139-216.

Monkkonen, E. "Estimating the Accuracy of Historic Homicide Rates: New York City and Los Angeles." In *The Varieties of Homicide and Its Research: Proceedings of the 1999 Meeting of the Homicide Research Working Group,* 13-21. Washington: U.S. Department of Justice (1999).

Morris, A. "Criminal Insanity." *Washington Law Review* 43 (1968): 583-622.

Nedry, H.S. "The Friends Come to Oregon: 1, Newberg Meeting." *Oregon Historical Quarterly* 45 (1944): 195-217.

Oberdeck, K. "Not Pink Teas: The Seattle Working-Class Women's Movement, 1905-1918." *Labor History* 32 (1991): 193-230.

Palmer, B. "Discordant Music: Charivaris and Whitecapping in British North America." *Labour/Le Travail* 3 (1978): 5-62.

Pfeifer, M. "Midnight Justice: Lynching and Law in the Pacific Northwest." *Pacific Northwest Quarterly* forthcoming, 2003.

Phillips, J., R. Gartner, and K. De Luca. "Incarcerating Holiness: Religious Enthusiasm and the Law in Oregon, 1904." In *People and Place: Historical Influences on Local Culture,* ed. J. Swainger and C. Backhouse. Vancouver: UBC Press, forthcoming (2003).

Platt, A., and B. Diamond, "The Origins of the 'Right and Wrong' Test of Criminal Responsibility and Its Subsequent Development in the United States: An Historical Survey." *California Law Review* 54 (1966): 1227-60.

Richards, K.D. "Regulars and Militia: Washington's Post-Frontier Military." *Columbia* 9, 1 (Spring 1995): 6-11.

Ross, D.F. "The Spirit of M'Naghten." *Gonzaga Law Review* 9 (1974): 806-15.

Rotundo, E.A. "Learning About Manhood: Gender Ideals and the Middle-Class Family in Nineteenth-Century America." In *Manliness and Morality: Middle-Class Masculinity in Britain and America, 1800-1940,* ed. J.A. Mangam and J. Walvin, 35-51. New York: St. Martin's Press, 1987.

Schwantes, C. "Free love and Free Speech on the Pacific Northwest Frontier." *Oregon Historical Quarterly* 82 (1981): 271-93.

–. "Protest in a Promised Land: Unemployment, Disinheritance, and the Origins of Labor Militancy in the Pacific Northwest, 1885-1886." *Western Historical Quarterly* 13 (1982): 373-90.

Scott, R.J. "Small-Scale Dynamics of Large-Scale Processes." *American Historical Review* 105 (2000): 472-79.

Slotkin, R. "Apotheosis of the Lynching: The Political Uses of Symbolic Violence." *Western Legal History* 6 (1993): 1-15.

Strange, C. "Murder and Meanings in U.S. Historiography." *Feminist Studies* 25 (1999): 679-97.

–. "Wounded Womanhood and Dead Men: Chivalry and the Trials of Clara Ford and

Carrie Davis." In *Gender Conflicts: New Essays in Women's History*, ed. F. Iacovetta and M. Valverde, 149-88. Toronto: University of Toronto Press, 1992.

Sutton, J.R. "The Juvenile Court and Social Welfare: Dynamics of Progressive Reform." *Law and Society Review* 19 (1985): 197-245.

Taiz, L. "Applying the Devil's Work in a Holy Cause: Working-Class Popular Culture and the Salvation Army in the United States, 1879-1900." *Religion and American Culture* 7 (1997): 195-223.

–. "Hallelujah Lasses in the Battle for Souls: Working and Middle-Class Women in the Salvation Army, 1872-1896." *Journal of Women's History* 9 (1997): 84-107.

Taves, A. "Knowing Through the Body: Dissociative Religious Experience in African and British-American Methodist Traditions." *Journal of Religion* 73 (1993): 196-213.

Tighe, J. "Reforming the Insanity Defence in the Progressive Era." *Bulletin of the History of Medicine* 57 (1983): 397-411.

Umphrey, M.M. "The Dialogics of Legal Meaning: Spectacular Trials, the Unwritten Law, and Narratives of Criminal Responsibility." *Law and Society Review* 33 (1999): 393-423.

Warren, J.R. "An Explosion of Savagery." *Portage* 9 (1988): 12-15 and 28-29.

Welter, B. "Female Complaints: Medical Views of American Women." In *Dimity Convictions: The American Woman in the Nineteenth Century*, ed. Welter, 57-70. Athens, OH: Ohio University Press, 1976.

THESES AND OTHER UNPUBLISHED WORK

Bogue, B., and S.B. Yunker. "Proved Up on Ten Mile Creek: The Story of the Early Settlers of Lane County, Oregon." Bound typescript, n.d., available at Waldport Public Library.

Corvallis Commercial Club. *Benton: The Blue Ribbon County of Oregon*. Corvallis, 1920.

Jacobs, L.K., et al. "The Stauffer-Will Farmstead: Historical Archeology of an Aurora Colony Farm." University of Oregon Anthropological Papers, 1981.

Marks, L. "Hysterical Frenzies and Religious Legitimacy: Women, Sexuality, Madness, and Religion in North American and British Psychiatry, 1850-1890." 1995.

Martin, B. "History of Corvallis, 1846-1900." MA thesis, University of Oregon, 1938.

Pfeifer, M. "'Midnight Justice' in the Pacific Northwest: Lynching and Law in Washington, Oregon and Idaho, 1882-1919." Unpublished paper available at <http://academic.evergreen.edu/users5/pfeiferm/PacificNorthwestLynching.html>.

Reynolds, M.K. "Corvallis in 1900," n.d.

Robeck, C.M. "The Dog Days of Summer: 1906." 2001.

Saltvig, R. "The Progressive Movement in Washington." PhD dissertation, University of Washington, 1966.

OTHER ACCOUNTS OF THE CREFFIELD STORY

Beam, M. "Crazy After Women." In *Cults of America*, ed. M. Beam, 35-58. New York: McFadden Books, 1964.

Crew, L. *Brides of Eden: A True Story Imagined*. New York: HarperCollins, 2001.

Holbrook, S. "Death and Times of a Prophet." In *Murder Out Yonder: An Informal*

Study of Certain Classic Crimes in Back-Country America, ed. S. Holbrook, 1-21. New York: Macmillan, 1941; also in *Wildmen, Wobblies and Whistle Punks,* ed. S. Holbrook, 41-60. Corvallis, OR: Oregon State University Press, 1992.

–. "Murder Without Tears." *Sunday Oregonian* 4 parts: 8, 15, and 22 February, and 1 March 1953.

–. "Oregon's Secret Love Cult." In *Grand Deception: The World's Most Spectacular and Successful Hoaxes, Impostures, Ruses and Frauds,* ed. A. Klein, 16-23. Philadelphia: Lippincott, 1955; also in *American Mercury* 40 (1937): 167-74.

Hynd, A. "Prophet Joshua and His Holy Rollers." In *Murder, Mayhem and Mystery: An Album of American Crime,* ed. A. Hynd, 265-73. New York: Barnes, 1950.

Johnson, E.A. "History of the Benton County Courthouse." Unpublished, c. 1988, Benton County Historical Museum.

McCracken, T., and R. Blodgett. *Holy Rollers: Murder and Madness in Oregon's Love Cult.* Caldwell, ID: Caxton Press, 2002.

McDonald, M. "Roll Ye Sinners Roll: The Story of the Creffield Cult, Corvallis, Oregon, 1903-1909." Unpublished, 2002.

Mathison, R. "Franz Creffield: Naked Reformer." In *Faiths, Cults, and Sects of America,* ed. R. Mathison, 301-05. Indianapolis: Bobbs-Merrill 1960.

Miller, T. *The Quest for Utopia in Twentieth-Century America.* Vol. 1. Syracuse, NY: Syracuse University Press, 1998, 113-14.

Nash, J.R. *Encyclopedia of World Crime.* 2 vols. Wilmette, IL: Crime Books, 1989, vol. 1, 815, and vol. 2, 2191.

–. *Murder, America: Homicide in the United States from the Revolution to the Present.* New York: Simon and Schuster, 1980: 182-84.

Parrott-Holden, J. "Joshua the Second: The Man Who Put the Hex on San Francisco." *Columbia* 11, 4 (Winter 1997-98): 35-37.

Pintarich, D. "The Gospel According to Edmond Creffield." In *Great Moments in Oregon History,* ed. D. Pintarich and W. McCormack, 105-10. Portland: New Oregon Publishers, 1987.

Stanton, C.K. [pseud. for S. Holbrook] "The Enigma of the Sex-Crazed Prophet." *Front Page Detective* (January 1938): 4-9 and 108-10.

Thompson, L. "Nemesis of the Nudist High Priest." *Startling Detective* 42 (March 1951): 5-11.

Underwood, S. [pseud. for S. Holbrook] "Blonde Esther and the Seducing Prophet." *True Detective Mysteries* 27 (March 1937): 10-15 and 92-94.

Index

Printed and bound in Canada by Friesens

Set in Adobe Garamond

Design: Brenda and Neil West, BN Typographics West

Copy editor: Judy Phillips

Proofreader: Jillian Shoichet